Tackling Racism in Europe

An Examination of Anti-Discrimination Law in Practice

Martin MacEwen

BERG
Oxford/Washington, D.C.

First published in 1995 by
Berg Publishers Limited
Editorial offices:
150 Cowley Road, Oxford, OX4 1JJ, UK
13590 Park Center Road, Herndon, VA 22071, USA

Library of Congress Cataloging-in-Publication Data

A catalogue record for this book is available from the Library of Congress.

British Library Cataloguing in Publication Data

A catalogue record for this book is available from the British Library.

ISBN 0 85496 857 1 (Cloth)
1 85973 047 7 (Paper)

Printed in the United Kingdom by WBC Bookbinders, Bridgend,
Mid Glamorgan.

Contents

List of Figures and Tables

Anti-Discrimination Law in Europe: A Context to Evaluation

The Aim of this Study

Unquestionably, Europe is experiencing a period of momentous change. The collapse of the monolithic structure of the Soviet Union, the fragmentation of Yugoslavia, the re-unification of Germany and the creation of the European Union are all changing the map of Europe. With these changes have come a host of problems, not least of which are the inter-ethnic conflicts now raging in many of the recently formed and emerging states. These conflicts are often violent, and there is no doubt of the need for urgent political remedies.

However, there is a danger that attention will focus too strongly on the urgency of solving these conflicts and will be deflected from the fragile and at times precarious social relationships between the more stable communities of Western Europe and the minority groups which exist within them. Today in Western Europe the post-Second World War emigrants from the Caribbean, Asia, Africa and the Middle and Far East, who were often invited into Europe to help fuel the engine of industrial recovery, are now classed as the new settlers. Their legitimate hopes and aspirations for equal opportunity within pluralist democracies and within a tolerant European Union have been frustrated not only by overt racism, manifested in incitement, intimidation, physical violence and harassment, but also in the pervasive, persistent and equally corrosive racial discrimination which they meet in every aspect of life.

The first states to ratify the International Convention for the Elimination of All Forms of Racial Discrimination (ICERD, 1965) were quick to suggest that discrimination was alien to the naturally harmonious race relations existing within their own territories.[1] Today, however, there

---

1. M. Banton, 'Effective Implementation of the UN Racial Convention', *New Community*, Coventry, 1994, vol. 20, no. 3, 1994, pp. 475–487.

is a healthier acceptance that all is not well in the state of Denmark or in her 11 or more colleagues in the Union. But not all states have accepted that a legal framework outlawing racial discrimination and enabling or requiring positive action is a necessary, if insufficient, prerequisite to effecting social change in order to promote equality of opportunity. Article 119 of the Treaty of Rome has brought the subject of equal opportunity for women within the competence of the European Union, and the Social Charter has been designed, at least in part, to create a level playing field in the enlarged free market. There is now a need for the European Union to make racial equality one of its primary concerns, and there is a particular need for an anti-discrimination directive.

The principal aim of this book is to provide a straightforward overview of anti-discrimination law and its context in a representative selection of European states. It is also intended to make comparisons between states and to examine what opportunities exist for the European Union to introduce its own legislation to promote more effective measures against racial discrimination.

An important reference point for national legislation is the body of international law to which all member states are signatories. In the field of human rights there is a wealth of international agreements setting out standards in areas such as education, employment and civil and political rights as well as race relations, to which the majority of European states adhere. Recently, the European Community incorporated the European Convention on Human Rights (1950) into its jurisprudence and the European Court consciously interprets Community Law with a view to compliance with the Convention. Accordingly, this study also provides an overview of relevant international obligations and their enforcement provisions, not only to discover any differences in application by member states but also to explore the scope for their incorporation into Community Law.

Clearly, the social context in which anti-discrimination law is located may differ from one country to the next and may inform what the law covers and how it is enforced. Accordingly, this book also presents case studies of anti-discrimination law in four core states of the European Union, France, the Netherlands, Germany and the United Kingdom, and in three peripheral states, Denmark, Ireland and Greece. The aim of these case studies is to outline the social context in which the laws are placed as well as the nature of the laws themselves. Forming anything more than tentative conclusions from this study will be problematic because of the number of variables which affect the law in each member state as well as Community law itself. Nonetheless, an attempt is made to draw out those common features and models of good practice which may encourage opportunities for further study and for legal reform.

Ethnic Minorities in Europe

The history of human kind is in some ways the history of human mobility. There have been many kinds of population movements throughout history, whether voluntary or forced, peaceful or violent, gradual or sudden. Immigration is by no means a twentieth-century phenomenon in Europe and there have been many earlier movements. However, earlier migrant groups such as the Italian and Polish communities in France no longer view themselves as having any allegiance other than to their country of adoption.[2]

Following the Second World War, however, many European countries experienced a significant new wave of immigration in the 1950s and 1960s. Opportunities for labour were created by the need to rebuild and expand the European industrial base and there was large-scale recruitment of unskilled migrant workers from southern Europe, North Africa and colonies or former colonies of many European states. One of the myths of post-war immigration was that the immigrants would return to their home countries, a myth found frequently in the perception of migrants as well as the host community itself. However, when the recession which followed the oil crisis in the early 1970s reduced opportunities for cheap labour and created severe unemployment in immigrant communities, few immigrants or their settled families wished to return. Primary immigration in many European countries virtually ceased at that period but secondary immigration, of wives and dependents to effect family reunion, continued during the late 1970s and 1980s.

A new trend developed in the late 1980s and early 1990s, which witnessed an unprecedented number of refugees seeking asylum in Western Europe, particularly from Eastern Europe and Africa. In 1992 450,000 asylum seekers sought refuge in Germany alone. Significant increases in asylum seekers have also been experienced by the Scandinavian and Benelux countries, Spain, Portugal, Italy, France, the UK and Greece.

The creation of the European Community by the Treaty of Rome in 1956 and its development into the European Union following the Single Europe Act in 1988 and the Maastricht Agreement in 1991 were initially driven by economic considerations, the prospect of wealth facilitated by free movement of capital, labour and establishment. Later there came the prospect of monetary union – deferred no doubt by the collapse of the ERM – and the creation of a European nationality, at least in the sense of

2. Council of Europe, *Community and Ethnic Relations in Europe: Final Report of the Community Relations Project of the Council of Europe*, Council of Europe, Strasbourg, France, 1991, document MG-CR (91) 1 final E.

the absence of internal customs and borders and the conferment of a right on individuals to move within the Union subject to their being nationals of a member state. The impact of this development will not materialise for some time, but it does increase the difference between citizens and non-citizens and gives rise to a well-founded fear that members of visible minorities are those most likely to be subject to oppressive policing over their status.[3]

States determine entitlement to citizenship, that is, who has a right to belong to the state and who does not. The basis for that judgment is largely untrammelled. There is no binding international convention which sets out standards to be applied by state signatories, and wide differences of approach exist within Europe. Thus third-generation Turkish settlers in Germany may be denied citizenship, classified as guest workers and suffer systematic discrimination on the grounds of their nationality.[4]

At present the position of minorities in Europe may be characterised under five generic headings as follows:

1. *State Diversity.* There is a recurring myth that European states were formed by the occupation of a particular geographical region by a single dominant cultural group. While this may be an attractive political concept, in reality most European states were created by the merger of a number of ethnic minorities, for whom the classification 'immigrant' has either never been apposite or has been inappropriate in recent years. Even the insular United Kingdom has Welsh, Irish, Scottish and English cultural groups in addition to other long-established minorities such as Jewish and Romany peoples. In Ireland the division between the British Protestants of Ulster and the Catholics of the Republic is a relic of fairly distant immigration and more recent colonialism. The current conflict between the Protestants and Catholics in Ulster serves to illustrate the complexity of inter-ethnic conflicts; in this instance there are divisions along the lines of religion, language, cultural identity and ethnic and national origins, and the result has been a clash of class and social hierarchies and of power, privilege and resultant discrimination.

State diversity is also represented in indigenous communities which straddle state borders. In France and Spain the Basque communities have long sought for identity and recognition within states which have been less than supportive of cultural diversity. In addition, many countries have distinctive indigenous communities such as the Bretons in France, the

3. See T. Bunyon, *Statewatching the New Europe*, Statewatch, London, 1993.
4. Thus comprehensive car insurance premiums for Turks is three times that of Germans and for Greeks it is one and one-half times greater, irrespective of the longevity of residence or driving experience (information provided at Anglo-German Conference in Berlin, November 1993).

Catalans in Spain and the Pomacs in Greece. As a consequence it would be erroneous to categorise ethnic homogeneity of European states as a norm.[5]

2. *Settled Communities*. Migration in earlier periods by groups such as Romany Gypsies into Greece and northern Europe and Jews from eastern to western Europe has led to the development of long-established ethnic groups. In some cases there has been reciprocal migration, such as that between Germany and Denmark which has led to the development in these countries of Danish and German minorities, respectively.

3. *Refugees*. Since the Second World War there has been a significant increase in the number of refugees in Europe. Many of these have come from Africa, but there have also been many European exiles from the Ukraine, Poland and Lithuania who have settled in the UK, France and Germany. More recently, refugees from Vietnam, Sri Lanka and Iran have settled in Europe, becoming in some cases naturalised citizens.

4. *Colonial Immigration*. In the mid-twentieth century countries such as the UK, France, Portugal and the Netherlands have decolonised most or all of their dependent territories. One consequence has been the take-up of rights of immigration to the 'mother' country, particularly in the 1960s when the large, expanding European labour markets were receptive to immigration in order to meet labour and skill shortages.

5. *Guest Workers*. Those states such as Germany, Spain, Switzerland and Italy, with a less significant colonial past, responded to post-war labour shortages in their home markets by employing immigrant workers. Some states such as Switzerland looked for a source of labour inside Europe, particularly in Italy; Spain, France and Portugal sought labourers in North Africa, while Germany, the Netherlands and France were receptive to labourers from Turkey.[6]

Immigrants in Europe today fall into one of three principal categories of residential status. First, there are those with irrevocable rights of residence; these are usually classified as citizens. Second, there are denizens who have residential status but have more limited rights of residents, and do not have citizenship. Third, there are those most commonly classified as 'guest workers', who are subject to severe

5. Anthony D. Smith, *The Ethnic Origins of Nations*, Blackwell, London, 1988.
6. M. MacEwen and A. Prior, *Planning and Ethnic Minority Settlement in Europe: The Myth of Thresholds of Tolerance*, Research Paper No. 40, Edinburgh College of Art/ Heriot-Watt University School of Planning & Housing, Edinburgh, 1992.

restrictions on residents by virtue of their 'temporary' status, although the nature of this status and restrictions varies considerably from one state to another. Of the 13 million members of visible ethnic minorities resident in Europe today, probably more than two-thirds are non-citizens.

These classifications are important for a number of discrete reasons. Firstly, settled ethnic minority communities will establish nationality by the second generation in those countries which recognise the law of *ius soli*, meaning that citizenship is acquired by reason of birth within the country concerned. Conversely, those countries which recognise the acquisition of citizenship by reason of descent or *ius sanguinis* will have a significant number of second- or even third-generation immigrants who remain classified as 'foreigners'. Germany is a particularly important example of this latter case, with its large population of Turkish immigrants who are not recognised as citizens. There are significant differences in the respective rights of citizens and aliens from state to state, but in general it is clearly advantageous to be classified as a citizen. For example, in some countries only citizens may be hired for civil service jobs, a classification which may extend all the way down to teachers in local community schools.

It can be seen from the above that states often reserve the right to discriminate against immigrants, both in the immigration process itself and in the status and privileges afforded to non-nationals and also in the conferment of citizenship. In exercising its right to discriminate in these matters, the state may, and indeed is likely to, delineate categories of applicants by reference to their racial or ethnic origin. The extent to which a state does not discriminate arbitrarily in this fashion will be a symbol of its good faith and will in turn affect the credibility of its anti-discrimination law.

As a consequence of the variety of immigration patterns (let alone rights assigned to relatives and dependents in respect of family reunification) Western Europe, or Europe defined by membership of the European Community, is characterised by diversity. This diversity may be found in areas such as the longevity of settled communities, in its religious allegiances, in its linguistic expression, in its cultural forms and aspirations and perhaps most importantly in the legal status and social position of its residents.

Multi-Ethnic Societies

Today in most states of Western Europe immigrant communities account for between one and five per cent of the total population (see Table 1). In respect of particular localities within states ethnic minorities may constitute a much more significant proportion of the total population: the

Table 1.1 Population Size and Foreigners in EC Countries (1988); Table 2 in Sarah Spencer (edit) 'Immigration as an Economic Asset: the German Experience', Trentham Books, London, 1994, p. 43

	Thousands				Per cent			
			Workers					
	Population (1)	Foreigners (2)	Foreign (3)	EC (4)	(2):(1)	(3):(1)	(4):(1)	Foreign Employment
Belgium	9,884	853.2[b]	187.0	140.8	8.6	1.9	1.4	6.4
Denmark	5,130	128.3[b]	45.5	12.4	2.5	0.9	0.2	1.4
West Germany	61,451	4,489.1	1,577.1	472.7	7.3	2.6	0.8	7.7
France	55,884	2,785.0[a]	1,172.5	589.3	5.0	2.1	1.1	6.4
UK	57,065	1,736.0[c]	820.9	398.2	3.0	1.4	0.7	4.2
Greece	10,010	193.4[b]	24.9	6.6	1.9	0.3	0.1	0.9
Ireland	3,538	–	19.9	16.1	–	0.6	0.5	2.7
Italy	57,441	429.4[d]	57.0	14.0	0.8	0.1	0.0	–
Luxembourg	375	96.8[b]	58.8	55.9	25.8	15.7	14.9	33.2
Netherlands	14,760	568.0[b]	175.7	86.2	3.8	1.2	0.6	3.1
Portugal	10,305	89.8[b]	30.5	6.8	0.9	0.3	0.1	0.6
Spain	38,809	354.9	57.0	22.0	0.9	0.2	0.1	0.2

Sources: Population (middle of the year): OECD, *Main Economic Indicators*, 1991. Foreigners: Statistisches Bundesamt, *Statistisches Jahrbuch für das Ausland*, 1990. Foreign workers and EC workers: Statistisches Bundesamt, *Statistik des Auslands*, 1990. EUROSTAT, *Sozialporträt Europas*, Luxembourg 1991.
a Statistisches Bundesamt, *Länderbericht Frankreich*, 1989; b 1987; c 1985; d 1981

inner cities of Britain, France and the Netherlands, for example, may have up to one-third of their population from ethnic minority groups. Given the longevity of settlement of many of Europe's ethnic minorities, the classification of 'immigrant communities' is becoming less accurate as a description of these groups. It is also misleading with respect to the extent to which the minority groups are integrated into the societies in which they are now settled. The same can be said of ethnic minorities in the United States, Canada and Australia. The ethnicity of minorities may contrast with that of dominant groups in respect of culture, race (or more accurately physical appearance) and language, and national origin may remain a dominant factor in the psyche of a particular group's identity, but their residential status means the classification of 'immigrant' is becoming increasingly irrelevant.

It is clear that immigrants do not constitute a single homogeneous group. Arabs, Indians, Chinese, Africans and Caribbeans have little or nothing in common with one another culturally and face different kinds of problems in the host society. It is also apparent that serious conflicts can arise in the relationships between different immigrant groups, which not infrequently stem from the fact that different groups are required to live in proximity in the relatively disadvantaged parts of large cities.[7] However, that common experience of relative disadvantage and discrimination may bring groups together, thus justifying the composite political description 'black' where the common experience of oppression of 'racialised minorities' demands a united opposition. National, ethnic, racial and cultural diversities have become a characteristic feature of European society, especially in the larger cities where most of the newcomers have settled. In addition to the experience of discrimination, being a member of an 'ethnic minority group' is also likely to imply other shared characteristics including inadequate participation in the major institutions of the established society such as employment, education, housing and social services, and reduced possibilities for influencing democratic decision-making processes. Further, the marginal position of these groups in society is passed on to successive generations.[8]

Ethnocentric Power

However, while the majority of European states are multi-cultural and have multi-ethnic populations, the organs of state and the ideologies which underpin them are mono-cultural. The formation and consolidation of

7. Council of Europe, *Community and Ethnic Relations in Europe: Final Report of the Community Relations Project of the Council of Europe*, p. 9.
8. Ibid., p. 9.

nation-states have largely been dependent on the centralisation of government power and the promotion of a common culture, religion, language and way of life. Citizens were encouraged to relate their identity with group-identity and the identity of the nation-state itself. This monolithic approach to nationhood does not, of itself, deny ethnic diversity but it does mean its marginalisation and subjugation; the dominant norms are held to be of greater value and minority groups are expected to undergo a process of cultural adjustment or 'acculturation' to ensure that their own ways of life, attitudes and approaches do not clash with or threaten the legitimacy of those associated with the 'national identity'.

While such expectations are common throughout Europe, there are nonetheless both overt and covert differences in the approaches of public agencies to diversity. In the case of France, for example, the centralist nature of the state promoted the ideology of mono-culturalism, leading to assimilationist policies towards minority ethnic groups. In his analysis of the ethnic origin of nations, Anthony Smith observed that if it is true that those units which stand the best chance of forming nations are constructed around an ancient ethnic core, then both 'history' and 'landscape' become essential vehicles and moulds for nation-building. History and landscape are unearthed and appropriated to form the mythology and symbolism of poetic spaces and golden ages which cast their own spell of nationalism. The process of turning motley groups into an institutionalised nation requires the projection of a sense of belonging and identity in order to unify and integrate the nation. Authenticity and autonomy are provided through a symbolic framework, which supports the mythology of the past and translates it into a model for future action and achievements. Those institutions which are common to all citizens, such as the education system, become part of the ideological framework through which the mythology of the past is projected through the adoption of uniform values. Thus the English public schools, the German gymnasia and the French Lycees and Grand Ecole provide the vehicle through which a sense of nationality and identity is transmitted to the younger generations, and the specifics of each national system such as curricula, examinations and teaching practices become a badge of ownership, identity and pride.[9]

The highly centralised nature of French administration owes much to the status and tradition of the monarchy and the need to evolve a Paris-based royal French mythology and symbolism to combat tendencies of localism and provincialism and even ethnic diversity represented by the

9. Anthony D. Smith, *The Ethnic Origins of Nations*, Blackwell, London, 1988, p. 134.

Breton, Alsatian, Provencale and Basque cultures. In other words, ethnic diversity was perceived as a threat to central control. But such central control is not a necessary prerequisite to nation formation; in India the multiplicity of divisions in caste, region, language and even religion, while dominated by Hindu beliefs, are accommodated to a large extent in the decentralised nature of its parliament and other institutions. Further, neither the adoption of tight centralist control nor the tolerance of diversity are guarantors of continuity and stability in inter-ethnic relations; the recent disturbances in Assam and in Kashmir and the bombings in Calcutta and Bombay, as well as those in London and Manchester and the arson attacks on holiday homes in Wales, demonstrate that inter-ethnic relations are always precarious.

Colonial expansion, particularly in Britain, France and the Netherlands, has intensified the need for a sense of belonging and cultural identity. Expatriates needed to reinforce their links with the 'mother country'. At the same time, Christian evangelism among the colonial populations, trading expansion and even the more mundane opportunities for travel and adventure were undertaken in the name of a claimed innate superiority of the coloniser over the colonised. Opportunities for exploitation were frequently legitimatised by being transformed into the obligation for cultural, social and linguistic conversion. This proselytisation not only alienated and devalued the indigenous culture in the eyes of the coloniser, but also divorced the colonised from their own heritage even to the point of zombification.[10] Inevitably those who suffered most from such oppression were the slave communities, who were removed both physically and psychologically from their roots and self-identity.

In modern Europe the existence of ethnocentric state power remains evident but does not go unchallenged, partly because of its association with a crude expression of nationalism. As Benedict Anderson observed:

> In an age when it is so common for progressive, cosmopolitan intellectuals (particularly in Europe?) to insist on the near pathological character of nationalism, its roots in fear and the hatred of the Other, and in its affinities with racism, it is useful to remind ourselves that nations inspire love, and profoundly self-sacrificing love.[11]

10. F. Fanon, *The Wretched of the Earth*, MacGibbon and Kee, London, 1965.

11. B. Anderson, *Imagined Communities: Reflections on the Origin and Spread of Nationalism*, Verso, London, 1983 as quoted in David McCrone, *Understanding Scotland: The Sociology of a Nation*, Routledge, London, 1992, p. 201.

Inevitably, then, there is a tension between the state's de facto recognition of increasingly plural societies and its desire to protect and foster those legitimate sentiments of national identity which attracts such passionate support from its citizens.

Regionalism and State Integrity

In Eastern Europe the drawing back of the veil of totalitarian control and the establishment of state democracy has revealed many unresolved tensions and conflicts. The disintegration of the Soviet Union and the re-emergence of independent states such as Lithuania, Estonia and Latvia and the Caucasian republics has in some cases resulted in open warfare. In Yugoslavia, it has become clear that Tito's control over ethnic divisions had done little to assuage conflicting aspirations for dominance not only in Slovenia, Croatia and Serbia but, as we are now witnessing, in Bosnia, Kosovo and Macedonia. But it is not only in totalitarian states that ethnic groups have begun to assert themselves. In Canada the constitutional referendum in October 1992 provided an opportunity not just for the Quebecois but also for the indigenous peoples, the Inuit and the Cree Indians and those of mixed descent, the Metis, to question their association within the English-dominated Canadian Federation. In the case of the indigenous 'nations', which do not have an established power base, treaties and agreements are being reexamined so as to determine the most effective way for renegotiating the relationships between the peoples and the state.

There are thus considerable tensions between existing states which, as we have seen, are frequently an association of multifarious ethnic groups but are nevertheless intent on upholding the existing centralised bureaucratic structures – complete with networks of economic, diplomatic and military ties – and minority groups who are intent on asserting their own ethnic or cultural identity. In many cases these ethnic groups are also intent on creating their own nation-state to mark the boundaries of their interests.

In the European context the aspirations of settled minority ethnic communities do not generally include formal 'independence', even within a federal conglomeration. More frequently aspirations focus on the legitimacy of language and culture, and ethnic groups seek to create a power base which will promote recognition of these within a state dominated by other norms. The European Community's decision to create a Committee of Regions, as part of the Maastricht Treaty, may provide a mouthpiece for localised minority groups. However, the principal concern of minority groups throughout member states of the European Community is to achieve a power base within existing structures for promoting equality of opportunity and redressing a significant power imbalance in contra-distinction to that realisation within alternative or parallel structures.

Visible and Non-Visible Minorities

In any given European state, ethnic minority groups are likely to share a number of common interests in promoting their own culture, language and traditions against centrist pressures for assimilation and in their most extreme form, denial. Nonetheless, visible minorities are much more frequently identified as 'aliens' irrespective of their national origin or current citizenship, and are also much more frequently the subject of racial attacks and harassment as well as discrimination in housing, employment and education. In the UK, there is much evidence to demonstrate that the discrimination experienced by visible minorities reflects, not their cultural divergence from dominant norms, but the fact that they are seen and perceived to be 'different'. The extent of racist violence and harassment catalogued in the Glyn Ford Report[12], together with evidence from national studies including those by the Home Office, the Policy Studies Institute, the Commission for Racial Equality (CRE) and Scottish Ethnic Minorities Research Unit (SEMRU) in the UK, confirms the vulnerability of visible minorities in comparison with others. Moreover, the specific evidence of discriminatory practice in education, employment and the provision of goods, services and facilities provided in these studies demonstrates further that it is the perception of being different by reason of race (or more accurately the perception of race) that triggers off discriminatory treatment.

Some commentators have suggested that xenophobia or the fear of foreigners is the factor triggering off discriminatory treatment rather than visible differences from the 'norm'. Thus in France the fact that many of the Moslem population are immigrants from Morocco or Algeria may justify a view that their experience of discrimination is based on their apparent foreignness. But equally many Moslems, whether their ancestors came from North Africa or elsewhere, are French nationals, have been resident in France from birth, are fluent French speakers and are 'French' by any objective test; yet they still suffer from systemic discrimination. Similarly in Germany, any explanation of the harassment of Turks and Gypsies – many of whom, like French Moslems, are second- and third-generation residents – as mere xenophobia ignores the essentially racist

12. G. Ford, *Report of the Committee of Inquiry into Racism and Xenophobia*, by a Committee of the European Parliament with Mr Glyn Ford, MEP as rapporteur, Office for Official Publications of the European Communities, Luxembourg, 1991.

manner in which German nationality is conferred. It seems difficult to conclude that xenophobia is materially different from racism in most of its manifestations, and it is the visible identity of the victim which is the telling factor in the vast majority of cases of racism. Clearly, however, there are also other grounds for discriminatory treatment, and those who wish merely to discriminate on religious grounds may use colour as a form of convenient, if not always accurate, shorthand to identify deviants from religious norms.

Nationality and Citizenship

Formally, the European Community is not concerned with ethnicity nor indeed with race; the Treaty of Rome of 1956, the Single Market of 1986 and the European Union of 1990 confer rights, benefits and obligations on the basis of nationality. Thus freedom of movement of workers, establishment and capital, and indeed freedom to settle with one's family, is dependent on citizenship of a particular state within the European Community; and citizenship is defined by that state itself and not by the European Community. For fairly pragmatic reasons the European Community has determined that it is for the individual state concerned to determine who becomes a citizen and who will benefit from the expanding rights conferred by the treaties and agreements and the European laws thereunder.

But the concept of a Europe without frontiers for nationals, that is without passports or customs controls between member states, is equally built on an assumption that so-called permeable boundaries in Spain, Italy, Portugal and Greece will be shored up and tighter national controls on immigration will protect the member states from an influx of non-nationals from other states. In consequence this means not only fairly tight controls on visitors but also a common view of the treatment of refugees. If there are no passport controls, then non-nationals who gain entry to one European Community state have access to all. The only method of controlling or checking the legitimacy of the movement of third-party nationals on the removal of border checks is to 'stop and search', either randomly, on receipt of information of illegal entry or, most worryingly, on the assumption that a black person is more likely to be a non-national than a white person. However, despite the impact of these provisions on race relations within the European Community, there has been little institutional concern about the consequences of the abolition of internal frontiers.

The legal status of immigrants varies from one European country to another; in the United Kingdom, Commonwealth citizens have many of the rights of British citizens whereas in most other countries of the

European Community there is a clear distinction between the status of nationals and foreigners. But even in countries where most post-war immigrants have not acquired nationality, a status akin to citizenship may be acquired and the children of long-stay migrants may acquire the nationality of their country of residence. The test applied for the acquisition of citizenship also varies considerably. In the United Kingdom, the British Nationality Act of 1981 adopted the 'patriality' test first introduced by the Immigration Act of 1971. The patriality test means that immigrants can acquire citizenship if their parents or grandparents were born in the UK, and excludes from citizenship others including citizens of the Commonwealth or dependant territories who have no such links. Previously, the British Nationality Act of 1948 had created two principal forms of citizenship, that of the United Kingdom and Colonies and that of a citizen of the Commonwealth and British subject,[13] but the Act did not recognise any difference in immigration status between these two categories. It was the Commonwealth Immigrants Acts in the 1960s which introduced invidious distinctions between these categories; this had the effect, and clearly the purpose, of enabling white Australians, New Zealanders and Canadians (people from the Old Commonwealth) to achieve settlement status more readily than those from the New Commonwealth states of India, Pakistan and the former African colonies.[14]

France, in keeping with the traditions of a centrist state, originally viewed its colonies as an extension of metropolitan France and accordingly conferred French citizenship on their inhabitants. But immigrants who were thus accepted as part of French society were then expected to assimilate French cultural norms. The French approach insisted on formal equal rights for all individuals on the premise that institutional recognition of cultural minorities denies the integrity of the state.[15] Today the French state has clearly moved away from this total assimilationist view, but there is still a strong insistence on the unitary character of the state and official use of the term 'ethnic minorities' remains limited. However, the term 'immigrants' becomes less appropriate to describe people, many of whom were born in France and have French nationality. The term 'populations of immigrant origin' is now passing into widespread use and a new range of official bodies has been developed to coordinated policies for integration. Thus the

13. Ann Dummett and Andrew Nicol, *Subjects, Citizens, Aliens and Others: Nationality and Immigration Law*, Law in Context series, Weidenfeld and Nicolson: London, 1990, p. 137.

14. Ibid.

15. Council of Europe, *Community and Ethnic Relations in Europe: Final Report of the Community Relations Project of the Council of Europe*, p. 13.

traditional French distinction between nationals and aliens, which has been important in respect of the conferment of rights and obligations, has been attenuated by the recognition of minority communities within the category of French citizens. The distinction has also been eroded by the de facto requirement within the European context to provide equal rights to EU nationals and, through various agreements, rights to some third-country nationals who do not enjoy French citizenship.

Germany, whose colonial dependencies were few, has with limited exceptions neither sought nor welcomed permanent settlers from foreign countries but has accepted large numbers of guest workers, principally from Turkey, to meet the needs of the domestic labour market. In Germany, however, citizenship is normally acquired through descent (*ius sanguinis*) and second- and even third-generation immigrants do not automatically acquire citizenship and are generally referred to and considered to be 'foreigners'. The very rigid approach to the conferment of nationality on the settled Turkish community is in sharp contrast to the facility with which 'ethnic' Germans acquire citizenship irrespective of their tangible association with their 'mother country'.

While recognition or conferment of nationality remains the most important and perhaps most effective formal guarantee of rights recognised by the state, obtaining a secure residential status remains important for any non-citizen. European states have frequently adopted additional measures to cope with new situations arising from recent immigration: either rules and legislation have been adapted or completely new pieces of legislation and other measures have been introduced. Some European countries gave recognition to certain religions with a strong following amongst immigrants and even provided them with equal status to the dominant host religion. France belatedly provided the right of association to minorities after 1981, but other European countries were frequently more generous, providing immigrants with a certain longevity of residence with the right to vote and to be elected at the local municipal level of government.

The study 'Community and Ethnic Relations in Europe', conducted by the Council of Europe, illustrates that there is great variety within the European Community as to the rights and the extent of rights extended to non-citizens.[16] There is also evidence of a direct correlation between extending rights to non-nationals and the expectation that they will become nationals by naturalisation. The naturalisation rate is particularly high in Scandinavia, where resident foreigners have been given many opportunities for participation in decision-making processes, but is much

16. Council of Europe, *Community and Ethnic Relations in Europe*, Council of Europe, Strasbourg, France, 1990.

lower in Germany and Switzerland, countries which have extended few rights to foreign nationals.

Even a superficial examination of the experience and practice of difference states within the European Community regarding how they confer citizenship and how they treat foreigners is sufficient to conclude that few if any rules are immutable. It is primarily the value judgments of the states concerned, or more accurately the value judgments of their elected governments, which determine the circumstances in which citizenship is conferred and the extent to which rights are conferred on foreigners, including rights of settlement and rights to participate in local democratic institutions.

Class, Ethnicity and Social Status

While the focus of this book precludes an examination of the sociology of race including how, why and with what impact social stratification affects discrimination both within member states of the European Community and within the European Community itself, there is clear evidence of the interaction between social status, ethnicity and racial discrimination.[17] From a British perspective it is important to acknowledge that class, frequently manifested by schooling, accent and social status, are clear predictors of life chances: a recent analysis of senior civil servants in the Scottish Office demonstrated the importance of public school upbringing, of graduation from Oxford and Cambridge universities and of being schooled outside Scotland. In the context of anti-discrimination law it is important to mention that no contemporary European state outlaws directly class or social status as a basis of discrimination. Nonetheless, in so far as contemporary anti-discrimination legislation on the grounds of race, as exemplified by Section 1 of the Race Relations Act of 1976, provides that indirect discrimination is unlawful unless justified on non-racial grounds, by the same token where class and other prejudices result in disproportionate lack of opportunity for a section of applicants who are identifiable on racial grounds, then members of that section will have a valid claim for discrimination. While class has never been accepted as a justifiable basis for discrimination it would be naive to suppose that courts do not re-define class, both consciously and otherwise, as some more acceptable equivalence such as 'well-mannered', or 'sympathetic' which may then be perceived to be justifiable.

17. John Solomos in *Race and Racism in Contemporary Britain*, Macmillan, London, 1989, provides a useful overview of the subject while the sociology of race is given a succinct position statement in Haralambos (ed.), *Sociology; New Directions*, Causeway Books, Lancashire, 1985.

Much of the contemporary debate on ethnicity also goes beyond the boundaries of this book. Nonetheless the term 'ethnicity' has an important ideological underpinning.[18] Ethnic groups cannot remain untouched by ideologies, particularly racial ones. To the extent that ethnicity has been used as a substitute or euphemism for 'race', it may reinforce subordination in a system of 'internal colonialism' where the colonial relationship affects both the dominant and subordinate groups in their perception of their own role. Robert Blauner refers to internal colonialism as a process in which colonised groups who are minorities within a structure of white bureaucratic control have their culture depreciated or destroyed and are confined to low-status social positions: this in turn affects their self-conceptions and they tend to view themselves as inferior in much the same way whites view them.[19] The categorisation 'ethnic minority' may consequently be part of the semiotics or sign language by which groups are categorised and assigned subordinate roles and responsibilities. In contrast with class, however, discrimination on the basis of ethnicity constitutes racial discrimination, which is prohibited under major international conventions. For most purposes, ethnicity is defined as a composite of culture, language, religion and national origin. Anti-discrimination law thus may serve to protect not only individuals but the cultural heritage of minorities from attrition by policies of assimilation and integration.

Inequality – of what?

The concepts described above may be characterised as aspects of inequality. Because the formulation of anti-discrimination law is based on the premise that law is capable of promoting equal treatment and protecting the most vulnerable against arbitrary discriminatory practice, there is an inevitable conceptual interdependence between inequality and anti-discrimination provision.

The concept of inequality carries descriptive, normative and rhetorical connotations. The descriptive connotation is dependent upon establishing a basis for comparison and describing the influences or circumstances which give rise to social differentiation: to the extent that inequality becomes descriptive it is synonymous with diversity and does not therefore carry with it the badge of social evil.

In the case of racial inequality, the history of science, anthropology, literature, sociology and law demonstrate that these disciplines frequently

18. E. Cashmore and B. Troyna, *Introduction to Race Relations*, 2nd edition, The Farmer Press, Basingstoke, 1990, p. 145.
19. Robert Blauner, *Racial Oppression in America*, Harper and Row, New York, 1972.

espoused concepts of genetic differentiation to justify the superiority of white or western society and white people over black people by the assertion of innate differences which justified inequality through reference to natural selection.[20] Today there is much greater conviction in, and commitment to, a belief that all persons are created equal and should enjoy rights and fulfil obligations on the basis of equal treatment. But in the debate on questions of normative inequality, the central question becomes 'inequality of what?' – that is, what is the normatively significant domain of inequality?

The reality of human existence is diversity and there is no necessary assumption that the promotion of equality in one aspect of life will not decrease diversity in others. A study by Amartya Sen on the normative aspects of inequality demonstrates that there is wide diversity of what kind of equality is sought by different states and by different regimes; for some it is equality in the distribution of welfare that is central, while for others it may be equal liberty, equality of primary goods, equality under the law or equality of influence – that each should account for one, and none for more than one. Each theory assigns value to equality, and in each case this value derives from a more basic concern to render the theory itself impartial, free from arbitrary discrimination that would pose clear and direct threats to the possibility of any ethical theory.[21] Sen argues that freedom of choice is central to a meaningful understanding of equality, while recognising that this freedom has limitations: thus 'freedom from drought' may not appear to render substantial choice for those subject to its ravages. Freedom in this context is the existence of the means and capability to take positive steps not only to ameliorate the immediate experience but to reduce the likelihood of recurrence.

Rights and freedoms are concepts which are inextricably linked, as is illustrated by the European Convention on Human Rights and Fundamental Freedoms (1950). In many works, however, rights and freedoms are often categorised in a manner reflecting the particular theories, institutions, instruments or even idiosyncrasies which the author is trying to promote.[22] An important distinction should be made between the theories and concepts of the empirical positivists on the one hand, and those of the natural rights adherents, whose approach is based on God-given or *a priori* moral assumptions which are not open to empirical

20. See M.D. Biddiss (ed.), *Images of Race*, Leicester University Press, Leicester, 1979, and J.R. Flynn, *Race, IQ and Jensen*, Routledge and Kegan Paul, London, Boston and Henley, 1980.

21. See Amartya Sen, *Inequality Re-examined*, Clarendon Press, Oxford, 1992, and A. Hamlin, 'Complex Ruminations on the Simplest of Ideas', *The Times Higher Education Supplement*, London, 30 Oct. 1992.

22. Scott Davidson, *Human Rights*, Open University Press, Buckingham, 1993.

verification, on the other. According to the former doctrine, which is permeated by the thinking of David Hume and the distinction between 'is' and 'ought', that which 'is' is verifiable and of concrete value; neither rights nor freedoms therefore have any meaning unless they are deliverable. In legal discourse, in order to exist rights and freedoms must be recognised and enforced by the courts. Austin took this argument to its otiose conclusion by suggesting that the law was the law because it was recognised as such by the courts and enforced by the state; the command of the sovereign, bolstered with the requisite procedural support of the state, was the primary law-making entity, and any law could be recognised provided it was enforced by the courts.[23]

Consequently for the positivists it was the process of recognition that determined the character of law and not the inherent attributes of what it was attempting to do. Thus the laws of Nazi Germany, including the racist differentiation between Aryans and non-Aryans, principle Jews and Gypsies, were de facto law and thus de jure law. The apparently amoral approach of the positivists was attenuated to a degree by the utilitarian doctrines of Bentham. To the utilitarian positivists the litmus test of acceptability was the application of the pleasure principle; on the premise that most things in life give pleasure or inflict pain, the utility of any measure would be assessed by seeing if it gave greater pleasure than pain to more people.[24] But this might lead to the tyranny of the majority over minorities: minority groups would have no claim to protection if their disadvantage (or pain) was outweighed by the advantage (or pleasure) given to numerically stronger groups.

More recently Hart has sought to introduce a different positivist test of the validity of law, thus maintaining the distinction between law and morality.[25] He has argued that the legitimacy of law is derived from the community which it seeks to direct, in essence an argument similar to the 'social contract' theories of Rousseau and Locke which otherwise fall into the natural law camp. On that basis it would be possible to protect minorities because they comprise a distinct element within the broader community and pluralist societies would only support or legitimate laws which promoted that essential respect. But whatever interpretation is placed on positivism it cannot disguise the inherent difficulty of finding a sound home for human rights and the concept of equality within this

23. See, for example, R.M.W. Dias, *Jurisprudence*, 3rd edition, Butterworths, London, 1970, Chapter 14, pp. 381–404.
24. J. Bentham, in H.L.A. Hart and J.H. Burns (eds), *An Introduction to the Principles and Morals of Legislation*, Athlone Press, London, 1982; David Hume, *A Treatise on Human Nature*, Fontana Collins, London, 1970; Davidson, *Human Rights*, pp. 1–62.
25. H.L.A. Hart, *The Concept of Law*, Clarendon Press, Oxford, 1971.

philosophical framework.

Utilitarianism is built on the assumption that individual needs must give way to those of the community. Dworkin argues that it is a tenet of liberal democratic society that equal respect and concern must be a principle qualifying the drive to maximise happiness on behalf of the greatest number.[26] When community drives threaten to violate respect for individual rights then the latter should be upheld over the former. By combining the approaches of Hart and Dworkin within a positivist utilitarian framework, there is scope for requiring the protection of both group and individual rights under local and international law.

One of the most important recent contributions to the literature on rights has been that of Rawls.[27] In his social contract theory, all persons are in an original position of equality regarding the distribution of power and freedom but are hidden from their own personal situation by a 'veil of ignorance'. Rawls contends that in this situation a rational person will apply two principles of justice: first, everyone will have the most extensive rights to basic liberties compatible with the same rights being given to all others and, second, the impact of the state on social and economic inequalities must be organised to benefit the least advantaged, thus promoting equality of opportunity in the distribution of 'primary goods' such as liberty, income and wealth.

Clearly not all contemporary authors are concerned equally about the distributional impact of legal systems. Nozick has postulated a theory based on the idea of the minimal state which is confined to a night watchman role.[28] The moral precepts of the state, again based on a variation of the social contract theory, include a right to life, liberty, property and contract, and freedom from criminal activities such as assault, robbery and fraud, which threaten the enjoyment of these rights. Beyond those constraints the individual is allowed to do what he or she wishes. The state must not assume a welfare function or promote the redistribution of wealth, as this would interfere with individual freedom; this is Nozick's essential criticism of utilitarianism. In this minimal state it would seem that equality would have no place as a principle: accordingly historical or inherited disadvantages, though clearly limiting choice and freedom from arbitrary constraints for the individual as well as the group, would not be compensated for or diminished by state activity.

To diminish inequality both Sen and Rawls argue in support of a capability approach which in essence means the provision of resources, or in Rawls' terminology 'primary goods', to optimise choice. Sen

26. R. Dworkin, *Taking Rights Seriously*, Duckworth, London, 1971.
27. John Rawls, *A Theory of Justice*, Oxford University Press, London, 1972.
28. R. Nozick, *Anarchy, State and Utopia*, Basic Books, New York, 1974.

recognises that the concepts of inequality and equality are exceedingly complex and consequently making any statements about them are highly problematic. There is agreement, however, with Rawls in that where critical choices are to be made regarding future actions, whether at a governmental or individual level, there must be both a structure and infrastructure which enables and facilitates the conferment of benefits in comparative terms to the least well-off.

Whether or not the development of a coherent theoretical rights framework will promote the advancement of human rights and anti-discrimination law at national and international levels is clearly debatable. Indeed, if the UN were to have waited until its members had agreed a common theory before drafting legal instruments it is improbable that any of the international conventions mentioned in this book would have been passed. In fact, the passage of these laws reflects the recognition of *realpolitik* by the members of the bodies concerned; they have been more concerned to abolish torture, for example, than to examine in detail what torture is, what is wrong with it and why people practice it. The developed if imperfect structure of international law can be seen as a reflection of a compelling need to respond – or at least be seen to respond – to urgent and critical problems. The common enemy of apartheid, for example, was the binding agent which created the International Convention Against All Forms of Racial Discrimination in 1965.

Although differences in state ideologies on human rights have been played down in order to achieve agreement on international conventions and protocols, it remains generally true that the liberal democracies of the West placed much greater emphasis on individual rights and on civil and political rights than did the socialist and Marxist states. The latter in turn placed greater stress on community development and economic and social rights. With the collapse of the Soviet Union and other communist and Marxist states, the ideologies they supported received such a blow that many predict their imminent total demise. In intellectual terms, however, there is still a case to answer as to the best way of addressing both group and individual interests, and it would be unwise to simply assume that promoting the primacy of individualism will necessarily lead to more protection for community rights. This general political debate is still ongoing. More specifically, race relations and anti-discrimination law provide an important link between individual and minority group rights, and it is possible that these could serve as a testing ground more generally for international law on human rights.

As anti-discrimination law is a branch of human rights, and human rights protection is now firmly enshrined in international law, anti-discrimination law has become a separate branch of public international law attracting its own legal theories and scholarship. Davidson gives a useful introduction to this area from a human rights perspective.[29] For the present, it will suffice to make a couple of general observations about this. If we consider 'law' to be that which is constantly observed and which ensures that breaches are systematically penalised, then we are forced to confront the central dilemma of international law. It is generally the sovereign state, through the local remedies rule, rather than the UN or other international body (IB) which must ensure the observance of the law. The sanctions which an IB can impose are seldom compelling, and these bodies cannot insist on redress for individual grievances.

In the field of human rights, international law has had to break new ground by seeking to extend to individuals, as well as states, the opportunity to question the actions of governments, institutions and persons otherwise outside the arena of public law. As the last report of Austria to the CERD illustrated, states have been slow to accept responsibility for seeing that private organisations do not discriminate in areas such as recruitment or promotion; particularly when discrimination is indirect and stems from policies such as the imposition of age barriers, and where the institution may not be aware that these policies are creating disadvantage.

Equality and Political Theory

In political theory there is a clearly-marked division between right-wing and left-wing approaches to equality. In the right-wing view there is a presumption that economic benefits will filter down through society, and the adoption of policies which stimulate growth will best serve the poorest of society in absolute if not comparative terms. Equality here means the right of the individual to compete in society and enjoy economic benefits. Clearly the poor are initially disadvantaged in this competition, and 'leg-up' programmes such as urban renewal, job creation, work-training and education priorities may be permissible to offset this; however, the market must not suffer major distortion or growth will not be optimised and trickle-down benefits will in turn be affected.

Put crudely, the right frequently sees equality in terms of equality in the market place or equal competition, but not in terms of social equality or the creation of a level playing-field. The perceived danger of state action to assist any disadvantaged group is that this action creates a dependency culture and kills off initiative by failing to provide adequate reward. The market is perceived to be fair in the sense that it achieves a random distribution of benefits in cases where there is not enough to reach

29. Davidson, *Human Rights*, pp. 1–62.

everyone; thus justice is perceived to be done.[30]

In contrast, the left take a view that the existing demonstrable inequalities on the basis of race are neither an inevitable reflection of market forces nor a situation which will be remedied by formal access to equality of opportunity. Accordingly, effective anti-discrimination law must address not only existing discriminatory practice but also inherited disadvantage. Another point of departure for the left is that the present climate of recession, or its immediate aftermath, and the spirit of individualism against social values fosters a destructive competition and an ideology of individual materialism. Disadvantaged groups thus have, and perceive there to be, little hope of improvement, which results in their severe alienation from dominant norms. This leads to both physical consequences, such as unemployment, and emotional and psychological consequences such as delinquency, crime and the longer-term crystallisation of inequality by closing down opportunities for advancement.

Equal Opportunity Law and Policy

The application of political theory requires governments to adopt practical policy measures, which are usually but not necessarily underpinned by law. Certainly some states have accepted the law as a prerequisite,[31] but it is generally accepted that law alone will be inadequate to effect change; legislation must be integrated with complimentary policy measures. We may characterise law and policy in this field as comprising one or more of the following approaches:

First, the *equal treatment approach* depends on establishing formal equality. This has been described as the colour-blind approach because there is a presumption that if all people are 'equal' they must be treated identically. The criticism of this approach is that it leaves indirect discrimination untouched because it does not involve any formal differentiation. For example, housing allocation policies which require an applicant to be on the waiting list for a particular period or to have a relation resident in the preferred locality are likely to discriminate against newcomers. Similarly word-of-mouth recruitment, while no doubt cheap and effective, will merely perpetuate the established composition of the workforce and thus discriminate against black people.

Second, the *level playing-field approach* accepts the fact that indirect discrimination will have created historical patterns of disadvantage which

30. Goodwin, 1992.
31. See Home Office, *Racial Discrimination*, Cmnd 6234 at para. 23, HMSO, London, 1985.

the equal treatment regime will not have addressed. This approach therefore seeks to tackle 'pre-entry' handicaps by encouraging the conditions which will enable minorities to compete fairly. In housing, for example, access to a Housing Association may be restricted by a failure to advertise vacancies in the minority press, or by restricting information to English publications. At work promotion may depend on a standard of English which goes far beyond the needs of the job. The level playing-field approach attempts to seek out these handicaps and correct them. The emphasis of this approach is on gatekeepers such as employment agencies, estate agents, interviewers and promotion boards. A criticism has been that, while it may strive to have everyone start on equal terms, once competition for social and economic advantage is on, the traditionally disadvantaged will fall behind, producing much the same outcome as before.[32]

Third, the *equal outcome approach* focuses attention on the end result of policies and programmes, imposing an expectation that ethnic minorities will be reflected proportionally in, for example, the workforce, education and housing allocations. In so far as this approach accepts the legitimacy of quotas as a means of achieving the desired result, there are a number of criticisms.[33] In particular the result may involve the less well-qualified, and potentially less deserving, getting a job, a house or promotion to make up the numbers, and in doing so discriminating against better qualified white applicants who feel no great need to shoulder the burden of rectifying historical disadvantage. Such reverse discrimination is often unlawful, but perhaps more importantly it is seen to be unfair; it denies everyone a fair chance and is in breach of the concept of natural justice. Moreover it may perpetuate practices which are discriminatory by producing simplistic solutions.[34]

Fourth, the *equal opportunities approach* is similarly concerned about outcomes but rejects the legitimacy of quotas and takes a longer-term view of when proportionality will be achieved. Essentially this approach is a systemic one, being as much concerned about attitudes, processes and policies as about outcomes, while frequently testing the value of the system by the extent to which it delivers improvement in practice. Because this approach accepts the need to monitor, ethnic record-keeping is required and targets are set to establish goals and gauge progress towards

32. Ian Forbes and Geoffrey Mead, *Measure for Measure; A Comparative Analysis of Measures to Combat Racial Discrimination in the Member States of the European Community*, Equal Opportunities Study Group, University of Southampton/Department of Employment, Sheffield, 1992.

33. See John Edwards, *Positive Discrimination*, Tavistock Publications, London, 1987.

34. Martin MacEwen, *Housing, Race and Law*, Routledge, London, 1991.

them. While legislation does not need to underpin this process, it is unlikely that it will be widely adopted outside the public sector and the major employers without a legal framework. An example of the equal opportunity approach imposed by law is provided by the Canadian Federal Employment Equity Act (section 4) which requires larger employers to prepare plans setting goals and targets and to report annually on progress to the Minister of State for Employment.[35]

The advantage of the equal opportunity approach is that it is designed to sustain improvement by effecting systemic change permeating the whole organisation, and to encourage an ethos which will not only facilitate a questioning of traditional methods but also install the capability to effect change and to monitor its effects. There is always a danger that the pursuit of current fashion will produce short-term successes only; nonetheless, there is an obvious parallel between this approach and contemporary views of stimulating organisational change and improvement through 'customer care', through quality systems and through total quality management.

Motives for Anti-discrimination Law

Differences in political views regarding the normative value of the concept of equality and the policies which should be followed in turn affect the development and implementation of anti-discrimination provisions. Moreover, there is evidence that the political values which are applied to justice and equality are culturally-bound. Our preference for one form of analysis and explication over another is less the product of applied logic and more a reflection of the dominant social values in which we are placed.[36] As a consequence, when in a democratic state the government in office wishes to seek a mandate from the electorate and at the same time affirm its intention to achieve equality of opportunity, it may negotiate 'solutions' to discriminatory practices which are little more than palliatives from the perspective of minority groups but which are acceptable to the majority. Indeed much of the history of race relations has been bound up in ideas about electoral tolerance.[37]

From the perspective of state psychology there are probably three

35. See Ian McKenna in report of Scottish Ethnic Minorities Research Unit (SEMRU) to Home Office in four volumes, 1992; the first volume was later published as, *Anti-discrimination Law in Four English Speaking Countries*, SEMRU and Commission for Racial Equality, Edinburgh, 1992; vol. 1, p. 106.

36. Warnke, 1992.

37. See G. Bindman and A. Lester, *Race and Law*, Penguin Books, Harmondsworth, 1972, and Jack Greenberg, *Race Relations and American Law*, Columbia University Press, New York, 1959.

principal motives behind the promulgation of anti-discrimination law provisions:

1. First, there is a motive 'to do good': such a motive is frequently evangelical and may be driven by a sense of guilt at the evident inequality of social opportunities between racial groups. Such motives may become manifest in top-down programmes driven at a political level, with preset targets and budgets and, more often than not, little flexibility in accommodating local opinion and knowledge.[38]

2. Second, a state may want to 'look good'. States are frequently concerned about their own public image and will go to some lengths to avoid being categorised as racist, xenophobic or exploitative. Motives may include the necessity to comply with international regulations, or the need to improve relationships with other states and minority groups resident there; for example, Germany's relations with the Danish government are often affected by the existence of the Germany minority group in Denmark. States will also be concerned about their domestic public image. The result may be the passage of legislation outlawing discriminatory practices in a range of situations but the legislation will often lack the necessary teeth to secure compliance. A particular example in Britain is Section 71 of the Race Relations Act of 1976: this supposedly imposes a duty on local authorities by obliging them to 'make appropriate arrangements with a view to securing that their various functions are carried out with due regard to the need . . . to promote equality of opportunity and good race relations between persons of different racial groups.' As Lord Hailsham observed during the passage of the legislation, this was a cosmetic measure; the Home Secretary has never taken any action against any local authority for ignoring it.

3. The third motive might be classified as seeking to 'be just', by which is implied a more conscious realisation that self-interest goes beyond controlling social tensions created by racial inequality. There is an attempt to promote much more substantial harmonious inter-ethnic relations, through the adoption of measures which seek to marry the promoted ideology of equality of opportunity with practical measures which will secure tangible movement towards its delivery.

There may also be more direct pressures for the creation of anti-discrimination law, including the need to control racial unrest in the form of riots, racial attacks and harassment and international pressure such as

38. See the critique of the British Urban Programme by Stewart and Whitting, *Ethnic Minorities and the Urban Programme*, SAUS, Bristol, 1983.

trade sanctions (as exemplified in Rhodesia and South Africa) or the effecting of trading agreements such as Lome. There have been pressures from indigenous peoples such as the Aborigines in Australia, the Maoris in New Zealand, the Inuit in Canada and the American Indians in the USA, all of whom have demonstrated the resurgence of their self-identity by demanding that the state reassess processes of acculturation and the effective delivery of equal opportunities on both an individual and a group basis.

Purpose and Function of Anti-Discrimination Law

Given the complexity of issues, pressures and motives which affect the drafting of legislation, the expectations of what the legislation will achieve may differ significantly within states as well as between them. Frequently the expected outcomes are not made explicit, thus making judgments difficult: this is true in most European Community states.

If we consider anti-discrimination law in five principal areas, namely the provision of goods, services and facilities, education, employment and housing, and the enjoyment of political and legal rights, then we can see what the law is intended to cover. However, the mere recital of the law can mask intentions. The absence of anti-discrimination law in housing, for example, may be counterbalanced by public and grant-aided private or voluntary sector programmes which effectively ameliorate disadvantage. Further, the presence of legislation is no guarantee of its delivery; in law, voting rights were conferred on all citizens of the USA, but in practice some Southern officials showed considerable ingenuity in thwarting these rights through tactics such as the manipulation of literacy tests. In this case, as soon as old practices were stamped out by tedious, case-by-case litigation, new ones were invented.[39]

In its first annual report, the British Race Relations Board (as it then was) summarised the role of legislation as:

1. Providing an unequivocal declaration of public policy.
2. Providing support to those who do not wish to discriminate but feel compelled to do so by social reasons.
3. Providing protection and redress to minority groups.
4. Providing for the peaceful and orderly adjustment of grievances and the release of tension.
5. Reducing prejudice by discouraging the behaviour in which prejudice finds expression.

39. See Arthur Larson, 'The New Law of Race Relations', *Wisconsin Law Review*, 1969, No. 2.

Modern commentators have suggested that further roles be added, including:[40]

6. Reducing systemic discrimination by changing policies and practices which result in indirect discrimination.
7. Establishing standards by which public and private behaviour may be measured and improved and by creating a forum (the enforcement agency) to articulate such standards.

The extent to which states will emphasise the role of legislation, either to control extreme acts of violence and to stem civil unrest or as a mechanism for social engineering to achieve radical change, is less likely to depend on the stated objectives and roles, even where these are clearly articulated, and more on the relative weight given to the relevant sections of the legislation by those responsible for review (usually the government of the day) and those responsible for enforcement (the police, the public prosecution service or a special agency). Pareto has sought to explain this gap between apparent expectations and delivery by suggesting that much of our social action is of a non-logical kind.[41] We do not establish goals and then seek the best way of achieving them; rather we have sentiments requiring expression and then seek to provide, frequently in retrospect, a logical explanation for the resultant action. Rex suggests that in race relations both personal and group interaction are more likely to be informed by sentiments associated with conflict, oppression and exploitation than with any rationalisation provided by the participants.[42] With respect to statecraft it may be argued that governments will have a gut response to particular issues but will seldom have the insight required to analyse the reasons behind this response. Accordingly, it is probably wise to suspend belief in official explanations as they are frequently divorced from a social context and a knowledge of actual outcomes.

Whatever the immediate purpose of state anti-discrimination provision, its content is likely to reflect at least some elements which have their origins in legislation found elsewhere. The influence of international conventions provides some common elements in anti-discrimination legislation, but there is also the fact that racialised minorities in different states are likely to suffer similar experiences. Consequently, criminal law must address common problems such as racial assault and harassment,

40. See, for example, C. McCrudden, D.J. Smith, C. Brown and J. Knox, *Racial Justice at Work – the Enforcement of the Race Relations Act 1976 in Employment*, PSI, London, 1991. See also MacEwen, *Housing, Race and Law*, and SEMRU, *Anti-discrimination Law*.

41. See John Rex, *Race and Ethnicity*, Open University Press, Milton Keynes, 1986, and Wilfred Pareto, *The Mind and Society: A Treatise on Sociology*, Dover Books, 1963.

42. John Rex, *Race and Ethnicity*, 1986.

incitement to racial hatred and the publication of various forms of racist material. With respect to discriminatory practice, the law will need to address common issues such as direct discrimination, that is, discrimination based directly on colour or on ethnic or national origins, and will particularly be obliged to do so when dealing with employment and the provision of services by the state and its agencies.

When dealing with discriminatory practices, the state will need to choose between using criminal law and civil law. Criminal law is more obviously in the public domain, with prosecutions in most states instigated by a public prosecution service following formal investigation of offences by the police. The advantage of using criminal law over civil action is that it sends an explicit message that discrimination is an offence against the state as well as the individual or group. Penalties may also be more severe, including fines and, in extreme cases, imprisonment. However, in many cases civil proceedings may offer the individual more effective remedies, because:

1. The standard of proof is less exacting; the test of liability is the balance of probability, whereas in criminal proceedings it is 'beyond reasonable doubt' and therefore much more onerous.

2. In many jurisdictions there may be a right of silence in criminal proceedings, whereas in civil cases there is no defence of self-incrimination and the respondent will be obliged to testify before a court or tribunal. On occasion, as in Britain, the court may draw adverse inferences if the respondent fails to provide information requested without reasonable explanation, or to offer a reasonable account of events which might challenge that of the pursuer.

3. Civil remedies are better geared to righting individual wrongs by tailoring redress to the specific issues arising in the case. Thus the courts may order reinstatement for a dismissed employee, prevent a houseowner from selling on a discriminatory basis (safeguarding the interests of a prospective purchaser), order monetary compensation to someone refused entry to a pub or require the recognition of equivalent qualifications to the normal university entrance requirements. In contrast, while courts in criminal cases may be able to provide some monetary redress to individual victims this does not usually happen and the range of remedies is much more restricted.

4. In civil cases the pursuer keeps control of proceedings, either personally or through a solicitor, while in criminal cases the victim is often kept completely in the dark regarding the process and may even be

unaware of its conclusion. This control includes settling on an extra-judicial remedy, a process contrasting with the all-or-nothing character of criminal proceedings.[43]

What is less uniform in both civil and criminal jurisdictions, possibly reflecting not only the perception of equality, the political attitude of the government in power and the purpose and pressure of introducing legislation, is the approach towards indirect discrimination. Indirect discrimination occurs where various tests and requirements are imposed in a non-discriminatory fashion but which nonetheless result in disadvantage for a particular racial group or groups. The same factors which influence attitudes towards indirect discrimination will influence the extent to which the state will apply anti-discrimination provisions to the private sector.

The extent to which civil and political rights as well as social and economic rights are addressed in anti-discrimination law is uncertain and unpredictable. As we have noted above, the status of 'citizen' will usually entail as a matter of course the conferment of civil and political rights. But frequently when these rights have been conferred formally they have then been denied in practice. In Europe, it is unusual for anti-discrimination legislation to address the conferment of civil and political rights beyond the formal equality provided to all citizens. It must be recognised, however, that whatever the content of any anti-discrimination law, it is frequently embedded in an existing structure of countervailing ideology which reflects both contradictory legislation and also the processes and the personnel – the court system and the access to legal aid, the lawyers and the judges – which are there to sustain it.

Anti-discrimination Law in Europe

When looking at the position of European states and the Council of Europe and the European Union, two questions spring to mind. Is there machinery at a European level which makes responses to discrimination distinct, and is the problem of discrimination in Europe distinct from that in other regions of the world? The first question is tackled in Chapter Three of this book, which deals with the various European bodies which have jurisdiction or influence over the issue. There may be a supplementary question about the extent to which the European organs are mirrored by those of North and South America, Southeast Asia, Australasia, Africa and in other parts of the world, but it is beyond the scope of this book to

---

43. Banton, 'The UN Racial Covenant', London, similarly lists four advantages of the civil system which covers largely the same ground but with a slightly different emphasis.

explore that issue. A 'regional approach' to the analysis of human rights has been attempted by a number of authors both on a general basis (Davidson, Brownlie and Thornberry), and on a more specific level by Beddard (for Europe), Buergenthal et al (for the Americas) and Bello (for Africa).[44]

As to the question of whether there is a specific European dimension, there would seem to be four areas where there are problems specific to Europe. These are the changing patterns of economic relations, the north-south divide and the subsidiary issue of sustainability, political upheavals within Europe and the dynamics of cultural identity and minority rights.

With respect to economic change, a couple of trends seem to be both long-lasting and important. First, while world markets are more organised on a regional basis, the GATT discussions in 1993 and the agreements that followed in 1994 illustrate that self-sufficiency within a regional network such as the EEC will give way to greater inter-regional trade. Any protected market within a region or its associates (the vulnerability of the Caribbean banana trade to the EU countries under the Lome Convention illustrates the point) will either have to compete in a larger arena or go under. If this leads to the further erosion of established trade and production and, because of the volatility of long-term investments, short-termism then those sections of the workforce which are most vulnerable, both skilled and semi-skilled, will include a disproportionate number of ethnic minorities.

It is also apparent that ethnic minorities in Europe are a comparatively aging section of the larger population and their demands for pensions, health care, sheltered housing and other services will increase. However, this coincides with a general European trend to stem investment in the public sector generally and to limit health and housing support in particular. Minority groups will be disproportionately affected by these changes, partly because of their increased representation in the communities affected but also because their members will have secured less insurance (such as investment in private housing which produces capital growth) against the cuts. Homelessness and begging have increased significantly in the UK in the past decade; the extent to which this becomes a European trend and that minorities become more visibly impoverished will increase the prospects of scapegoating and

44. See Davidson, *Human Rights*, 1993; Ian Brownlie (ed.), *Basic Documents on Human Rights*, 3rd edition, Clarendon Press, Oxford, 1992; P. Thornberry, *International Law and the Rights of Minorities*, Clarendon Press, Oxford, 1991; R. Beddard, *Human Rights and Europe*, 2nd edition, Sweet and Maxwell, London, 1980, (for Europe); T. Buergenthal, R. Norris and D. Shelton, *Protecting Human Rights in the Americas*, Engel, Kehl-am-Rhein, 1990, (for the Americas); and E.G. Bello, 'The African Charter on Human and Peoples Rights', *Hague Recueil*, 194, 1985–6, pp. 13–268 (for Africa).

victimisation, feeding the flames of xenophobia and racism which are now all too evident across Europe.

The Brand Report[45] addressed the problem of the so-called north-south divide. It is true that with the economic growth in Southeast Asia in particular, as exemplified by South Korea, Malaysia, Singapore and Hong Kong, the old hegemony of economic power is under threat, but much of the emerging competitiveness of 'third world' countries has been built on cheap labour, a factor which is unlikely to remain static. There is still a very significant difference in income between the north and south; investments channelled into sustainable growth may lessen the divide but there is also concern about environmental factors, such as Europe exporting its toxic waste to poorer recipients and the third world domestic economies accepting low standards of environmental control in order to sustain short-term growth. It is also evident that the developed world, having exploited resources indiscriminately in the past, now assumes that it can impose costly standards on others without commensurate assistance. The effect of these changes is not entirely predictable but it seems likely that the economic pressure on many individuals and families to move from developing to developed countries will remain and the EU will continue to be a prime target for economic migrants.

The countries of the south are also more vulnerable to floods, earthquakes and drought and there is little reserve in their economies to tide them over these disasters, adding to the conditions encouraging or even necessitating migration. While the events in the former Yugoslavia remind us that tribalism is not confined to the developing world, the extent of killing and unrest in Rwanda and Somalia explain the fact that 60 per cent of Europe's refugee and asylum seekers are from other continents. That proportion is unlikely to change.

There is also a north-south divide within Europe. Traditionally, northern European countries have been characterised as relatively stable, prosperous, liberal democracies and southern countries are relatively unstable, less well-off countries run by oligarchies or dictatorships. Sweden, Denmark, France and Germany would fit into the first category, while Portugal and Spain immediately after the Second World War, Greece under the Colonels after 1967, and Italy with its problems of minority government and the Mafia fall into the latter category. There is further an east-west boundary with membership of the European Community, NATO and the Council of Europe and former association with the Soviet Union defining the division.

45. Willy Brandt, *North-South: A Programme For Survival*, the report of the Independent Commission on International Development Issues (chaired by Willy Brandt), Pan Books, London and Sydney, 1980.

However this picture is no longer accurate. Not only have the dictatorships in Europe been replaced by democracies but the differences in economic prosperity are waning, partly due to the EEC regional infrastructure and development funding and the equalising influence of the Common Agricultural Policy, and partly because the decline in some heavy industries such as coal, steel and shipbuilding on which a number of the northern states had a traditional dependence. More generally, the traditional activities of states are increasingly vulnerable unless they are underpinned by a feature of local significance; an example might be the production of Scotch whisky because the quality of Scottish waters appears to give it a qualitative edge on production of whiskies elsewhere. Thus while Bordeaux wines may retain a pre-eminence amongst connoisseurs, the improvement in viniculture techniques elsewhere in Europe, not least from Australian exponents, has led to a highly competitive expansion in good quality wines within the EEC as well as from Romania, Bulgaria and Hungary. The car industry in the UK is now minimal and in France it is under threat while SEAT expands in Spain.

It seems highly improbable, however, that primary immigration into any EU state will be encouraged, not only because of the perceived need to shore up permeable boundaries but also because there has been a tangible change in attitudes towards throw-away migrant labour. Consequently the experience of Japan, whose cheap labour was indigenous, being overtaken in some industries by Korea and now threatened by the enormous potential of China both as a consumer and as a producer, may be repeated in European states and in the European Union itself.

The globalisation of trade is also reflected in the trend by eastern bloc and other countries to join the EU in the wake of the demise of the USSR. While the EU has expanded by the addition of Finland, Sweden and Austria in 1995 there are a number of countries waiting in the wings including the Baltic states, Turkey, Poland, the Ukraine, Slovenia and Hungary. But one of the considerations of membership has been that of human rights; the Baltic states with their 'ethnic' definition of citizenship, and the treatment of the Kurdish minority in Turkey provide examples where membership would be incompatible with the EU's espousal of the European Convention of Human Rights and the Rights of Minorities Protocol (see Council of Europe recommendations 1134, 1177 and 1203).[46]

46. D. Gomien, 'The Rights of Minorities under the European Convention on Human Rights and the European Charter on Regional and Minority Languages', in J. Cator and J. Niessen (eds), *The Use of International Conventions to Protect the Rights of Migrants and Ethnic Minorities*, The Churches Commission for Migrants in Europe, Strasbourg, 1993.

The third dimension to change within Europe relates to the political shift to the right. Governments in France, Germany, the UK and Italy (the four members of the EU with the largest voting power) are all right-of-centre and oppose any expansion of state spending on social welfare. In Italy the election of Berlusconi to the premiership, dependant on the support of the Northern League (a right-wing anti-immigrant party with fascist allegiances), is a development particularly threatening to the promotion of a common anti-racist front in Europe. The experience in the UK after 15 years of Thatcherism is that the social and structural contribution to racism is largely denied by government and there is little effort to counterbalance discrimination by the adoption of positive action programmes.

All this augers badly for the development of a concerted European dimension to the issues of both racial harassment and discrimination. But not all of the portents are negative. The adoption of the protocol on Minorities and the Vienna Declaration and Programme of Action in 1993 by the Council of Europe provide illustrations that the moderate right may be persuaded to take action, albeit frequently under the mistaken belief that it is countries other than their own which need to do something.

The final reference to change in Europe relates to cultural identity and pluralism within states, to which earlier reference has been made. It is ironic that many European ethnographers such as Malinowski, Pritchard, Fraser and Meade travelled to far-flung places such as the Trobriand Islands, the island of Tikopia and the Samoas to study the customs of the exotic with so little self-awareness that their own domestic practices were similarly worthy of study. Now the sociology of race relations is well developed, and it is not the purpose of this book to add to that literature. However, there are some trends which seem relevant. First, by the extension of nationality to immigrant minorities, many western states have signalled an acceptance that they are de facto multi-cultural. The extent to which they will adapt their mono-cultural institutions to accommodate such change is of critical importance.

Second, it is apparent that some states feel threatened by their loss of cultural integrity not merely within their boundaries but beyond. While Christianity dominates the religious map of Europe, to the east and south the Moslem faith holds sway. The historical enmity between the two is epitomised at its worst in the Bosnian conflict, but is also evident in the religious intolerance within states.

In France the Minister for Culture, M. Jacques Toubon (Jack Allgood to his unkind critics), introduced a law banning non-French words unless included in an approved dictionary. While the Constitutional Court in a decision in July 1994 ruled this law unconstitutional as it was in breach of the Declaration of the Rights of Man of 1789, the fact that the proposal had widespread support illustrates the state of siege that some states perceive themselves, their culture or their language to be under. Because English is the most widely spoken language next to the various Chinese spoken languages, it has not been threatened in the same manner although it has not hesitated to adopt a host of French phrases and expressions.

As indicated earlier in this chapter, concern about identity is far from a new experience but the promotion of regionalism within the EU, effectively by-passing national fora in the Committee of the Regions, the creation of new states with national identities in the aftermath of the USSR and the assertion of state sovereignty to counterbalance the centralising and monochromatic influence of the EU are factors which may promote a call for further recognition of minorities as separate cultural entities. That call has so far been met with a fairly cool response, the states concerned being eager to define what or whether national entities exist within their boundaries. It may be argued that the European Union and its members are in a stage of transition: there is an opportunity for both to guide the development of their societies by the promotion of genuine pluralism and by the use of stringent legal measures to stem racial discrimination. How far along that road each has travelled at international and national level is the focus of the chapters that follow.

−2−

Anti-Discrimination Obligations Imposed by International Law

Introduction

The purpose of this chapter is to describe the principal legal obligations imposed by international law in the area of racial discrimination, to which a significant number of EU States are signatories and which are consequently likely to be of relevance to both the immediate and longer-term development of law within and by the European Union.

The right not to be discriminated against on racial grounds is a long-standing right in international law. It falls within the generic description of human rights referred to, *inter alia*, in Article 1 of the United Nations Charter, which has as one of its purposes '. . . promoting and encouraging respect for human rights and for fundamental freedoms for all without distinction as to race, sex, language or religion.' Similarly the 1948 Universal Declaration of Human Rights refers to 'All men being born free and equal in dignity and rights' (Article 1), and to everyone being entitled to the rights set forth in the Declaration ' ...without distinction of any kind, such as race, colour, sex, language, religion, political or other opinion, national or social origin, property, birth or other status.'

While neither the Charter nor the Declaration of the UN constitute formal instruments of international law, and therefore lack formal mechanisms to secure their observance, both are considered to be key documents which set expectations of performance applicable to all members. However, Article 2(7) of the Charter also affirmed the principle of non-intervention by the UN in matters essentially within the domestic jurisdiction of members, which appears to preclude international intervention in this field.[1] Nor did the Charter attempt to set out what the term 'human rights' actually encompassed, although this was remedied by the Universal Declaration which contained lists of civil and political rights and of economic, social and cultural rights, setting a common standard.

---

1. Scott Davidson, *Human Rights*, Open University Press, Buckingham, 1993, p. 12.

Karel Vasak[2] attempted to classify rights according to the French revolutionary slogan 'Liberty, Equality, Fraternity', categorising those rights falling under 'liberty' (civil and political) as first generation, those under 'equality' (economic, social and cultural) as second generation, and those under 'fraternity' (under which rubric group rights would fall) as third generation. This categorisation has political currency and is a useful tool for considering the relative merits of such rights and the countries that most benefit from their promotion; the adage that human rights begin with breakfast is a reminder to the first world about the importance of third-generation rights in many developing countries. But from a legal perspective, there is no underpinning of any rights hierarchy within the UN Charter and Declaration. The fact that anti-discrimination law, while evidently based in the second generation class, seeps through all three suggests that the strength of its support stems from different interest groups.

It is true, however, that when the UN mandated the Commission on Human Rights to draft a binding treaty to give the Universal Declaration legal force, a dispute arose over the relative priority of civil and economic rights and the appropriate mechanisms for enforcement, which led to the creation of two separate covenants. Both the International Covenant on Civil and Political Rights (ICCPR) and the International Covenant on Economic, Social and Cultural Rights (ICESCR) were open for signature in 1966 but did not come into force until a decade later. Greater immediacy was given to the former by requiring the rights in Article 2 to be respected and protected forthwith, while Article 2 of the ICESCR simply provides that states should recognise the rights described and implement them progressively by the adoption of specific programmes. The ICCPR established the Human Rights Committee to implement its provisions and to consider individual petition enabled by an optional protocol. The ICESCR is supervised by the existing Economic and Social Council, a political body which has other responsibilities and less expertise than the specialist committees such as the Committee for the Elimination of All Forms of Racial Discrimination.

As was observed in the opening chapter, the modern concept of a nation-state does not imply homogeneity of the ethnicity of its nationals. The Bahais in Iran, the Kurds in Turkey and Iraq, the Moslems in Bosnia, the Quebecois in Canada (as well as the Metis and Inuit), the Tamils in Sri Lanka and the Sikhs in India are examples of a worldwide phenomenon where minority groups exist as a significant element within states dominated by those of different so-called ethnic origins. Relative homogeneity of ethnic origins, as exists in Japan, is the exception rather

2. Karel Vasak, 'A Thirty-Year Struggle', *UNESCO Courier*, 1977, pp. 29–32.

than the rule. It is also evident that ethnic, religious, linguistic, cultural, historical and social differences between groups are of great variation and complexity: accordingly the identification of particular common themes and experiences is problematic, and this leads to difficulties of analysis and conclusion even where the legislative provisions are common or similar.

The description 'European', no doubt in keeping with other 'racial' descriptions such as 'Asian', disguises a rich multiplicity of ethnic groups within Europe. While the aspirations of Catalans, Bretons and Basques may have common currency in Europe, there are also many other indigenous minority groups with different and less-well publicised ambitions. This fact was confirmed in the 76 country monographs prepared by Capotorti for the United Nations Sub-Commission on the Prevention of Discrimination and the Protection of Minorities.[3] There is also evidence of ethnic linkage across continents; the Lapps in Finland form part of the circumpolar peoples of Eurasia and North America. But again these people, while showing some commonality, can be classified into 71 different groupings.[4] The debates prior to the adoption of the Declaration on the Elimination of All Forms of Racial Discrimination which preceded the eponymous Convention as well as the national reports to the Convention confirm not merely the rich diversity of ethnicity in Europe, but also the ways in which definitions and classification may recognise or deny a group's identity.

The Purpose of International Conventions

Clearly, conventions with the same stated objective which have been drawn up at different times or in different places may have emerged for different reasons, and may seek to provide redress or protection for peoples or groups easily identified as victims at a particular time. Thus post-war promotion by the United Nations of conventions and protocols to protect minorities against discrimination reflected the crimes of genocide against the Jews, Gypsies and Poles during the Second World War. While it is not the purpose of this book to trace the historical origins of any international convention, nor to dissect the nuances in the language employed from the debates and negotiations which preceded the agreements, these considerations may affect the contemporary relevance and application of a particular provision. More importantly, the real

3. Capotorti, monograph referred to in P. Thornberry, *International Law and the Rights of Minorities*, Clarendon Press, London, 1991, p. 3.
4. Siuruainen and Aikio, *The Laps in Finland*, Society for the Promotion of Lap Culture, Helsinki, 1977.

impact of anti-discriminatory provisions is likely to depend less on the inclusivity or exclusivity of definitions, and more on the nature of policing and enforcement to secure compliance.

However, it is also important to mention an underlying difference of approach to racial discrimination within the UK and within other European countries. Because the UK does not have a written constitution which addresses and defines the relationship between the state and its citizenry, there is a presumption in the UK that anti-discrimination provision is predominantly aimed at acts between citizens rather than acts between the citizen and the state. As a result, when a remedy is to be found it will usually be available to the citizen against other citizens as well as to the citizen against the state. In other countries where anti-discrimination provision, whether originating from international conventions or otherwise, is found within a constitutional document there may be a presumption that it protects the citizen against the state but there is not necessarily a presumption that it protects citizen against citizen.

Because constitutional documents are focused on the state they are more likely to provide remedies specifically for the citizen rather than, more generally, for residents. The position in the UK differs from that in many other European countries in that remedies in statute law are more commonly available to anyone falling within the geographical jurisdiction of the 'region' covered by the statute. In Denmark, for example, the official position is that equality of treatment and the principle of non-discrimination on the grounds of race, colour and ethnic origin are entrenched in Danish law[5], but the Constitution itself makes distinctions between citizens and non-citizens regarding detention without trial, appointment to the civil service and ownership of property. There is also evidence that third-country immigrants residing permanently in Denmark are treated less favourably than Danish citizens, refugees, Nordic citizens and EEC citizens with respect to family reunion, work permits for family members, social security provision and deportation.[6]

Finally, there is no underlying presumption of a model society which any of the international conventions is attempting unequivocally to promote. Thus, while there may be a presumption against apartheid, including separate but equal treatment of ethnic or racial minorities,[7] it

5. See Meredith Wilkie, 'Discrimination in Denmark' in *Nordic Journal of International Law*, The Danish Centre for Human Rights, Copenhagen, 1990, vol. 59, no. 1.
6. Ibid., p. 48 ff.
7. The US Supreme Court decision in *Plessy v. Ferguson*, 163 U.S. 537 (1896) institutionalised (or confirmed the legal acceptability of) the common practice of providing separate provision for whites and blacks with the purely notional proviso that the provision should be equal; of course it seldom was: see J. Greenberg, *Race Relations and American Law*, Columbia University Press, New York, 1959.

does not necessarily follow that any signatory to the various conventions will pursue a policy of assimilation, whereby most aspects of separate identity will be lost in the dominant culture, integration, whereby some diversity may be respected but monolithic if elastic norms will prevail, or a pluralistic approach, whereby the norm is diversity and there is no expectation of conformity to the behaviour, language, religion or culture of the dominant group.

The Domestic Application of International Obligations

National constitutions tend to specify either that the courts apply the norms of international law directly (monist constitutions) or that they apply such norms only when special legislation has been passed (dualist constitutions). In fact this distinction is often less than clear-cut, and is of little benefit when explaining the different approaches that states adopt towards the implementation of international obligations. The UK is considered to have a monist constitution because there is no special legal hierarchy of domestic or other law but, because the courts will not recognise international law which conflicts with municipal law unless enacted by parliament and because the executive (through the monarch) sanctions accession to international obligations independently from the legislature, it also has the characteristics of a dualist system.

However, for our purposes the important test is whether the ratification of an international treaty results in any remedies for breach being made available in the municipal courts to those adversely affected. Frequently there is no straightforward answer to this question. To again use the UK as an example, there is a presumption that domestic statute law will be interpreted in conformity with treaty obligations, provided there is no conflict; but where there is conflict, the statute will take precedence. British courts have refused to allow the provisions of the European Convention on Human Rights, for example, to take precedence over domestic law. In *Brind and Others v Secretary of State for the Home Department (1991) 1 All ER 720*, the House of Lords upheld the legality of delegated legislation, the Home Secretary's directive prohibiting the direct broadcasting of the statements of named organisations in Northern Ireland, which was in breach of Article 10 of the Convention. The decision stated further that the Home Secretary was not even obliged to consider the implications of the Convention before issuing the delegated legislation; such a requirement, in the view of Lord Ackner, would be tantamount to incorporating the Convention into 'English' domestic law (commonly 'municipal law') by the back door.

One of the implications of incorporating the European Convention on Human Rights and other conventions into the law of the European Union is that states are obligated to enforce EU law. In the UK the European Communities Act of 1972, as amended, makes EU law part of municipal law as it is in other member countries, a point which is expanded in the next chapter.

It is thus evident that the impact of international obligations is not uniform amongst the signatories to conventions. Many countries with written constitutions have entrenched clauses in these constitutions protecting both minority groups or individuals who are members of racial minorities against arbitrary racial discrimination by the state or by individuals or groups within the state. In some countries, such as Greece for example, it is the practice to incorporate international conventions into domestic law so that the law courts of first instance are obliged to give cognisance to those conventions and to secure their enforcement. In other countries, such as the United Kingdom, the practice is to pass domestic legislation such as the Race Relations Act of 1976 which, whether designed for that function or otherwise, gives effect to international obligations. In countries such as Ireland and Denmark, however, the written constitution does not obviously implement all international obligations against discrimination and there has been no systematic attempt either to incorporate international obligations into domestic law or to pass national legislation which meets these obligations. In such cases as these there may be a presumption that the common law or jurisprudence of the courts, in applying the more general principles reflected in the national constitution or in relevant criminal or civil codes, will be interpreted so as to give effect to the undertakings to which the countries have been bound.

In addition to these formal differences of approach to the implementation of international obligations by EC member states, it is also evident that there will be wide differences of policy and practice, both by central government and by regional and municipal authorities, in the interpretation and application of these obligations. As a consequence, the mere signature of a state to a specific obligation is neither a guarantee that the obligation will be observed nor an indication that mechanisms have been adopted which will secure compliance.

A Statement of International Obligations

The following are the most important international obligations relevant to European states in the area of anti-discrimination law:

1. United Nations (UN): International Convention on the Elimination of all forms of Racial Discrimination (ICERD), 1965.
2. UNESCO: the Convention against Discrimination in Education, 1960,

and the 1962 Protocol.
3. UN: the International Labour Organisation (ILO) Discrimination (Employment and Occupation) Convention, 1958 (ILO No 111).
4. UN: International Covenant on Civil and Political Rights (ICCPR), 1966.
5. The Council of Europe; The European Convention on Human Rights and Fundamental Freedoms (ECHR), 1950.

In addition to the above conventions, covenants and protocols, the Slavery Convention of 1926 and the Protocol of 1953, the Supplementary Convention on the Abolition of Slavery, the Slave Trade and Institutions and Practices similar to Slavery of 1956, the Convention on the Prevention and Punishment of the Crime of Genocide of 1948 and the UN Conventions relating to the Status of Refugees in 1951, the Status of Stateless Persons in 1954, and the International Convention on Economic, Social and Cultural Rights (ICESCR, as mentioned earlier) are relevant but of less central importance to individual anti-discrimination provisions. The application of most of these provisions to the member states of the European Union is summarised in Table 2.1.

From the above list, it is evident that anti-discrimination protection is offered at a global level by the UN through the original Charter and, more saliently, through the Universal Declaration, while protection at a European regional level is organised through the Council of Europe, which by the beginning of 1994 had 32 members. To some extent the European regional system of protection consciously replicates and expands on the global system, and provides in a number of instances a more effective mechanism for enforcement as exemplified by the ECHR and the work of its own Commission and Court.

A recent area of increased international activity has been the protection of migrant workers and their families, as exemplified by the International Convention on the Protection of the Rights of All Migrant Workers and their Families of 1990. While this convention has as its goal the reaffirmation of rights within existing human rights provisions, it also applies these provisions to all workers irrespective of nationality and therefore has the potential to significantly expand the class of beneficiaries.[8] However, three years after the Convention was approved, only two states had ratified it and three others had signed; twenty states must ratify the Convention before it comes into effect and it may be some

8. S. Hune, 'Equality of Treatment and the International Convention on the Protection of the Rights of All Migrant Workers and Members of Their Families', in J. Cator and J. Niessen (eds), *The Use of International Conventions to Protect the Rights of Migrants and Ethnic Minorities*, The Churches Commission for Migrants in Europe, Strasbourg, 1994, p. 82.

time before this happens. The European Convention on the Status of Migrant Workers of 1977 (in force in 1983) had by 1993 been ratified by seven states (France, the Netherlands, Norway, Portugal, Spain, Sweden and Turkey) and signed by a further five (Belgium, Germany, Greece, Italy and Luxembourg). This Convention focuses on nationals of one contracting country who have been authorised to seek employment in another contracting country, but undocumented or irregular migrant workers are not covered.

Of greater longevity is the European Social Charter of 1961, which came into effect in 1965 after ratification by five states. The Social Charter is the counterpart of the ECHR (1950) in that it addresses economic and social rights and has played an important role in harmonising social policies in Western Europe. Among the seven articles considered to be the 'compulsory nucleus' is Article 19 dealing with the rights of migrant workers and their families. Charter rights are to be enjoyed without discrimination on the grounds of race, colour, sex, religion, political opinion, national extraction or social origin.[9] By 1993 the Charter, open for signature to Council of Europe members only, had been ratified by 20 states including the then 12 members of the EC.

Most of the rights defined by the Charter relate to work and working conditions, including health and safety, remuneration, collective bargaining, vocational guidance and training: there are also rights associated with social security, social and medical assistance and medical and welfare benefits. An additional protocol which addressed, *inter alia*, the rights of workers to information and participation in decisions relating to the working environment has now been ratified by three states, sufficient to give it effect, and had been signed by thirteen by the end of 1993. There is also an amending protocol adopted in 1990, which was designed to improve the supervisory machinery by increasing the role of the Parliamentary Assembly and non-governmental organisations (NGOs); by January 1994 this protocol had yet to come into effect, as it required ratification by all contracting parties and only five had ratified it by that date.

Because the supervisory machinery cannot be considered judicial control and the interpretation of the various committees charged with different functions are not binding on the contracting parties, the relative merits of the Charter in promoting anti-discrimination rights have not been examined in this study. It is acknowledged, however, that the cut-

---

9. In the preamble to Neissen and de Lary de Latour, 'Equality of Treatment; the European Social Charter and the European Convention on the Legal Status of Migrant Workers', in Cator and Niessen (eds), *The Use of International Conventions to Protect the Rights of Migrants and Ethnic Minorities*, p. 94.

Table 2.1 Application of International Conventions, etc. to EU member states: extracted from United Nations Human Rights International Instruments 1994

A	B	C	D	E	F
	Austria	Belgium	Denmark	Finland	France
International Covenant on Economic Social and Cultural Rights (ICESCR)	X	X	X	X	X
International Covenant on Civil and Political Rights (ICCPR)	Xa	Xa	Xa	Xa	X
Optional Protocol to the ICCPR	X		X	X	X
Second Optional Protocol to the ICCPR aiming at the abolition of the death penalty	X	s	s	X	
International Convention on the Elimination of all Forms of Racial Discrimination (ICERD)	X	X	Xb	X	Xb
International Convention on the Suppression and Punishment of the Crime of Apartheid (ICSPCA)					
International Convention against Apartheid in Sports (ICAS)					
Convention on the Prevention and Punishment of the Crime of Genocide	X	X	X	X	X
Convention on the Non-Applicability of Statutory Limitations to War Crimes and Crimes against Humanity					
Convention on the Rights of the Child	X	X	X	X	X
Convention on the Elimination of All Forms of Discrimination against Women (CEAFDW)	X	X	X	X	X
Convention on the Political Rights of Women	X	X	X	X	X
Convention on the Nationality of Married Women	X	s	X	X	
Convention on Consent to Marriage, Minimum Age for Marriage and Registration of Marriages	X		X	X	s
Convention against Torture and other Cruel, Inhuman or Degrading Treatment or Punishment	Xc	s	X	Xc	Xc
Slavery Convention 1926	X	X	X	X	X
1953 Protocol amending the 1926 Convention	X	X	X	X	X
Slavery Convention of 1926 as amended	X	X	X	X	X
Supplementary Convention on Abolition of Slavery: Slave Trade and Institutions and Practices Similar to Slavery	X	X	X	X	X
Convention concerning the Traffic in Persons and of the Exploitation of the Prostitution of others		X	s	X	
Convention on the Reduction of statelessness	X		X		s
Convention relating to the Status of Stateless Persons		X	X	X	X
Convention relating to the Status of Refugees	X	X	X	X	X
Protocol relating to the Status of Refugees	X	X	X	X	X
Convention on the rights of migrant workers and the members of their families					

Source: Human Rights International Instruments, Chart of Ratifications as at 30 June 1994, United Nations.

a, Declaration recognising the competence of the Human Rights Committee under article 41 of the International Covenant on Civil and Political Rights; b, Declaration recognising the competence of the Committee on the Elimination of Racial Discrimination under article 14 of the International Convention on the Elimination of All Forms of Racial Discrimination; c, Declarations recognising the

G	H	I	J	K	L	M	N	O	P	Q
Germany	Greece	Ireland	Italy	L'xbourg	N'lands	Norway	Portugal	Spain	Sweden	UK
X	X	X	X	X	X	X	X	X	X	X
Xa		Xa	Xa	Xa	Xa	Xa	X	Xa	Xa	Xa
X		X	X	X	X	X	X	X	X	
X		X	s	X	X	X	X	X	X	
X	X	s	Xb	X	Xb	Xb	X	X	Xb	X
X*										
X*										
X	X	X	X	X	X	X		X	X	X
X*										
X	X	X	X	s	s	X	X	X	X	X
X	X	X	X	X	X	X	X	X	X	X
X	X	X	X	X	X	X		X	X	X
X		X		X	X	X	s		X	
X	s	s	s		X	X		X	X	X
Xc	Xc	s	Xc	Xc	Xc	Xc	Xc	Xc	Xc	Xd
X	X	X	X		X	X	X	X	X	X
X	X	X	X		X	X		X	X	X
X	X	X	X		X	X		X	X	X
X	X	X	X	X	X	X	X	X	X	X
X*			X	X		X	X	X		
X		X			X	X			X	X
X	X	X	X	X	X	X			X	X
X	X	X	X	X	X	X	X	X	X	X
X	X	X	X	X	X	X	X	X	X	X

competence of the Committee against Torture under articles 21 and 22 of the Convention against Torture and Other Cruel, Inhuman or Degrading Treatment or Punishment; d, Declaration under article 21 only; s, Signature not yet followed by ratification; X, Ratification, accession, approval, notification or succession, acceptance or definitive signature; *, Ratification, accession, approval, notification or succession, acceptance or definitive signature which have been given only by the former German Democratic Republic before the reunification.

off point for this study is somewhat arbitrary as both the interpretations and recommendations of the committees are looked on as 'judgments and rulings' and the compilation of these are seen as the 'case law' of the Charter.

In similar vein, while the Conference on Security and Cooperation in Europe (CSCE) has promoted minority rights through a 'process' or general framework for political consultation and consensus-building among its member states, there is no legal structure for securing observance of the principles it has adopted. However, the CSCE is of significance in a number of respects, not least because it extends geographically from Vancouver to Vladivostock, from North America to Eurasia with some 53 participating states.[10] The CSCE is a relative newcomer to the field of minority rights. As the ending of the Cold War diminished the need for attention to issues of security, the CSCE began instead to focus on a growing shared concern for democracy and human rights. This trend was exemplified in the 1990 Copenhagen meeting of the Conference on the Human Dimension, which resulted in far-reaching commitments as to how governments should formulate policy on minority issues. The 1991 Geneva meeting of experts on national minorities issued a report adding a 'shopping list' of constructive measures adopted by states to address national minority matters, noting that these were of legitimate international concern and not within the exclusive provenance of the internal affairs of the state concerned; these were added to the measures adopted in the Charter of Paris of 1990.

While the CSCE now has, as a result of the Helsinki Meeting in 1992, a High Commission of National Minorities which has called for reports on a number of subjects (including the Roma, referred to in the previous chapter) its legal basis as a treaty-instrument or process is dubious; it has therefore not been examined in depth. Participating countries have declared their 'understanding that the CSCE is a regional arrangement in the sense of Chapter VIII of the Charter of the United Nation'. Consequently the fact that its legal status is uncertain does mean that it may not be empowered to make a valuable contribution to the promotion of human rights generally and of minority rights in particular.[11]

As Davidson has observed,[12] while treaties normally give rise to reciprocal rights between states, in the case of human rights the various covenants, conventions and their protocols are more in the nature of unilateral legally-binding commitments supervised by international

10. K. J. Huber, 'The CSCE and Minorities', in Cator and Niessen (eds), *The Use of International Conventions to Protect the Rights of Migrants and Ethnic Minorities*, p. 42.

11. Ibid., p. 41.

12. Davidson, *Human Rights*, p. 75.

institutions. Moreover, it is the individual citizen or, on occasion, the denizen on whom these rights are conferred and who ultimately may seek redress from those institutions. The local remedy rule applies for both regional and global rights, requiring the individual to seek redress in the relevant domestic courts or tribunals, but there is no requirement to seek a 'regional' remedy before a global one. Consequently once the domestic route has been exhausted the applicant may choose between regional and global remedies, and will no doubt weigh up the relative merits of each in terms of jurisdiction, *locus standi*, costs, speed and the likelihood of any decision being implemented.

An obvious weakness of such unilateral obligations in international law and political practice is that countries may withdraw from them formally upon giving notice, or informally by refusing to submit reports or respond to the jurisdiction of the international court and by refusing to implement any judgment. Greece at the time of the 1967 military junta was in flagrant breach of a number of Articles of the ECHR from which it ultimately withdrew: the sanctions of the European Human Rights Commission and the European Court made little if any impact at the time.

The International Convention of the Elimination of All Forms of Racial Discrimination

The Convention defines racial discrimination as:

> Any distinction, exclusion, restriction or preference based on race, colour, descent, or national or ethnic origin which has a purpose or effect of nullifying or impairing the recognition, enjoyment or exercise on an equal footing of human rights and fundamental freedoms in the political, economic, social, cultural or any other field of public life.[13]

The Convention forbids particular acts which arbitrarily differentiate between individuals in the enjoyment of human rights. While the Convention does not condemn or prohibit distinctions by the state which are based on the fact that the person is or is not a citizen, it does not justify private citizens making distinctions on the grounds of citizenship.[14]

The Convention enables special measures to be taken 'for the sole purpose of securing adequate advancement of certain racial or ethnic minority group or individuals requiring such protection as may be necessary in order to ensure such group's or individual's equal enjoyment

---

13. Article 1.1.
14. E. Schwelb, 'The International Convention on the Elimination of all forms of Racial Discrimination', *International and Comparative Law Quarterly*, 1966, vol. 13, p. 996 ff.

or exercise of human rights and fundamental freedoms.' Moreover, the Convention actually requires states to take such measures when circumstances so warrant to ensure the adequate development and protection of the groups identified and to guarantee full and equal enjoyment of human rights and fundamental freedoms.[15]

By 1994, 134 states had become parties to the Convention and 6 states had signed but not ratified (Benin, Bhutan, Grenada, Ireland, Turkey and the USA).[16] Thornberry has observed that the Convention is supported by states to a greater extent than any other comparable human rights instrument. The Convention does not explicitly deal with religious groups, but it does deal with 'racial' discrimination and gives the term a wide meaning. During the drafting of the Convention consideration was given to measures against anti-Semitism, racial segregation and apartheid, Nazism, genocide, neo-Nazism and other forms of racial discrimination.[17] For various reasons these measures were not adopted. Concern was expressed by the Arab states in particular, who were anxious to guard against charges of anti-Semitism as well as to condemn Zionism; a representative of Sudan emphasised that the Arab-Israeli conflict was 'not an expression of anti-Semitism in a religious or racial sense, but a dispute between Arabs on the one hand and Zionism as a political movement and Israel as a state on the other.'[18] At the time of the drafting of the Convention there was still a convenient assumption that racism was a product of colonialism; however, this 'noble lie' has outlived its utility.

The Convention includes an exemption of temporary measures which discriminate in favour of minorities to promote their interests. McKean has suggested that this exemption was not an exception to the principle of anti-discrimination but a corollary to it, demonstrating the fruition of the work of the sub-Commission on Human Rights of the United Nations and the method by which the twin concepts of discrimination and minority protection can be fused into the principle of equality.[19]

Article 2 of the Convention sets out the state's obligations in detail beginning with a general requirement 'to pursue by all appropriate means and without delay, a policy of eliminating racial discrimination in all forms and promoting understanding among all races . . .' The state must not

15. Article 1.4.

16. United Nations General Assembly A/47/18, *Report of the Committee on the Elimination of Racial Discrimination*, 22 September 1992, 47th Session Supplement No. 18.

17. See United Nations document E/CN4/L.710, E/3873; Schwelb, 'The International Convention on the Elimination of all forms of Racial Discrimination'; and Thornberry, *International Law and the Rights of Minorities*, p. 264.

18. United Nations document A/C.3/SR.1302 para. 16.

19. W. McKean, *Equality and Discrimination Under International Law*, Open University Press, Oxford, 1983, p. 159.

'sponsor, defend or support racial discrimination by any persons or organisations and must bring its laws into conformity with the Convention's requirements.'[20] Each state is required to 'prohibit and bring to an end, by all appropriate means, including legislation as required by circumstances, racial discrimination by any persons, group or organisation' (Article 2 [1] (d)).

Article 3 makes express reference to racial discrimination and apartheid, while Article 4 requires states to 'condemn all propaganda and all organisations which are based on ideas or theories of superiority of one race or group of persons of one colour or ethnic origin' or which attempt to justify or promote racial hatred and discrimination in any form. The states must undertake to adopt immediate and positive measures to be exercised with due regard to 'the principles embodied in the Universal Declaration of Human Rights and the rights expressly set in Article 5 of this Convention.' In Europe, Belgium, France, Italy, the UK and Malta have all made reservations or given 'interpretations' of this Article.[21]

Article 5 lists the particular rights which are expressly protected. These include equality before the law, security of the person (political rights), freedom of movement, freedoms of thought, conscience, opinion, expression and peaceful assembly (civil rights), and the rights to work, housing, health, education and to equal participation in cultural activities (economic, social and cultural rights). Article 6 requires the state to provide effective national remedies, while Article 7 imposes an obligation to educate against prejudice and to promote inter-racial understanding.

Part 2 of the Convention contains the measures for implementation. Article 8 provides for the establishment of a committee of 18 experts elected by member states but serving in a personal capacity; membership reflects equitable geographical distribution, the different cultures and legal systems of member states, and the need for high moral standing and acknowledged impartiality of appointees. Signatories are obliged to submit reports on the implementation of the Convention every two years, or otherwise when the Committee has requested (Article 9 [1]). The Committee (termed the Committee on the Elimination of Racial Discrimination, or CERD) makes annual returns to the Secretary-General to the General Assembly of the United Nations, and these may include suggestions and general recommendations based on the reports received. However, the Committee's work suffers from handicaps. In its return for 1992 the Committee observed that in a period of global transition where the cohesion of states has been threatened by brutal ethnic strife and social peace has been challenged by new assertions of discrimination, it was in

---

20. See Articles 2 (1)-(a), (b) and (c).
21. Thornberry, *International Law and the Rights of Minorities*, p. 269.

the paradoxical situation of having to deal with a much increased workload in a greatly diminished period of time. The Committee met for only two weeks out of the scheduled six in that year, owing to financial problems stemming from the failure by member states to honour assessed contributions.[22]

Inter-state complaints may be entertained by the Committee under the procedure set out in Articles 11 to 13, and this includes the potential for creating a subordinate *ad hoc* Conciliation Committee in cases of particular difficulty. With respect to the right of individual petition, Article 14 provides two potential provisions, neither of which are mandatory. First, where a state party declares that it recognises the competence of the Committee then the Committee may receive and consider communications from individuals or groups of individuals within the jurisdiction of that state who are claiming to be victims of a violation by that state party of any of the rights of the Convention. Second, a state party may agree to establish or indicate a body within its national legal order which shall be competent to receive and consider petitions from individuals, and groups. According to Thornberry,[23] the protection of the prerogatives of sovereign states has been a prominent feature of all international petitioning procedures, and the precautions evident in the procedure set out in Article 14 represent an interesting manifestation of the lengths to which caution can be taken while still admitting a validity of individual petitions. Of the European Community states in 1994, only Denmark, France, Italy and the Netherlands have made declarations recognising the competence of CERD under Article 14; Norway and Sweden have made similar declarations.

Although the ability to petition by parties other than states is not mandatory, it does reflect a progressive approach to human rights law. This is also true of the specific recognition of the right of 'groups of individuals' to petition: that recognition appears to be 'general and comprehensive',[24] including groups defined by race, ethnicity or language. Ultimately, where a dispute between two or more states over the interpretation or the application of the Convention has not been settled by negotiation or the procedures set out in the Convention, then reference may be made to the International Court of Justice for decision unless the disputants agree to another mode of settlement.

While the Convention has been signed by all members of the European

22. Paraphrased from letter of transmittal dated 14 August 1992 conveying the Committee's report for 1991–1992.

23. Thornberry, *International Law and the Rights of Minorities*, p. 269.

24. See N. Lerner, *The International Convention on the Elimination of All Forms of Racial Discrimination*, 2nd edition, Alphen Ann Den Rijn, Sijthoff and Noordhoff, Holland, 1980.

Community except Ireland, and the language deployed expresses wide-reaching obligations on the part of states to take action to eliminate discrimination at all levels, it has a significant number of weaknesses. First, although the definition of discrimination is broad, there is some doubt as to whether it encompasses indirect discrimination. Examples of the latter include the situation where a particular practice such as an obligation to wear a hat at work, which is not directly discriminatory but may have an adverse impact on a group such as the Sikh community. There is thus a view that, because the convention refers to distinctions based on race, any distinctions on other grounds would not be in breach even if they result in disadvantage and are in no way related to appropriate qualifications for the job or the service to which they have been applied. However, that is not a necessary conclusion: a number of international lawyers are of the view that the Convention does cover indirect discrimination.[25]

Second, while the opportunity for individuals to make complaints is enabled, this depends on the agreement of the state and most states have not availed themselves of this provision. The Committee received only one individual complaint between 1969, when the Convention came into effect, and 1992. It is safe to conclude therefore, given the knowledge that widespread discrimination does take place throughout Europe, that individuals do not see the complaints procedures as offering a meaningful avenue of redress.

Third, in common with most international conventions, the sanctions for non-compliance are largely ineffective. The requirement of states to submit reports on a regular basis, even where observed, does provide an opportunity for monitoring the extent to which the requirements have been implemented; but it is clear that the adoption of specific comprehensive and positive measures to counteract racial discrimination have not flowed from the Committee's own reporting to the other organs of the UN.

Fourth, there is no specific obligation placed on signatories to demonstrate that individuals are provided with appropriate remedies for acts of discrimination, or that there are effective state systems for monitoring and review.

Finally, the relatively recent procedure adopted by the CERD of appointing a rapporteur from its members to focus on the reports of one or more countries has improved the ability of CERD to question national reports more effectively. Similarly the decision to consider the position

---

25. See discussion in I. Forbes and J. Mead, *Measure for Measure*, Department of Employment, Sheffield, 1992.

of a country which has failed to report by sharing the wisdom of members and the information which they have accessed has improved the potential for accountability.

The UNESCO Convention

The Convention on the Elimination of All Forms of Discrimination was only one product of the Sub-Commission of the UN Commission on Human Rights. The former's terms of reference had been extended in May 1949 to making recommendations concerning the prevention of discrimination of any kind relating to human rights and fundamental freedoms, and the protection of racial, national, religious and linguistic minorities. But by September 1951 the Security Council had decided that it should be discontinued; the Sub-Commission had taken its job too seriously and had upset the Commission. It had the audacity to promote legislation with bite and enforcement with real teeth. As J.P. Humphrey, a former director of the human rights division of the UN secretariat, observed, 'the Sub-commission had been led down the perilous road of minorities by member states who had then conspired to ambush it and attempted to liquidate it'.[26] The Sub-Commission was saved, however, by the General Assembly which asked the Council to review its decision, and this led to a second and very fruitful phase of activity with the Sub-Commission concentrating now on education rather than the legislative activities stymied by the Commission. This move was in keeping with US opposition to international efforts to promote the enforcement of human rights.

During the 1950s and early 1960s the Sub-Commission was concerned with a series of reports on anti-discrimination policies in employment and education in association with the ILO and UNESCO as well as with slavery, in particular with the information supplied by states under the Supplementary Convention of 1956, and with apartheid in South Africa and discrimination in Rhodesia. According to Humphrey, apart from the great issues of war and peace, there has been no issue with which the UN has been more concerned than that of discrimination, and in this the Sub-Commission has played the most imaginative and constructive role.

The UNESCO Convention against Discrimination in Education 1960 was preceded by and owed its origins to a study of the topic by the Sub-Commission.[27] The UNESCO Convention was adopted by the General

---

26. See McKean, *Equality and Discrimination Under International Law*, p. 76 ff.
27. United Nations, *Study of Discrimination in Education*, Special Rapporteur Ammoun, UN Doc E/CN. 4/Sub.2/181/Rev. 1.

Conference in 1960 and entered into force in 1962.[28] The Convention was clearly in keeping with UNESCO's own purpose as expressed in its constitution:

> ... to contribute to peace and security by promoting collaboration among nations through education, science and culture in order to further universal respect for justice, for the rule of law and for human rights and fundamental freedoms which are affirmed by the peoples of this world, without distinction of race, sex, language or religion, by the Charter of the United Nations.

The Convention is directed against discrimination in education based on any 'distinction, exclusion, limitation or preference' based on race, colour, language, religion, political or other opinion, national or social origin, economic condition or birth, and which has the purpose or the effect of nullifying or impairing equality of treatment in education. Article 1 continues more specifically to prohibit the deprivation of access to education, limiting the quality of provision, giving separate education, or inflicting conditions 'incompatible with the dignity of man', all by reference to the above distinctions in application both to individuals and groups. In Article 2, an exception is made allowing for the separate provision of education for linguistic or religious reasons where this is in keeping with parental wishes, is optional and is of the same standard as other provision. Thus in the UK for example, the provision of separate schools for Catholic and Moslem minorities would not de facto breach the convention.

While the general tenor of the provisions in the Convention are integrationist in the sense of favouring universal and common education, some important recognition is given to cultural identity. Article 5 states that it is essential for states to recognise the right of members of national minorities to carry on their own educational activities including the maintenance of schools and the use or teaching of their own language.

The right to teach minority languages is subject to the educational policy of each state. Moreover, the fact that states are not obliged to provide or even to enable minority group provision confirms an evident reluctance to derogate from the state its right to determine how it runs its internal affairs, and whether or not certain activities are seen by the state as prejudicing 'national sovereignty' (Article 5(1)(c)). Further, unlike the general convention against discrimination, there are no effective provisions for petition; the Convention does not respect cultural rights in any substantial manner and where a dispute arises the balance is clearly

28. 11th Conference, UNTS, 429, 93; see Thornberry, *International Law and the Rights of Minorities*, p. 287, and Marks, 'UNESCO and Human Rights', *Texas International Law Journal*, 1977, vol. 13, p. 35.

in favour of the state.[29]

In 1978 UNESCO adopted a Declaration on Race and Racial Prejudice at its General Conference. Essentially, the Declaration is simply a position statement; it is not a binding treaty. However, having been adopted unanimously and by acclamation,[30] the Declaration carries a certain weight. It articulates in Article 1 a 'right to be different' for both individuals and groups and, in the preamble, condemns forced assimilation of the 'members of disadvantaged groups'. While endeavouring to ensure that differences are not used as a pretext for discriminatory practices and apartheid, the Declaration evaluates cultural distinctions and the legitimacy of group personality in a dynamic changing social environment and recognises that a museum-like preservation of cultural integrity also has inherent dangers.

The International Labour Organisation: Discrimination (Employment and Occupation) Convention 1958

This Convention (ILO No. 111) had been ratified by nine of the twelve European Community countries by the end of 1994, the exceptions being Ireland, Luxembourg and the United Kingdom. The Convention requires each signatory to undertake to declare and pursue a national policy to promote, by methods appropriate to national conditions and practice, equality of opportunity and treatment in respect of employment and occupation, with a view to eliminating any distinction in respect thereof (Article 2).

Article 1 (1[a]) defines discrimination in a similar manner to the UNESCO Convention as: 'Any distinction, exclusion or preference made on the basis of race, colour, sex, religion, political opinion, national extraction or social origin, which has the effect of nullifying or impairing equality of opportunity in treatment in employment or occupation.' Article 2 qualifies this definition by providing that any distinction, exclusion or preference in respect of a particular job based on the inherent requirements thereof shall not be deemed to be discrimination. The state, by Article 3, is required to enact 'such legislation . . . as may be calculated to secure the acceptance and observance of this policy'.

In common with the Convention on the Elimination of All Forms of Racial Discrimination (ICERD), this Convention begs the question of whether or not indirect discrimination is encompassed by the definition; again there is reference to 'any distinction . . . made *on the basis* of race',

---

29. Thornberry, *International Law and the Rights of Minorities*, p. 290.
30. See N. Lerner, 'New Concepts in the UNESCO Declaration on Race and Racial Prejudice', *Human Rights Quarterly*, vol. 3, no. 1, 1981, p. 48.

implying that only direct discrimination is covered, since indirect discrimination is defined by reference to the effects of a situation or practice which is not apparently based on racial grounds. However, the International Labour Organisation, amongst others, views that indirect discrimination is covered.[31]

As Wilkie has observed,[32] ILO 111 requires state parties to take measures to promote not only equality of treatment but also equality of opportunity. Indirect forms of discrimination which have the effect of undermining equality of opportunity must be eliminated. As with the Racial Discrimination Convention, ILO 111 requires special measures to be taken by state parties where necessary to eliminate discrimination in employment, and there is a specific obligation to enact appropriate legislation to ensure equality of opportunity in employment, to promote education programmes on the issue, and to repeal inconsistent legislation and administrative instruction. The 1988 report of the Committee of Experts on the application of conventions and recommendations emphasised the comprehensive nature of the Convention in its application to public employment, vocational guidance, vocational training and placement services under the direction of a national authority, not only in rendering racial discrimination unlawful but also in placing an obligation on the state parties to implement an equal opportunity policy to cover these activities. The Convention applies equally to the spheres of public and private employment.

With respect to the progressive nature of equal opportunity policies, the ILO Expert Committee emphasised that the absence of a policy in this area, far from signifying a lack of discrimination, would tend to imply the existence of discrimination: 'Once rigorous action gets underway and new measures are adopted to implement the principle of equality of opportunity and treatment, the existence of problems will, in practice, be brought to the surface, thus requiring further progress.' The Committee of Experts also made it clear that the simple affirmation of the principle of equality before the law by a state may be an element of an equal opportunity policy but it cannot, in itself, constitute a policy within the meaning of Article 2 of the Convention. According to the 1988 report:

> . . . the content of the national policy should . . . draw its information from the principle of the Convention: it is essential that it should be designed to promote equality of opportunity by eliminating all distinctions, exclusion or preference in law and practice; that it should cover the different grounds of discrimination expressly referred to and lastly, that it should provide for the

31. See International Labour Organisation Report of Committee of Experts, *Equality in Employment and Occupation*, ILO, 1988, p. 23.
32. Wilkie, 'Race Discrimination in Denmark'.

implementation that the principle of equality of opportunity and treatment in all fields and occupation.

Thus the Convention expects affirmative action programmes to be drawn up by the signatories with the express purpose of providing preferential treatment in education and training for disadvantaged racial minorities. The purpose of these special measures is to enable disadvantaged racial minorities to compete on an equal footing with other members of national societies. The Expert Committee also recognised, however, that while special measures had to be adopted in order to enable disadvantaged minorities to compete on an equal footing, it was also necessary for employers to understand the concept of 'reasonable accommodation' and themselves promote the principle of equality of access to employment. Where an employer refused to accommodate particular needs regarding religion or disability and to make the necessary changes in the workplace, that refusal might in itself constitute an act of discrimination.[33]

The principal weakness of the Convention is its failure to require state parties to establish supervisory mechanisms through a designated agency for the purpose of promoting a general application of the policy of equality. While it is true that the recommendations made by the Committee of Experts have identified models of good practice in this respect, the Convention suffers the common problem of being largely unenforceable.[34] It is also noteworthy that a country has no obligation to enact legislation if it 'calculated' that it would be ineffective; the United Kingdom, with Canada, ensured the recording of this interpretation in the *travaux preparatoires*.[35]

The UN Covenant on Civil and Political Rights (1966)

The UN adopted two provisions in the mid-1960s which had an impact on political and social rights. The Covenant on Civil and Political Rights and the Covenant on Economic, Social and Cultural Rights were both adopted in 1966 and both came into effect in 1976.[36] The former, drafted by the Commission on Human Rights, elaborated the civil and political rights set out in the Universal Declaration, including the rights to life,

33. International Labour Organisation Report of Committee of Experts, *Equality in Employment and Occupation*, ILO, 1988, p. 146: discussed in Wilkie, 'Race Discrimination', p. 76 ff.
34. See C. W. Jenks, *Human Rights and International Labour Standards*, Stevens, London, 1960.
35. See McKean, *Equality and Discrimination Under International Law*, p. 127.
36. See Thornberry, *International Law and the Rights of Minorities*, p. 141 ff. and p. 269 for background description.

liberty and security, privacy, peaceful assembly, a fair trial and equality before the law, the rights of members of ethnic, religious and linguistic minorities, freedom from inhumane treatment, freedom of thought, conscience, religion, expression and association and the right to self-determination. The last, along with the rights of minorities, were additions to the Declaration. Such rights were subject to both general and specific limitations.

The Covenant established a Human Rights Committee with two functions, to consider reports from states and to deal with complaints of violations from states (Articles 28 to 45). A protocol enabled complaints from individuals to be received, but there was no requirement to incorporate the provisions of the Covenant into domestic law. The Committee reports annually to the General Assembly.

Article 2 of the Covenant on Civil and Political Rights has been described as a key provision.[37] Article 2 (1) requires that 'each state party to the present Covenant undertakes to respect and to ensure to all individuals within its territory and subject to its jurisdiction, the rights recognised in the present Covenant without distinction of any kind such as race, colour, sex, language, religion, political or other opinion, national or social origin, property, birth or other status.' The corresponding provisions in Article 2 (2) of the Convention on Economic, Social and Cultural rights provide a similar definition, but unlike its sister Covenant and the ILO and UNESCO Conventions it refers to 'discrimination' rather than 'distinction'. The difference between these terms was thoroughly debated: delegates preferred 'distinction' because the Charter and the Universal Declaration both employed it and 'discrimination' would introduce a different shade of meaning implying action. McKean has suggested that the arguments in favour of retaining 'distinction', however, were far less cogent than those adduced by the Committee the previous year in favour of 'discrimination'. One argument in favour of using the term 'discrimination' was that it had acquired a much richer legal meaning, while the deployment of 'distinction' required reservations to be made to accommodate special measures of protection and to legitimate action designed to safeguard and protect the rights of certain socially and educationally backward groups of the population. These measures were then, perhaps somewhat unhelpfully, described as 'protective discrimination'.

Also somewhat surprisingly, Article 4 (1) employs the term 'discrimination' in the derogation clause:

---

37. UN document A/C3/S.R.1257, 237; McKean, *Equality and Discrimination Under International Law*, p. 148 ff.

> . . . in times of public emergency which threaten the life of the nation and the existence of which is officially proclaimed the states parties hereto may take measures derogating from their obligations under this Covenant to the extent strictly required by the exigencies of the situation provided that such measures are not inconsistent with their obligations under international law, and do not involve discrimination solely on the grounds of race, colour, sex, language, religion or social origin.

One reason for the lack of clarity in the terminology employed was that the composition of the drafting committees changed frequently, with the result of there being little continuity between sessions.

Although the Covenant on Civil and Political Rights recognises the universality of its listed rights – they are described as applying to 'every human being', 'everyone', 'all persons' – the Covenant does not avoid all distinctions between aliens and nationals. Article 25 requires that 'every citizen' shall have the right to participate in public affairs, and have equal access to public service 'in his country', while Articles 12 and 13 make distinctions between aliens and nationals with respect to entry and expulsion from a country and the protection of aliens from being arbitrarily expelled from a country of lawful residence without certain conditions being satisfied. The extent to which any state may make a legitimate distinction between rights of aliens and nationals is unclear, although Ramcharan concluded that 'a distinction between aliens and citizens is permitted only where explicitly provided by the Covenant'.[38] In the European context this is important when considering the case of third world nationals who are resident in member countries of the EC but who are not nationals of any. Accordingly some states take the view that aliens are excluded from access to particular rights or freedoms described in the Convention; many states are unwilling to accept immigrants who voluntarily take the state's nationality as being 'minorities' and consequently are even less disposed to accept the notion that foreigners are recipients of minority rights.

A particular example is given in Article 27, which is designed to protect the identity and culture of a particular group. If a group resident in a particular nation-state has not been given the nationality of that state then, although they may individually have rights associated with 'the prevention of discrimination', they may not be protected as a minority group. Accordingly they may not be able to expect the state to provide access to rights and freedoms defined in the Convention such as those relating to language and educational provision. Article 27 essentially

---

38. See Ramcharan, 'Equality and Non-discrimination', in L. Henkin (ed.), *The International Bill of Rights: the Covenant on Civil and Political Rights*, Columbia University Press, New York, 1981.

addressed itself only to the community aspects of religious observance, culture and language. While there has been some debate as to whether or not the negative phrasing of Article 27 represents 'a classic example of restrictive toleration of minorities',[39] some have argued that there are good reasons for making the state into a spectator in the struggle between weaker parties and the majority in that the state is under no obligation to render assistance to the former. This reflected the fact that the new African and Asian delegates to the United Nations wished to expend greater energy on creating a common pool of resourcing, rather than on the provision of positive help to the development of each linguistic group.[40]

Thornberry[41] has explored the meaning and application of Article 27 in some depth because of its potential importance, but its practical impact is still far from clear. A far from atypical example of the ambivalent attitude of signatories is given by a French Government interpretation that the Article did not apply:

> Article 2 [of the French constitution] declares that France shall be a Republic, indivisible, secular, democratic and social. It shall ensure equality of all citizens before the law, without distinction...of origin, race, or religion. It shall respect all beliefs.

Since the basic principles of public law prohibit the distinction between citizens on the grounds of origin, race or religion, France is a country in which there are no minorities and, as stated in the declaration made by France, Article 27 is not applicable as far as the Republic is concerned.[42]

On 16 December 1966 the General Assembly approved resolutions adopting the International Covenant on Economic, Social and Cultural Rights and the International Covenant and Optional Protocol on Civil and Political Rights. These instruments came into force on 3 January 1976, 23 March 1976, and 28 March 1979 respectively. The first case under the Covenant and Protocol was *Lovelace v. Canada* (1981, A/36/40, 166). Sandra Lovelace, who was born and registered a Maliseet Indian, complained that she had lost her status and rights as an Indian in accordance with the Indian Act of Canada by marrying a non-Indian in 1970; she pointed out that an Indian man who married a non-Indian women would not similarly lose his status. The Human Rights Committee

---

39. Robinson, 'International Protection of Minorities: a Global View', p. 89.
40. See Verdoodt, 'Ethnic and Linguistic Minorities in the United Nations', pp. 71–72.
41. Thornberry, *International Law and the Rights of Minorities*, p. 269.
42. Report to the Human Rights Committee ST/HR5 (1987), 35. In fact France gave an explicit reservation in respect of this Article but the position of other countries was similar without the reservation.

decided that the essence of the complaint was the effect of the Indian Act in denying Sandra Lovelace Indian status and the right to live on a reserve. Article 27 of the Covenant was deemed to be the most directly applicable in this case. The Committee concluded:

> Whatever may be the merits of the Indian Act in other respects, it does not seem . . . that to deny Sandra Lovelace the right to reside on the reserve is reasonable or necessary to preserve the identity of the tribe . . . therefore . . . to prevent her recognition as belonging to the band is an unjustifiable denial of her rights under Article 27 of the Covenant, read in the context of the other provisions referred to.[43]

Another case involving loss of status as a member of an ethnic group concerned *Kitok v. Sweden*, which was determined by the Human Rights Committee on 27 July 1988. Kitok was a member of the Sami community, who were by law divided into two groups, those who engaged in and enjoyed rights regarding reindeer herding and those who did not. Under the Swedish Reindeer Husbandry Act of 1971, Mr Kitok had lost his right to participate in reindeer husbandry as a member of the Sami community because he had engaged in a different livelihood for a period of three years. The Committee, taking note that Mr Kitok was permitted, albeit not as of right, to graze and farm his reindeer and to hunt and to fish, concluded that a violation of Article 27 had not taken place. An analysis of the terms 'reasonable', 'objective' and 'proportionality' was used to decide this issue, and the Committee stressed the importance of the context in which national legislation took effect.

Despite the evident limitations of the Covenant exemplified in Mr Kitok's case, both covenants do provide some practical safeguards against a state's intrusion into community ways of life. But while the covenants may provide some safeguards against cultural genocide by the state in its crudest forms, there is little protection against a slow but calculated policy of assimilation which removes the life-support systems of minority identity. The covenants have shown that they can protect individual rights in some instances such as the Lovelace case, but they are less effective at the protection of groups.

The European Convention on Human Rights

It is generally agreed that of all the new procedures established for protecting human rights, the machinery set up by the European

---

43. Thornberry, *International Law and the Rights of Minorities*, p. 179 (individual opinion of Mr Nejib Bouziri).

Convention on Human Rights and Fundamental Freedoms of 1950 is the most effective:[44]

> Article 14 of the Convention states that the enjoyment of the Rights and Freedoms enumerated 'will be secured without discrimination on any ground such as race, colour, sex, language, religion, political or other opinion, national or social origin, association with a national minority, property, birth or other status'.

However, the final provisions modified the original proposals in two important ways: first, there was no reference to a guarantee of equality before the law, and second, there was no general protection against discrimination on racial grounds, because protection was limited to the rights and freedoms guaranteed in the Convention. Both the American Convention on Human Rights (Article 24) and the United Nations Covenant on Civil and Political Rights, referred to above (Article 26), include the principle of equality before the law without discrimination and it is regrettable that the European system did not allow the Commission and the Court to interpret such a clause aided by the experience of other jurisdictions with similar provision.

In the discussion of alternative forms of the Article, the rapporteur charged with proposing alterations to the draft concluded that the Article could not retain the provision of equality before the law since a general non-discrimination clause might cause insoluble problems, for instance with regard to the treatment of foreigners.[45] It was also feared that this would produce a large number of applications, and investigating the facts of complaint would involve the Commission in too much work. Opposition was such that even a muted version which restricted the proposed guarantee to equal protection in the application of the law was found unacceptable and rejected.[46] While Article 14 provides for the enjoyment or the rights and freedoms in the Convention without discrimination, this enjoyment is qualified by Article 16 which provides that nothing in Articles 10, 11 and 14 shall be regarded as preventing the contracting parties from imposing restrictions on the political activity of aliens.

Two propositions have emerged from the interpretation of Article 14; either there cannot be a breach of Article 14 unless another article of the Convention has simultaneously been violated, or the Article applies the

---

44. See McKean, *Equality and Discrimination Under International Law*, p. 205; A. H. Robertson, *Human Rights in Europe*, Oceania, Manchester, 1963; and F. G. Jacobs, *The European Convention on Human Rights*, Oxford University Press, Oxford, 1979.
45. McKean, *Equality and Discrimination Under International Law*, p. 210.
46. See documents 1564, 55 and H (65) 16.

principles of non-discrimination to the enjoyment of all rights and freedoms set out in the Convention. However, in the case *Albert Grandrath v. the Federal Republic of Germany* (1966),[47] it was decided that Article 14 may be violated in a field dealt with by another article of the Convention although there is otherwise no violation of that article. That decision of the Commission (the body responsible for determining the first reference), was affirmed by the European Court of Human Rights in a Belgian-language case in 1968; in *Marckx v. Belgium* it was also held that, although Article 14 had no independent existence, it may play an important autonomous role by complementing the other normative provisions of the Convention and the Protocols. Later cases have suggested that courts may take a teleological approach to the interpretation of Article 14, providing a very broad application of the article, perhaps even beyond the confines of the rights and freedoms articulated in the Convention; although Judge Fitzmaurice has adopted a strictly literalist interpretation emphasising that the European Court of Human Rights is a court of law and not a court of ethics.[48]

While it has been observed that both the Commission and the Court have made a marked contribution to the development and understanding of the principles of the equality of individuals under international law, there are clear limits as to what the European Convention covers. In the current climate of civil unrest, it is notable that the Convention does not deal with discrimination in general nor with incitement as a separate issue. However, in 1965 the Consultative Assembly of the Council of Europe unanimously adopted a model law on incitement to racial, national and religious hatred which members of the Council were encouraged to adopt.

The Commission and the Court have considered a large number of applications some of which have led to changes in the domestic law of the signatories to the Convention. Because of the limitations described, however, and because of the increasingly long period between application and result (the average waiting period was 5 years in 1992) the Convention has made little impact on reducing racial discrimination. Some changes have been proposed; for example at the meeting of the Council of Europe in Vienna in October 1993, a declaration was adopted which agreed the amalgamation of the two organs, the Court and the Commission, into a single court. At the time of writing, however, there is no commitment to pass a protocol to the Convention which would extend the prohibition of discrimination beyond the rights declared in the Convention.

---

47. Application No. 2299/64, Report of Commission adopted 12 December 1966.
48. McKean, *Equality and Discrimination Under International Law*, p. 214 ff.

Recent Initiatives

In 1988 the Council of Europe adopted a draft charter, the European Charter for Regional or Minority Languages, the text of which was then considered by a committee of experts. The draft is designed to protect languages 'belonging to the European cultural heritage' which are identified territorially but spoken by a minority within any given state. It is not clear whether Kurdish or Romany would fall within the qualifying definition in Article 1, although it is proposed that the state contracting to the Charter would determine which languages did so qualify.[49] The two main objectives of the charter are to promote and to protect the use of languages in education, the media, the public services and more generally in social, cultural and economic activities. Trans-frontier links are envisaged, and minority groups would be able to petition in the event of alleged breach of undertakings.

The European Convention for the Protection of Minorities is to be considered by the Council of Europe following the adoption of a draft in February 1991. A principal objective will be to protect and develop minority identity in cultural, religious and linguistic expression against any forced attempts at assimilation. There is a growing acceptance within the Council of Europe that the Convention on Human Rights fails to give adequate protection to minorities.[50]

In 1985 the UN adopted the Declaration on the Human Rights of Individuals who are not nationals of the country in which they live.[51] In recognising that many people now live in countries of which they are not nationals, the Declaration seeks to protect these people's language, culture and traditions. To that extent it can be characterised as conferring a right to resist integration into the life of the host country.[52]

Domestic Application of Conventions and Treaties

This chapter has described the obligations imposed by international law. However, it is essential to retain a sense of perspective about the practical opportunities available to individual litigants or groups when seeking to

49. P. Thornberry, *Minorities and Human Rights Law*, the Minorities Rights Group, London, 1991.

50. D. Gomien, 'The Rights of Minorities under the European Convention on Human Rights and the European Charter on Regional and Minority Languages', in Cator and Niessen (eds), *The Use of International Conventions to Protect the Rights of Migrants and Ethnic Minorities*.

51. UN Doc: A Res. 40/1449.

52. R. Lillich, *The Human Rights of Aliens in Contemporary International Law*, Manchester University Press, Manchester, 1984, p. 55.

achieve remedies when these obligations are breached. In doing so it is perhaps relevant to identify the questions which need to be addressed with respect to any particular obligation :

1. Does the group which is adversely affected know of the existence of a relevant obligation imposed by the convention?
2. Is the state a signatory of the convention, and if so, has it expressed reservations which exclude the application of particular provisions relevant to the alleged breach?
3. Does the state allow petition by individuals (as opposed to petition only by other state signatories) to seek a remedy?
4. Has the state incorporated the convention or an equivalent legal obligation into domestic law?
5. If so, has the complainant exhausted all state remedies available?
6. Is there a state or voluntary agency responsible for providing advice and assistance to the complainant, and is legal aid available?

3

Anti-Discrimination Law in the European Community

Introduction

At time of writing, the European Union is in a state of flux. The British Presidency of the European Council in the latter half of 1992 succeeded in resolving the problems created by the Danish referendum rejecting the Maastricht Agreement, but GATT negotiations raised difficulties in the Community, particularly with France. Speculation in currency markets undermined confidence not only in the European Exchange Rate Mechanism but also in the long-term prospect of monetary union, of which the ERM was intended to be a precursor. It had also become apparent by this point that the eleven signatories of the Protocol which comprises the Social Chapter of the Maastricht Treaty were increasingly frustrated by the United Kingdom's failure to address the structural causes of the recession and to provide resources through the Regional and Social Fund to bring Europe back to work. At the same time, racism began to feature prominently in the European headlines, with most concern being expressed over the resurgence of Nazism in Germany. However, while the development of the European Union, as it became in 1993, remains uncertain, it is still appropriate for the purposes of this study to chart developments and to provide a tentative prognosis as to the future direction of change in the area of anti-discrimination law on the grounds of race.

The body of European Community Law comprises both primary and secondary legislation. The primary legislation is found in the Treaty of Rome of 1957, the Single European Act of 1986, the European Union Act of 1992 and other amendments which have been effected to the original Treaty from time to time. Signatories of the European Community, unlike signatories of most international agreements, conventions and protocols, are obliged to incorporate this primary legislation into domestic law, which in effect binds national courts to give recognition to the primacy of European Community Law over domestic law even where the latter conflicts with and has been enacted subsequent to the European Community provisions.

In addition to the three foundation treaties, the ECSC (relating to coal and steel), the EAEC (relating to atomic energy) and the EEC (or what was then called the common market and is now the European Community) along with the annexes and protocols, which supplement these treaties, subsequent treaties and agreements such as the Merger Treaty in 1965 and the various treaties of accession may also be considered as a primary source of Community law. The foundation treaties are 'self-executing' which means that when ratified they automatically become law within all member states:[1] they must be applied directly by municipal courts, and therefore need not await a local legal instrument to give them effect.

The institutions of the European Union or Community (the terms are now being used without distinction), that is the Council of Ministers, the Parliament and the Commission as well as the European Court of Justice, are established by the foundation treaties as supranational institutions, with supranational powers which enable them to function. The treaties do not explicitly incorporate general or specific rules of international law, and generally the European Court has developed Community law within the context of the primary sources rather than by reference to international law sources for the purpose of interpreting not only the treaties but legislative acts made under the treaties. In the words of Advocate-General Lagrange:

> ... our Court is not an International Tribunal, but is concerned with a Community which has been created by six states and which resembles more a federation than an international organisation ... The Treaty ... although concluded in the form of international treaties and undoubtedly being one, nevertheless also constitutes, from a substantive point of view, the character of the community. As a consequence the legal provisions derived from the Treaty must be viewed as the internal law of the community.

However, in the case *Van Duyn v. Home Office* (1974) ECR 1337 the Community Court upheld the principle of international law that although a state has a duty to receive its own nationals it has no such duty towards the nationals of another state. Nevertheless, Community nationals may claim right of entry by virtue of a directly applicable provision contained in the EC Treaty.

Members may enter into conventions which may create additional inter-state rights but not which derogate from rights provided by the treaties. Article 220 of the Treaty of Rome, as amended (hereafter 'the Treaty'), provides that states may negotiate conventions to secure a

---

1. See D. Lasok, J. Bridge and W. Bridge, *The Introduction to the Law and Institutions of the European Communities*, 3rd edition, Butterworths, 1982.

protection of rights and abolition of double taxations for tı.
and these conventions would have the force of treaties and ʟ
and probably cognisable by the European Court as a source of Coı.
law.[2]

Secondary sources of law are those which are derived from ᵥ
founding Treaty. They are in essence delegated legislation and theı.
validity and scope are tested against criteria laid down in the treaties.
According to Article 189 of the Treaty, both the Council of Ministers and
the Commission are empowered to make regulations, directives and
decisions in accordance with the specific functions and purposes of the
Treaty itself. Regulations of a general scope are 'binding in their entirety'
and are 'directly applicable' in all member states (Article 189 (2)). In
comparison with regulations, directives issued by the Council and the
Commission are 'binding as to the result to be achieved, upon each
member state' to which they address but the choice of the method is left
to the state concerned (Article 189 (3)).

Unlike regulations, therefore, directives are not meant to be an
instrument of uniformity even when a directive which is addressed to
several states simultaneously has the same objective. The Community
usually sets a time limit upon the implementation of the directive. Like
regulations, directives have to be reasoned or motivated and based on the
Treaties. It appears that directives have a direct effect on signatories as
member states but not on individuals; while the Belgian Conseil d'Etat
held that Directive 64/211, which purported to coordinate the rules of
deportation of foreign nationals, had such effect in Belgium, the French
Conseil d'Etat did nor recognise that the same directive had effect in
France.[3] Also, in cases where a directive is clear, precise and unconditional
and the period for compliance has expired, then that directive may have
direct effect. Thus in *Marshall v. Southampton and South West Hampshire
District Health Authority* (1986), it was held that Article 5 of the Equal
Pay Directive of 1976, in its application to non-discrimination regarding
pensionable age, had direct effect because the period for compliance had
expired and the provisions were unequivocal.

Immigration Law and the EU

As noted in Chapter 1 immigration pressures in European states stem from
a number of separate but frequently interlinked sources. The collapse of
the Eastern bloc has led to ethnic reunion, most notably in Germany but
also in Greece and in Finland, while many ethnic Russians are returning

2. Ibid., p. 93.
3. In *Minister of the Interior v Cohn-Bendit* (1979) Dalloz 155; (1980) 1 CMLR 543.

from the former republics of the Soviet Union. The demand for cheap labour in Europe after the Second World War led to steady immigration until the 1960s which was followed by secondary immigration of dependants. Political and economic pressure as well as flood, drought and other natural disasters have substantially increased the number of refugee and asylum seekers in the 1980s and 1990s. Some description of how individual countries have responded to these pressures is given in the following three chapters, but the question of whether at the European Union level there are both policies and laws which either reflect or guide municipal or state practice is addressed here.

It may be argued that the existence or otherwise of a European dimension to immigration is peripheral to our concern with equal opportunity for minorities within Europe. However, given the fact that minority groups are disproportionately affected by immigration law and policy impacting on family reunification, and on the stringency of controls exercised by the police and immigration officials at external borders – let alone their increasing intrusion into the verification of immigration status internally, whether with regard to access to housing, employment, social welfare and community support facilities – in practice the relationship between immigration and equal opportunity policies is manifest. This was clearly illustrated by the CRE investigation into the British Home Office Immigration Department, when the Divisional Court of the Queen's Bench held that the Commission for Racial Equality remit of promoting equal opportunities included the right to express concern over discrimination in the Department even if this discrimination did not contravene any existing legislation.[4]

The individual sovereignty of the state within the European Union is powerfully expressed not only in the right of the state to confer citizenship but also in its control over state access, i.e. who gets into the state and on what conditions. While states have been slow to accept restriction on this authority, their accession to international treaties, as illustrated in the previous chapter, suggests that where there are reasons for accepting common standards and approaches such as the recognition of bona fide refugees under the terms of the Geneva Convention, which all members have ratified, then some concessions are negotiable. That willingness to compromise resulted in the Ad Hoc Group on immigration, which was set up in London in 1986 during the UK presidency.[5] Like the TREVI group, which was established in 1975 to coordinate measures to combat

---

4. See *Home Office v. CRE* (1980) RDLR 50.
5. See A. Cruz, *An Insight into Shengen, Trevi and other European Intergovernmental Bodies*, Churches Committee on Migrants in Europe (CCMG) Briefing Paper No. 1, Brussels, 1990.

terrorism within EC member states, and which now extends to international crime and drug trafficking with police matters falling within the ambit of the TREVI 1992 Group, the Ad Hoc Group is not formally part of the EU and its decisions are not accountable thereto. This has attracted criticism to the effect that there is a democratic deficit in the informal coordination of immigration policies, the promotion of agreements (such as the Dublin Convention relating to the reception of refugees) and the imposition of penalties on carriers, mainly airlines, which take passengers including legitimate refugees without relevant documentation. The attraction of developing a community-wide approach to immigration is that this would provide a shield against criticism from national MPs and non-governmental organisations, and would also provide a palatable solution to problems which may appear intractable at the national level, particularly when constitutional rights may need to be modified.[6]

As noted above, the Single Europe Act of 1986 and the European Union Act of 1992 have brought some aspects of immigration policy within the competence of the EU, either directly or indirectly through special inter-governmental arrangements. Article K(9) of the 1992 Act provides that immigration (considered under Justice and Home affairs) may be brought within the competence of the Community institutions by extension of Article 100c; the decision to do so would have to be by a unanimous vote of the Council of Ministers on the initiative of either the European Commission or a member state. Until that transfer takes place, however, the deliberations of the inter-governmental meetings will not be fully reported and the priorities informing the development of a European immigration policy are unlikely to be made explicit. It is obvious that there are important differences of approach to this issue by member states and the UK, for example, has no preconceived social or economic goals which underpin its immigration policy. In 1971 the Home Office stated to the Select Committee on Race Relations and Immigration:

> Immigration law in this country has developed mainly as a series of responses to, and attempts to regulate, particular pressures rather than as a positive means of achieving preconceived social and economic aims.[7]

Although Britain had an open-door policy to immigration in the late 1950s and early 1960s, thereafter UK governments have been fairly consistently opposed to immigration from the New Commonwealth. The

6. See A. Cruz, *Community Competence over Third Country Nationals Residing in an EC Member State*, CCME Briefing Paper No. 5, Brussels, 1991.

7. Discussed in Ann Dummett, 'Objectives for Future European Policy', in Sarah Spencer (ed.), *Strangers and Citizens*, IPPR/Rivers Oram Press, London, 1994.

rights of British subjects to settle were altered by the Immigration Acts of 1962, 1968 and 1971, and they were stripped of citizenship of the UK by the British Nationality Act of 1981; the rights of dependants to join their families in the UK were also limited. Such a closed textured debate on immigration, where the firm but fair slogan reflects not only its superficiality but also its inherent dishonesty, contrasts with the situation in France where immigration policy is seen as an element within the central economic plan and in Germany were it is recognised as an integral part of economic policy. But Spain and Italy, countries of traditional out-migration, have only come to accept the need for a European dimension because of concerns about illegal immigration from North Africa and Albania respectively.

A common policy on immigration is a natural precursor to the abolition of border controls within the EU, which was planned for the end of 1993 but failed to emerge by that point. Such a development is of potential benefit to ethnic minority groups. There is continuing concern that the UK approach of imposing restrictive external controls and either maintaining border checks or insisting on increased stop-and-search policing to control illegal immigration will dominate the framework of emerging EU policy. The dangerous formula, black-equals-alien-equals-illegal immigrant, is beginning to be recognised by the European institutions as a potential by-product of the covert inter-governmental discussions which will determine the agreements which these institutions will inherit.[8]

Equality and EU Legislation

While the provisions of the European Community are generally intended to impose obligations on states they also define rights for individual nationals of the state. However, states also define the status of nationals and such rights are not generally extended to third-country nationals who are not citizens of any EU member state, even if they are settled with rights of residence (or 'denizens'). Accordingly, the rights and obligations created by EU treaties and agreements are generally addressed to citizens. One of the principal objectives of the Treaty of Rome was the creation of a Common Market with the provision of unhindered movement of capital, goods and establishment. In the Single European Act of 1986, the free movement of nationals within the EU is also affirmed and this reinforces as a primary law within the competence of the Treaty provisions

8. See, for example, EP Directorate General for Research, *Immigration Policy and the Right of Asylum in the Member States of the European Community*, Working Paper W3, European Parliament, Brussels, 1992.

issues of discrimination on the basis of nationality between member-state nationals. There is nothing in the Treaty of Rome, however, which expressly prevents discrimination against persons, not on the grounds of their nationality but on the grounds of their racial or ethnic origin; nor has there been a systematic development of Community law in respect of non-discrimination against non-EU nationals with residency status within any country of the EU.

Article 119 of the Treaty of Rome addresses the provision of equal pay for equal work between men and women. This Article requires that member states 'ensure and subsequently maintain the application of the principle that men and women should receive equal pay for equal work'. The European Court of Justice has ruled that Article 119 has direct effect and confers rights on individuals. Accordingly, it must be applied in all domestic courts regardless of the wording of domestic legislation. As noted previously, Article 119 has given rise to secondary legislation and to some non-binding instruments, including recommendations, memoranda and resolutions. As is the general practice, the European Commission formulates proposals for directives mainly on the basis of programmes of action agreed by the Council of Ministers, taking into account the views of EU advisory committees and the views of the European Parliament.

For equality legislation, the Advisory Committee on Equal Opportunities for Women and Men is a principal source of advice. This Committee is composed of representatives from official equality agencies such as the Equal Opportunities Commission in the UK. When formulating proposals, the European Commission sends its draft to the Council of Ministers and in turn the Council requests the views of both the European Parliament and the Economic and Social Committee. In the European Parliament, proposals may be considered by a number of committees including, for equality legislation, the Committee on Women's Rights and the Committee on Social Affairs and Employment.

Once passed, legislation is enforced through the European Commission's power of infringement proceedings and by the right of individuals to rely on the provisions of European Law in their national courts and tribunals. The European Commission has in the past instituted infringement proceedings against the United Kingdom in relation to the Equal Pay Directive and the Equal Treatment Directive. Infringement proceedings against the UK for failing to provide for equal pay for work of equal value led to the Equal Pay (Amendment) Regulations of 1983, which came into force in January 1984. Infringement proceedings for failure to require the elimination of discrimination in collective agreements, and for excluding from the scope of the Sex Discrimination Act 1975 small firms employing fewer than five persons from private households, led to relevant changes in the original Act by the Sex Discrimination Act 1986.

In addition to the Equal Pay and Equal Treatment Directives (75/117 and 76/207 respectively), the European Commission has issued the following: the Directive on Social Security, providing for equal treatment for men and women in state social security (86/7/EEC) and implemented in 1984; the Occupational Social Security Directive (86/378/EEC) providing for equal treatment in occupational pension schemes for employees and self-employed people; and a directive on equal treatment for self-employed men and women in agriculture (86/613/EEC) which was adopted in 1986 and relates to the principle of equal treatment of self-employed people and the spouses of self-employed people.

European Community Law and Anti-Discrimination Law on the Grounds of Race

While Community law to protect persons from racial discrimination has not been developed, there have been a number of reports to the European Parliament. These have called for the 'review and amendment of national legislation against political extremism, racism and racial discrimination'. Moreover, while there is no explicit provision within Community Law which addresses racial discrimination, Chapter 1 of Title 111 on Social Policy (comprising Articles 114 to 122) may be referred to as implicit justification for accepting competency within the subject area. Article 118 in particular relates to the Commission's responsibility of promoting cooperation between member states in the social field, including employment, labour law and working conditions.

As we have observed, there is a possibility that Community law may absorb international conventions including the European Convention on Human Rights and Fundamental Freedoms. The recognition of such conventions as a source of Community law is to be found in the judgment of the European Court of Justice in *Defrenne* v. *Sabena* 149/77 (1978) ECR 1365. In this case the court had to decide whether or not sex discrimination was prohibited, when it clearly fell outside Article 119 of the Treaty. Although the answer was in the negative because at that time no rule of Community law had been developed, the court considered that there was a potential competency to develop law relating to fundamental human rights outside the treaty provisions: 'The court has repeatedly stated that respect for fundamental personal human rights is one of the general principles of Community Law, the observance of which it has a duty to ensure . . .'

Council Directive 76/207/EEC relates to equal treatment for men and women, and in its preamble in support of the Council's competence in this area the Directive invokes Article 235 which enables the Community to take measures not otherwise specified in the Treaty to enable the pursuit of the stated objectives. In the absence of any specific Treaty powers, the reference in Article 2 to the harmonisation of living and working conditions was seen to be a central objective of the Treaty. By extension, there is then a case for invoking Articles 235 and 2 in order to justify the competence of an equal treatment Directive which covers race as well as gender, as both would further the objectives of harmonisation. Moreover, Directive 75/117/EEC on equal pay for men and women, which relates more closely to the explicit competence of the Community under Article 119, also states that: 'It is desirable to reinforce the basic laws by the standards aimed at facilitating the practical application of the principle of equality in such a way that all employees in the Community can be protected in these matters.'[9]

A further question relating to competence is whether the EU can legislate not merely with respect to the Community nationals and their families, but also to non-nationals and their families resident within the Community. Given the extent of arbitrary discrimination based on nationality and the high proportion of visible minority denizens who are not nationals the exclusion of the latter from Community competence would seriously undermine the impact of a non-discrimination directive. But it is the nature of the Community to deny or confer benefits to non-nationals and it therefore seems a harsh and spurious logic to claim that equality of treatment, within the competence of the Community, may not be extended to denizens in defined circumstances. There is also some case law of the European Court which suggests competence regarding third-country nationals.[10] Moreover, and alluding to the positivist view of law referred to in the opening chapter, if the Community members and institutions recognise the Community's competence, which is clearly in keeping with the various declarations and resolutions of the Community referred to in this chapter, then this competence will be given effect in member states. In the event that existing Treaty provisions become a real impediment to Community law against racial discrimination, Article 236 makes it possible to amend the Treaty to accommodate such provision.

Recognition of the European Convention of Human Rights as a potential source of Community law is endorsed by a further reference to the Convention in the preamble to the Single European Act of 1986. While

9. Ann Dummett, 'The Starting Line: A proposal for a draft Council Directive concerning the elimination of racial discrimination', in *New Community*, 1994, vol. 20, no. 3, pp. 530–538.
10. Elspeth Guild, *Protecting Migrants Rights: Application of EC Agreements with Third Countries*, Briefing Paper No. 10, Churches Committee for Migrants in Europe, Brussels, 1992.

the *Defrenne* case looked at equality in the context of an ILO Convention, it would seem equally competent for the European Court to make reference to the UN Convention on the Elimination of All Forms of Racial Discrimination which, as noted earlier, provided in Article 2 (d) that: 'Each state shall prohibit and bring to an end, by all appropriate means, including legislation as required by circumstances, racial discrimination by any persons, group or organisation.' Similarly, Article 26 of the International Covenant on Civil and Political Rights requires of domestic law that signatories prohibit any discrimination on the grounds covered including racial ones and there is clear potential for the development of Community law in this area.

Concern within the Community about the rise of fascism and racism, while far from a dominant central focus, is not new. The Committee of Inquiry into the rise of Fascism and Racism in Europe (the Evregenis Report) of 1985 was followed by a Declaration against Racism and Xenophobia made jointly by Parliament, Council and Commission in 1986. The Committee of Inquiry into Racism and Xenophobia (the Glyn Ford Report) of 1990 provided a survey of racism and xenophobia in all member states and concluded with 77 recommendations for change. A number of those recommendations implied the competency of the European Community to draft directives on anti-discrimination provision; Recommendation No. 31 asked the European Commission to draft a directive on a community framework of legislation against racial discrimination while recommendation 33 suggested the creation of a Residents' Charter and the preferment of a Residents' Card providing free movement guarantees to third-country nationals (non-EEC nationals, resident within member states). At time of writing there is a draft External Borders Convention which proposes a three month visa-free travel period in the EU for EU-resident third-country nationals, and the Communication of the Commission to the Council and Parliament on immigration and asylum policies, in making the predictable link between strict inflow controls and policies of integration, acknowledges the need to provide a measure of increased mobility for third-country nationals (TCNs in common parlance).

The joint Declaration of 1986 against racism and xenophobia made it incumbent on all institutions as well as individual member states to take appropriate measures to combat all forms of intolerance, hostility and use of force against any person on grounds of racial, religious, cultural, social or national differences. But neither this Declaration, nor the resolution passed by the European Parliament on the same day, is of binding force; both are statements of expectation similar, perhaps, to the UN Declaration. Whether these will also lead to more tangible legal instruments has yet to be seen.

In 1990 the Council of Ministers adopted a further resolution against racism and xenophobia, but it acknowledged that responsibility for taking action lay primarily with member states. As yet there is a lack of resolve, particularly by the Council of Ministers, to secure the promotion of Community legislation against racial discrimination. The De Piccoli Report on Racism and Xenophobia to the European Parliament in April 1993 reiterated the need for action at a national level, while the 1994 annual report on human rights by the EU committee on Civil Liberties and Internal Affairs regretted the lack of progress in adopting the Council of Europe's Plan of Action against racism announced in Vienna in October 1993. It also regretted the absence of a Community Directive against racial discrimination and the failure of Ireland to ratify the ICERD.

There is of course an argument that a Community Directive on racial discrimination is superfluous; with extensive membership of ICERD, with recognition of the European Convention by members and Community institutions and with a growing body of legislation at domestic level is there any need for further protection at the Community level? Dummett has stated the arguments in favour of a directive, which are summarised as follows:

1. The Community's acknowledgement of rights in constitutional and international law requires action to remedy obvious breaches caused by racism and xenophobia.
2. In the single market, racial discrimination will interfere with free movement of persons and services by preventing the victims from obtaining jobs, housing and services.
3. Variations between the levels of protection afforded by states will discourage minorities from moving to states were the protection is small or non-existent.
4. Prompt action is required for the proper functioning of the single market.

As the single market has increased the likelihood of discrimination against non-Community nationals within states, as opposed to at the frontiers, it is fitting that the Community takes action to protect those interests which it professes to promote, such as equal opportunity, but which it has in fact undermined. The concept of a single market makes certain assumptions regarding equality of treatment for workers in the areas of health and safety, working conditions and non-discrimination on the grounds of gender. Equality of competition between states also implies the adoption of common standards against discrimination in the workforce, housing and services; as states have failed to achieve such commonality despite the adoption of standards in international charters and conventions, the Community with its greater powers of enforcement should invoke a directive to achieve that end.

Within the context of the United Kingdom response to Maastricht, a number of developments suggest continuing opposition to the incorporation of any provision relating to racial discrimination. The Treaty of European Union agreed in Maastricht is wider in scope than any previous EC treaty. It expands many of the existing responsibilities of the European Community and brings in new policy areas both within the Treaty of Rome and outside it. The Treaty also introduces a concept of union citizenship and increases the decision-making powers and rights of inquiry of the European Parliament, but it does not resolve one inherent conflict in this area. The freedom of movement of citizens is a right created and enforced by the Community, but the definition of citizenship is something which remains within the sole competence of the individual member states. The principal rights to be afforded to citizens are as follows:

1. Every citizen will be free to remove and reside freely within the territory of any member state; the Council will take necessary decisions to implement these measures by unanimity.
2. Citizens will have a right to vote and stand as a candidate at any local election in any EU country outside their own; detailed arrangements are to be agreed before the end of 1994.
3. A similar right would be given to citizens to vote and stand as candidates for the European Parliament (wherever resident), subject to rules to be agreed before the end of 1993 (i.e. before the then impending European Parliament elections).
4. Any union citizen in a non-EC country should be entitled to diplomatic or consular protection from any member state. Again the rules would have to be agreed between member states by the end of 1993.
5. Citizens would have the right to petition the European Parliament or to apply to the Ombudsman.

The Maastricht Treaty leaves justice and home affairs as an inter-governmental pillar of the union treaty, although it does enable the European Commission to be associated with decision-making and it has given the Commission limited powers of initiative. The provisions of the Treaty identify certain common areas of interest, including immigration and asylum policy, the crossing of the Community's external borders, combating drug addiction and fraud, and judicial, customs and policy cooperation. In these areas, joint positions and joint action can be taken by the Council of Ministers (the Council) which can then decide that certain measures can be adopted by qualified majority. Only member states will have powers of initiative in criminal matters, but the Commission will be fully associated with this work.[11]

While there is an obligation that the European Parliament should be informed and consulted and its views taken into consideration, it is clearly the Council which will play the major role in this area and, as importantly, it is the Council which will determine any movement away from inter-governmental competence, which is outside the formal decision-making process, to the deliberative and consultative mainstream of community life. However, special mention was made under the Justice and Home Affairs and Immigration pillar to the European Convention on Human Rights and to the Convention on the Status of Refugees in that policy and decisions of the EU and its members would have to have regard to the protection 'afforded to persons persecuted on political grounds'. It is also noteworthy that a Union-wide system for exchanging information between European police forces (Europol) is to be set up under the inter-governmental pillar.

It is difficult to articulate a sound and logical argument which would justify competence in these matters while at the same time excluding competence in relation to racial discrimination. There is one argument which is purely political and relates to the social policy; if racial discrimination is considered exclusively an aspect of EU social policy, then, to the extent that the Social Chapter has inter-governmental rather than Community competence, it remains outside the mainstream of Community action. As a result of British opposition to the draft treaty provisions on social policy, there has been no change to the existing social articles in the Treaty of Rome as modified by the Single European Act, although eleven member states have concluded an agreement for the implementation of the 1989 Social Charter (from which the UK also excluded itself) as a protocol to the Maastricht Agreement. In effect the member states have agreed that eleven of the members can borrow the Community institutions en bloc, with the Commission, Parliament and Court of Justice doing their normal jobs and the Council adopting measures by unanimity in some cases and qualified majority in others. This majority will now consist of 44 votes out of 66 instead of 54 out of 76, with a requirement for further alteration to accommodate the accession of Sweden, Austria and Finland from 1995. The matters to be agreed by majority include health and safety, working conditions, information and consultation of workers, equality at work between men and women and the integration of persons excluded from the labour market. Unanimous voting will be required for social security and social protection of workers,

11. See briefing note of the Commission of the European Communities ISEC/B25/ 92 dated 29 September 1992.

the protection of workers made redundant, representation and the collective defence of workers and employers, conditions of employment for third-country nationals and financial contributions for promoting jobs. While pay, rights of association, the right to strike and the right to impose lock-outs are not covered by these provisions, the inclusion of equality at work between men and women, the reference to employment for third-country nationals and the reference, *inter alia*, to working conditions all suggest a fairly broad and expanding competency under the social agreement, which might well have also included anti-discrimination provisions on the grounds of race.

The abolition of the Wages Council by the UK Government and its stance against the provision of a minimum wage in the European Community may be seen as a challenge to the creation of a level playing-field in which the true competition promoted by the market can take place. Eleven of the member states have recognised the need for a level playing-field and, by analogy, would be bound to accept the logic of anti-discrimination law contributing to such provision in the same way that regional and social disparities attract appropriate compensatory measures. Essentially, the UK Government sees an expanding EU social policy as intrusive to domestic economic policy and something to be resisted.

Nonetheless the continuing racial warfare in Bosnia in 1993, the growing concern about the rise in fascism and racism in Europe and the political realisation that, at some juncture, some action must follow the fairly constant stream of pronouncements about racism have all resulted in a small but significant shift away from the subsidiarity black hole, wherein all energy at community level is consumed in exhorting states to adopt the comprehensive measures against racism which the community itself will not enact. At Edinburgh in December 1992 the Council stressed the importance of states 'implementing fully their policies for integrating legal immigrants' (MNS, 8 January 1993),[12] and stated its conviction that vigorous and effective measures must be taken throughout Europe to combat xenophobia. It stopped short, however, of advocating a Community Directive, although such a proposal was welcomed by Commission officials and some politicians including the British Prime Minister.

12. See A. Cruz (ed.), *Migration News Sheet*, monthly journal of the European Information Network, CCME, Brussels.

The European Community and Formal Links with Overseas Countries

Introduction

Because of the wide variety of differing links between member states and former dependent territories, of special links with 'foreign countries' such as the Vatican City in the heart of the Italian capital and, perhaps of over-riding importance, because of the relative autonomy with which member states have developed their relationships with such territories and the status of their residents as nationals, there is understandably much confusion surrounding the legal status of Europe's independent countries, overseas territories and autonomous regions within the framework of the treaties forming the European Community.[13] These special relationships would appear to fall into three categories:

1. The French Overseas Departments which now form part of France;
2. European or nearby regions of member states which enjoy autonomous or semi-autonomous status, and;
3. Independent countries and territories referred to in Part IV of the Treaty of Rome and which retain ties of varying strength with a member state (these are listed in Annex 1 to the Council decision of 25 July 1991).

French Overseas Departments

Following a French legal decision taken on 2 August 1984, the French Overseas Departments of Reunion, Guadeloupe, Guiana and Martinique have the status of regions or Departments which are an integral part of the French Republic. Accordingly, within the terms of Article 227 of the EC Treaty, these territories comprise part of the European Community. There is special provision under Article 227 relating to French Overseas Departments which indicates that only certain provisions of the Treaty would apply to the islands, although the Court of Justice has held that all the provisions of the EC Treaty and secondary law applied to the French Overseas Departments since 1960. However, the Council can adopt specific measures in order to meet the special needs of these territories, and in 1987 the Commission created an inter-service group in order to carry out a comprehensive study of these regions' problems connected

---

13. See background report of the European Commission, *The European Community's relations to French Overseas Departments, European autonomous regions, overseas countries and territories and independent countries within EEC boundaries*, 10 December 1992, No. ISEC/B33/92, London.

with the establishment of the Single Market in 1993.[14] That study was reported to the Council and a programme called Poseidom, creating a legal framework for the Community's contribution to the economic and social development of the islands, was adopted by the Council in December 1989. While that programme contains detailed regulations concerning agriculture, taxes, regional cooperation, transport and structural funds, it does not attempt to prevent the full participation of French citizens from French Overseas Departments in the activities of the EEC on equal terms with other member nationals.

Spain and Portugal

Spain has two autonomous regions on the Mediterranean coast of Morocco, the cities of Ceuta and Melilla. Under Article 25 of the Spanish Accession Act, the derogations from the Treaty exclude both Ceuta and Melilla from the Community's Customs Territory and from application of the common commercial fisheries and agricultural policy.

In contrast the Canary Islands, also an autonomous region of Spain situated in the Atlantic Ocean, enjoy the same status as the two Moroccan cities but will be gradually incorporated over a transitional period into the custom territory of the Community, accompanied by suitable measures to compensate for their insular character and remoteness.[15] The Canary Islands are subject to a programme of options called Poseican, similar to those applied to the French Overseas Departments, with the object of adapting the regulations in relation to agriculture, fisheries and taxation to fit with EC policy over a period of time.

Portugal has two autonomous regions, the islands of the Azores and Madeira in the Atlantic Ocean. By virtue of the 1985 Portuguese Act of Accession, the islands are both politically and economically part of the Community. On 14 April 1989 the European Parliament, with support from the Economic and Social Committee, resolved that the Azores and Madeira should be afforded special treatment from the Community and the Poseima programme was adopted by the Commission on 26 June 1991 based on the same principles as the Poseidom programme for French Overseas Department.

Britain

Although the Channel Islands and the Isle of Man are not formally part of the United Kingdom but belong to the UK's head of state, the Queen,

14. Ibid., p. 1.
15. Ibid., and the decision of the Council dated 26 June 1991.

the UK has responsibility for foreign relations and external defence and retains ultimate responsibility for their government. The islands' relationship with the Community is governed by Articles 25–27 and Protocol 3 of the UK Act of Accession of 1972, with the Protocol stating that the islands are included in the EC customs territory. However, the Protocol provides that the Treaty provisions relating to free movement of workers and rights of establishment do not apply to the islanders. Nationals of all EU countries must receive identical treatment within these territories, and all islanders enjoy the same rights as UK citizens in the UK but not, as stated, in the rest of the EC.

Gibraltar was included under Article 227 of the Treaty of Rome which relates to European territories for whose external relations a member state is responsible. Accordingly, while Gibraltar through the UK has negotiated certain exemptions from the common custom tariffs, the Common Agricultural Policy and the need to apply VAT, Gibraltarians have the right of free movement and establishment in the Community. Although the debate between the UK and Spain regarding sovereignty is ongoing, by an agreement in 1984 all restrictions between Gibraltar and Spain were removed and the free movement of persons, as well as of vehicles and goods, was then permitted.

Following the British Nationality Act of 1981, which came into effect in 1983, the nationality status of both Commonwealth citizens and citizens of the remaining dependent territories, principally Hong Kong, was altered. For these people, access to and free movement within the European Community is now dependent on having British nationality; neither Commonwealth citizens nor citizens of independent territories are any longer classified as 'British subjects' or 'Citizens of the United Kingdom and Colonies' by reason of birth in their respective category of territories. Indeed the *ius soli*, by which anybody born in the United Kingdom obtained rights of citizenship by dint of birth, was removed by the 1981 Act. Only a person born in the UK and resident for ten years, one of whose parents became a British citizen or who had become settled in the UK, may apply for registration as a British citizen. Otherwise, a minor born in the UK may apply for British citizenship, but discretion remains with the Home Secretary unless the person is entitled to registration by reason of statelessness.

While the exercise of any discretion vested in the Secretary of State under the 1981 Act must be done without regard to the race, colour or religion of any person who may be affected (Section 44(1) of the 1981 Act), the Home Office is not required to give reasons for the grant or refusal of an application under the Act. This sub-section was not in the original Bill but was moved by the government at committee stage (Standing Committee, Column 1909) in response to criticism and pressure, notably from the Catholic Commission for Racial Justice. Timothy Raisen, then the responsible minister, said in moving the amendment that it was 'in no sense intended to suggest that recent governments or the present one, or future ones, have acted or are likely to act in a discriminatory manner . . .' He thought the value of the provision 'is that it will do something to offset . . . fears and apprehensions and to show those concerned that we believe that they are entitled to be treated fairly and, in particular, not to be discriminated against.'

Raisen also referred to the fact that the United Kingdom had ratified the International Convention on the Elimination of All Forms of Racial Discrimination. Article 1(3) of the Convention states: 'nothing in this Convention may be interpreted as affecting in any way the legal provisions of party states concerning nationality, citizenship or naturalisation, provided such provisions do not discriminate against any particular nationality.' However, although the majority of visitors to the UK in the past decade between 1980 and 1990 have been white, it remains likely that children born of black parents are disproportionately affected by these provisions of the 1981 Act and the safeguards provided by Section 44 are not substantial. Nonetheless, it should be recognised that the British government provided that persons settled in the UK under the provisions of the previous legislation between 1981 and the Act coming into effect in 1983 could register as British nationals; consequently the vast majority of both black and white settled residents in the UK are British citizens and are entitled to the provisions of free movement within the European Community.

Significantly, Hong Kong citizens granted settlement rights in the UK prior to or after 1997 (when Hong Kong is returned to China) will not automatically become British citizens and therefore will not have entitlement to free movement within the EEC. It is also noteworthy that the 1981 Act created a unique category of citizen (the British Overseas Citizen) which entitles the holder to be and to go nowhere.

Independent Countries within EU Countries

The principality of Andorra in the eastern Pyrenees, whose sovereignty is exercised by the President of France and the Spanish Bishop of Urgel, is outside the scope of the EC Treaty and not part of the European Community.

Monaco is not a member of the European Community and is considered by the EC as a foreign country, although it has been part of the customs territory of the Community since 1984 and EC rules of circulation of goods apply.

Both San Marino and the Vatican City, though closely linked with Italy, are formally outside the scope of the EC Treaty and are considered by the EC as foreign countries. Accordingly there are no rights of free movement or settlement.

Third-Country Nationals

One of the objectives of the Single European Act of 1986 and the Maastricht agreement has been to create a Europe without internal frontiers. However, because third-country nationals, even those permanently and lawfully resident in the community, do not benefit directly from access to employment, self-employment or residence rights across the Community, the provisions of Article 48–66 of the EC Treaty which set out free movement rights with regard to work, establishment and services cannot generally be directly relied upon by third-country nationals. Third-country nationals may acquire rights by reason of family ties with someone who is an EU national and has acquired rights of free movement; consequential rights of family settlement and reunion may then arise. Following the case of *Singh* (C-370/90), it appears that European Community rights of settlement afforded to third-country nationals for the purposes of family reunion may supersede restrictions imposed by national states. It would also appear that EU companies have some rights to move workers without free movement rights to other member states in order to provide services (see the *Rush Portuguesa* Case, C-113/89, [1990] E.C.R. I-1417).[16]

Under Article 238 of the European Community, agreements have been entered into with countries such as Turkey, Poland and Hungary, and with 69 African, Caribbean and Pacific states included in the Lome IV Convention. A particular agreement has been entered into between the European Community and the EFTA countries (Austria, Finland, Liechenstein, Norway, Sweden and Switzerland), and in addition the European Court of Justice has established that directly enforceable rights regarding employment and/or social security benefits exist as a result of the relationships between the European Community and both Turkey and Morocco. Following a series of decisions by the European Court of Justice, it seems that Turkish workers can rely on the interpretation of Association Agreements to ensure that those workers with rights of residence cannot be discriminated against in member states on the grounds of their nationality. Accordingly with respect to working conditions, Turkish workers have acquired the same rights as EU nationals but do not have protection against discrimination on racial grounds.

---

16. The analysis in this section is based on material by Guild, *Protecting Migrants' Rights*.

In common with the Association and Cooperation Agreements relating to Turkey, Algeria, Morocco and Tunisia, and with the Czech and Slovak Federal Republics, Hungary and Poland, the Lome Conventions are 'mixed' in that they contain obligations on the part of the Community as an entity and also on the member state. It is also clear from the jurisprudence of the European Court of Justice that the Lome Conventions are self-executing and are capable of giving direct effect. In *Razanatsimba* (Case 65/77, [1977] E.C.R. 2229), the Court considered Article 62 of Lome I, which contains a non-discrimination provision on the treatment of Association Community Party (ACP) nationals, but held that the wording of that Article, which requires treatment on a non-discriminatory basis, did not mean either that an ACP national must be treated like an EU national or that one ACP national must be treated as favourably as any other ACP national in a member state. It seems, however, that the wording of Annex VI of Lome IV is substantially clearer, prohibiting discrimination 'in relation to its own nationals', which means nationals of a member state. Accordingly it is expected that the European Court of Justice would come to a different conclusion when determining a current application.[17]

There is some uncertainty as to the status of a Declaration to a Convention between the European Community and a third country. In the *Grimaldi* case (C-322/88, [1989] E.C.R. 4407), the European Court of Justice found that even though a recommendation does not have binding force it does have some legal effect. National courts are bound to take such recommendations into consideration in order to decide disputes submitted to them, in particular where these cast light upon the interpretation of a national measure. The Court also decided that the legal form of a measure does not determine its nature; the Court itself must decide whether the content of a particular measure is wholly consistent with the form attributed to it, and only when a provision is sufficiently precise, clear and unambiguous that it gives rise to rights and obligations may it be considered as being directly applicable. In the view of Guild, Annex VI to the Lome Convention IV is sufficiently clear, precise and unambiguous to give rise to directly applicable rights, but, even if that is not the case, following the decision in the *Grimaldi* case national courts must give consideration to the recommendations or declarations in the interpretation of a national provision.[18] In both the Eastern European Agreements and the Association and Co-operation Agreements the prohibition against discrimination based on nationality is limited to

17. Ibid., p. 23.
18. Ibid.

workers who are legally employed; the agreements also extend to working conditions, pay and social security benefits linked to employment.

Agreement on the European Economic Area

As from 1 January 1993, this Agreement entitles nationals of EFTA state countries all free movement rights which were previously available only to EU nationals, although transitional provisions with regard to Liechtenstein and Switzerland delayed reciprocal free movement for EU nationals to those states. As a consequence of this Agreement, EFTA nationals are the first to have full free movement rights within the Community. There is a particular concern that such rights should be granted to non-EC nationals and non-EC residents while other third-country nationals, who have a much closer connection to the Community by reason of being denizens, are not granted similar rights.

Conclusions

Simpson[19] has attempted to describe the dangers of increasing unemployment following the elevation of free market forces as a moral imperative within the expanded legal framework of the Community. Unemployment increased by half a million in the year following the completion of Single Market. There has also been a disproportionate regional impact within member countries[20] and on particular industrial sectors. It has been argued that the existing sections of the European population who are socially and economically disadvantaged and, in particular, the black communities will be most adversely affected by the development of the Single European Market. Moreover, while the 'Charter of Fundamental Social Rights' unveiled by Ms Vasso Papandreou, the Social Affairs Commissioner, in May 1989 indicated some form of protection for the least well-off, many were disappointed that the Charter as it was then outlined was narrow in focus, and its concern was with the particular rights of workers rather than with the more general rights of people. More extensive rights had originally been suggested in the address to the TUC Conference in September 1988 by Jacques Delors, the then President of the European Commission, when he set out five themes of protection:

19. Alan Simpson and Mel Read, *Against the Rising Tide*, Spokesman Publications, Nottingham, 1991.
20. The Neuberger Report.

1. Freedom of movement of peoples across national boundaries.
2. The establishment of a set of guaranteed rights including health and safety at work.
3. The provision of high quality training for the unemployed.
4. The development of a regional strategy within Europe to tackle marginalisation, under-development and economic decline, and
5. Guaranteed minimum rights providing every citizen with an assured subsistence income and defined rights for all in relation to health care and public services.

The down-grading of the Social Chapter to the status of an annex to the Maastricht Agreement came about through the opposition of the British government and British employers to the notion of fundamental rights for workers, citizens and residents. This represented such a major collision of interests and basic philosophies that the Social Chapter could neither be progressed as an entrenched element of the agreement nor be sustained in any comprehensive fashion beyond the provision of particular rights of workers; an extension to include citizens or all residents was not politically possible. But with the establishment of a Europe without frontiers from 1993 onwards, it is the enhancement of rights of citizens in respect of free movement and, as part and parcel of that process, the removal of border checks for such citizens, which heightens and sharpens the contrast with the residual rights of third-country nationals within the EC.

The legitimate area for discrimination on the basis of nationality, which was previously focused on border crossings, will now be extended to random checks within any member state of the EC, by the police to determine rights of abode, by employers to determine rights of employment and by government, both local and central, to determine rights of access to services such as the health, public housing, and social security support. In effect, the existence of national frontiers which facilitated systematic checks for all entrants whether nationals or not has in the past led to a *de lege* and, despite occasional passport raids by the police on employers to check the status of employees, a de facto presumption that any resident is legitimate. The removal of frontier checks for everyone and the retention of restrictions on the rights of movement for third-party nationals has simultaneously shifted the balance of presumption. As noted earlier (the Glyn Ford Report) there are 13 million non-EU nationals who have rights of residence within individual EU states; it is this sizeable community which has been deprived of its rights of equal treatment, and because the majority of EU nationals are white and the majority of third-country nationals with a legitimate right of residence but restricted to one country in the EU are black, there is no doubt as to what shorthand will be used to justify either random or systematic checks on the legitimacy of residence.

It is an ineluctable conclusion, therefore, that the creation of a single European market has exacerbated the circumstances in which racial discrimination is likely to take place. Yet, despite the rise in racist activity and xenophobia throughout Europe, evidenced not merely by the aberrations of the lunatic fringe but also by the election successes of so-called respectable elements such as the Northern League in Italy in November 1993, the Community has failed to grasp this nettle and to address the necessity of incorporating anti-discrimination legislation within the principles of European Law.

The discussion of both primary and secondary legislation has suggested that the conclusion that anti-discrimination provision is not competent within the existing framework of European law is ill-founded or, in the kindest terms, is based on a selective and very narrow view of legislative legitimacy. This conclusion is sustainable on the evidence, as is illustrated by the introduction of other provisions to protect the interests of a genuine competitive market.

There is some evidence that the activities of the far right and extremist organisations are increasingly being coordinated at European level,[21] but there is also more encouraging evidence that communities and groups are becoming more alive and informed about the threat and are taking individual or joint action in order to counteract it. This is exemplified by the Declaration against racism by Karlsruhe city in July 1990, the emergence of the Standing Committee on Racism in Europe (SCORE) in the UK and the increased networking facilitated by the European Forum for Migrants established by the European Commission. It remains far from clear, however, whether such activities will provide sufficient momentum either at the national level of member EU states or at the supranational level of the European Commission itself to convince the Council of Ministers that model anti-discrimination law is not only desirable, but is necessary and even overdue. As has been observed earlier, specific anti-discrimination legislation on the grounds of race is only one element within any strategy to promote equal opportunity within Europe, and no element of that strategy, including legislation, can be effectively sustained without concomitant policy measures backed by political will, resources and real determination.

Elements of such necessary policy ingredients were to be found in the 77 recommendations of the Glyn Ford Report, but unfortunately the political reaction to the Report has been characteristic of the general European ambivalence which has inhibited the translation of policy into

21. Simpson and Read, *Against the Rising Tide*, p. 65.

practice at the European level. While it is the nature of the European Council to reflect the lowest common denominator of tolerance in relation to progressive measures, it must be acknowledged that the attitudes and policies of member states may differ widely. In order to inform the debate on how anti-discrimination law will be progressed at a European level, we turn now to the experience of a selection of member states.

4

Anti-Discrimination Law in Three Peripheral EC States: Denmark, Ireland and Greece

This chapter provides a commentary on three 'peripheral' European states, Denmark, Ireland and Greece. This study is complementary to the study of four core states which is provided in the next two chapters. Because the EC or European Union comprised twelve member states at the end of 1994, it was felt that some selectivity of study would be necessary and that, in keeping with the Community's own view of its core and peripheral region, it was expedient to examine the experience and response to racism and xenophobia using a similar 'geographical' approach.

Clearly the purpose in making this comparison is to examine variances in practice between member states of the European Community but in doing so there is no supposition that these states share a common experience of ethnic minority settlement or of approaches to the issue of anti-discrimination law. In Western Europe there are two principal legal systems in operation; the civilian, or Romano-Dutch, system which is most commonly used, and the common law system which is shared by Ireland and the UK. Civilian systems are said to be based on deductive judicial interpretation; a code relating to criminal or civil law will set out the basic principles and a cadre of professional judges will apply and interpret such principles without undue reliance on previous case law. Common law systems are said to be characterised by inductive judicial interpretation, in which the courts will look for case precedent to a much greater extent in providing a guide for interpretation of a particular statute. Statutes are judged on their own merits rather than within the broader context of a legal code.

A significant practical difference between the two is the fact that the legislation in common law systems is frequently more detailed; this helps to explain the fact that the Race Relations Act of 1976 is the most comprehensive in Europe. When judges approach statutes either without any preconceived notion that there is a basic principle behind the statute 'o achieve equality of opportunity or that, even if previous case ...ows such a principle, it may clash with other legal preconceptions which demand priority, then the legal draftsmen may attempt to anticipate these problems by being much more explicit about what the legislation covers (and what it doesn't) than would be necessary in a civilian system, both to avoid misconstruction and to accommodate or counter past statutory interpretation. In the field of racial discrimination, this is illustrated by an amendment to the Race Relations Act 1968 which defined racial grounds as including 'race, colour, or ethnic or national origins'. The House of Lords, in *Ealing LBC v. Race Relations Board, ex parte Zesco* (1971) RDLR 1, held that a London Borough was entitled to refuse to put Mr Zesco on its housing waiting list on the grounds of his current nationality. The fact that he had been resident in the locality for 20 years and had served in the RAF during the Second World War may have suggested that the decision to discriminate against Mr Zesco was arbitrary, illogical and morally insupportable, but a narrow construction of the meaning of the statute was applied by the court and Ealing's attitude was upheld by the law.

To get around that judicial interpretation, the Race Relations Act of 1976 included explicit reference to 'nationality' as well as national origin. But, in order to enable central government to discriminate on the grounds of current nationality or any other racial ground, conflicting legislation (including subordinate provisions delegated to Ministers of the Crown) was given express exemption. Thus Section 75(5) of the Act exempts rules restricting employment to persons of a particular birth, nationality, descent or residence (the last would have only come under the Act through the provisions relating to indirect discrimination) who may be employed by the Crown or by any public body prescribed by regulations.[1]

All EU member states have written constitutions, excepting the UK. Such constitutions commonly set out basic human rights which the state seeks to guarantee against any contradictory legislation. These two differences, that between civilian law and common law and that between written and unwritten constitutions, indicate that we may expect both Ireland, the only EC common law state with a written constitution, and the UK to be distinctive and therefore worthy of examination.

Having chosen Ireland because of its common law system, the need for a geographical spread among the countries chosen for analysis suggested the inclusion of Greece in the south and of Denmark in the north. While geography is seen as an important determinant of trade

---

1. See R. White, M. MacEwen, K. Miller and I. McKenna (eds), *Race Discrimination Law Reports*, Commission for Racial Equality, 2 vols, 1990, vol. 1, p. 59, for summary of regulations.

opportunities within the community, it is also an important feature affecting immigration pressure from refugees. These and other differences are alluded to more fully in the individual descriptions that follow. In fact, there are equally compelling arguments in favour of the inclusion of Portugal or Spain, neither of which have passed extensive legislation against discrimination and both of which have histories of colonial expansion and recent immigration. However, a final and less respectable factor, the accessibility of source materials and the author's limited knowledge, prevailed in favour of Greece, the founder of modern democracy.

Anti-Discrimination Law in Denmark

Introduction and Historical Background

Denmark's immigration policy has for many years been influenced by the fact that the country borders Germany and the European Community to the south and the other Nordic countries to the north. By decision of the Danish parliament, or Folketing, on 1 April 1955 the German minority was granted certain rights exceptional to those granted to other foreign minorities, such as the right to speak its own language, start its own schools, participate in local Danish elections, own newspapers and have access to other German-language media, and the right to maintain religious and cultural connections with Germany. To some extent these special provisions for the German minority in Denmark reflect a desire to create conditions which would encourage similar treatment of the Danish minority living in Germany.[2]

The close cultural and linguistic links between the Scandinavian countries was the major reason for the establishment of the Nordic Council in the 1950s which gave rise, *inter alia*, to rights of unrestricted access and movement of any citizen of one member of the Nordic Council to and within the territory of all others. These provisions were extended to Greenland and the Faroe Islands when home rule was granted.

Traditionally, Denmark has been characterised by a homogeneity of ethnic origins. Today, however, almost 3 per cent of Denmark's 5 million people are non-citizens, and it is the non-citizens who comprise the vast majority of the ethnic minority groups resident in Denmark despite the presence of immigrants such as Greenlanders, refugees and others who have acquired citizenship.

2. Meredith Wilkie, 'Race Discrimination in Denmark', in *Nordic Journal of International Law*, vol. 59, FASC. 1, The Danish Centre of Human Rights, Copenhagen, 1990, p. 5 ff.

Denmark's ethnic minorities fall into a variety of categories. First, there are about 45,000 Greenlanders, who are Inuits.[3] Second, in 1988 there were just over 23,000 citizens of other Nordic countries resident in Denmark, comprising 17 per cent of all non-citizen residents. It may be misleading, however, to classify citizens of the Nordic Council, which comprises Norway, Sweden, Finland, Denmark and Iceland, as being distinguishable on ethnic grounds. Third, almost 20 per cent of non-citizens resident in Denmark are EC citizens; this group numbers 26,875 people, the bulk of whom are from Germany and the UK. Finally there are the so-called third-country residents, the majority of whom come from other European countries (30 per cent) mainly from Turkey and the former Yugoslavia; some 22 per cent come from Asia with Pakistan and Iran being principal sources of immigration. Table 4.1 shows the foreign citizens resident in Denmark as of 1 January 1989.

Thus in addition to immigration stemming from the freedom of movement facilitated through membership of the Nordic Council and the EC, Denmark has accepted settlers from Germany, refugees from Hungary and, from 1968, a significant number of guest workers from Turkey, the former Yugoslavia, Pakistan and Morocco. Because of rights of family re-unification, the numbers of such ethnic groups have continued to grow despite subsequent policies restricting primary immigration. In addition

Table 4.1 Foreign Citizens resident in Denmark at 1.1.89: source Meredith Wilkie, 'Victims of Neutrality, Race Discrimination in Denmark', in *Nordic Journal of International Law*, 1990, vol. 59, Fasc. 1

Country of Citizenship	Persons	%
Turkey	26,072	18.4
Great Britain	9,968	7.0
Norway	9,937	7.0
Yugoslavia	9,149	6.4
Sweden	8,178	5.8
West Germany	8,131	5.7
Iran	7,715	5.4
Pakistan	6,454	4.5
Stateless Palestinians	4,800	3.4
Sri Lanka	4,338	3.0
USA	4,202	3.0
Other Nationalities	43,072	30.3
TOTAL	142,016	100.0

Source: Danmarks Statistik 1 January 1989 and O. Hammer, DEN KULTURELLE UDFORDRING: AT ARBEJDE MED INDVANDRERE OG FLYGTNINGE (Social-politisk Forlag, 1989), p. 93.

3. Ibid., pp. 5 ff.

to settling an earlier influx of Hungarian refugees, Denmark accepted about 26,000 refugees between 1979 and 1988 including Iranians, Kurds from Turkey, Tamils from Sri Lanka and stateless Palestinians, Chileans, Poles and Vietnamese. Despite the longevity of residence of many Danish settlers, only about 12 per cent of immigrants and refugees have taken Danish citizenship since 1978, as shown in Table 4.2.[4]

Table 4.2 Refugees taking Danish Citizenship since 1978: source Meredith Wilkie, 'Victims of Neutrality, Race Discrimination in Denmark', in *Nordic Journal of International Law*, 1990, vol. 59, Fasc. 1

Nationality	Number of Persons	Per cent of Total Immigrant Population
Pakistan	1,453	22.5
Poland	1,450	37.6
West Germany	1,273	15.7
Vietnam	868	25.7
Morocco	659	na
Yugoslavia	657	7.2
Turkey	638	2.4
Philippines	557	na
Great Britain	557	5.6
India	540	na
TOTAL	17,209	12.0

Source: O. Hammer, op cit, pp. 96–97.

In common with many other western European countries, Denmark recruited its guest workers in 1968 and 1969 during a period when labour supply was low and there was a continuing need to perform the less attractive tasks – the dirty, boring, hazardous and arduous work – which many Danes preferred to avoid and from which their education and expectations disqualified them.[5] Despite the recession following the oil crisis in 1972, many guest workers remained; the tightening of primary immigration which Denmark imposed in common with many other western European countries did not stem from secondary immigration. Many of those who were already settled chose to remain rather than risk returning home and then not being allowed back into the host country once the doors to further immigration were shut, and these exercised rights of family reunification and brought their families to join them in Denmark.

The 1983 Aliens Law established administrative and appeal procedures for the protection of the rights of immigrants. The same law liberalised

4. Also see T. Hammer, *European Immigration Policy: A Comparative Study*, Cambridge University Press, Cambridge, 1985, pp. 96–97.
5. Wilkie, 'Race Discrimination in Denmark', p. 17 ff.

Denmark's asylum procedures by providing certain safeguards including the extension of equal rights to non-Convention refugees, but both the amendments to the law in 1986 and other changes in administrative practices and processes have largely diluted the more expansive view of immigration represented in the Act. Current practice means that third-country nationals now have little prospect of achieving immigration to Denmark. Even visiting Denmark as a tourist has become virtually impossible for many non-whites, and the requirement for nationals of certain countries (even short-stay visitors) to obtain a visa before entering the country is now administered so rigorously that genuine business visits, family and holiday visits and other bona fide intentions have been frustrated by the government's refusal to grant the necessary visas.[6]

Racism in Denmark

Quraishy and O'Connor observe that racism in Denmark, in common with most European countries, spans the full spectrum.[7] It ranges from the usual stereotyping of non-white immigrants as hordes of foreigners overrunning the virgin land, through the stigmatisation of foreign cultures (especially Islam) as alien and threatening, to institutionalised racism on the part of the police, the immigration authorities, the municipal councils and public agencies in general.

Typically, immigrants or foreigners are blamed for Denmark's economic problems such as rising unemployment and crime rates, and although less than half of Denmark's 3 per cent foreign nationals are 'non-European', frequently the 'foreigner' is identified as being Moslem and thus a cultural threat from the third world. The Glyn Ford Report[8] stated that events in inter-community relations during the four years from 1987 were causing growing concern about the extent of racial prejudice in Denmark. The Report noted Wilkie's conclusion that foreigners were denied equal opportunities, in violation of many international conventions signed and ratified by Denmark, to the extent that in some state-run job centres employers were actually asked whether they were prepared to hire an immigrant for a certain job; employers could refuse foreigners employment with impunity.

There has been an increasing number of attacks on immigrants and refugees since 1985. On 12 July 1986, some 2,000 'rockers' launched a

6. Ibid.

7. Quraishy and O'Connor, 'Denmark: No Racism By Definition', in *Europe Variations on a Theme of Racism*, Institute of Race Relations, London, vol. 32, no. 3, January–March 1991.

8. G. Ford, Report drawn up on behalf of the Committee of Enquiry into Racism and Xenophobia, The European Parliament, Luxembourg, 1991, pp. 55–56.

concerted attack against a hostel which accommodated 247 asylum seekers from Iran, Sri Lanka and Lebanon, to protest against the influx of refugees.[9] In 1987 a representative of the *Fremskritspartiet* (Progress Party) referred on a local radio station to refugees as 'the vast hordes of terrorists pouring in over us from the Middle East and Sri Lanka who "bred like rats"'. The Progress Party, which pledges to expel Moslems and refugees from Denmark, increased its share of the vote from 4.8 per cent to 9 per cent at the election of 10 May 1988. Local councils have voted against the reception of 'even more people of foreign origin taking residence in Ishoj' and in another Copenhagen suburb, Farum, there was a proposal in 1988 to hold a referendum on whether the municipality should make 25 homes available to refugees. In the seaside resort of Gilleleje youths broke into a hotel where Lebanese asylum seekers were staying and stabbed two people, necessitating the movement of the refugees to a more secure place.[10]

There is also evidence that racial violence is not confined to the activities of so-called extremists groups, but is to be found within the fabric of traditional institutions in Denmark. The police, whose racist behaviour is frequently backed up by the courts, were involved in shooting and killing an unarmed Palestinian refugee; the culprit escaped conviction by pleading that he thought the Palestinian was preparing to take up a karate position. In contrast an Iranian refugee who was chased for several blocks by a policeman for no apparent reason, and who then stabbed and killed him, was given life imprisonment.

Violence is not the only manifestation of prejudice and discrimination. A Tanzanian visitor whose papers were in order and who was allowed in the country to visit his fiancée was then sent home by the police, who thought he was seeking asylum. In this instance, and in many others, the police failed to call in an interpreter. It is alleged that the Danish police constantly subject blacks to arbitrary treatment, including searches, harassment, arrest and being told to stay away from public places.[11] There is also evidence of racism throughout the prison service, and the Justice Department has been accused of purposely delaying some Tamils' applications to bring close relatives from Sri Lanka to Denmark.[12]

It would also appear that racism and prejudice are becoming increasingly acceptable, as various forms of xenophobia are being articulated through political groups such as the 'Danish Society', which has in turn had a significant effect in influencing several newspapers to

---

9. *Migration News Sheet*, August 1986.
10. Reported in the *International Herald Tribune* on 30 July 1990.
11. Quraishy and O'Connor, 'Denmark: No Racism By Definition', p. 11.
12. Ibid., p. 116.

take a fiercely anti-discrimination stand. Other right-wing groups include the DNSB (the Nazi organisation), the National Party and the Danish Chapter of the Ku Klux Klan. While many of these groups are marginal, they feed off and into the right wing of more traditional parties, forcing racism into the mainstream of Danish political life.

Discrimination in Housing

Public housing in Denmark is the responsibility of individual municipalities, where housing is built and administered by non-profit-making housing associations. While public housing is not always the cheapest form of housing available, waiting lists are common in the major urban areas due to the general under-supply of housing. Central government controls both funding and quotas, and national legislation determines entry qualifications and consequent allocations. General rules applying to municipal governments include an obligation not to discriminate on the basis of race in respect of allocations, and these and other rules are designed to ensure that decisions are objective and based on reasonable criteria while still allowing the municipal governments a major say in allocation policy.

It was noted earlier that some municipalities have acted in a discriminatory fashion; Ishoj, for example, has directed housing associations to impose a limit of 10 per cent of 'foreigners' in each public housing building in the municipality.[13] That direction, effective since mid-1970s, was referred to the Director of Public Prosecutions and then to the Ombudsman, both of whom concluded that such discrimination was not unlawful because dispersal of the Turkish population, at whom this measure was directed, would enhance integration and was therefore in the Turkish community's own self-interest. In mitigation, it should be said that some Turkish representatives had been consulted and had agreed to the implementation of the policy.[14]

The Prohibition of Discrimination

International Obligations.   Denmark has become a party to a number of the various international obligations against racial discrimination which were described in Chapter 2. In 1971 Denmark ratified the International Convention on the Elimination of all forms of Racial Discrimination

13. Wilkie, 'Race Discrimination in Denmark', p. 29.
14. For discussion on discrimination in housing allocation policies generally and the impact of indirect discriminatory allocation rules, see Martin MacEwen, *Housing, Race and Law*, Routledge, London, 1991, pp. 216–250.

(ICERD) and Denmark is one of the relatively few states which has accepted that the Committee established by the Convention may receive and consider communications from individuals or groups who claim to be victims of violation by the state under the terms of Article 14.[15] Denmark established a commission through the Ministry of Justice in order to examine Danish legislation and to review its concordance with the obligations imposed by the Convention; the commission concluded that there was a potential conflict between compliance with the Convention in all respects on the one hand, and the aim of the Danish Constitution to respect the rights of individuals to express their views on the other. By mid-1992 it was understood that there had been no individual complaints made to the committee under Article 14.[16]

Other conventions and treaties of which Denmark is a signatory include the European Convention on Human Rights; as noted earlier, Article 14 of this convention prohibits racial discrimination in terms of the various rights described, but it extends only tentatively beyond these boundaries. Denmark has also ratified ILO 111 (the Discrimination (Employment and Occupation) Convention of 1958), the UN Covenant on Civil and Political Rights of 1966 and the UNESCO Convention against Discrimination in Education of 1960.

It is generally accepted that the Danish courts, when in doubt about the interpretation of a domestic provision, prefer the interpretation that best complies with existing treaty obligations. There is also a presumptive rule that new legislation will be interpreted in a manner consistent with the treaty obligations, and the courts will presume that such obligation has not been enacted by parliament with the intention of conflicting with international obligations. However, it would seem that if there is a direct conflict then the international obligation must give way to domestic provision.[17] While three Danish Supreme Court decisions from 1989 have confirmed that the Danish courts of law and other authorities are under an obligation to base their interpretation of Danish law on such international obligations, there is still some doubt as to the complete applicability of these obligations. Civil rights movements have argued for the incorporation of international obligations into domestic law in order to ensure that the decisions of the courts and the municipal

15. See R. Plender, 'Human Rights of Aliens in Europe', in the Council of Europe, *Directorate of Human Rights in Europe*, Martinus Nijhoff, 1985, p. 33 ff.

16. See Danish Draft Report, *Comparative Assessment of Legal Instruments Implemented in the Various Member States of the European Community to Combat all Forms of Discrimination, Racism, Xenophobia and Incitement to Hatred and Racial Violence*, the Danish Centre for Human Rights, Copenhagen, 1992, p. 9.

17. C. Gulmann, 'Denmark', in F. G. Jacobs and S. Roberts (eds), *The Effect of Treaties in Domestic Law*, Sweet and Maxwell, London, 1987, vol. 7, p. 92.

authorities are in complete accord with them.

Between 1956 and 1990, 218 individual complaints against Denmark of breach of the European Human Rights Convention were raised with the European Commission; ten were considered by the Commission and seven were also considered by the European Human Rights Court. By the beginning of 1991, 17 cases had yet to be settled; none of these concerned Article 14 of the European Convention and no other cases of racial discrimination have been determined under Article 14.

By ratifying the optional protocol of the Covenant on Civil and Political Rights (CCPR), Denmark accepted the competence of the United Nations Human Rights Committee to receive and consider complaints concerning violations of the rights established in that Convention. According to its annual report, the Committee had not considered any Danish individual complaints by the beginning of 1991.

The Danish Constitution. The current Danish Constitution dates from 1953; Section 17 protects the individual's civil and political rights against discrimination by the state on the basis of religion but does not cover racial discrimination. Protection of personal liberties against discrimination on religious and political grounds is provided by Section 71. Because the Danish Constitution provides against arbitrary discrimination, it would appear that there are implicit and explicit requirements for equality before the law which would serve as the basis for actions against discrimination on the grounds of race, against any public authority in the exercise of its legal obligations.[18]

However, at a constitutional level there are no explicit provisions which prohibit racism, racial discrimination or xenophobia, and the Supreme Court has been reluctant to declare laws *ultra vires* because they are in breach of the Constitution. That option remains a possibility. More importantly, the courts will require an interpretation of existing provisions to accommodate a presumption of equality before the law and the absence of arbitrary discriminatory treatment including that on racial grounds.

Section 1 of the Constitutional Act provides that the Constitution applies to all parts of the Kingdom of Denmark including Greenland and the Faroe Islands. Thus Denmark cannot be considered to be a federal state. However, Section 82 of the Act provided local government with the right to establish an element of autonomy, and this has enabled the

---

18. See Danish Draft Report, *Comparative Assessment of Legal Instruments Implemented in the Various Member States of the European Community to Combat all Forms of Discrimination, Racism, Xenophobia and Incitement to Hatred and Racial Violence*, p. 16.

so-called 'Home Rule Acts' for Greenland and the Faroe Islands. Because the Danish Constitution refers to both Danish citizens ('Borger') and to 'persons', there is some doubt as to whether protection provided by the Constitution extends in all cases to non-national residents or visitors. Clearly some provisions are explicit in their conferment of rights only on Danish citizens, including the right to vote in general elections (Section 29) and eligibility for parliament (Section 30). A Danish Act of Election to Local Government and County Councils provides that foreign citizens may after three years of permanent residence in the municipality obtain suffrage and eligibility in local elections.

As Denmark is a signatory to ILO Convention 111, the Discrimination (Employment and Occupation) Convention of 1958, the state is bound to uphold the principles of equality of treatment in employment and to respect such provision in the interpretation of constitutional rights. However, a statement of constitutional rights, whether vague or specific, is one thing and providing effective implementation and the provision of remedies is another. Denmark asserted, in its second report to the Committee on the Elimination of Racial Discrimination, that constitutional guarantees ensured that the individual has rights to bring acts of discrimination before law courts or other public institutions, and ensured equal treatment before these organs. To date, no case has been brought under the Constitution to ensure such equality for either citizens or non-citizens, and the substantiation of the rights provided by the Constitution is clearly in question.

Penal Code.   Under Section 266b of the Penal Code (as altered by Law No. 288 in 1971 and a further minor amendment in 1987), a criminal offence is created whenever any person, publicly or with the intention of wider dissemination, makes a statement or imparts other information by which a group of people are threatened, insulted or degraded on account of their race, colour, national or ethnic origin, religion or sexual orientation. Those convicted are liable to a fine or up to two years imprisonment. Prosecution, exceptionally, can be made only by the police and there are only about two convictions per annum. One of these included the 'Green Jackets' who, prior to an election, had been invited to comment on immigration issues and had made racist responses. Although convicted by the Supreme Court of aiding and abetting the offence committed by the 'Green Jackets', the reporter who conducted the interview gained some sympathy from those arguing for freedom of expression.

The Race Discrimination Act of 1971.   This Act is limited in scope although the definition of discrimination – race, colour, national or ethnic origin or religion – is fairly broad.[19] It does not include indirect discrimination, but it includes refusing to serve in (or to serve on like conditions) or give access to a place, performance, exhibition, meeting or the like that is open to the public, and discrimination in the conduct of a trade or business, or a non-profit undertaking. While a violation of this Act is a criminal rather than civil offence, prosecution is conducted by the police rather than the Director of Public Prosecutions and the penalty, as a criminal offence of the lowest category, is limited to a fine or up to six months imprisonment. Neither discrimination in employment nor discrimination in the public sector is covered. According to the Danish returns for ICERD, there were only seven prosecutions from 1985 to 1989 inclusive; there were many more under Section 266b of the Penal Sanction Code during the same period, and 13 convictions under 266b between 1985 and 1991. It appears that proof is a particular problem under the 1971 Act, as a defendant has generally only to deny a racial motive for the courts to dismiss the charge; the use of statistical evidence appears to be either ignored or inadmissible.

The Ombudsman.   The powers of the Ombudsman embrace the whole of public administration in Denmark, including civil servants and military personnel and the administration of local municipalities. The Ombudsman may investigate complaints against individuals as well as departments, and where he finds evidence of illegal activity he may order the prosecution services to take appropriate action. He may order a department to initiate disciplinary action, or he may merely express an opinion on a referral. However, he does not have the power to quash a decision nor to reverse one.[20] The precise nature of the powers and obligations of this post are set out in the Ombudsman Act of 1954 (No.203 of 11.6.1954) as amended and directives of the Folketing thereunder, but these do not expressly extend to cover discriminatory acts or omissions in public administration. Moreover, the government has never considered the possibility of providing the Ombudsman with special powers in this area.[21]

Theoretically, the Ombudsman will take international obligations into account when considering the legitimacy of any complaint, and a decision may lead to general changes in policy and practice as well as of specific benefits to the complainant. There is little evidence, however, that this

19. Ibid., Chapter 6 for discussion of impact.
20. Wilkie, 'Race Relations in Denmark', p. 50, and M. Herlitz, *Elements of Nordic Public Law*, P. A. Norstedt and Soners Forlag, Stockholm, 1969.
21. Danish comment to the International Human Rights Committee in 1980.

potential has been realised when dealing with racial discrimination complaints.

Discrimination in Ireland

Introduction and Historical Background

The history of inter-ethnic relations in Ireland has been dominated by that country's fraught relationship with Great Britain from before 1800 until independence in 1922, and by the Catholic-Protestant divide. The Protestant ascendancy in the Pale was based on religious discrimination, which had its historical roots in English immigration and overlordship. With independence, the Catholic majority 'beyond the Pale' was assured of political dominance by means of constitutional provisions. As Smith has observed, its island location did little to help strategically-placed Ireland escape from invasions and repressions by the government and settler communities.[22]

Though there was recognition that the Irish were the rightful inhabitants of the country, the growing religious divergences following the Reformation exacerbated English denigration of indigenous culture and identity. However, the Celtic Catholic traditions and the role of the clergy in the local Irish communities survived British repression and Puritan missionary endeavours and were ultimately reflected in the new constitution. Predictably, the persecution and discrimination which the Catholic majority suffered had reinforced the religious content of Irish ethnicity, resulting in the establishment of Catholicism as the State religion in the new constitution.

Today, Ireland has a population of 3.5 million, the mobility of which has been characterised by emigration rather than immigration. With its relatively high rates of unemployment, Ireland is not seen by potential migrants as being particularly attractive, a fact illustrated by the relative paucity of asylum applicants. There were less than 100 of these in 1989[23] while there were 11,500 applicants to the UK in the same year.[24]

There is a small but growing Irish population of African, Asian and Caribbean origin; the 1981 census statistics indicated there were 20,000

22. A. Smith, *The Ethnic Origins of Nations*, Blackwell, Oxford, 1986.
23. PE 139.156, Working Document by Patrick Cooney quoted in Ford, p. 85; see also PE 140.128, p. 2, quoted in Ian Forbes and Geoffrey Mead, *Measure for Measure: A Comparative Analysis of Measures to Combat Racial Discrimination in the Member States of the European Community*, Equal Opportunities Study Group, University of Southampton/Department of Employment, Sheffield, 1992, p. 47.
24. 'Asylum Statistics United Kingdom 1990–91', *Statistical Bulletin*, Home Office, London, 1992, Issue 12/92, Table 8.1.

Asian and black immigrants in the country, who then comprised less than 0.6 per cent of the population. In the last ten years that population has increased and has been added to by Middle Eastern immigrants and descendants of the original immigrants. According to Tannam,[25] the concentration of minorities in the cities would suggest that 10 per cent of the population of Dublin may be black or non-white by the end of the 1990s.

Ireland also has a significant traveller community, numbering in the region of 21,000, and travellers are seen as the largest and most significant visible minority which is now estimated to be between 1.5 per cent and 2 per cent of the total population. According to the Glyn Ford Report more than 70 per cent of the travelling population now have fixed accommodation, and with the waning of their traditional trades and livelihoods the majority now live on the periphery of urban centres.

Racism and Discrimination

According to Cooney, Ireland 'has been remarkable free' of problems relating to racism and discrimination because of the absence of large numbers of 'foreigners'.[26] Such complacency is not reflected in the Report on Racial Discrimination in Ireland compiled by 'Harmony' in 1990.[27] An opinion poll of February 1991 indicated that 24 per cent of the Irish population considered that people of a different race or colour should live in separate districts, and 12 per cent admitted that they were racially prejudiced. Minority groups of African and Asian descent face racism in all aspects of their lives, and recent figures on non-EC nationals suggest that only a third are economically active.[28] Apparently there is still a presumption in Ireland that Irish society is principally Catholic, white and heterosexual.

Racism has been expressed in incidents such as repeated attacks on Jewish shops in Dublin's south inner city in 1986, barring travellers from a public meeting in a Dublin hotel in 1987, and youths laying siege to a Dublin Corporation flat occupied by a Moroccan and ultimately forcing both the Moroccan man and his Irish wife to leave the area in 1987. In

25. M. Tannam, *Racism in Ireland Sources of Information*, Harmony, Dublin, 1991, p. 14.

26. See G. Ford, *Report of the Committee of Inquiry into Racism and Xenophobia*, Office for Official Publications of the European Communities, Luxembourg, 1991, p. 60.

27. See *Racial Discrimination in Ireland: Realities and Remedies*, Harmony, Dublin, 1990.

28. D. De Jong and M. Zwamborn, *Equal Treatment and Discrimination in Europe*, International Alert and the Netherlands Institute of Human Rights, the Netherlands, 1991, Appendix V. See Forbes and Mead, *Measure for Measure*, p. 47.

the same year, racist slogans were daubed outside the family home of an Irish woman and her black British husband; thereafter the family were denied a transfer from their Dublin council flat on the grounds that that ordeal might be repeated elsewhere and it was beyond the capability, if not the responsibility, of the housing authority to deal with it. In addition to discrimination in housing, there is also ample evidence of discrimination in respect of employment; it is claimed that discrimination and prejudice are the normal daily experience of travellers of all ages.[29]

Prohibition of Discrimination

International Obligations. Uniquely amongst EC member states, Ireland is not a signatory of the Convention against Racial Discrimination (ICERD). Ireland is also one of three EC countries not to have ratified ILO 111 on Discrimination in Occupations and in Employment. Ireland is a signatory to the European Convention for the Protection of Human Rights and Fundamental Freedoms (under the auspices of the Council of Europe); between 1959, when the Convention became operable by reference to the European Court of Human Rights, and 1991, six cases had been referred to the Court, none of which involved Article 14 either directly or indirectly.[30] This represents less than 2 per cent of the 345 cases considered by the Court during this period. The European Commission on Human Rights received 5,500 provisional files in 1991, of which 1,648 were registered; of the latter only seven were from Ireland.[31]

Ireland is also a party to the Convention on the Prevention and Punishment of the Crime of Genocide (1948), the International Covenant on Civil and Political Rights (1966) and the Community Charter of the Fundamental Social Rights of Workers, adopted by eleven of the twelve member states of the European Community in December 1989. Ireland has not ratified the UNESCO Convention Against Discrimination in Education. None of the Conventions or Covenants to which Ireland is a signatory has been incorporated into domestic law, which would be required in order to give them direct effect.

The Irish Constitution. Article 40(1) of the Irish Constitution of 1937 provides that 'all citizens shall, as human persons, be held equal before the law'. Although this provision refers to citizens, the Irish Courts have

---

29. Fifth Report, Committee to Monitor the Implementation of Government Policy on Travelling People, Dublin, 1989, p. 4.

30. European Court of Human Rights, *Survey of Activities 1959–1991*, Council of Europe, Strasbourg, January 1992.

31. European Commission of Human Rights, *Survey of Activities of Statistics 1991*, Geneva, 1992.

interpreted this as being a fundamental right applicable to all people regardless of nationality. However the question of whom the equality principle is intended to address has so far escaped specific consideration by the courts. Litigation has shown that the Article is conceived of as being addressed to the state, and that individuals in their private and business relationships are not affected by it. Racial discrimination by private citizens in their commercial dealings and other relationships are considered, if at all, under special legislation rather than under the constitution.[32] In *Quinn's Supermarket v. Attorney General* (1972) IR 1, Justice Walsh said:

> this provision is not a guarantee of absolute equality for all citizens in all circumstances but it is a guarantee of equality as human persons . . . relating to their dignity as human beings and . . . is a guarantee against inequality grounded on an assumption or indeed a belief, that some individual or individuals or classes of individuals, by reason of their human attributes, or their ethnic or racial, social or religious background, are to be treated as the inferior or superior to other individuals in the community.

It therefore appears that the courts will limit the guarantees provided by the Constitution to situations in which the discrimination relates to essential rather than contingent features of an individual's existence.

Domestic Law: Civil Code. With regard to employment, there is specific legislation which may be interpreted as restricting discrimination on racial grounds. Section 6(1) of the Unfair Dismissals Act 1977 provides that every dismissal shall be presumed to be unfair unless the employer demonstrates that there are 'substantial grounds justifying dismissal'. Moreover, Section 6(2) provides that a dismissal is deemed automatically unfair if it resulted wholly or mainly from, *inter alia*, the race or colour of the employee; similarly selecting employees for redundancy on racial grounds would also be unfair. But the Act does not generally guarantee rights to employees, prospective employees or ex-employees, nor does it extend rights to employees with less than one year's service (excepting dismissal on the grounds of pregnancy).

Domestic Law: Criminal Code. There are no special provisions which make racial discrimination unlawful in the areas of service provision or housing. The Prohibition of Incitement to Racial Hatred Act 1989 makes

32. See M. St. John, 'Racial and Ethnic Discrimination in the Republic of Ireland', in the Runnymede Trust Report prepared and edited by Ann Dummett, *Report on Racial Discrimination and the Law in EEC Countries*, for the Social Affairs Commission of the European Economic Community, unpublished, 1986, p. 48.

it an offence to engage in activities, including the use of words in public places or at public meetings or publishing, distributing or broadcasting material, where these are threatening, abusive or insulting and are intended, or are likely, to stir up hatred 'against a group of persons in the state or elsewhere on account of their race, colour, nationality, religion, ethnic or national origins, membership of the travelling community or sexual orientation'.

Certain local acts such as the Dublin Police Acts make it an offence to use words or conduct calculated to bring about a breach of the peace. Words or conduct calculated to influence violent behaviour or passions, including racial hatred and disharmony, may also under certain circumstances amount to a breach of the peace. In addition there are two actions in tort, one relating to intimidation and another relating to conspiracy, which in civil law may be used to protect the rights of the individual. However, there is no evidence that these have been used extensively or effectively to defend against racial discrimination.[33]

Access to Law.   In general, legal aid provisions are poor. Claims can be brought before industrial tribunals without legal representation, but there is no record of any cases which concern racial discrimination in employment.[34] Special help is provided for representatives of the traveller community through a number of organisations such as the Dublin Travellers Education and Development Group, the Irish Travellers Movement and the National Federation of Irish Travelling People. Harmony provides support to the minority communities of African, Asian and Middle East origin and the indigenous black Irish population, as well as campaigning for comprehensive anti-racist legislation, ratification of ICERD and proper monitoring.[35] In its third report of 1987, the committee set up to monitor the implementation of government policy on travelling people requested that the government introduce legislation to make it illegal to discriminate against anyone because of race, colour, creed, or membership of a minority community. However, this along with similar requests from Harmony and other organisations working in this area, has fallen on deaf governmental ears.[36]

The government policy statement of July 1984, concerning Ireland's travelling people, did make particular commitments and led to the formation of the committee referred to above to oversee the implementation of a comprehensive programme. Positive measures in that

---

33. Ibid.
34. Forbes and Mead, *Measure for Measure*, p. 48.
35. *Racial Discrimination in Ireland: Realities and Remedies*, p. 12.
36. Ibid., p. 17.

programme include the creation of special funds from the national lottery earmarked to provide services for young travellers, the provision of 500 places at special training centres and the issuing of specific instructions to departments to provide special assistance. However, as Forbes and Mead have observed,[37] at both governmental and administrative levels, racial discrimination is not considered to be a serious problem in Ireland and it is considered that it would be too costly to introduce effective legislation with the appropriate machinery for enforcement.

Michael Kelly has observed that it is the social uniformity of the country which supposedly explains the lack of any explicit guarantees or protections for racial or other minorities. The experience of the Irish Council for Civil Liberties, however, would suggest that the existing minority groups do experience a high level of social intolerance and are all the more vulnerable for being few in number and generally ill-organised.[38]

Discrimination Law in Greece

Introduction and Historical Background

In contrast to Ireland, Greece has neither, at least in recent years, been subject to colonial subjugation nor has it been a country which has only experienced emigration. However, many of Greece's immigrant population are people of Greek origin returning home as qualified professional workers or returning to retire. In common with Ireland, the visible minority is a small proportion of the total Greek population.

In 1987–88 it was estimated that only 0.6 per cent of the population were visible minorities and were therefore susceptible to discrimination on the basis of colour or origin.[39] The largest minority groups are of Turkish and Cypriot origin. In addition to the 60,000 'documented' foreign residents in Greece, of which the Turkish community comprises about half, it has been estimated that there are in the region of 70,000–200,000 illegal immigrants in Greece.[40] According to one report, it is

37. Forbes and Mead, *Measure for Measure*, p. 48.

38. M. Kelly (ed.), *Annual Report for the Irish Council for Civil Liberties*, Irish Council for Civil Liberties, Dublin, 1986.

39. M. Werth and H. Komer, 'Immigration of citizens from third countries into the southern member states of the European Community', in *Social Europe*, Commission of the European Community, Brussels, 1991, p. 62. There are also groups of Pakistanis and Iranians but not enough to comprise a significant element of the visible minorities according to the Ford Report.

40. De Jong and Zwamborn, *Equal Treatment and Discrimination in Europe*, p. XXVI.

government policy not to grant citizenship 'to coloured people in general even if the formal conditions specified by law are fulfilled'.[41]

The majority of Greek citizens who are also members of minority groups are found in Western Thrace, in the provinces of Evros, Rhodope and Xanthy. The Moslem minority in these provinces includes 40,930 Turkish speakers, and in addition there are 31,000 Pomaks and 14,000 Gypsies. The presence of the Turkish minority stems from an agreement on the exchange of Greek and Turkish populations on 30 January 1923, when Turkish subjects of Greek Orthodox faith resident on Turkish soil were exchanged for Greek subjects of Moslem faith resident on Greek soil. The Greek inhabitants of Constantinople, as it then was, the boundaries of which were defined by the law of 1912, were exempted from this agreement, and the Moslem inhabitants of Western Thrace who had settled in the region east of a line defined in the 1913 Treaty of Bucharest were also exempt. Although the Pomaks are frequently identified with the so-called Moslem or Turkish minority, on linguistic grounds they cannot be said entirely to belong to this category as their language is Greek mixed with Slavonic elements. Ethnically, the Pomaks may be descended from the ancient Thracians (Agrians).[42]

The break-up of Yugoslavia, the process of ethnic cleansing in Bosnia and the potential for inter-ethnic conflict in Kosovo has focused public attention on the most southerly Yugoslav region of Macedonia, and in turn on the position of minorities in the Greek province of Macedonia. Macedonia, in modern terms, is a region of the Balkan peninsula lying athwart Greece, Yugoslavia (or former Yugoslavia) and Bulgaria. It is one of the most ethnically mixed areas in Europe; at one time it lay wholly outside the north of Greece but since the second Balkan war of 1913 when Bulgarian Macedonia was greatly reduced, the larger part of the region was taken from the extreme south-west of Bulgaria to form the Greek province of Macedonia. An exchange of populations took place with Turkey in 1923 following the Treaty of Lausanne and again with Bulgaria in 1930; the existing boundaries largely stem from the Balkan Pact of 1953. The legitimacy of Macedonian ethnicity is currently a matter of political concern. The Greek government argues that Tito's decision to recognise the 'Macedonian' language and province within Yugoslavia was

41. See P. C. Panangopoulos, 'Supplementary Points to the Report on the Legal Aspects of the Social Integration of Persons who are Nationals or come from Third Countries outside EEC and permanently resident in Greece', unpublished, 1989, quoted in De Jong and Zwamborn, *Equal Treatment and Discrimination in Europe*, p. XXV.

42. Report on Racial Discrimination and the law in EEC Countries, Runnymede Trust Report prepared and edited by Ann Dummett for the Social Affairs Commission of the European Economic Community, unpublished, 1986; submission by Ioannis Toulias p. 20.

based largely on the expedient self-interest of the regime and not the existence of a separate cultural identity in Macedonia.

Racism and Discrimination in Greece

The government of Greece by the colonels, established after a coup in 1967 and lasting until 1974, was essentially fascist and left evidence of torture and general brutality. The legacy of that regime can be found in the politics of a number of right-wing organisations.[43] In 1990 there were violent riots in Komotini in Western Thrace, with conflict between Orthodox Christians and Moslems. The first independent Moslem MP, elected in June 1989, was sentenced to eighteen months imprisonment in 1990 for disturbing the peace and inciting discord; his imprisonment and that of another Moslem leader sparked off the clashes, which resulted in the death of one Christian and injuries to nineteen people.

While the 120,000 strong Moslem minority in Western Thrace was provided with particular protection by the Treaty of Lausanne between Greece and Turkey in 1923, the state's relationship with its Moslem minority has led to a diplomatic row between Greece and Turkey and complaints by the Moslem community of harassment by Greek authorities. There are also complaints of bureaucratic obstacles to obtaining permits for building houses and for improving existing homes with sanitary and heating facilities, to obtaining loans from State-controlled banks, and to getting driving licences and permission to drive tractors.[44]

While there are few reports that similar problems are experienced by the Macedonian population or the Jewish and Armenian communities, it is evident that attempts to assimilate the gypsy population in Greece have not succeeded; the majority are still living apart from Greek society. The experience of ethnic minority employment suggests that discrimination is related to colour and there is evidence of substantial variation in rates of pay. Foreigners with work permits are known, in some cases, to earn 50 per cent less than their Greek counterparts.[45] There is evidence of rising xenophobia in the shipyards and the building industry, where increasing competition for jobs has led to protectionist policies.[46]

43. *Europe Variations on a Theme of Racism.*
44. Ford, *Report of the Committee of Inquiry into Racism and Xenophobia*, p. 54.
45. Forbes and Mead, *Measure for Measure*, p. 44.
46. Werth and Komer, 'Immigration of citizens from third countries into the southern member states of the European Community', p. 97.

Anti-discrimination Law

International Conventions. Greece is a signatory to the International Convention on the Elimination of all Forms of Racial Discrimination, the Convention on the Prevention and Punishment of the Crime of Genocide and the European Convention on Human Rights and Fundamental Freedoms, but is not a signatory to the International Covenant on Civil and Political Rights of 1966. Greece is now a signatory to the UNESCO Convention against Discrimination in Education, and in May 1984 Greece ratified ILO Convention 111 on Discrimination in Occupations and Employment. By reason of Article 28(1) of the Constitution, those conventions to which Greece is a signatory constitute an integral part of domestic law:

> The generally recognised principles of International Law, as well as International Conventions which have been adopted by law and have entered into force in accordance with the conditions provided therein, shall be an integral part of domestic Greek law and shall prevail over any contrary provision of Law. The principles of International Law and International Conventions shall be applicable to aliens on a reciprocal basis.

As a consequence, no domestic law either previous to or subsequent to any convention signed by Greece may contain provisions at variance with such a convention when it has been given effect. Litigants in Greece whose rights are not fully protected by Greek domestic law could rely, at least in theory, upon the conventions in the Greek courts directly as these are stated to be an integral part of domestic Greek law.

Constitutional Provisions. Article 5(2) of the 1975 Constitution stipulates that all persons living within Greece should enjoy full protection of life, honour and freedom, irrespective of nationality, race, language, religious or political belief. While these provisions are couched in generous terms, with reference to 'all persons' rather than just Greek citizens and 'race' as well as language and religion, there is some doubt as to the practical application of such general clauses. In particular there is doubt as to whether rights against discrimination in the provision of services, education and housing and employment are necessary derivatives from the expression 'life, honour and freedom'.[47]

Article 22 of the Constitution concerns the right to work. Paragraph 1 provides that work constitutes a right and should enjoy the full protection of the State, which seeks to create conditions of full employment for all citizens and to promote the moral and material advancement of the rural

---

47. See also Forbes and Mead, *Measure for Measure*, p. 45.

and urban working population. The same paragraph also provides that all working people, irrespective of 'sex or any other distinction', shall be entitled to equal pay for equal work. The reference to 'any other distinction' would, by implication, incorporate race and colour, while the reference to 'all working people' appears to extend to the private and public sector, to part-time and full-time workers, and to citizens and non-citizens.

Other Legislation.   In addition to the incorporation of ICERD and ILO 111, there are two provisions of Greek domestic legislation which make specific reference to racial discrimination. Law 927/1979 criminalises 1) the public incitement of acts which may engender racial discrimination or hatred, 2) the public expression of ideas which are offensive to other persons because of their racial or national origin, and 3) the refusal in one's professional capacity as a provider of goods or services to supply them to an individual on the basis of that person's racial or national origin. As noted previously, Greece has ratified ICERD (in 1972) and these provisions were passed to give effect to the requirements imposed by ICERD to introduce measures to combat incitement to racial hatred and discrimination in the provision of goods and services. With respect to employment, Law 1264/1982 entitles foreign nationals as well as Greek citizens to enjoy membership of and participation in trade unions, and it has subsequently been accepted that foreign nationals in Greece are free to form their own associations and unions. Greece has failed to introduce specific legislation pursuant to all the requirements of ICERD and ILO 111 relating to employment, but as these two Conventions are incorporated into domestic law they provide protection against discrimination not otherwise specifically covered (for example in the area of recruitment).

Article 4 of the Greek Civil Code stipulates that foreign nationals shall enjoy civil rights on an equal basis with Greek nationals; there is no evidence, however, that this provision has proved effective with respect to racial discrimination. Article 20 of the Constitution and Articles 62, 63 and 110 of the Civil Code provide for equal treatment in terms of legal proceedings and in the bringing of civil legal actions. Article 105 of the Introductory Act to the Civil Code provides that the state shall be obliged to pay compensation for any unlawful act or omission committed by its institutions in the execution of their public duties, unless the act or omission in question is the result of a failure to observe a provision enacted in the public interest. The individual offender and the State shall be equally responsible, subject to the special provisions relating to the responsibility of ministers. By Article 106, this obligation applies to the municipalities, communes and other public law entities.

It is also possible to appeal on the grounds of abuse of authority by a public authority (this includes an organ of central or local government or public corporation) to the Council of State in order to have an action annulled when it is in violation of the Constitution. There is no evidence, however, that these provisions have been applied in cases of complaints of racial discrimination.

While there are no general anti-discrimination provisions which cover education, the laws of 694/1977 and 695/1977 regulate the foundation and operation of Moslem schools in Western Thrace. Special provision is made for the election of a management committee and for the provision of the Turkish language and Moslem religion within the curriculum. In 1986 over 255 minority schools were in operation in Western Thrace, including elementary, secondary and high schools as well as Islamic seminaries.

Civil and political rights, access to the civil service, the conferment of offices and honours and the practice of any profession or work in any industry are not subject to any religious test. Consequently, Greek subjects who belong to the minority groups enjoy, both legally and practically, the same protection and guarantees offered to other Greek subjects.[48] Particular recognition of the rights of the Moslem minority are found in the Law of 2345/1920 by which, under Moslem law, muftis are appointed as salaried Greek civil servants. The mufti exercises judicial authority over Moslems in Greece in matters of marriage, divorce, alimony, guardianship, trusteeship, rights over minors, Islamic wills and succession in the absence of a will. There is provision for Greek courts to ratify the decisions or recommendations of the mufti in the above cases.

Conclusions

The circumstances of immigration and settlement by ethnic minorities in the three peripheral countries examined above confirm the views expressed in Chapter 1 about the diversity of experience and the variety of responses at the institutional level. Certain common themes emerge from this comparison. Firstly, racism is an everyday experience for visible minorities in each of the three countries; the fact that the victimised population is relatively small in both comparative and absolute terms does not suggest that minorities are less vulnerable in key areas such as access to housing, employment and education, although overt racism is probably less common than indirect discrimination.

Of the three countries surveyed, only Denmark has sought to list

---

48. Dummett, 'Report on Racial Discrimination and the law in EEC Countries', p. 28.

discriminatory legislation, but having done so it has done little to remedy the faults detected. Both Denmark and Greece therefore appear to be in breach of ICERD Article 2(d), which requires each state party to take 'effective measures to . . . rescind . . . laws . . . creating or perpetuating racial discrimination wherever it exists'. As Ireland is not a party to that convention its failure to protect minorities does not constitute a breach of these provisions, but at the same time Ireland has done less than either Denmark or Greece to make concessions to a multi-racial society, even with regard to the travelling community which is the country's only sizeable minority. Special treatment is afforded the German minority in Denmark and the Moslem 'Turkish' minorities in Greece which enables support for linguistic and cultural divergence from the 'norm', but in neither state is there evidence of any profound governmental support for more general anti-racist strategies which might be underpinned by domestic legislation.

–5–

Anti-Discrimination Law in Core EC States: Part I: France and the Netherlands

Having examined three peripheral states in the previous chapter, four core EC states, France, the Netherlands, Germany and the United Kingdom (or more accurately, Great Britain) are studied in this and the next chapter. Northern Ireland represents a special case and is not covered in this analysis.

Some of the reasons for choosing Great Britain have already been alluded to: the UK is exceptional in not having a written constitution, it is one of two EC states which has a common law system, it has (in Great Britain, though not in Northern Ireland) the most comprehensive anti-discrimination provisions in a single statute of any EC country and it was one of the earliest to legislate against racial discrimination. In common with the UK, the Netherlands and France have recent colonial histories which have influenced patterns of immigration as well as political and social attitudes towards citizens and other immigrants and migrants from overseas. This separates them from the other major European states, Italy, Germany and Spain, for while the latter have had more or less significant colonial adventures none has been affected to the same extent by post-colonial immigration.

Germany, both old West Germany and the now unified Germany, is a special case politically, particularly because of its open espousal of racist ideologies under the Third Reich, and has very little in the way of domestic anti-discrimination legislation. However, Germany is not atypical in its current approach, which is that citizenship is the basic requirement for equal treatment within the European Community; similarly its experience of racist attacks, anti-semitism and xenophobia are unfortunately far from unique, nor is the governmental response to explain that experience in terms of opposition to the enjoyment of rights of asylum seekers and refugees. Nevertheless, there are some particular aspects of the German situation which make for intriguing study. In addition to the history of the holocaust, there is the diaspora of the 1.5

million Turkish population, guest workers and their families, for whom German nationality has never been on serious offer but who bear the brunt of racial attacks and discrimination. The generous reception for refugees, guaranteed until recently by the Constitution, has been offset by the lack of effective legislation against racial discrimination and by ambivalence towards erstwhile 'foreign German' immigrants from the east, the Sinti and Roma communities and the 40,000 to 50,000 black Germans.

With respect to Spain and Italy, until comparatively recently both have been countries of emigration to the more prosperous north. Indeed there is evidence that Spaniards and Italians have also suffered discrimination on racial grounds in those countries in which they were seeking employment. During the 1960s a large number of Iberian workers were employed in Germany, Switzerland and Belgium, and many bars in Brussels then displayed notices: 'No entry for Spaniards, Africans and North Africans'.[1] Although inter-EC national xenophobia is an aspect of racial discrimination and a subject worthy of study in itself, it is not the focus of this work, which concentrates on visible minorities which for the most part originate outside the EC. Both Spain and Italy do have small minority groups and while neither have adopted many legislative measures to combat racial discrimination, a case for selecting either for this study could be argued. The Evrigenis Report (1985) played down the extent of racism in Italy but the Ford Report (1991) redressed this, noting violent incidents against immigrants in Florence, Rome, Varese, Turin, Caserta, Catania, Livorno, Matera and Milan in 1990 alone. The dossier issued by Documentacion Social of Caritas Espanola in 1987 shows a disturbing degree of racism in Spain.[2]

Despite arguments in favour of including other states, the choice of France, the Netherlands, Germany and Britain was essentially pragmatic. Three of these states have at least acknowledged the need for central government action and have attempted to use legislation and to develop policy to combat racism and racial discrimination. Germany represents something of a paradox; it has been a fairly assiduous member of international conventions and has had the most generous constitutional provisions regarding asylum seekers and refugees, but at the same time, Germany has proved one of the most reluctant of all the EC states to match international intentions with domestic practice.[3]

1. Carr in *Race and Class*, Institute of Race Relations, London, January–March 1991, vol. 92, no. 3.
2. *Los Immigrantes en Espana*, Documentacion Social, Caritas Espanola, 1987, p. 376.
3. There have been a number of studies of anti-discrimination law in Europe which have informed this work, in particular the study by Forbes and Mead (1992) for the Department of Employment which provides a useful snapshot of the employment law in

France

Introduction

Because of France's colonial past, a significant number of French citizens originate from overseas. In addition, and forming a greater percentage of the total resident population, France has a significant number of non-French citizens, estimated in 1983 at 8 per cent of the total population. Apart from EC citizens and North Americans, the major groups were Algerians, Moroccans, Asians, Tunisians and Turks. Paris, Lyons, Marseilles and other urban areas were the focus of ethnic minority group concentration. Table 5.1[4] shows a 3 per cent increase in the foreign population of France between 1985 and 1990 but this increase is less than half the percentage increase of all other EC countries. Figure 5.2[5] indicates the high relative proportion of immigrants from the North African countries of Morocco, Tunisia and Algeria amongst the foreign population living in France; just under four in every ten foreign nationals come from those countries, although a large number of Moroccans and Algerians living in France are French citizens by virtue of the fact that they arrived in France before their country of origin became independent. There is evidence from the 1990 census, however, that a significant number of French citizens of Algerian origin consider their nationality to be Algerian when by law it is French.

Table 5.1[6] shows that Portuguese and Italians made up a significant minority of foreign nationals resident in France between 1980 and 1990, but there has been a comparative decline in the number of Spanish residents. In 1988 the Algerian minority was approximately 850,000 or 1.5 per cent of the population, and remained the largest single ethnic group. The numbers of Moroccans had increased most sharply of all, by nearly 14 per cent to 560,000 or 1 per cent of the population. Immigration

---

the then 12 member states of the EC. The twelve-part study commissioned by the European Union of the relevant law in member states has been published but only in a stilted summary form *Legal Instruments to Combat Racism and Xenophobia* (European Commission, 1993). The periodic reports of states parties to the CERD have also provided useful background information as well as various reports to the EC, such as Ford (1991) and Evrigenis (1988) on racism and xenophobia in Europe and those to the Council of Europe, particularly those associated with the inquiry into 'Community Relation' from 1988 to 1991. From time to time the ILO and other bodies have commissioned comparative studies (see Dex: MIG WP.59, 1992) and papers presented to seminars, such as the International Conventions held in Strasbourg in November 1993 (Cator and Niessen, 1994), have proved useful.

4. The population of foreign nationality in different countries in Europe, 1980–90.
5. Population Trends No. 69, Autumn 1992: 10C.
6. Changes between 1980 and 1990 in most frequent country of foreign nationality.

Figure 5.1 Foreign Nationals in Selected European Countries (1949–1990): John Haskey, 'The immigrant populations of the different countries of Europe: their size and origins', in Population Trends No. 59, Autumn 1992

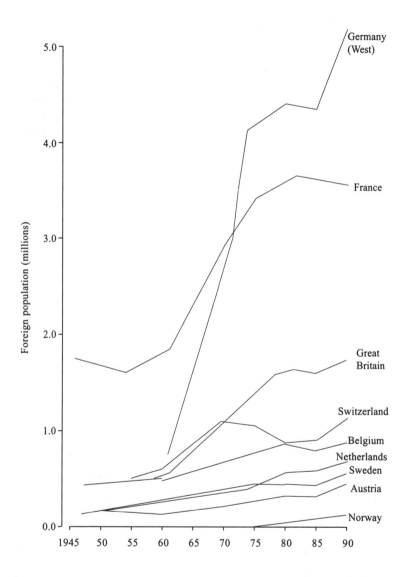

Sources: Census data from UN Demographic Yearbooks, French censuses, SOPEMI 1992.

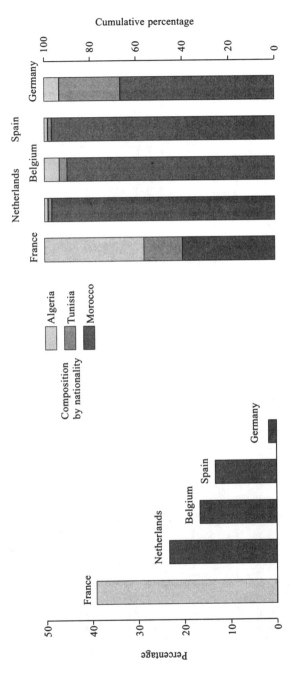

Figure 5.2 Maghreb Nationals resident in certain European Countries, John Haskey, 'The immigrant populations of the different countries of Europe: their size and origins', in Population Trends No. 59, Autumn 1992, 10c

Table 5.1 Foreign Nationals resident in selected countries of Europe between 1980 and 1990; John Haskey, 'The immigrant populations of the different countries of Europe: their size and origins', in Population Trends No. 59, Autumn 1992

Country of residence	Year											Percentage change:			Percentage of total population in 1990
	1980	1981	1982	1983	1984	1985	1986	1987	1988	1989	1990	1980–85	1985–90	1980–90	
EC countries															
Belgium	0.89	0.89	0.89	0.89	0.90	0.85	0.85	0.86	0.87	0.88	0.90	− 4	+ 7	+ 2	9
Denmark	0.10	0.10	0.10	0.10	0.11	0.12	0.13	0.14	0.14	0.15	0.16	+15	+37	+ 58	3
France*			3.44			3.47					3.58		+ 3		6
Germany (West)	4.45	4.63	4.67	4.53	4.36	4.38	4.51	4.63	4.49	4.85	5.24	− 2	+20	+ 18	8
Italy	0.30	0.33	0.36	0.38	0.40	0.42	0.45	0.57	0.65	0.49	0.78	+42	+85	+161	1
Luxembourg	0.09	0.10	0.10	0.10	0.10	0.10	0.10	0.10	0.10	0.10	0.10	+ 4	+ 6	+ 10	28
Netherlands	0.52	0.54	0.55	0.55	0.56	0.55	0.57	0.59	0.62	0.64	0.69	+ 6	+25	+ 33	5
Spain							0.29	0.33	0.36						
Great Britain†		1.65		1.70	1.56	1.63	1.76	1.78	1.76	1.85	1.74		+ 7		3
Other European countries															
Austria	0.28	0.30	0.30	0.28	0.27	0.27	0.28	0.28	0.30	0.32	0.41	− 4	+52	+ 46	5
Finland	0.01	0.01	0.01	0.02	0.02	0.02	0.02	0.02	0.02	0.02	0.03	+33	+55	+105	0.5
Norway	0.08	0.09	0.09	0.10	0.10	0.10	0.11	0.12	0.14	0.14	0.14	+23	+41	+ 74	3
Sweden	0.42	0.41	0.40	0.40	0.39	0.39	0.39	0.40	0.42	0.46	0.48	− 8	+24	+ 15	6
Switzerland	0.89	0.91	0.93	0.93	0.93	0.94	0.96	0.98	1.01	1.04	1.10	+ 5	+17	+ 23	16

Source: Derived from SOPEMI 1992; EAPS reports; French Censuses; Labour Force Survey for GB.

* Excludes some of French nationality who declared themselves as Algerian.

† Estimates liable to sampling variability.

from Turkey, Cambodia, Vietnam and Tunisia had increased the visible minority to 4 per cent of the total population.[7]

The Runnymede Trust Report on France (1986) indicated at that time a level of 14 per cent unemployment amongst ethnic minority workers in comparison with 8.75 per cent in the total population.[8] As Forbes and Mead have observed,[9] these figures, together with the pattern of ethnic minority dominance of the unskilled labour market, demonstrate the disadvantage suffered by those minorities; concentration at the lower end of the employment market is usually associated with less job security, fewer opportunities for advancement and higher levels of unemployment. Although one explanation for this employment pattern can be found in the lack of suitable education, training and resultant qualifications amongst ethnic minority groups, there are also restrictive requirements for professional qualifications and diplomas which impede access for aliens. Lack of qualifications may also result in lower wages and poorer working conditions. Public sector employment in France is available to French nationals only, regardless of qualifications.

After World War II there was an influx of migrants in France which lasted until the 1960s. This influx was frequently clandestine and in contradiction to the edict of 2 November 1945, but was necessary in order to oil the engines of post-war French reconstruction. In 1966 the French Minister of Labour declared, 'clandestine immigration is not a bad thing in itself, because if we were to apply the International Regulations and Agreements strictly, we would probably not have enough hands.'[10] But by the end of the 1960s, the French government wished to regain control of immigration flows and set up bilateral agreements with the labour-exporting countries. In 1972, the Marcellin-Fontanet circulars of 23 February and 5 September made it necessary once more for an immigrant to have employment in order to obtain a resident permit. Illegal immigration continued, and it was estimated by the end of the 1970s that 300,000 persons were illegal immigrants. On 10 January 1981 the 'Loi Bonnet' imposed new and more stringent conditions on entering and residing in France, and increased the number of people expelled on account of illegal residence.

7. Ian Forbes and Geoffrey Mead, *Measure for Measure: A Comparative Analysis of Measures to Combat Racial Discrimination in the Member States of the European Community*, Equal Opportunities Study Group, University of Southampton/Department of Employment, Sheffield, 1992.

8. Runnymede Trust Report prepared and edited by Ann Dummett, Report on Racial Discrimination and the law in EEC Countries, for the Social Affairs Commission of the European Economic Community, unpublished, 1986.

9. Forbes and Mead, *Measure for Measure*.

10. French section on immigration by Jacqueline Costa-Lascoux in Dummett, Report on Racial Discrimination and the law in EEC Countries.

In a review on the immigrant situation in France of May 1981, Stanislaus Mangin was extremely critical of the law, and more importantly the policies and practices, affecting the condition of immigrants in France. Following the election of President Mitterand, the government was committed to a three-pronged approach; first, to clean up the situation inherited from the past which disadvantaged immigrants and their children; second, to regularise the position of illegal immigrants generally and to promote new rights providing equality of treatment with French nationals, including the adoption of international cooperation agreements with the countries of immigrant origin; and third, to promulgate clear, objective and precise rules concerning the immigration situation. While some of these objectives have been pursued through changes in domestic legislation and policy, pan-European attempts to harmonise approaches to immigration and asylum seekers within EC countries have ensured the present restrictive approach to immigration and family reunification.[11]

Evidence of Racism and Discrimination

In 1986 twenty people of ethnic minority origin were murdered in France, all but one of whom were North Africans or French citizens of North African origin. In at least half of these cases there was no rational explanation for the attack and the motives were clearly racial.[12] In addition to these murders, there have been numerous violent attacks resulting in amputations, physical and mental handicap, or permanent and complete paralysis of the victims. A number of these incidents have been attributed to excessive and unjustifiable violence by the police although most go unrecorded; one exception was an incident where a black doctor suffered substantial injuries, which were inflicted by the police when he tried to respond to an emergency call. In 1991 a French youth of Algerian origin was shot three times in the back at close range by a policeman who felt threatened; the policeman was accompanied by another policeman and the youth was handcuffed.

Opinion surveys show that between 73 per cent and 81 per cent of French people believe the French National Front to be a racist party and 76 per cent believe that it is incapable of governing. However, 31 per cent of respondents have agreed with the views of Le Pen on immigration, and 18 per cent would favour him for the post of Immigration Minister.[13]

11. Ibid.
12. G. Ford, *Report of the Committee of Inquiry into Racism and Xenophobia*, Office for Official Publications of the European Communities, Luxembourg, 1991, p. 61.
13. Ibid., p. 63.

President Mitterand has himself expressed the view that the 'threshold of tolerance' of immigration had been reached in the 1970s. These and similar 'official announcements' are no longer atypical, and have tended to legitimate the adoption of a right-wing stance towards immigration and immigrants by a broad section of political opinion in an attempt to regain ground lost to the National Front.

In education, the mayors of three municipalities (Beaucaire, Casseneuil and Montfermeil) have, in open defiance of the Ministry of Education, refused to register non-EC children in local schools in order to 'shock' the authorities into curbing immigration. One communist mayor of another municipality expressed an 'understanding' of this kind of action and made such strong attacks against blacks and Arabs that his own party took action against him. There have also been a number of incidents where Moslem girl pupils have been banned from schools because of their refusal to remove their headscarves. The press has been lively and vitriolic in its exaggeration of the influence of Islamic fundamentalism, and has fuelled the notion of the Islamic threat to the Christian state.

Implicit and explicit preferences for French nationals in employment are matched by the everyday practice of allocating housing in a discriminatory way, without the discrimination being made directly in terms of national origin.[14] Discrimination is a frequent occurrence in public places such as cafes, restaurants, shops and places of entertainment. There is also evidence of discrimination by estate agents and property owners.

In common with many other states, France has adopted measures against racism not as part of a proactive stance but as a reactive political concession, when murders and violence reached an embarrassing level and caused protests from the governments of North African countries. The decision of the prime minister to establish an inter-ministerial unit on racist violence followed the bombing of an immigrants' hostel in Nice in 1988; proposals to strengthen the existing legislation, which were given their first reading in May 1990, followed the murder of three North African youths and the results of opinion surveys showing extensive racism in French society.

Anti-discrimination Provisions

International Obligations. On 7 March 1966 France ratified the United Nations Convention on the Elimination of all forms of Racial Discrimination (ICERD). Subsequently the definition of discrimination used in the Convention has been adopted in French domestic law. France

---

14. Costa-Lascoux, in Dummett, Report on Racial Discrimination and the law in EEC Countries, p. 8.

is also one of four members of the EC (the others being Denmark, Italy and the Netherlands) which has declared its recognition of the competence of the Committee on the Elimination of Racial Discrimination to receive and consider communications from individuals from within its jurisdiction who claim to be victims of a violation under the terms of Article 14(1) of ICERD.

In common with all other member states of the EC, France has ratified the 1951 Convention relating to the Status of Refugees and the 1967 Protocol thereto. France is also a signatory to ILO Convention No. 111 on discrimination in occupations and employment. France is a signatory to the ILO Convention No. 97 which aims at ensuring equality of opportunity and treatment between migrants and national workers. However, France is not a signatory to ILO Convention No. 143 (ratified by only two member states, Italy and Portugal) which aims at providing protection to undocumented or clandestine migrant workers.

The legal status of migrant workers in the member states of the Council of Europe is covered by the European Convention on the Legal Status of Migrant Workers, which has been ratified by seven Council of Europe members including France. In common with other EC members, France is a signatory to the European Convention on Human Rights and, along with Portugal and Spain, it has ratified the European Convention on Establishment. As with all EC members excluding the UK, France is a signatory to the European Social Charter.

France has ratified the UNESCO Convention on Education of 1960, and the UN Covenant on Civil and Political Rights of 1966 and its optional Protocol. Article 27 of the Covenant on Civil and Political Rights adopts a pluralist approach to minority rights in so far as it is designed to protect community language, culture and religion; France filed a reservation to this Article because it does not formally recognise minority groups. France has also ratified the International Covenant on Economic, Social and Cultural Rights of 1966.

According to Section 55 of the Constitution of 1958, once an international convention has been ratified by parliament it supersedes national law and, theoretically, when there is conflict with national law then the convention may be applied directly. However, neither judicial nor administrative authorities have yet expressed an opinion on the direct application in domestic law of the various articles of either of the UN covenants or the other conventions listed so far as not otherwise incorporated into domestic legislation. There is also no evidence that litigants assume the direct applicability of these provisions when seeking a remedy.[15]

15. Forbes and Mead, *Measure for Measure*, p. 36.

Constitutional Provisions.   Article 2 of the 1958 French Constitution provides that:

> France is a republic, indivisible, secular, democratic and social. It shall ensure the equality of all citizens before the law, without distinction of origin, race or religion. It shall respect all beliefs.

The preamble to the 1958 Constitution refers to the Declaration of the Rights of Man and of the Citizen of 1789 which affirms the principle of equality before law, and to the preamble to the Constitution of 1946 which firmly condemns all forms of racial discrimination.[16]

The Constitutional Council reaffirmed in 1991 that because the French people were indivisible without distinction of origin, race or religion, minorities, in this instance the Corsican people, could not be recognised by the legislature.[17] The Council has interpreted the constitution as conferring rights to all residents and not just to French citizens, thus affirming that arbitrary discrimination on the grounds of nationality is unconstitutional,[18] but the constitution also allows different treatment for those in different situations, and equality may be restricted in the public interest if there is a rational link between the restriction and the objective of the law. The Constitutional Council has also decided in effect that not all elections are expressions of national sovereignty and therefore need to be restricted to French nationals; non-citizens are thus eligible to participate in local elections.

To summarise, the French constitution can be said to be characterised by three elements; the principle of equality, the refusal to recognise minorities, and the increasing movement away from nationality as the basis for asserting human rights and freedoms. But in practice, seeking a constitutional redress for racial discrimination has not proved easy. A decision of the *Conseil d'Etat* in July 1991, in referring to the Declaration of the Rights of Man of 1789 and the Preamble to the Constitution of 1946, asserted that the legal norms extended to individual rights. This decision may provide some opportunity for jurisprudence in the area of human rights to be developed by reference to constitutional guarantees, but it seems likely that specific legislation against racism and discrimination will prove the more effective avenue for individual litigants.[19]

16. See J. Costa-Lascoux, *Anti-discrimination in Belgium, France and The Netherlands*, report prepared for the Committee of Experts on Community Relations, Council of Europe, Strasbourg, 1990 (MG-CR).
17. C.C.91.290 D.C., quoted in Legal Instruments to Combat Racism and Xenophobia.
18. C.C.89.269 D.C.
19. See Part IV of the Report of the European Commission (1992).

Legislation Creating Criminal Offences. The Act of 1 July 1972 which implemented obligations under ICERD addressed first racist utterances or writings by making amendments to the Press Act of 1881, and second racial discrimination by amending several articles of the Criminal Code, thereby creating new criminal offences. In the former case there are specific offences and penalties for the utterance of defamation and insults, the penalties for which are greater when they are made publicly than privately and which expressly include defamation or insults of a racist or discriminatory nature. Similarly, by an amendment to the Press Act of 1881, there is an express prohibition of incitement to racial hatred when that incitement is directly provoked.

Associations whose declared purpose, by virtue of their constitutions, is to combat racism are themselves enabled to initiate proceedings under the above legislation; these associations include the League against Racism and Anti-semitism (LICRA), the Movement against Racism and in favour of Friendship between Peoples (MRAP) and the Human Rights League. These three, amongst others, have brought actions against newspapers and authors of pamphlets with respect to insults or defamation of a discriminatory nature. The police are also able to initiate proceedings through the prosecution service.

Although there have been a number of successful prosecutions under the above provisions there have also been a number of acquittals, some arising out of the difficulty of defining racist remarks within the meaning of the law. The Metz Court has held that 'while it is traditionally possible to lampoon certain ethnic groups, this is only possible if it is done in moderation in order to denounce certain oddities such as dress or accent but without ever impugning the respectability of the persons or groups concern.' One interpretation is that writings or drawings, which would be intolerable if printed in newspapers with a normal news-giving mission, will not be taken seriously by readers of the weekly magazine *Charlie Hebdo*, who are familiar with its outrageous style and caustic satire.[20]

In addition to incitement and defamation, certain acts of discrimination are rendered unlawful by the Criminal Code, as follows:

1. The provision of goods or services. Article 416, paragraphs 1 and 2, provide for the penalties of imprisonment between two months and one year and/or a fine of from 2,000 to 20,000 francs for refusal to provide goods or services to an individual or legal person, or for making an offer of such condition on membership or non-membership of a particular

20. Costa-Lascoux, *Anti-discrimination in Belgium, France and The Netherlands*, p. 13.

ethnic group, race or religion. The term 'legal person' includes any association, company or its members.

2. Refusal of employment or dismissal. Article 416-3 renders the same penalties for refusing to hire or dismissing a person on the grounds of his or her origin, sex, family status, membership or non-membership of a racial group, or making an offer of employment subject to conditions based on the origin, sex, family status or membership or non-membership of a racial group.

3. Economic activities. Article 416-1 imposes like penalties on anyone who, by act or omission, impedes the exercise of any economic activity under normal conditions of any individual or legal person by reason of the latter's national origin, or his or her real or supposed membership of a particular ethnic group, race or religion.

4. Access to public services. Article 187-1 imposes penalties against any person who, in an official public capacity, denies another the benefit of a legitimate right on the grounds of the latter's sex, family status or membership or non-membership of a particular ethnic group. Penalties range from two months to two years and/or a fine of between 3,000 and 40,000 francs.

Changes in the law designed to make the penalties for racism more effective include a stipulation that, regardless of the type of discrimination, it is no longer possible to deny criminal liability on the grounds of a 'legitimate motive'. This defence has been frequently employed in the past.[21] With respect to discrimination by employers, anyone in the organisation who has the right to hire or fire can be held liable. This provision is designed to avoid complex legal issues which could otherwise arise because of the legal status of the parties or the allocation of responsibility for fault between the employer and employee acting within or outside his or her scope of employment.[22] As a result employers cannot deny liability for their employees by arguing that the employee is solely responsible for his or her actions. Under a 1991 amendment to the 1972 law, a conviction for certain offences may lead to the offender being barred from public posts and being denied the right to stand in elections.[23]

---

21. Ibid., p. 14.
22. See Forbes and Mead, *Measure for Measure*.
23. See Ford, *Report of the Committee of Inquiry into Racism and Xenophobia*, p. 62.

Civil Actions. With respect to employment-related complaints, the work code or *code du travail* provides the framework for more detailed legislation which is found in the *code d'emploi.* Copies of the code are available at all workplaces and inform complainants of significant rights of protection against less equal treatment. Employees can ask for their contracts to be drafted in a language of their choice and a complainant can take a case to one of the 400 labour inspectors who deal with all labour matters. The trade union concerned also has the right to pursue complaints.

All such complaints are pursued through civil action by written submission to the magistrate of the *Tribunal de Grande Instance.* The magistrate has a supervisory responsibility to ensure that all necessary elements of the case are made available and considered, and he or she is empowered to call for full and further documentation. While the procedure is lengthy and burdensome, the optional presence of an advocate can ensure that the complainant is fully informed of progress.

It is a characteristic of civilian systems that the judiciary have a responsibility to investigate and to seek out what is relevant, and then ensure that this is presented to the court. In contrast, in common law systems the judge has been compared with a referee whose primary responsibility is to overview the contest between the pursuer and the defender so that no unfair advantage is obtained by one party at the expense of the other; it is not the task of the judge, therefore, to ensure that the court is informed of all relevant facts. It may be argued that in cases of technical difficulty the pursuer requires the guidance of the court and this may be more likely to happen in the French system. In practice the distinction may be overstated; in British employment tribunals, which follow similar procedure to courts but have greater latitude in the admission of evidence, it is fairly common for the chair to guide the complainant so that the case presented makes appropriate use of the available information, and French tribunals still have comparatively little experience of discrimination complainants. A Council of Europe Report (MG CR (90) 5) of December 1989 noted the very small number of convictions for discrimination in France; most people were afraid to complain and most who did complain were unsuccessful.

Pursuing Complaints. The major obstacle to bringing a successful complaint of discrimination before the courts lies predictably in the provision of evidence; this is compounded on occasion by problems associated with registering the complaint. With regard to the former, in employment cases it seems that an employer need only omit to give the reason for his selection decisions to escape prosecution in recruitment cases, and in the latter instances there is evidence that the amount of monetary deposit which complainants who wish to sue for damages are required to pay has had the effect of dissuading the victims of offences from initiating court proceedings.[24]

A number of circulars have been issued by successive Ministers of Justice to improve the effectiveness of the Act but several trenchant difficulties remain. In particular, indirect discrimination is not effectively covered in some cases because of the need to demonstrate that refusal of the employment or service required was based on racial grounds. There are also practical difficulties in persuading people to testify.

Costa-Lascoux has suggested that the area in which discrimination is most common and its consequences most serious is that of housing. As has been noted, Article 416 provides for the prosecution of estate agents and private landlords for discrimination in this area, but conviction clearly depends on the ability of the pursuer to provide adequate evidence and call appropriate witnesses in order to prove his or her case. However, agent provocateurs may be used to demonstrate an intention to discriminate. Costa-Lascoux has also provided a breakdown of the convictions under the 1972 Act between 1984 and 1987 and these are replicated in Table 5.2.[25]

The provision for the posting of local notices publicising conviction for an offence was exemplified in a case heard by the eleventh section of the Paris Court of Appeal in November 1974, which gave a decision against a building manager who was fined 500 francs and required to pay 3,000 francs in damages to each of the plaintiffs. The judgment, as required by law, was posted publicly in the building for a period of fifteen days.

While the intimation of an intention to discriminate on the basis that a 'tolerance threshold' had been exceeded led to the conviction of a president of a town centre association for incitement to racial hatred in the Criminal Court of Marseilles in 1985, the same reason, the need to limit the number of minorities to a level acceptable to the local white community, has been used by public agencies and local housing authorities with impunity.

There is no evidence that the government has introduced positive action programmes, as required by ICERD Article 2(2) to help racially disadvantaged groups. In civic education, however, Section 2 of Law No. 89-548 of 2 August 1989 contains the following:

School Curricula, at every stage in the school, [should] include subjects designed to acquaint pupils with the diversity and wealth of the cultures

24. MG-CR (88) 14, p. 6 and MG-CR (90) 2, p. 15.
25. MG-CR (90) 2, p. 18.

Table 5.2 Convictions in France under 1972 Act between 1980 and 1992; Jacqueline Costa-Lascoux, 'French Legislation against Racism', in New Community 1994, vol. 20, no. 3, pp. 371–379 at p. 377

Year	Actions			Threats		
	Against the 'Maghrébins'	Others	Total	Against the 'Maghrébins'	Others	Total
1980	17	3	20	29	6	35
1981	14	9	23	20	3	23
1982	34	9	43	32	23	55
1983	65	3	68	81	15	96
1984	45	8	53	85	17	102
1985	50	20	70	91	7	98
1986	40	14	54	93	2	95
1987	39	7	46	68	12	80
1988	51	13	64	108	27	135
1989	44	10	54	188	49	237
1990	37	15	52	202	81	283
1991	34	17	51	251	66	317
1992	17	11	28	62	49	111
TOTAL	487	139	626	1,310	357	1,667

Victims of racism since 1980

Year	Anti-Maghrébin racism		Other racism		Total	
	Wounded	Killed	Wounded	Killed	Wounded	Killed
1980	9	–	1	–	10	–
1981	1	–	1	–	2	–
1982	10	–	1	–	11	–
1983	33	5	–	–	33	5
1984	11	2	5	2	16	4
1985	23	5	6	–	29	5
1986	10	3	1	–	11	3
1987	29	3	2	–	31	3
1988	39	3	12	–	51	3
1989	22	1	9	–	31	1
1990	29	1	6	–	35	1
1991	7	–	7	–	14	–
1992	9	–	6	–	15	0
TOTAL	232	23	57	2	289	25

represented in France. Civics classes are one of the means by which the school must inculcate in pupils respect for the individual, his origins and his differences.

The competence of a court or tribunal to deal with a complaint is co-terminous with the gravity of the offence which is classified in three types of infractions:

1. A simple infringement dealt with by a police tribunal.
2. A delict or criminal wrong which is dealt with by a correctional tribunal.
3. A serious crime which goes to the *Cour d'Assis.*

The simplest form of process is by complaint to the Commissioner of Police, submitting written details of the infraction and of the people involved along with proofs and copies of any documents. Although this procedure is free and the police will help with identification, there are a number of procedural drawbacks; delays are likely to occur, and the complainant is kept in the dark about the progress of the complaint.

Assessing the Legal Provisions

As far as criminal law is concerned, there is case law evidence that legislation concerning incitement and racist publications has had some impact. Several prosecutions under this legislation have received wide coverage in the media.[26] With reference to refusal of goods or services and discrimination in employment or housing, however, conviction indicate the woeful success rate of complainants and suggest that employers and others are becoming more adept at avoiding the intentions of the legislators and frustrating the onerous burden of proof which rests with the complainant. The provisions which enable qualifying associations to initiate proceedings have undoubtedly assisted complainants in deciding whether or not to pursue complaints and in determining the appropriate avenue to follow. There remain, however, four major obstacles in the system:

1. The rules of evidence and procedure relating to proving discrimination, and the failure of that definition to encompass indirect discrimination, limits the potential impact of the existing law.
2. The low level of successful prosecutions in both criminal and civil cases suggests that the onus of proof on the complainant or prosecution is unrealistically high; there is too great a willingness on the part of the courts and others to accept apparently innocent explanations.

26. MG-CR (90) 2, p. 19.

3. Ethnic minorities in France are generally at a significant economic and social disadvantage particularly in terms of access to employment and housing. Differences identified with 'cultural discrimination', including religion and dress, frequently deflect actions based directly on colour or racial origin. Thus refusal of a service on the grounds of the applicant's poverty, appearance or demeanour may be accepted where it is not transparently a subterfuge for racist intention.

4. Despite the support of registered associations, there is no effective system of class action to ameliorate racial discrimination against a group regarding housing or employment. The effect of individualising complaints has been to minimise the public perception of their importance and the impact of remedies awarded by courts and tribunals.

In common with the other legal systems studied, French law is as much a victim of the economic, social and political situation in which it is placed as it is an instrument for fashioning change. With respect to racism and discrimination, the climate of political opinion is a substantial impediment to effecting radical change; the state's reference to 'the threshold of tolerance' has the effect of legitimising certain xenophobic expressions in the public reaction to physical concentrations of immigrants whether in housing, education or employment. The law in France, as in many other EC states including Germany, Belgium, Italy, Spain and Portugal, has been largely negative and has not sanctioned positive discrimination. Public employers are not set targets for the employment of ethnic minorities, there are no obligations to publish annual reports on the implementation of equal opportunity initiatives, and there is little incentive to pursue policies designed to improve the provision of goods and services through monitoring and review. Historically, the French attitude towards cultural diversity has always been ambivalent. The legacy of French colonialism and what Franz Fanon has referred to as the 'zombification' of the colonised through the process of cultural attrition has done nothing to create a climate of mutual respect between French and other cultural traditions.[27]

It has become common in Europe to express fear of Moslem fundamentalism, to see both an east-west and north-south divide in terms not merely of poverty and wealth but also in terms of democracy and freedom against theocracy and restriction, and to view Western values as progressive and liberating, for example in areas such as equality for women and the development of the rights of children, but under increasing threat from retrogressive cultural invasion. France, with its views about

27. F. Fanon, *The Wretched of the Earth*, MacGibbon and Kee, London, 1965.

the integrity of the state and the French values it symbolises, has been particularly reluctant to embrace pluralism and cultural diversity as an enriching experience.

The Netherlands

Context and Historical Background

The Netherlands, like Britain, has a legacy of immigration and settlement by ethnic minorities connected with its colonial past and the links consequently established between the Netherlands and its dependencies in Surinam, the Molluccas and elsewhere. After the Second World War, the need for mainly unskilled labour attracted immigrants, mostly males from the former colonies; in addition, a significant number of Turkish and Moroccan immigrants settled in the Netherlands. The period of primary immigration in the 1960s and 1970s was then followed by more restrictive emigration policies, which virtually excluded all further primary emigration but permitted family unification. There are now approximately 700,000 members of ethnic minorities living in the country, of whom only 100,000 are Dutch nationals. According to an estimate in 1992, ethnic minorities comprise 5.3 per cent of the population.

The Surinamese form the largest 'immigrant' group in the Netherlands with 190,000, followed by the Turks (160,000), the Moroccans (120,000) and 50,000 Dutch Antilleans from the Caribbean. The Mollucans, from the Molluca islands in Indonesia, number about 40,000 and there are similar numbers of Gypsies.[28] Immigrants from other EEC countries, principally Germany, Belgium, France, UK, Italy, Ireland and Luxembourg, number 161,000 and are a larger group than the Turkish minority, but they are neither viewed nor classified as immigrants. There are also some 300,000 European-Indonesians who formed the first large group of immigrants leaving Indonesia after independence.

It is the Mollucans who have perhaps the most unusual history of the immigrant minorities. Mollucan soldiers had been part of the colonial army fighting the Indonesians. On being demobilised, they were transferred by the government to barracks in the Dutch countryside. The Mollucans had been promised an independent republic of South Molluca by the Dutch but a formal agreement in the 1980s freed the Dutch of that commitment in exchange for a programme enabling the Mollucans to leave the camps and integrate into the labour market. One element of that

---

28. *Race and Class*, January–March 1991, p. 119.

programme was affirmative action to bring 1,000 Mollucans into government service.

Neither the Turkish nor Moroccan immigrant groups had any colonial connection with Holland, but migrant labourers were offered employment during the 1950s and 1960s and then resisted pressure to leave after the economic crises of the 1970s. By the end of the 1970s it had become clear that the immigrants were permanent residents in the Netherlands, and despite the lack of employment opportunities for unskilled labour following completion of industrial reconstruction, the unemployed migrants remained.

In general, government policy towards the emerging pluralist society has moved towards one of integration with preservation of cultural identity, by formally promoting multicultural events and awareness training. In 1986 legal immigrants were given the right to vote in local government elections, and all major political parties now have non-white candidates campaigning in their communities. There is also evidence of the presence of ethnic minorities in the media, trade unions, educational institutions and in an increasingly large cross-section of public and social activities.

About 50 per cent of the ethnic minority groups live in the four largest cities, Amsterdam, The Hague, Rotterdam and Utrecht, where they comprise 15 per cent to 20 per cent of the total population. Generally ethnic minorities are concentrated in older districts where social services are poorer and where they may form a majority of the total population.

Racism and Discrimination

The Ann Frank Foundation in Amsterdam, which records and monitors racial incidents, chronicled in 1986 the following incidents: attempts to set the mosque of Deventer on fire; swastikas being daubed on the car of a vicar who had helped refugees and the homeless (his car was later set on fire); racist attacks on Surinamese, Moroccans and Turks; and a Surinamese and an Antillian being shot at by the police without evident provocation.[29]

The far right in the Netherlands has enjoyed a partial revival since 1989 with the election of Hans Janmaat, leader of the *Centrum Demokraten* (CD), to a seat in the Dutch parliament. Although the CD is small, with a membership of just over 1,000, there are other racist and fascist parties including the *Centrum Partij '86*, the Jongeren Front, the Action Front of National-Socialists and the *Consortium de Levensboom*. The last is led by Florie Rost van Tonningen, the widow of one of the leading Dutch

29. Ibid., pp. 122–124.

collaborators with the Nazis during World War II, who is an international figure in neo-Nazi circles.[30] While the Ford Report suggested that in comparison with countries such as Germany, France and the UK, racial discrimination takes a less aggressive form in the Netherlands, there is clear evidence of institutionalised and subtle forms of racism which is nonetheless harmful to those who suffer it. The employment situation for ethnic minorities in Holland has been described as 'disastrous', as the average rate of unemployment amongst that group is three times that of the host community. There is also evidence that well-educated members from ethnic minorities have difficulty in obtaining employment. A report to the Minister of Justice of 10 February 1988 concluded that ethnic minorities had absorbed racial discrimination instead of using the legal means available to combat it. Discrimination at work and in daily life had been accepted as a normal social phenomenon and reflective of the 'cold, crude, hard and reserved' behaviour of the Dutch people.[31] A further example of discrimination was found in recruitment and selection procedures, where a survey found that half the personnel officers interviewed admitted making use of racial stereotyping before coming to decisions.[32]

Anti-discrimination Law

International Obligations. The Netherlands has ratified the following International Conventions and Obligations:[33]

1. The UN Convention for the Elimination of all forms of Racial Discrimination
2. ILO 111 the Convention Against Discrimination in Occupations and Employment
3. The UN Covenant on Civil and Political Rights
4. The UNESCO Convention on Discrimination in Education
5. The UN Convention on the Prevention and Punishment of the Crime of Genocide
6. The Council of Europe European Convention on Human Rights and Fundamental Freedoms

30. Ford, *Report of the Committee of Inquiry into Racism and Xenophobia*, p. 35.
31. Ibid., p. 69.
32. H. Hoogihemsmstra, Equal Opportunities for Minorities getting a job? Recruitment and Selection Process on the Labour Market for Un- and Semi-skilled Personnel 1991, pp. 1–6.
33. For a comparative view of the anti-discrimination legislation operating in the UK and the Netherlands and the handling of complaints see Anita Brocker, 'A Pyramid of Complaints: The Handling of Complaints about Racial Discrimination in the Netherlands', in *New Community*, Commission for Racial Equality, London, July 1991, vol. 17, no. 4, pp. 603–616.

7. The Council of Europe Convention on the Legal Status of Migrant Workers
8. The Social Charter of the European Community

While in Dutch legal theory international obligations have direct effect without the need for legislation or statutory directive, the precise scope of the application of such conventions is controversial and far from clear-cut. It has been observed, however, that Dutch lawyers are showing a growing awareness of the importance and possible uses of these conventions because they can be used to test the validity of pieces of national legislation.[34] From an example where the International Covenant on Civil and Political Rights was applied in a case concerning unemployment benefit for a woman, it is increasingly evident that lawyers are appealing to conventions more frequently, with the result that judges take such conventions more seriously. It would appear, however, that where there is domestic legislation the courts cease to apply the obligations imposed by the conventions; such domestic provision is, therefore, given greater weight than the convention itself. In addition to lawyers making reference to these conventions there is also evidence that non-governmental organisations are playing a significant role in stressing their importance, which in turn contributes to judicial awareness.[35] But while such obligations may have direct effect, there is some doubt as to whether their application extends beyond the state to the individual.

The Dutch Constitutional Provisions. Article 1 of the Dutch Constitution of 1983 provides that all persons in the Netherlands shall be treated equally in like circumstances. Discrimination on the grounds of religion, belief, political opinion, race, sex or on other grounds is not permitted. While individuals are not entitled to take direct action against other individuals on the basis of this Article, individuals who are subject to racial discrimination by the state do derive protection from this provision.[36] While the constitutional provisions restrict membership and the franchise of parliament and provincial councils to Dutch citizens, in the amended Constitution such restrictions are not applied to municipal elections. The Constitution limits basic social security rights to Dutch nationals but because international treaties extend rights to non-citizens, the Dutch administrative courts give cognisance to such obligations.[37] As far as racial

34. Forbes and Mead, *Measure for Measure*, p. 56.
35. Ibid.
36. See CCPR/C/10/Add.3. and PE139.213.P5 as well as discussion in Forbes and Mead, *Measure for Measure*.
37. Contribution by Thomas Hessels, in Dummett, Report on Racial Discrimination and the law in EEC Countries.

discrimination is concerned, the principles of non-discrimination are elaborated in the Criminal Code, the Civil Code and the Labour Laws.[38]

Other Legal Provisions. Particular provision against racial discrimination is found in the Criminal Code, the Civil Code and the Labour Laws. The Criminal Code, as amended in 1971, provides under Article 90 a definition of discrimination as follows:

> Any form of distinction, any exclusion, restriction or preference, the purpose or effect of which is to nullify and impair the recognition, enjoyment or exercise on an equal footing of human rights and fundamental freedoms in the political, economic, social or cultural or any other field of public life.

Apparently, public life is to be contrasted with domestic life rather than private life.[39]

Article 137 of the Penal Code covers racial insult, incitement to hatred, discrimination and violence on racial grounds; it is also an offence to publicise or disseminate racist material. The penalties include fines of up to 10,000 guilders or imprisonment for up to one year. An editor or distributor who has been convicted twice for the same violation within five years may be disqualified from further pursuance of his or her occupation.

Article 429 makes it a criminal offence to take part in or to support in any other material way activities which are aimed at discriminating against people on racial grounds. Article 429 also penalises racial discrimination in the exercise of a profession, business or trade and in the offering of goods or services. Offences carry penalties of imprisonment for up to two months or a fine of up to 10,000 guilders. Positive action is enabled under this article where the discrimination is to facilitate ethnic or cultural minority groups counteracting existing inequalities. The provisions of Article 429 further prohibit discrimination in the recruitment of new employees and in terms and conditions for existing employees, including promotion and dismissal. The courts have held that these provisions cover not only direct but indirect discrimination; thus if a language requirement was imposed inappropriately and unnecessarily for a particular job or qualification, which resulted in a disproportionately low representation of minority groups, or a particular minority group, this would be unlawful. However, if the requirement could be shown to be relevant for the job in question it would be considered lawful, whether or not the impact was disproportionate. In this respect the interpretation of the Dutch courts

---

38. Roger Zegers de Beijl, *Although Equal Before the Law* . . ., ILO Working Paper, ILO Office, Geneva, 1991.
39. Forbes and Mead, *Measure for Measure*, p. 57.

mirrors the statutory provisions expressed in Section 1 of the British Race Relations Act of 1976.

Article 429 of the Penal Code was introduced in 1971 to give effect to obligations imposed by the Netherlands' ratification in 1971 of the Convention Against Racial Discrimination (ICERD). It should be noted that a 10,000 guilder fine (about £3,000) is not inconsiderable. Individuals who believe that they have been discriminated against and where the offence is covered by the Penal Code may complain to the police, who are under a duty to investigate a complaint. In practice, cases have proved difficult to pursue and the sanctions imposed have been slight, particularly under the employment provisions where the biggest fine imposed to date has been £25.[40]

The Civil Code. Under Articles 15 and 16 of the Civil Code the court is empowered to dissolve racist organisations on application by the Public Prosecutor. The purpose or effect of such organisations must be to discriminate on racial grounds or to provoke violations of public order and morality. Under 162 Book 6 of the New Civil Code anyone who has suffered damage from an unlawful discriminatory act (including contravention of the Penal Code) may seek compensation; in cases of criminal offence the court may simultaneously impose a penalty and order compensation under Article 1401.[41]

Anti-discrimination Regulations. The Labour (Collective Agreements) Act of 1927 was amended in 1971 to nullify any provision which restricted employment on racial grounds. Similarly an Act on Equal Competition, also of 1971 and also implementing the Dutch ICERD Obligations, renders null and void competition agreements which are discriminatory on racial grounds. Article 28 of the Act on Works Councils empowers such Councils to act against discrimination in companies. In addition to explicit provisions in subsidiary legislation, the minister responsible for a particular area may specify that anti-discrimination requirements be included in the interpretation of rules. Thus the Minister of Social Affairs officially ordered that statutes and rules in the field of social work should contain the condition that social services should not be refused to any client on the grounds of religion, belief, race or nationality.

The Dutch courts have provided a broad interpretation of the term 'race' which extends to colour, descent and national and ethnic origin in a fashion similar to that of ICERD. While this interpretation does not

40. Ibid.
41. See MG-CR (90) 2, p. 25.

extend to cover current nationality, in a number of cases the courts have considered that making a distinction between nationals and non-nationals may constitute a form of unlawful indirect discrimination.[42]

There have also been some amendments to legal provisions preventing non-nationals being employed in the civil service. An Act of 20 April 1988 permitted the employment of foreign nationals in the public service, and there are now only a limited number of posts for which Dutch nationality is required as a precondition: these include posts in the judiciary, military services, police force, representation of the Netherlands government abroad, and certain positions involving confidentiality. Under the Foreign Workers (Employment) Act foreign nationals, whether EC members or not, need only hold a valid resident's permit allowing them to enter into paid employment in order to be eligible for employment as civil servants. Section 5 of the Act, applying the European Convention on the Legal Status of Migrant Workers, provides that:

> The terms for entering into, continuing, or terminating a labour contract with an employee who is of a nationality other than Dutch, and who resides in the Netherlands, may not be less favourable than the terms that apply to an employee with Dutch nationality.

Discriminatory Provisions in Dutch Legislation. In 1983 a report drawn up by Baune and Hessels provided an inventory of legislation and ministerial orders effecting distinctions on the grounds of nationality, place of residence, language, religion, culture and race.[43] The report identified some 1,300 different regulations, 80 per cent of which had a negative discriminatory impact on ethnic minorities. The government's response was slow and defensive, and a statement by the Minister of Home Affairs in 1985 suggested that most laws did not discriminate or were justified in doing so where they did.[44] As a consequence, some discriminatory provisions relating to religious holidays and differences in social security provisions remained unaltered. However, some recognition of pluralism in Dutch society can be found in the regulations of 1957 and 1980, which allow the slaughtering of cattle to comply with Jewish and Moslem religious customs respectively.

---

42. I. Asscher-Vonk, 'The Netherlands', in *Bulletin of Comparative Labour Relations*, 1985, p. 173.
43. See H. H. M. Baune and T. Hessels, *Minorities and Minor Rights*: An Inventory of Dutch Acts and Regulations which Distinguish between Citizens and Aliens, WODC no. 35, The Hague, 1983; Hessels, 'Racial Discrimination in The Netherlands', Landelijk Bureau Racismebestrijding, Amsterdam, in Dummett, Report on Racial Discrimination and the law in EEC Countries, p. 20.
44. Hessels, 'Racial Discrimination in The Netherlands', p. 20.

The Ombudsman. In 1983 the Dutch national ombudsman gave his first public verdict on racial discrimination by public authorities, concerning a complaint by a cadet of racial discrimination at the military school. While the ombudsman found that the complaint was not sufficiently proved, he did declare in his verdict that public authorities had an obligation to take specific measures to implement the principle of equality as laid down in Article 1 of the Constitution, and were obliged to set a good example and provide a model of good practice for the general public.[45]

Access to the Law. Complainants seeking agency support in pursuing a complaint are most likely to use the services of the *Landelijk Bureau Racismebestrijding* (LBR), the Dutch bureau against racism similar to the CRE in Great Britain. The LBR was founded in 1985 by several ethnic minority organisations and the Netherlands Jurist Committee for Human Rights (*Nederlands Juristen Comite voor de Mensenrechten*). It is an independent organisation, but it is funded by the Department of Justice and is given official government recognition for the role it plays. Nonetheless it does not have any statutory competency and it is therefore essentially an advisory body, providing help, guidance and assistance to individuals, lawyers and local organisations.[46]

The bureau is currently involved in strategic test cases to pursue the most productive use of limited resources in financial, political and promotional terms. It has also commented on government policy as outlined in the *Minderhedennota* (policy document on minorities) of 1983, which comprises two elements, namely a restrictive immigration policy and a desire to improve the legal status of legally resident non-nationals.[47] The LRB has a network of some twenty local offices along the lines of Race Equality Councils in Britain. Unlike the Race Equality Councils, however, local offices do specialise in providing legal support to complainants as the bureau believes that an aggrieved individual can best be helped within his or her local environment. The aim is to have lawyers and local organisations acting against racism all over the Netherlands and to provide the necessary legal and social aid, generally on a free basis.[48]

The Bureau has declared consumer affairs, police and public prosecutions to be its main priorities and it has issued codes of practice, although these do not have any statutory effect, in the areas of housing

45. See *Bilthoven v. Ministry of Defence*, Rechtstraak, Vreendelingenrecht, 113, quoted in Ibid., p. 22.
46. MG-CR (89) 21, p. 6.
47. Hessels, 'Racial Discrimination in The Netherlands', p. 25.
48. Ibid.

and employment. The LBR has no formal powers to conduct investigations but it has undertaken research in structural forms of racial discrimination.

Other community and intermediary organisations include the National Bureau of Foreign Workers (NCB) which offers assistance to ethnic minorities. Unfortunately, the most common form of advice provided by the bureau is to advise clients to drop their complaints in the face of the daunting task of proving the treatment received was actually discriminatory. The same advice is often provided by the police, lawyers and the public prosecutors.[49]

Complainants who have attempted to pursue complaints under the Criminal Code have often had cause to complain about police treatment. Frequently their complaints have not been taken seriously, and on occasion complainants have been subject to harassment.[50] It has been estimated that only 5 per cent of complaints ever reach the stage of court proceedings. Accordingly, despite the availability of free legal assistance and advice and the pursuit of criminal violation at public expense, ethnic minorities are aware of the limited chances of a successful outcome, a fact reflected in the low level of complaints. This was a factor leading to revised instructions being issued to public prosecutors and the police in September 1993 on how to handle racial discrimination cases.[51] As yet there is no protection against victimisation for raising a complaint of racial discrimination although the Equal Treatment Bill of 1991 included such provision. Quotas have not been used either in employment or in housing although housing associations have employed both positive and negative targets in their allocations to ethnic minority groups.

Unlike the position in the UK, employment complaints represent a minority of all discrimination complaints brought before the Public Prosecutions Department, although there are significant fluctuations in numbers; between 1981 and 1984 forty-six employment cases produced eleven convictions while between 1985 and 1986, sixty-eight cases led to thirty-eight convictions. In 1987–88 twenty-two cases were brought with five convictions. In 1993 an Equal Employment Act was presented to Parliament but the trade and industry lobby resisted its adoption.[52]

49. Forbes and Mead, *Measure for Measure*, p. 59.

50. Ibid., p. 58.

51. P. Rodrigues, 'Racial discrimination and the law in the Netherlands', in *New Community*, Commission for Racial Equality, vol. 20, no. 3, April 1994, pp. 381–391.

52. Ibid., p. 389; see also Sharda Kartaram, Final Report on Legislation in the Netherlands Against Racism and Xenophobia, unpublished submission on behalf of Landelijk Bureau Racismebestrijding, Amsterdam to Directorate General for Work. Labour Relations and Social Affairs for the European Commission in Brussels, March, 1992.

Again in contrast to the focus of the CRE attention, the LBR has concentrated on test cases in housing rather than in employment.

The decision in the *Binderean* case in 1983 recognised that statistics could demonstrate a pattern of discrimination, showing in that case under-representation of ethnic minorities in housing association allocations. This has encouraged an examination of 'pattern and practice' by investigation agencies and complainants. The government has also responded to statistical patterns; where statistics showed that members of ethnic minorities, older employees and women were more likely to lose their jobs in collective dismissals, the Ministry of Social Affairs and Employment gave explicit instructions concerning the responsibility of Employment Offices to observe the strictures of international treaties, the Constitution and the Penal Code and 'to oppose and fight discrimination as far as it affected recruitment, dismissals and training opportunities'. This has led in turn to the provision of training facilities dedicated to members of ethnic minorities and of a number of programmes which recognise the disadvantages suffered by ethnic minority groups.

Positive action is permitted under the terms of ICERD and consequently it is legitimate for an employer to favour a member of an ethnic minority seeking employment, but only where his or her qualifications match those of any other applicant. The Minister of Social Affairs and Employment requested local authorities by circular in 1983 and by a follow-up communication in 1985 to 'give preference to members of minority groups on the recruitment of personnel, provided they are qualified for the job', and 'to give extra attention to minority groups in the allocation of contracts to third parties'.[53] Further anti-discrimination policies are to be found in the contract compliance system operated by local authorities and central government is considering making such practices a requirement: it is currently under consideration.[54]

Conclusions

While Dutch anti-discrimination law displays a number of very positive aspects, it is piecemeal and fails to deliver effective remedies for individual complainants. It demonstrates a diversity of approaches from criminal sanctions through to constitutional and civil remedies and ultimately to the prospect of mediation through the ombudsman. The broad definition of discrimination which includes indirect discrimination, the ability to bring actions with respect to indirect discrimination and the relevance of statistical patterns of discrimination to support particular

53. Hessels, 'Racial Discrimination in The Netherlands', p. 27.
54. PE139.239:3.

complaints of discrimination, particularly in the housing and employment field, extend beyond contemporary provisions in many other EC states. The opportunity for positive action in employment and housing allocations and the provision of an explicit government policy on structural discrimination and disadvantage against minority groups form part of an array of positive measures in the Dutch system.

Despite these positive aspects, however, there is evidence of continuing discrimination and disadvantage particularly with respect to employment. This evidence, together with the low level of complaints and even lower numbers of successful proceedings, suggest that the avenues available for complainants, the support provided, the evidence required in order to prove the complaint and the remedies available, broad as they appear to be, are in some measure inadequate both in achieving effective redress for individuals and in securing a change in practice to promote equality of opportunity in the private, voluntary and public sectors.[55]

Costa-Lascoux has suggested that the Dutch system, in common with the British system, exemplifies an approach based on a policy enabling the representation and emancipation of minorities which uses positive discrimination to fight against negative discrimination. This is in contrast to the system in France and Belgium, which is based on equal rights for all citizens with no institutional recognition of minorities.[56] It has been suggested that there is a risk that the former system may actually further stigmatise minorities by accentuating socio-cultural differences and, by facilitating minority lobbies, exacerbate a reflex of intolerance on the part of the host community.

However, there is little evidence that this hypothesis is substantially true. In neither the Netherlands nor in the UK has positive action through training, education or housing programmes led to more than marginal racial discrimination against the host community, nor is there evidence that recognition of minority groups as having legitimate identities has caused a white backlash. The contrast between France and the Netherlands does demonstrate a difference of approach and a failure to resolve potential conflicts between an individualistic approach (which all four countries share in the area of complaint resolution) and an approach based on the pursuit of policies designed to compensate for past disadvantage with an emphasis on positive action and the setting of targets with effective monitoring and policy review.

55. See discussion in A. Bocker, 'A pyramid of complaints', *New Community*, 1991, vol. 17, no. 3.

56. Costa-Lascoux, *Anti-discrimination in Belgium, France and The Netherlands*, p. 26.

—6—

Anti-Discrimination Law in Core EC States: Part II: Germany and Great Britain

In this chapter the examination of core states is concluded with studies of Germany and Great Britain. In Germany the law is technically post-unification but, given the virtual absorption of the German Democratic Republic into the legal and constitutional norms of the German Federal Republic, in essence it is the legal regime of the latter which is the subject of this study.

Germany

Categories of Minorities in Germany

Ethnic minorities in reunified Germany fall into five principal categories:

1. minorities from established communities,
2. guest workers, those post-war immigrants who sought employment in an expanding West German economy,
3. dependents of guest workers who were permitted to settle either temporarily or permanently as a process of family reunification,
4. refugees and asylum seekers from Europe and elsewhere who have been permitted to settle in Germany,
5. so-called ethnic Germans, who have been permitted, as a matter of policy and law, to repatriate to Germany because of their language and cultural links irrespective of their national status.

The first category, ethnic minorities settled within Germany, include the following major groups; the Danish minority in Schleswig-Holstein, the Sorbian minority in Brandenburg and Saxony, the Sinti and Romany Gypsies (a proportion of whom do not have German nationality) and the Jewish community which numbers about 40,000 with the largest concentrations in Berlin, Munich and Frankfurt-am-Maine.

Settled Communities. The Danish minority totals roughly 50,000, although precise figures are not known.[1] Special recognition was given to the Danish minority following the Kiel Declaration of 16 September 1949 and the joint Bonn/Copenhagen Declaration of 29 March 1955 by the German and Danish governments, which conferred the following rights on the resident Danish minority in Germany:

1. The cultivation of Danish customs and culture.
2. The promotion of the Danish language both spoken and written, and the admissibility of Danish before courts and administrative authorities.
3. Access by the Danish minority to public funds on an equal basis to other German citizens.
4. Recognition of the special interest of the Danish minority in cultivating its religious, cultural and social ties with Denmark, in a fashion reciprocal to that of the German minority in Denmark itself.

This special recognition of the Danish minority enables the establishment of Danish schools and kindergartens through the Danish School Association, which has about 8,000 members. These schools include the Duborg Grammar School in Flensburg and a secondary modern boarding school in Laderlund, with a Danish Adult Education Centre in Jarplund near Flensburg. The cost of the Danish Minorities Culture and Welfare Activities is met by the Danish government, the Danish Border Association (made up of numerous smaller organisations), the Schleswig-Holstein Land and private funds. Danish language newspapers include the *Flensborq Avis*.

The Sorbian minority comprises 60,000 people, most of whom live in Oberlausitz and Niederlausitz in the State of Saxony and Land of Brandenburg. This group is descended from the Western Slavs; it has been in existence for about 600 years and its languages (both high and low Sorbian) are maintained to the present day. According to Article 35 and Protocol 14 of the German unification Treaty the Sorbs have the following rights:

1. Freedom to participate in the distinctive Sorbian culture and traditions.
2. Freedom to maintain and further develop Sorbian culture and traditions.
3. Freedom to cultivate and preserve the Sorbian language and public life.

1. ICERD, 12th German Periodic Report, Centre for Human Rights, Geneva, 1993, p. 7.

In October 1991 a 'Foundation for the Sorbian People' was established in Bautzen, with the dual purpose of promoting Sorbian culture and international understanding and cooperation with other national groups and minorities in Europe. In 1992 the Foundation received 41 million Deutschmarks in government funds, half from the Federal Government and half from the two Land involved. As of February 1993 Sorbian was taught in 56 schools providing tuition for 5,400 pupils.[2] Section 184 of the Code of Civil Procedure is modified by the unification treaty referred to enabling Sorbian to be spoken in court in Sorbian areas, specifically at the Bautzen regional court.

As with the Jewish community, the Sinti and Romany Gypsies were persecuted on racial grounds under the National Socialist government of the Third Reich. It is estimated that about 70,000 Sinti and Romany Gypsies now live in the Federal Republic of Germany, but it is not known how many of them have German nationality. Since January 1991, the Office of the Central Council of German Sinti and Romany and the Documentation and Cultural Centre have been financed by the Federal Government of Germany, with the Land of Baden-Wurttenberg assuming a 10 per cent share of the Centre's overheads. One objective of the Centre is to promote the language, traditions, customs and ways of life as well as the documentation of literature and history (including the period of Nazi tyranny) of the Sinti and Romany people. The Federal Council attempts to represent the interests of this ethnic group in public affairs, dealing with issues of restitution, the recognition of the Sinti and Romany as an ethnic group within Germany and the protection of their portrayal in the press and media. The Federal Government and North Rhine/ Westphalia have entered into arrangements with Macedonia (the former Yugoslav territory) to promote the repatriation of non-German Sinti and Romany whose applications for asylum had been refused.

The German Central Welfare Office estimates that 34,000 Jews live in Germany today, but the Jewish community itself estimates the population to be nearer 40,000. Given that around 4 million Jews were killed in the Holocaust, the Jewish proportion of the total German post-reunification population of 80 million people is very small. The Federal Government provides funds for the promotion of key Jewish institutions including the Central Council of Jews in Germany, the German Coordination Council of the Societies of Christian Jewish Cooperation and the International Council of Christians and Jews, as well as institutions dealing with academic research into Jews and Judaism such as the Central Archive for Research into the history of Jews in Germany, the College of Jewish Studies and the Leobaeck Institute.

2. Ibid., p. 8.

Guest Workers. Between 1952 and 1955 the development of the labour market in the Federal Republic of Germany was characterised by a decline of unemployment and a significant rise in vacancies for employment. With the increasing demand for labour, German companies began looking beyond state boundaries for employees. By 1960, of the one-quarter of a million foreign workers in Germany 44 per cent came from Italy with others coming from Greece, Spain, Yugoslavia and Turkey. During the 1960s, recruitment agreements were signed between the Republic of Germany and Spain (1960), Greece (1960), Turkey (1961), Portugal (1964), Morocco (1960 and 1966), Yugoslavia (1968) and Tunisia in the same year.[3] The Federal Government saw its responsibility as the provision of manpower for the expanding economy. The trade unions, while protecting wages of local workers, sought equal treatment for guest workers; but in general the social requirements of incoming workers in terms of family reunion, the education of children and the provision of housing was considered little and late.[4]

By 1968, 5.2 per cent of the workforce within the Federal Republic was non-German, increasing to some 10.3 per cent by 1971. By March 1991, that proportion had slightly diminished; the number of alien workers amounted to 1.8 million, comprising 8 per cent of the workforce. At the same time the unemployment rate amongst non-Germans was 10.7 per cent, considerably greater than for German nationals. Today in Germany there are in the region of 600,000 workers from Turkey, 300,000 from Yugoslavia, 180,000 from Italy, 106,000 from Greece, 61,000 from Spain and 43,000 from Portugal; because the nationals of the last four countries are also EC nationals, their movement is not subject to restriction within the European Union.

In the last thirty years major changes have occurred in the non-German population. Some 44 per cent of aliens resident within Germany are women, a figure which has increased substantially through the process of family reunion.[5] According to the Federal Ministry and Social Affairs BMA in 1992, 52.6 per cent of alien births in Germany were of Turkish parents (note that German legislation does not recognise *ius soli* as a basis for nationality). Thus while there have been many declarations of government that Germany is not an 'immigration country' the reality is different.[6]

---

3. Ursula Mehrlander, 'The Development of Post-War Migration and Refugee Policy', in Sarah Spencer (ed.), *Strangers and Citizens*, IPPR/Rivers Oram Press, London, 1994, p. 3.
4. Mehrlander, 1978: 115 Footnote quoted in Sarah Spencer (ed.), *Strangers and Citizens*, IPPR/Rivers Oram Press, London, 1994.
5. G. Schultze, 'Sociale Situation Auslandischer in Nordrhein-Westfalen', referenced in Spencer (ed.), *Strangers and Citizens*.
6. Spencer (ed.), *Strangers and Citizens*, p. 5.

Asylum and Refuge Seekers. Between 1953 and 1968 the number of persons seeking political asylum in West Germany totalled 70,000. That number had increased by 60 per cent in the following decade, and in 1979 alone the number of applicants was 51,000; in 1980 the number rose to 107,000 and remained around the 100,000 mark per annum up to 1990. The number then rose dramatically to 190,000, increasing again to 250,000 in 1991, and to 440,000 in 1992. There have been four major reasons for the dramatic increase in figures; repressive totalitarian political systems, economic difficulties, scarcity and destruction of natural resources, and the occurrence of ecological catastrophes.[7] There have also been dramatic changes in the countries of origin of asylum-seekers over this period. In 1981, 52 per cent of asylum-seekers came from the third world, 20 per cent from Poland and 13 per cent from Turkey. In 1992, 57 per cent came from Yugoslavia, Romania and Bulgaria.

While the GDR did not have a constitutional obligation to accept asylum- and refuge-seekers, it had entered into a number of inter-governmental agreements which had resulted in some 90,000 foreigners being employed there by 1989. The majority of these came from Vietnam (60,000) with others coming from Mozambique, Angola, Cuba, Poland and China.[8] The majority of these agreements were terminated in 1991 and 1992 around the time of reunification and over 90 per cent of the foreign workers then returned to their own countries, but between 6,000 and 8,000 workers, most of them Vietnamese, decided to remain in the Federal Republic of Germany until the time when their original contract expired.

German Unification: Ethnic Germans from Eastern and Southeast Europe. Between the erection of the Berlin Wall in August 1961 and 1980, approximately 600,000 people made their way from East to West Germany. In 1989 thousands of mostly young people from the GDR used their holiday in other socialist countries to reach the Federal Republic via embassies in Prague and Budapest; some 340,000 GDR citizens came to the Federal Republic in that year and a further 240,000 entered West Germany in the first six months of 1990. When German reunification became foreseeable in the middle of 1990, the number of GDR citizens coming to West Germany decreased significantly.[9]

According to the Federal Constitution (Article 116, paragraph 1) 'German' resettlers are not aliens but are German citizens. This Article is based on a provision in the Third Reich Constitution of 31 December

7. Opitz 1991, p. 9, ibid. 14.
8. ICERD, 12th German Periodic Report, p. 36.
9. Spencer (ed.), *Strangers and Citizens*, p. 6.

1937 which provides that anyone who has lived, or whose parents or grandparents have lived, in the former eastern territories of Germany (East Prussia, Pomerania, East Brandenburg, Silesia and Danzig) has a right to repatriation and recognition as a German citizen. After World War II approximately 4 million Germans, so classified, lived beyond Germany's eastern border. A fairly generous policy under the Federal Republic which has been continued by unified Germany has enabled many ethnic Germans from Poland, the Soviet Union and Romania, as well as a lesser number from Czechoslovakia, Hungary and Yugoslavia to return to Germany.

The reasons for granting favoured treatment to those of German ethnic origin related to characteristics such as descent, language, education and culture. Many of those repatriated, particularly younger migrants, had to learn high German as a foreign language.[10] Ethnic Germans did not appear to pose a problem regarding integration before 1987, when their numbers increased significantly. Attitudes on the part of the host German population seem to have changed around this time, due to growing problems associated with employment and housing.

Evidence of Discrimination and Racism

In common with many other European countries, Germany has experienced an increase in the number of violent attacks against foreigners in the past decade, and there appears to be a reluctance on the part of both the police and the public prosecutor's office to prosecute racially motivated violence or admit that racism was a motive in certain crimes. On 1 June 1983 a Hamburg court sentenced a band of skinheads to prison terms ranging from 3 to 10 years for the murder of a Turkish worker but, although the band had proven links with extreme right-wing groups in Hamburg, the judge refused to accept the view that the killing was racially motivated.[11] Similarly a court in Tubingen (Baden-Wurttenberg) accepted the argument by the defence that two men responsible for killing an Iranian asylum-seeker had mistaken their victim for a shoplifter.

The Turkish immigrant population of 1.5 million people bears the brunt of racial harassment, violence and discrimination. The journalist Gunther Wallraff, in his book and film on Turkish guest workers, has documented and exposed the extent of discrimination against them; most have insecure

10. K. D. Bade, *Deutsche im Ausland Fremde in Deutschland*, Munchen, 1992, p. 407.

11. Ian Forbes and Geoffrey Mead, *Measure for Measure: A Comparative Analysis of Measures to Combat Racial Discrimination in the Member States of the European Community*, Equal Opportunities Study Group, University of Southampton/Department of Employment, Sheffield, 1992, p. 82.

rights of residence and are quite defenceless against legislation that treats them as foreigners. There are many third-generation Turks who either do not have the opportunity to become German citizens or who do not wish to avail themselves of that opportunity because of the lack of dual nationality permitted in Germany. Those who are not German citizens suffer systemic discrimination because of their non-German status. In addition to the groups described above there are some 40,000–50,000 black or Afro-Germans in what was West Germany, many the offspring of liaisons between American GIs and German women, who also suffer discrimination on racial grounds, challenging the pretence that discrimination is only against non-nationals and that all Germans are treated alike.

Anti-Semitism has not been eradicated; two studies have concluded that as much as 20 per cent of the population still harbours overt anti-Jewish sentiments and anti-Semitism is latent in a further 30 per cent. The denial of the holocaust and the existence of Nazi gas chambers is reflected in Germany as part of an expanding international network with branches mainly in the USA, the UK and France.[12] However, anti-Semetism is only part of a more general atmosphere of intolerance. An opinion survey in September 1989 found that 75 per cent of West Germans felt that there were too many foreigners in the country, 69 per cent agreed that asylum-seekers were unfairly exploiting the social security system and 93 per cent favoured a reduction in the number of economic refugees. Racial hatred against Africans and Asians was shared by 20 per cent of respondents, the majority of whom supported the *Republikana*, the right-wing party which had significant successes in the late 1980s. The same survey also demonstrated antagonism to migrant workers, particularly to the Turkish population. After the events of August 1992 in Rostock, international attention has focused on the failure of the police to provide basic protection for refugees, but there is evidence that the police are themselves using violence against refugees, many of whom are held in 'concentration camps', and Amnesty International has argued that no person seeking asylum should be held in such camps.[13]

The extent of systemic discrimination against foreigners in Germany was illustrated at a conference in Berlin in November 1993.[14] In particular, evidence of discrimination in unemployment of guest workers, and of the difficulties experienced in obtaining housing and insurance was presented.

12. Ibid., p. 58.
13. T. Bunyan, *Statewatching the New Europe*, Statewatch, Nottingham, 1993, p. 156.
14. Now published in summary form; see Zig Layton-Henry and Czarina Wilpert, *Discrimination, Racism and Citizenship: Inclusion and Exclusion in Britain and Germany*, The Anglo-German Foundation, London, 1994.

The Law Against Discrimination

International Obligations. As of 31 December 1993, Germany was a signatory to 24 of the 25 international instruments on human rights listed in the Charter for ratification issued by United Nations. These include the International Covenant on Economic, Social and Cultural Rights, the International Covenant on Civil and Political Rights (together with the optional Protocol), the International Convention on the Elimination of All Forms of Racial Discrimination (ICERD) (but Germany is not a party permitting direct access to the Committee by individual complainants by reason of Article 14), the various Conventions relating to Equal Rights for Women and the Abolition of Slavery and Apartheid, the Convention relating to the Status of Refugees and its Protocol, and the Convention on the Reduction of Statelessness. Germany was not yet a signatory to the Convention on the Rights of Migrant Workers and Members of Their Families, but this Convention had only just been open for signature at that time.

In March 1993 Germany submitted its twelfth periodic report to the CERD, which was combined with the eleventh report which was due on 14 June 1990. Germany reported that it had fulfilled the obligation to punish the dissemination of racist ideas and incitement to racial hatred and racialist activities under the terms of Article 4(a) of that Convention, mainly by way of the Penal Regulation on Incitement of the People (Article 130 of the Penal Code) and Article 131 of the Penal Code, according to which anyone who disseminates such publications is liable to punishment. The dissemination of propaganda by organisations is prohibited under the constitution and the use of Nazi symbols and gestures is punishable under Articles 86 and 86a of the Penal Code.

It is the view of the German government that the ICERD does not oblige the governments to report on their treatment of foreigners because Article 1, paragraph 2 of the Convention expressly provides that it does not apply to distinctions, exclusions, restrictions or preferences made by a state party between citizens and non-citizens. This exception is of fundamental importance when viewing Germany's compliance with the ICERD and its constitutional provisions. As indicated above, the constitution does not provide any entitlement to nationality by reason of birth in the country or longevity of residence, and it expressly excludes dual nationality. The latter is particularly disabling with respect to the Turkish community because of the desire of many of its members to retain rights of citizenship of Turkey itself.

In terms of the European dimension, Germany is a member of the Conference of Security and Co-operation in Europe (CSCE) which has undergone important changes since 1989. The CSCE is referred to as a 'process' or a general framework for political consultation and consensus building amongst its fifty-plus participating states.[15] Despite the fact that the CSCE is a regional arrangement under the terms of Chapter VIII of the Charter of United Nations and does not therefore have any legal status, the Helsinki Final Act of 1975 included the following declaration (Principle X):

> The participating states on whose territory national minorities exist will respect the right of persons belonging to such minorities to equality before the law, will afford them the full opportunity for the actual enjoyment of human rights and fundamental freedoms and will, in this manner, protect their legitimate interests in this sphere.

The meetings of the conference have a 'conference on the human dimension' and the rights of minorities have been reaffirmed periodically.[16] The 1990 Copenhagen document of the CSCE recognised that to belong to a national minority (i.e. a non-dominant population that is a numerical minority within a state) is a matter of a person's individual choice (Chapter IV, paragraph 32). The CSCE has authorised political measures which have a new 'operational mechanism'; these have included short-term fact-finding missions, longer-term in-country missions and even multi-lateral negotiations to respond to conflicts with an inter-ethnic dimension such as those in Georgia, Nagorno-Karabakh and the former Yugoslavia. Longer-term missions have also been deployed to help prevent ethnic conflict in places such as Estonia and Latvia.

As a further result of the 1992 Helsinki meeting there is now a 'High Commissioner on National Minorities' based in the Hague. The High Commissioner had become involved in half a dozen countries by the end of 1993, but within the context of the European Union the only study of relevance was that relating to the Roma or Gypsies in the CSCE region. In the wake of the post-1989 changes in central and eastern Europe and the former Soviet Union, the problems confronting the Roma throughout Europe have greatly intensified, and it is clearly relevant in the German context that a study of the Roma and Sinti as a minority be undertaken.

In common with other European Union members, Germany is also a signatory to the European Convention on Human Rights and Fundamental Freedoms of 1950 under the auspices of the Council of Europe. There have been a number of German language cases taken to the European

15. K. J. Huber, 'The CSCE and Minorities', in J. Cator and J. Niessen (eds), *The Use of International Conventions to Protect the Rights of Migrants and Ethnic Minorities*, The Churches Commission for Migrants in Europe, Strasbourg, 1994, p. 41.

16. See Charter of Paris of CSCE Summit 21 November 1990, and P. Thornberry, *International Law and the Rights of Minorities*, Clarendon Press, London, 1991, p. 30.

Court; Article 6 of the Convention gives defendants who do not understand the language of the court the right to be provided with an interpreter. In one case the European Court of Human Rights had to determine whether the requirement for an applicant to pay for an interpreter at a trial constituted a violation of this Article (*Luedicke, Belkacem and Kok v. the Federal Republic of Germany*, ECHR 28 11 78 series A, No. 29). While the European Court held in favour of the applicants in this instance, it is generally recognised that there is a paucity of case law relating to minority rights of the European Convention; this is in large measure due to the lack of attention being paid to minority rights issues in the domestic courts of the states parties themselves.[17]

Constitutional Provisions. In the Constitution of the Federal Republic of Germany, which became applicable to the unified country, Article 3(3) prohibits discrimination on the grounds of sex, birth, race, language, national or social origin, faith, religion or political persuasion; these provisions, it is contended, apply to foreigners living in the republic. According to constitutional convention, when there is a conflict between the requirements of international conventions and the German constitution then the latter prevails. The approach of the German courts, however, is to try to construe domestic provisions so that they are in accordance with international requirements.[18]

It is also accepted that Article 3(3) directly binds only the legislature, the executive and the judiciary, as provided for by Article 1(3). Moreover Article 19(4) specifies that when an individual's right has been violated by a public authority recourse should be through the courts, and it therefore appears that Article 3(3) is primarily intended to ensure the protection of the individual against the exercise of government authority rather than the actions of third parties. In terms of, for example, public employment, which includes state government and local authority employment, constitutional redress would be provided to the individual against discrimination by the state. However, where the government contracts with a private employer who has responsibility for hiring and firing, then the employer is not covered by the constitutional provision; although it has been argued that Article 3(3) may have an indirect impact on private employers by requiring them to act fairly and reasonably.[19]

---

17. D. Gomien, 'The Rights of Minorities under the European Convention on Human Rights and the European Charter on Regional and Minority Languages', in Cator and Niessen (eds), *The Use of International Conventions to Protect the Rights of Migrants and Ethnic Minorities*, p. 56.
18. Forbes and Mead, *Measure for Measure*, p. 40.
19. Ibid., p. 41.

Protection Under Civil Law.   The Works Constitution Act as amended by Article 75(1) provides that every Works Council must ensure non-discrimination in employment and recruitment. This Act of 1972 was amended in 1989 and clearly extends to employers in the private sector. While the prohibited grounds for discrimination mention race but not colour, it is understood that discrimination on the basis of colour would be covered. Professor K. Heilbronner of the University of Konstant has advised that the law extends to indirect discrimination as well as direct discrimination, but there is no case law to demonstrate that the court would share that interpretation. There has been one case of an employer attempting to instruct the Labour Office not to send any foreigners; the employer was advised to discontinue this practice, which has since become illegal.

Because 43 per cent of all workers are in trade unions (50 per cent in the case of foreign workers), unions are important sources of assistance when seeking legal redress and the protection of employment rights. Unions are empowered to provide free legal advice to their members. Under the Works Constitution Act an employee can complain to the authority responsible for his employment, and the employer is obliged to advise how the complaint will be dealt with and the outcome of his grievance. There is also protection against victimisation. By Article 85 of the Act, the Works Council is empowered to hear grievances and instruct the employer to remedy them. Where the employer disagrees with the remedy the Works Council may appeal to the Conciliation Committee, which will act as an arbiter. Where a complainant can demonstrate better qualifications for a job, and the person who receives the job is of a different race, then the onus would shift to the employer to demonstrate that the appointment was not discriminatory on the basis of race. The evidence used may be either direct or indirect – such as production of statistical evidence showing a tendency to appoint a smaller proportion of minority applicants than majority ones.[20]

It should be noted, however, that German civil law makes no specific provision for compensation for the victims of racial discrimination. While racial discrimination is notoriously difficult to detect, particularly when it is indirect, even in cases where discrimination is apparent, remedies may not be available. Thus the Federal Insurance Supervisory Office (FISO) has reported receiving repeated complaints that German motor insurance companies are avoiding providing motor insurance to foreigners and in doing so are discriminating systematically, particularly against people of Turkish, Yugoslav and Greek nationality. Applications for auxiliary motor insurance (beyond the third party cover required by

20. Ibid., p. 42.

law) are being turned down systematically or, exceptionally, accepted only for higher premiums. It is the view of FISO that these procedures do not constitute a breach of the law, but the withdrawal of a private insurance company from an insurance contract has been held to be an infringement of the basic law (Article 3(3)) by the Berlin Regional Court in a decision in 1989.[21]

In housing there is also evidence of systematic discrimination by the application of strict quotas in relation to public housing allocations.[22]

The Criminal Code and Racial Violence and Harassment. Just as there are no specific legislative measures or policy provisions against racial discrimination in Germany, so there are no direct measures against racial violence and harassment. Damaged property and injury to persons are punishable offences under the Penal Code, which also include specific clauses relating to incitement and racial hatred (paragraphs 130 and 131); however, these do not explicitly cover discrimination on ethnic or national grounds.[23]

The absence of legal provision reflects in addition a lack of any national policy framework in which minorities have an integral place in society as of right. German unification in 1990 has added to the complexity of xenophobia. Anti-Semitism and neo-Nazism are still strong on the eastern side of the former border, manifested in demonstrations, daubings on public buildings and desecration of Jewish cemeteries.[24] According to the Ford Report there is evidence of support from the police for extreme right-wing political parties, and that the police and the public prosecutor's office prosecute racially motivated violence with reluctance. However, the German government has the view that 'legal instruments in force are sufficiently effective to counter undesirable elements'.[25] Moreover, government continues to link hostility to foreigners (*Auslanderfeindlichkeit*) with an increase in the number of foreigners resident in the country giving rise to problems of racial prejudices and hostility, as if racism and xenophobia were beyond governmental control.

Between September 1978 and March 1987, there were 1,382 criminal proceedings against suspected right-wing extremists.[26] A report from the

21. ICERD, 12th German Periodic Report, p. 39.

22. See Final Report of the Community Relations Project, *Community and Ethnic Relations in Europe*, ref. MG-CR (1991) 1 Final, Council of Europe, Strasbourg, 1991.

23. Robin Oakley, *Racial Violence and Harassment in Europe*, Council of Europe, Strasbourg, 1992, (MG-CR (91) 3 rev. 2), p. 29.

24. Ibid., p. 29.

25. G. Ford, *Report of the Committee of Inquiry into Racism and Xenophobia*, Office for Official Publications of the European Communities, Luxembourg, 1991, pp. 18, 52, and annex 3.3.

26. Kalinowsky, 1990: annex 3.

Federal Ministry of Justice (*Rechtsextreemismus und Strafrechtspflege*), stated that 183 charges were made against right-wing extremist organisations under Section 130 of the Penal Code and 50 charges under Section 131; over 50 per cent of these charges related to anti-Semitic activity. Twenty-one per cent of charges related to xenophobic activity, mostly under Section 130 of the Code.[27] There were no convictions against racist groups in 1990 and 1991 under Section 129 of the Penal Code.

Article 21.2 of the basic law enables the authorities to ban racist organisations. The federal constitutional court, upon application by the *Bundestag*, the *Bundesrat* or the federal government, has to determine the constitutionality of such organisations in applying a ban or otherwise. To date only two organisations have been banned under the Article, both in the 1950s; one was a national socialist group and the other a communist party. However, from 12 September 1964 and the coming into effect of the Association Act, a further five right-wing extremist organisations have been banned in Germany; the most recent of these was the *Nationale Sammlung* (the National Union), which was dissolved in 1989.

Federal Government Policy

The Federal Government claims to have a three-pronged policy with regard to foreigners living in Germany. Its aims are to integrate foreign workers and their families who have been living in Germany for some time, limit future immigration of foreign workers, and promote voluntary repatriation.

The 6 million foreigners in Germany constitute some 7.8 per cent of the total resident population. The German government, in its report to ICERD, states that integration is a process of becoming involved in the life of the community and requires some effort on the part of the foreigner; in particular the foreigner has to adjust to the values, standards and social norms in the country. Respect for German culture, the fundamental values enshrined in the constitution (separation of government and church, status of women, religious tolerance), a knowledge of German, the renunciation of exaggerated nationalistic or religious behaviour and integration at school and work (compliance with compulsory school attendance, vocational training also for women, in due time immigration of children) are basic prerequisites. Thus integration or incorporation into economic, social and cultural life in Germany appears to be not too distant from acculturation.

However, a new Aliens Act in 1991 has strengthened the legal position of foreigners and enabled them to plan their permanent residence or length

27. ICERD, 12th German Periodic Report, p. 21.

of stay with greater certainty. The Act provides for a limited extension of residence, a right of abode, subsequent immigration of spouses, the introduction of an independent right of abode for children who have subsequently immigrated, and the naturalisation of foreigners who were born and grew up in the country. A new provision is the right of young foreigners who have returned to their home country to return to Germany at a later date and settle there permanently. Through naturalisation, foreigners acquire German nationality and thus the right to vote.

Great Britain

Introduction

Great Britain comprises the countries of England and Wales, which share a common legal system, and Scotland which has a separate legal system, but excludes Northern Ireland which, despite being ruled directly from the Houses of Parliament in Westminster from 1972 following the prorogation of the Stormont Assembly in Belfast and despite having a similar legal system to England and Wales, has no statute law dealing with racial discrimination. Northern Ireland is unlike Great Britain in another respect in that it does have an explicit anti-discrimination law relating to religion, reflecting not only a desire to address the needs of the historically disadvantaged Roman Catholic minority, but also the pressure applied by the Republic of Ireland and the USA, the latter as a condition of investment.

In common with both France and the Netherlands, post-war Britain looked for cheap immigrant labour in order to fuel industrial expansion. It did so by turning to the New Commonwealth, in particular the West Indies and the Indian sub-continent. The push-pull factors of lack of job opportunities at home and the promise of employment and improved living standards in the UK attracted a significant number of migrants in the 1950s and early 1960s, and the immigration process was accelerated in East Africa by the Africanisation policies of newly independent states which encouraged Asian settlers to leave.

According to the 1991 census, visible ethnic minorities in Britain comprise 3 million or 5.5 per cent of the general population.[28] The largest ethnic minority groups within this population are those of Indian origin (840,800), Caribbean origin (499,100) and Pakistani and Bangladeshi origin (636,100). The black African population was put at 207,500 and

---

28. David Owen, *The Changing Spatial Distribution of Ethnic Minorities in Britain, 1981–91*, Centre for Research in Ethnic Relations, University of Warwich, Coventry, 1993, Table 2.

the Chinese at 157,500.[29]

The 1981 census showed that nearly 3.4 million people living in Britain were born overseas, with over half of these being white. Accordingly the word 'immigrant' is no longer an accurate description for Britain's black minority population, most of whom are now born in the UK. It is important to emphasise in the British context that the vast majority of people in the visible minority groups have British nationality and most are not first-generation immigrants.

Control of primary immigration into the UK has been increasingly strengthened first by the Commonwealth Immigrants Acts of 1962 and 1968 and then by the Immigration Act of 1971, the cumulative effect of which, when read with the immigration rules thereunder, was to deny the validity of a British passport (unless it was issued in Britain) for the purpose of gaining entry to and settlement status in the UK. From 1971, British citizens have had no right of residence in the UK unless they had a passport issued in the UK. The British Nationality Act of 1981 attempted to rationalise the relationship between nationality and immigration status, creating three forms of citizen; British citizens who have rights of residence in the UK, citizens of a British Dependent Territory (principally Hong Kong) who may have rights of residence in the dependent territory but not in the UK, and British Overseas Citizens who, it appears, uniquely amongst the citizens of the world, have no rights of residence anywhere.

While current immigration rules provide for family reunification with respect to dependents under eighteen years old living abroad, indirect racial discrimination occurs in many of the rules affecting immigration. This is exemplified in the primary purpose rule concerning marriages, by which the fiancé(e) living abroad must demonstrate that he or she did not marry for the primary purpose of joining the spouse to gain residence in Britain, and by the perpetual challenging of relatives as to whether they are 'related as claimed'. In addition there is evidence of discrimination in the administration of the law. The Commission for Racial Equality (CRE) found that the Immigration Service systematically discriminated on racial grounds and the conclusions reached by the CRE investigation have raised the legitimate question of whether or not the UK meets its international obligations with respect to protecting family unity.[30]

In addition to the Asian and West Indian minorities there are both citizens and residents originating from African states, including Ghana, Nigeria and Kenya as well as the white immigrant minorities from Canada, Australia, New Zealand and South Africa. Britain also houses a

29. Ibid.
30. See CRE, *Report of Formal Investigation into the Immigration and Nationality Department of the Home Office*, CRE Publications, London, 1985.

number of indigenous minorities; UK citizenship extends to Northern Ireland and citizens of the Republic of Ireland have rights of residence in the UK, and there are also Welsh and Scottish 'minorities'. It would, however, be difficult to justify 'racial' distinctiveness in these groups although linguistic and cultural traditions differ. Other communities such as the Jewish community (spread throughout the UK), Poles, Ukrainians, Lithuanians, Greeks and Cypriots may be said to have a more obviously distinctive cultural homogeneity.

Although there has been some administrative devolution to Wales through the Secretary of State for Wales and the Welsh Office based in Cardiff, the substantial fusion of England and Wales which began in the fourteenth century is reflected in the common legal system, local government and educational provision. Social work and housing also share a common basis of approach. In contrast, despite the union between Scotland and England in 1707, Scotland has retained its own legal system, its own form of local government, a separate educational system and a distinctive approach to many elements of local government including housing, police, water and social work. As a result, Scotland may yet require to be considered as a separate entity in terms of law and administration, including race relations.

Evidence of Discrimination

Evidence of racial discrimination in Great Britain is well documented. The Home Office, which is charged with the responsibility for race relations throughout Great Britain, has issued reports on racial discrimination in 1975 (Cmnd 6234: September 1975), on urban deprivation, racial inequality and social policy (Home Office 1976), on racial attacks (Home Office, 1981; Home Office, 1989). The Home Affairs Committee (HAC), a Committee of the House of Commons, has considered the operation of the CRE (HAC, 1981), racial disadvantage (HAC, 1981), and racial attacks and harassment (HAC, 1986 and Home Office 1992).[31] In addition the House of Commons Select Committee on Race Relations and Immigration (the precursor to the Home Affairs Committee), the Housing Corporation, the Commission for Racial Equality, Political and Economic Planning (now the Policy Studies Institute), the Runnymede Trust and various other bodies have provided a well-documented library of investigations and reports relating to discrimination and harassment on racial grounds in the UK.

31. See also *The British Twelfth Periodic Report to the Committee for the Elimination of Racial Discrimination*, United Nations Centre for Human Rights, Geneva, 1992, CERD/C/226 Add. 4.

The Commission for Racial Equality (CRE) is charged with a statutory responsibility under the Race Relations Act of 1976 for reporting on the implementation of the Act and making recommendations for change to the Home Office. Responsibilities include monitoring the effectiveness of the Act and recording the incidence of discrimination and number of complaints referred; these are summarised in the CRE's annual reports to the Home Secretary and Parliament. According to the CRE reports, while there is some evidence that racial disadvantage is diminishing it remains a significant problem. Unemployment figures in the spring of 1987–89 showed that unemployment among people of Pakistani and Bangladeshi origin was twice the rate of that among whites, and in comparative terms both West Indians and Guyanese were considerably worse off than their white counterparts. As Forbes and Mead have observed, the data and the evaluative reports on the experience of visible minorities with employment shows that there are systematic, if varied, disadvantages on the basis of colour and ethnic group.[32] Despite relative improvement in the employment position of the Indian minority, colour remains 'the decisive factor' when seeking employment.[33] In housing, MacEwen has documented the extent of racial disadvantage and indicated racial discrimination in both the public and private sector as well as the housing association sector.[34] CRE investigations into housing in Liverpool and Tower Hamlets (CRE, 1987 and 1988) demonstrated systematic discrimination in housing allocation policies, in the design and implementation of urban renewal policies and in the housing of homeless persons.

In England and Wales the third national survey of racial minorities, conducted by the Policy Studies Institute (PSI) in 1982, showed widespread disadvantage in each of the areas studied, especially housing, employment and education.[35] In Scotland the only national survey (of the cities of Glasgow, Edinburgh, Aberdeen and Dundee) was that conducted on behalf of the Scottish Office in 1989;[36] racial disadvantage was found in employment and in housing. Other surveys confirm the vulnerability of minorities to harassment and physical assault in Scotland, and there is little evidence that being a member of a relatively small and dispersed community, in comparison with the higher concentrations of ethnic

32. Forbes and Mead, *Measure for Measure*, p. 20.

33. T. Modood, 'The Indian Economic Success: a Challenge to Some Race Relations Assumptions', *Policy and Politics*, 1991, vol. 19, no. 3.

34. M. MacEwen, *Housing, Race and Law: The British Experience*, Routledge, London, 1991.

35. C. Brown, *Black and White Britain*, Policy Studies Institute, London, 1984.

36. Social Planning and Research, *Ethnic Minorities in Scotland*, The Scottish Office, Edinburgh, 1989.

minority groups in England and Wales, makes living more secure or improves the opportunities to compete more evenly with the host community. The fact that ethnic minorities have disproportionately high numbers of convictions for crime and numbers in prison suggests that on occasions minorities are the victims of the criminal justice system, and that one manifestation of structural disadvantage is alienation from social norms. In all societies, it is the most disadvantaged who will have the least to lose from crime and while strong social structures may inhibit criminal activity, the experience of discrimination, harassment and disadvantage will undermine the self-respect on which such structures depend.

Prohibition of Discrimination

International Obligations. The United Kingdom has ratified the following conventions and other obligations relating to discrimination, racism and xenophobia:

1. The UN Covenant on the Economic, Social and Cultural Rights of Minorities
2. The UN Covenant on Civil and Political Rights of 1966
3. The UN Convention on the Elimination of all Forms of Racism of 1965
4. The UNESCO Convention against Discrimination in Education
5. The European Convention on Human Rights and Fundamental Freedoms of 1950
6. The European Convention on Social Security

In addition to the above the UK is a signatory to, or has ratified, the following:

7. The Convention on the Prevention and Punishment of the Crime of Genocide of 1948
8. United Nations Convention relating to the Status of Refugees of 1951
9. United Nations Convention relating to the Status of Stateless Persons 1954

The United Kingdom has not, however, been signatory to the following:

1. The Fourth Protocol to the European Convention on Human Rights
2. The Optional Protocol to the International Covenant on Civil and Political Rights of 1966
3. The International Convention on the Protection of Rights for Migrant Workers and Members of Their Families of 1990
4. ILO Convention No 111 (Discrimination in Occupations and Employment)

The UK expressed reservations about the Covenant on Civil and Political Rights, specifically reserving the right to continue to apply from time to time such immigration legislation governing entry to, stay in and departure from the UK as the country deemed necessary, thus qualifying its acceptance of Article 12(4). The government also reserves the right to enact such nationality legislation as is deemed necessary in order to reserve the acquisition and possession of citizenship under such legislation 'to those having sufficient connection with the United Kingdom or any of its dependent territories'. This was expressed as a reservation concerning Article 24 (3).

When ratifying the Convention on the Elimination of Racial Discrimination, the UK also made a number of reservations and interpretative statements with respect to the requirement to make reparation or satisfaction in terms of Article 6. The UK expressed the view that it would fulfil its obligations if only one of the potential forms of redress was made available to bring the discriminatory conduct to an end. The government also made a position statement with respect to the Commonwealth Immigrants Acts of 1962 and 1968, stating that it did not regard these as involving any racial discrimination within the meaning of Article 1(1) or any other provision of the Convention. With respect to Article 4 which requires a party to the Convention to adopt further legislative measures in particular areas, the UK interpreted the application of the Article in the context of the universal Declaration of Human Rights and the rights expressly set forth in Article 5 of the Convention (in particular the right of freedom of opinion and expression and the right to freedom of peaceful assembly and association). The UK is not one of the four EC member states which allows individual petition under Article 14 of this Convention.

Neither the courts in England and Wales nor those in Scotland will give recognition to international treaties or obligations unless they are expressly incorporated into domestic legislation. Thus in *Kaur v. Lord Advocate* 1981 SLT 322 Lord Ross emphasised that the courts could take no cognisance of the European Convention on Human Rights even as an aid to construction; that decision was endorsed in a higher court, the Second Division of the Inner House of the Court of Session, in *Moore v. Secretary of State for Scotland* 1985 SLT 38. There may, however, be a presumption made by the courts that parliament did not intend to legislate contrary to its international obligations although a contrary statute would prevail against such a presumption: see Lord Denning's opinion in *R v. Secretary for Home Affairs et al, ex p Bhajan Singh* (1975) to all ER 1081. There is no apparent right of redress in domestic law for a person whose rights under the Convention have been found by the European Court of Human Rights to have been violated (*R v. Secretary of State for the Home*

Office, ex p Weeks (1988), the Times 15 March 1988), and the judiciary will not resort to the European Convention on Human Rights in order to fill a gap in domestic legislation (see *Malone v. Commissioner of Police of the Metropolis* (No. 2) (1979) 2 all ER 620, per Sir Robert Megarry VC, p. 648. It seems, therefore, that the UK courts will only refer to international treaty obligations and Conventions as an aid in construing domestic legislation or in applying the common law as it already exists.

The right of individual petition under Article 25 of the European Convention on Human Rights has led to a number of decisions by the European Commission on Human Rights in the area of racial discrimination, and to one particular decision by the European Court of Human Rights. With one exception, these cases concerned the UK's restrictive immigration and nationality laws. The European Commission has found that the UK has been in violation of Article 3 relating to 'degrading treatment' and of Article 8 relating to respect for family life, because certain provisions have had the effect of discriminating on the basis of both sex and race under the terms of Article 14 (see *East African Asians v. UK* (1973) 3 EHRR 76).

Constitutional Provisions. In those countries in which the constitution has over-riding legal force in the sense that it controls what other legislation may be passed or applied, there is often a constitutional court which applies and interprets the text of the constitution in disputed cases; examples are the Supreme Court in the USA and the Federal Constitutional Court in Germany. There may also be special constitutional provisions in centralised or unitary states, the purpose of which is to protect the constitution not so much against local government but against potential contravention by central government.

The United Kingdom has neither a written constitution nor a Supreme Court whose function, either primarily or significantly, is to protect constitutional conventions.[37] But while there is no single document establishing the relationship between the primary organs of government within the United Kingdom, nor one which sets out the particular powers of the crown, the cabinet, parliament and the courts of law, there is certainly an assemblage of laws, institutions and customs that, in the words of Bollingbroke, compose the general system according to which

---

37. See A. W. Bradley of *E. C. S. Wade and G. Godfrey Phillips: Constitutional and Administrative Law*, Ninth edition, Longman, London, 1977, pp. 1–41; also see K. C. Wheare, *Modern Constitutions*, 2nd edition, Oxford University Press, Oxford, 1966. For discussion of the nature of constitutional change and in Britain see N. Johnson, *In Search of the Constitution*, Pergamon Press, Oxford, 1977. For discussion of the constitutional implications of devolution and independence in application to Scotland see John P. Grant, *Independence and Devolution*, W. Green & Son, Edinburgh, 1976.

a community has agreed to be governed.[38]

Nor does the absence of a formal written constitution and a court to interpret it and secure its observance imply that there are no written constitutional documents. The Treaty of Union between England and Scotland and the Acts of Union of the respective parliaments in 1707 are clearly of a constitutional nature, and in their expression of certain inalienable rights they may be referred to in the courts as authoritative sources of law. Nonetheless, the United Kingdom parliament and the House of Lords in its capacity as the supreme court for all civil cases throughout the UK have established a Convention that parliamentary legislative powers are beyond challenge. As a consequence, and with the sole exception of EC provisions, any challenge against any legislative provision to the effect that it is in contravention of constitutional authority will not be successful.[39] While it is clear in the Treaty of Union between England and Scotland that certain matters were declared fundamental and unalterable, the Treaty made no provision for future amendment of itself nor for future renegotiation of the terms of the Union. Article 18 of the Treaty drew a distinction between public right, policy and civil government, and the laws concerning 'private right' which were declared to be unalterable unless to the 'evident utility' of the Scottish people. While the distinction between public right and private right with respect to racial discrimination might have notional importance in terms of the provisions of the Treaty, because the Treaty was largely silent on 'human rights' — which might be considered to be in the public domain — there would appear little point in arguing a constitutional case for the protection of such rights. As a consequence the sole access to remedial action against racial discrimination is through normal legislative provision and its interpretation by the courts and, exceptionally, through any residual common law provision not covered by statute.

Legislation.   Parliament has passed three acts dealing specifically with racial discrimination; the Race Relations Act of 1965 which was superseded by the Race Relations Act of 1968, which was in turn superseded by the current Race Relations Act of 1976. The vast majority of legislative provision relating to anti-discrimination law and equal opportunities is now found in the Race Relations Act of 1976 and for the

38. From a 'Dissertation upon parties' (1733), quoted in Wheare, *Modern Constitutions*, p. 2.

39. See *MacCormick v. Lord Advocate* (1953) S.C.396. It has been suggested by Bryce in *Studies in History and Jurisprudence*, vol. 1, p. 194, that, by fusing herself with Scotland in 1707, England altered the constitution of the enlarged state no further than by the admission of additional members to parliament and the suppression of certain offices in Scotland.

purposes of this discussion we shall confine our remarks to that Act.

The Race Relations Act of 1976 is comprehensive. It provides a broad definition of racial grounds to include race, colour, ethnic or national origin and nationality; it addresses both direct discrimination and indirect discrimination through the definitions in Section 1, and the scope of unlawful discrimination extends to both public and private sectors, education, housing, employment and training, and more generally to the provision of goods, services or facilities to the public or a section of the public. Racial discrimination includes segregation. It is also unlawful to victimise a complainant or to aid, facilitate or induce unlawful acts of discrimination. Employers and principals may be vicariously liable for the acts of their employees and agents, and there is express provision for clubs, partnerships, trade unions and employers organisations, vocational training bodies and the training commission. A positive but tortuous general duty is placed on local authorities, the Housing Corporation, Scottish Homes and Homes in Wales under Section 71 of the Act. The duty is 'to make appropriate arrangements with a view to securing that their various functions are carried out with due regard to the need' for eliminating racial discrimination and promoting good race relations.

Limitations and Exceptions. Limitations on the application of the Act are provided in particular instances. It is possible to discriminate in a private sale of domestic property by the householder where an intention to discriminate has not been adverted. There is provision for the domestic situation (the American description being a 'Mrs. Murphy' exemption) which enables lawful discrimination to take place in domestic households against prospective guests or tenants who are to live with the householder; an association or club which has less than twenty-five members is also considered 'domestic'. Further special arrangements are made for fostering. The Crown and its public servants are generally covered by the Act, particularly when they are providing a service to the public or a section to the public. It appears, however, that the police, the Immigration Department, the Inland Revenue and other public services are not covered by the provisions of the Act in areas such as the collection of taxation or the making of arrests on a criminal charge, which are regulation or control activities rather than the provision of facilities or services to the public.

There is also special provision for positive action in the field of educational and training in favour of a particular racial group, where that group has been under-represented in a particular sector of the workforce.

Dealing with Complaints. Complaints relating to employment go before industrial tribunals for determination. Complaints relating to public sector education go to the relevant Secretary of State for resolution in the first instance. All other complaints go to designated county courts in England and Wales or to sheriff courts in Scotland for determination. In complaints to the county or sheriff courts, applicants may be eligible for legal aid on means-tested criteria; in complaints to industrial tribunals legal assistance may be available but this would cover only the preparatory work, and not the actual representation before tribunals. In all instances complainants may seek to avail themselves of free support and assistance from the Commission for Racial Equality (CRE), the statutory agency established by the 1976 Act and charged with three functions:

1. to enforce the act
2. to promote equality of opportunity
3. to review the legislation and report such reviews periodically to the Secretary of State for the Home Office.

In recent years the CRE has received in the region of 1,500 individual complaints per annum; in 1991 there were 1,655 complaints, the majority of which (1,203) related to employment. The majority of non-employment complaints (245 in 1991) related to the provision of goods, facilities and services (Section 20) while there were some 67 complaints relating to housing (Section 21) and 63 relating to education (Section 17). Most complaints come direct to the CRE although a significant number (314 in 1991) are referred from one of the local Racial Equality Councils. In the same year some 52 complaints were referred to the CRE from solicitors with a lesser number referred from Citizens Advice Bureaux (42), law centres (34), trade unions (25) and other sources (23).[40] Although both the county courts and the sheriff courts are obliged to keep records of referrals under the Race Relations Act, their records are inadequate and it is not possible to gauge accurately the number of complaints other than those dealing with employment where the CRE has not been asked for assistance. The CRE itself represented some 400 complainants in 1991. In that year only 166 cases represented by the CRE were determined by the courts and tribunals; of the 147 employment cases, 101 were settled on terms and 19 were successful after a hearing.

As well as being empowered to assist individual complainants to seek remedies for unlawful discrimination under the legislation, the CRE is able to carry out formal investigations into patterns and practice of discrimination under Section 48 of the Act. Between the Commission's establishment in 1977 and December 1991 the CRE issued fifty-two

40. Commission for Racial Equality, *Annual Report 1992*, CRE, London, 1993, pp. 76–77.

reports on completed investigations. Of these twenty-three were in the field of employment, fifteen were on housing, nine were on services and five were on education provision. By 1992, eight further investigations had been embarked on but had not been completed.

Under the Act of 1976, the CRE assumed the joint responsibilities previously exercised by the Race Relations Board with respect to enforcement and the Community Relations Commission in the field of promotional and development work. Of the CRE's £14 million budget for the financial year 1991–92, over £4.5 million was spent on grant aid for employment of racial equality officers employed by the 91 Racial Equality Councils (RECs) partially resourced by the CRE. While the Racial Equality Councils are not statutory bodies, after a report by the PSI criticised the nature of the partnership between them and the CRE a new and formal partnership has been entered into which ensures that the RECs comply with work programmes approved by the CRE.[41]

The Racial Equality Councils (previously known as Community Relations Councils) are usually partly funded by local authorities; they originated over twenty years ago from a base of charitable, voluntary and church organisations. There has been a marked shift in the focus of their work from general advice to promotion of equal opportunity policies and race equality issues. While the RECs have no statutory responsibility for securing the enforcement of the anti-discrimination legislation, some of the larger Councils do provide representation for complainants. However, this has not been a strategic or significant element in any of the RECs' work. Because the 1976 Race Relations Act enabled complainants to pursue their own complaints (previously complaints could only be pursued before tribunals and courts through the Race Relations Board), there is potential for RECs increasing their representational work very substantially. However, the lack of focus in the agreed work programmes and the previous lack of training in legal processes and procedures provided either locally or centrally indicate that any such development is unlikely in the shorter term.

Other Legal Provisions. The Public Order Act of 1986 renders it unlawful to incite racial hatred, and the requirements to prove an intention to incite are less exacting than under the previous Public Order Act of 1936 as amended by the Race Relations legislation. Racial harassment may constitute a 'detriment' in terms of the Race Relations Act, rendering it unlawful for an employer to tolerate it at work. Both the employment

---

41. See P. Gay and K. Young, *Community Relations Councils: Roles and Objectives*, Policy Studies Institute in association with the Commission for Racial Equality, London, 1988.

and housing codes of practice issued by the CRE provide guidance on action to be taken to prevent racial harassment and to secure effective remedies following its occurrence, but there is no separate legal offence of racial harassment either in England and Wales or in Scotland. The extent to which the common law in each jurisdiction seeks to control racial harassment is discussed more fully in Forbes and in MacEwen but in neither jurisdiction is there any statutory recognition of racial attacks or racial harassment as an offence distinguishable from other forms of attack or harassment.[42]

A small number of promotional activities are enabled by other legislation but are less frequently resourced. Section 11 of the Local Government Act 1966 enabled local authorities to finance additional staffing for the purpose of improving the services provided to ethnic minority groups. A similar provision is made in Scotland, but the Secretary of State for Scotland has not authorised Section 11 funding. In England the annual funding under this section approximates £100 million; the provisions and monetary allocation are both under review. .

What's Wrong With the Legislation? The Commission for Racial Equality is charged with providing periodic reviews of the 1976 Act and its second review, following a period of extensive consultation, was submitted to the Home Office in 1992. While that review was not prefaced by a rigorous analysis of the workings of the Act, it was informed by a number of different studies and critiques including those by Brown and Gay (1985), McCrudden (1987), Dhavan (1988) and MacEwen (1991) as well as a series of studies and reports conducted by its own staff.[43] Accordingly ,while the CRE's second review may reflect an institutional view and lack the rigour which a more systematic statistical analysis and comprehensive review would have shown, the criticisms made of the legislation are both informed and incisive and reflect the authority instilled by very practical experience in handling complaints and pursuing investigations.

42. Duncan Forbes, *Action on Racial Harassment: Legal Remedies and Local Authorities*, Legal Action Group in London Housing Unit, London, 1988, and M. MacEwen, *Racial Harassment, Council Housing and the Law*, 1986, Research Paper, SEMRU, Edinburgh.

43. C. McCrudden, 'The Commission for Racial Equality: Formal Investigations in the Shadow of Judicial Review', in R. Baldwin and C. McCrudden (eds), *Regulation and Public Law*, Weidenfeld and Nicholson, London, 1987. See also C. Brown, C. Gay and P. Gay (1985), *Racial Discrimination: Seventeen Years after the Act*, Policies Studies Institute Paper No. 646, London, 1985, Rajeev Dhavan, *Why are there so few cases? On the Uses and Non-Uses of the Race Relations Act 1976*, unpublished report submitted to the CRE, London, 1988; and Forbes, *Action on Racial Harassment: Legal Remedies and Local Authorities*.

The review included a number of criticisms of the Race Relations Act of 1976 of which the following are the most important:

1. The definition of indirect discrimination, following the Court of Appeal decision in *Perera v. Civil Service Commission* (1983), was too narrow; while a 'condition or requirement' which was to the detriment of a particular racial group was explicitly covered by the legislation, the tolerance of a situation or the imposition of a preference which was not a complete bar to access to employment, for example (not being a 'condition or requirement'), was not covered.

2. The provisions relating to victimisation were felt to be inadequate in that the legal interpretation by the court had meant that complainants did not enjoy full protect (see *Kirby v. Manpower Services Commission* (1980) RDLR 1:12).

3. With respect to exemptions, the House of Lords has held in *ex parte Amin* that the expression 'provision of goods, facilities and services' in the 1976 Act applied only to activities analogous to those provided by private undertakings. As a consequence, areas such as immigration control, the prison system and many police activities fell outside the Act; it was felt that these should be included.

4. Because legal aid was not generally available to complainants coming before industrial tribunals, public resourcing in both race and sex cases relating to employment, was restricted to support from the CRE and legal assistance. It was recommended that a specialist division be established to hear all discrimination cases whether relating to employment or not, and that legal aid be made more widely available.

5. Under the 1976 Act, the CRE was empowered to seek responses to questionnaires from respondents but the courts had been reluctant to draw inferences from a failure to provide answers to such questions or from evasion in response. The recommendation was that tribunals should be under a duty to draw the inference that was considered appropriate.

6. With respect to formal investigations of named persons, the CRE currently must have reason to believe that unlawful acts of discrimination are taking place or have taken place. It was felt that this was unduly restrictive of the CRE's investigatory powers.

7. Following on formal investigations where discrimination has been found, the 1976 Act enables the CRE to issue Non-discrimination Notices. In addition to particularly bureaucratic requirements which have resulted in investigations becoming very protracted, there was some concern that the CRE was acting as both judge and jury in its own case. It was recommended that a transfer of the case be made from the CRE to a tribunal to issue a notice, on application by the

Commission, and that the tribunal also be given power to prescribe changes in the practice of the respondents, in order to promote equal opportunity.

8. It was felt that the power to award compensation following an investigation to those who had suffered unlawful discrimination was inadequate; the CRE or the industrial tribunal should have increased powers in this respect.

9. It was considered that the powers of industrial tribunals should be generally improved so that they might order appointment, promotion, reinstatement or increased compensation in discrimination cases, including those relating to indirect discrimination.

10. The current code-making powers of the CRE are restricted to employment and housing, although it has exercised discretionary powers to issue codes in education and other areas. The potential advantage of statutory code-making power is the resultant obligation placed on courts to take into account whether or not a respondent has complied with the code in the consideration of a complaint. Code-making powers should be extended to all areas encompassed by the law.

11. The 1976 Act does not require employers, whether in the public or private sector, to keep ethnic records or to monitor performance. The CRE proposed mandatory ethnic record-keeping, details of which would be passed to the Commission on request. The CRE suggested that employers be required annually to publish or make a statement available on the ethnic composition of their workforce; any interested person would have the right to obtain this information from the employer. With respect to non-employment, the Commission were again critical of the lack of any legal obligation to monitor, particularly in the housing sector. The CRE recommended that ethnic monitoring should be selectively prescribed, and that it should not be limited to the public sector as had been proposed in the previous review of the Race Relations Act in 1985.

12. The CRE had felt that its power to accept undertakings from respondents was too limited and inflexible, as well as being problematic regarding enforcement. It was recommended that these powers should be extended.

13. Section 71 of the Act placed a positive duty on local authorities to promote good race relations, and it was recommended that this obligation be more tightly defined and extended to all organisations providing a service or carrying on an undertaking of a public nature.

In addition to the above criticisms of the Act, the second review consultation document asked four critical questions:

1. Whether or not there should be a law to cover religious discrimination and incitement to religious hatred.
2. Whether or not the law on blasphemy should be completely abolished, or extended in some other form to cover all religions.
3. Whether or not there should be one organisation dealing with all discrimination under the banner of a human rights organisation (this would essentially mean combining the CRE and Equal Opportunities Commission with responsibility for sex discrimination, and creating a new body concerned, subject to the passage of appropriate legislation, with issues of disability).
4. How protection from racial discrimination could be extended to ethnic minorities in Europe.

Although the above criticisms were driven by the experience of the enforcement institution and not the spontaneous lobbying of complainants and ethnic minority groups, the broad nature of consultation procedures used to formulate these recommendations evinced a very positive response. With respect to those criticisms which promote the value of anti-discrimination provision, there were few fundamental disagreements with the CRE's recommendations for changes to the 1976 Act. With regard to the enforcement provisions, however, some commentators felt it desirable to separate the promotion of equal opportunities from enforcement, and to place responsibility for the former more positively on central and local government while leaving the latter as the sole responsibility of the CRE.

Clearly the enforcement agency, the CRE, has not been above or beyond criticism itself. The first report of the Home Affairs Committee for the session 1981–82 concerned the performance of the Commission for Racial Equality,[44] and endorsed the dual role of the Commission as an investigative and promotional body provided that its promotional work was dictated solely by the need to eradicate racial discrimination. The report did recommend, however, that much of the Commission's current promotional activity should more properly be carried out by government departments, and that the Commission should act more in the manner of other specialist law enforcement and advisory commissions. In doing so it would shed some of its multifarious functions which it had taken on (paragraph 81). With respect to complaints, it was felt that the Commission should follow up its production of a 'do-it-yourself' kit for discrimination complainants with a vigorous programme of training organisations and individuals in the necessary skills for aiding a

44. House of Commons first report for the Home Affairs Committee session 1981–82 Commission for Racial Equality, vol. 1, Report of the Minutes of Proceedings HC46-1 HMSO, London, 1982.

complainant at all stages of his or her case.

The Home Office was asked to report to the Committee on the possibility of extending legal aid to discrimination cases. With respect to formal investigations, the Home Affairs Committee seemed very much out of sympathy with the difficulties faced by the CRE; the Committee stressed the need for the CRE staff to act with discretion and courtesy, for publicity to be avoided and that major new investigations should reflect the limitations on resourcing. Although the CRE has effected a number of managerial and other changes in response to the Home Affairs Committee Report – for example its speed in carrying out formal investigations has increased significantly – it has remained subject to internal dissension and external criticism. A number of staff have complained of racial discrimination and lack of promotion opportunities, the public have complained of bureaucracy and inefficiency, and the CRE is frequently perceived to be a somewhat distant and aloof organisation. It has failed to develop an effective linkage between its funding of research activities and its investigatory and promotional work. It has also handled a number of situations very badly; one example is the production of the Race Discrimination Law Reports, hundreds of copies of which remain unsold in the Commission's basement.

But the organisation also has its strengths. In addition to honing its own skills in representing complainants and in conducting investigations generally, it has developed a more effective strategy in prioritising its enforcement activities. The CRE has frequently used its formal investigations effectively to direct change in housing, education and employment and has successfully put pressure on the public sector, principally central and local government, to secure beneficial change in practices. Its own codes of practice have set tangible and achievable targets in the various sectors in which they apply, and in its new partnership with Racial Equality Councils the Commission has demonstrated a willingness to listen and learn and to be responsive to legitimate external pressure for change.

Katznelson has suggested that institutions such as the CRE and local Racial Equality Councils have extended the colonial relationship between ethnic minority groups (the colonial dependents) and the government (the mother country) by providing a racial buffer, one function of which has been to diffuse the legitimate aspirations of the black communities for self-expression through subverting the creation and development of their own institutional frameworks.[45] It is probably true that if the Racial Equality Councils as well as the CRE had developed a more open and

45. Ira Katznelson, *Black Men, White Cities: Race, Politics and Migration in the United States 1900–30 and Britain 1948–68*, Oxford University Press, London, 1973.

perhaps less patronising relationship with ethnic minority groups in the period since the publication of that critique, it would now be difficult to argue with any conviction that these organs are instruments of central government which suppress and diffuse challenge. It may be argued however that the RECs, while frequently doing useful work, nonetheless do not give value for money and alternatives should be explored. It would be in keeping with the Conservative government's philosophy to consider private tendering for the negotiated programmes of work in a specific locality.

Judging the efficacy of the Race Relations Act of 1976 and its enforcement agency, the Commission for Racial Equality, is clearly problematic. In comparative terms, however, while the Race Relations Act may not be perfect it does carry significant weight and has fairly comprehensive coverage of both the public and private sector. Perhaps its most significant weakness remains its failure to impose sanctions which are strong enough to force major employers and service providers to review their practices in order to secure compliance in the short term. It is also evident that many potential complainants 'lump it or dump it'. They refused to pursue complaints because of the low prospect of success accompanied by the high risk of damaging relationships with employers and/or colleagues. Alternatively, having embarked on a complaint, they will 'dump' or abandon it because of the time and stress associated with pursuit.

With respect to the value of there being a specialist enforcement agency, the obvious question to ask is whether or not complainants would be better off without it. For all its faults the CRE has surely made a contribution not only to the support of individual complaints but also to promoting a better public awareness of the extent to which discrimination continues to take place and of the need for and means whereby equal opportunities may be pursued.

The Four Core States: Conclusions

A study of the legislation applying in the four core states does not suggest that the differences in philosophical approach between France and Germany on the one hand and the Netherlands and Britain on the other have determined the manner in which legal remedies have been provided. Similarly, while there may be important differences in the settlement patterns of visible minorities in the states examined, it would be hard to conclude that these have been instrumental in determining the legislative measures adopted. The experience of the Netherlands demonstrates that Roman law (civilian) systems can use both the criminal and civil codes to counteract racial violence and discrimination. All the countries studied had adhered to ICERD while both France and the Netherlands allow individual petition to the Committee. The influence of ICERD is most apparent with respect to incitement to racial hatred, where broadly similar criminal sanctions are employed by all the states but the extent of latitude given to the press and the balance struck with freedom of expression vary. The definitions of racial discrimination applied by the different states are also similar and follow the ICERD definition to a substantial degree, but there is no apparent standard with respect to indirect discrimination (on which ICERD is silent or at least muted). The German approach is essentially minimalist in terms of domestic legislation.

Perhaps the most striking distinctions are the following:

1. There is a fairly fastidious adherence on the part of the French and the Germans to the concept of one nation to the exclusion of diversity within the 'culture' of their nationals, despite the recognition of such diversity in non-national residents or denizens. It is apparent that the adoption of nationality is not merely an acceptance of the sovereignty of the state but also the acceptance of an exclusive cultural inheritance. The rationale underpinning this approach may be justified, not only by the need to promote the myths of common identity in order to secure state loyalty but also, in the case of France in particular, by the need to protect the cultural fabric from assimilation into the English-speaking world. However, the result appears to deny the importance of the cultural inheritance of minority groups and to breach the UN Covenant on the Protection of the Rights of Minorities regarding cultural, social and economic differences. Both the Netherlands and the UK appear to adopt a more open view of citizenship and to accept, at least in theory, the concept of a multi-cultural society. In a comparative study of Caribbean minorities in Britain and the Netherlands it was concluded that there was a continuous dialectical exchange between culture and structure.[46] It is not unreasonable to assume, therefore, that differences in approach to the notion of citizenship have influenced and will continue to influence the experience of ethnic groups including the nature of racism and discrimination.

2. On the assumption that the experience of discrimination in each of the states is proportional, i.e. that no one state provides an environment which is substantially better than that of any other in terms of the incidence of

---

46. J. Boissevain and H. Grotenbreg, 'Culture, Structure and Ethnic Enterprise: the Surinamese of Amsterdam', in M. Cross and H. Entzinger (eds), *Lost Illusions*, Routledge, London, 1988.

discrimination, then it can be assumed that a higher number of compla...
lodged and remedies granted by the courts is indicative of a relativel_y
more effective system. On that basis the UK system is better than the
Dutch, which in turn is better than the French or the German systems.
That conclusion is evidently simplistic and may ignore important
qualifications.

3. The feeling of minority groups regarding their sense of belonging to
the state may be considered as an indicator of how well law and policy
have combined to provide a receptive environment. This study is not of
sufficient breadth to arrive at firm conclusions; the four core states all
experience racism and discrimination but commentators have suggested
that the Netherlands has instilled racial tolerance as a norm in the social
fabric more successfully to-date than, arguably, the UK or France and,
certainly, Germany.

The final chapter of this book attempts to explore the rationale behind
the differences of approach of all the states studied to international
obligations, a constitutional framework and domestic legislation.

Approaching Analysis

Introduction

This chapter attempts an assessment of the relative merits of anti-discrimination provisions in the countries previously examined. It provides a commentary on the actual and potential impact of international conventions on domestic legislation and policy development in anti-discrimination law. It will be apparent that, in the absence of any convincing methodology adopted by any given state regarding the effectiveness of both international and domestic law, and of reliable statistical data on which to base conclusions, the diagnosis and prescription which are provided here will be selective and impressionistic: even if this chapter fails to provide the correct answers, it at least attempts to provide a list of relevant questions.

Perhaps the first and most obvious question is whether patterns of immigration and settlement, the nature of similarity and distinctiveness, attitudes towards self and group identity and the extent to which the country concerned promotes or experiences assimilation, integration or pluralism as the dominant norm are factors which influence anti-discrimination law provision. Our interest in this question must be a narrow one and is confined primarily to its impact on domestic law; i.e., does the experience of minorities within a state determine the legal measures adopted by the state to counteract discriminatory practice?

In looking at issues of immigration and settlement it may also be appropriate to ask whether there are any distinctive patterns which are particularly associated with either core states or the periphery. If there are distinctive patterns associated with one area or another, are these reflected in patterns of legislative response?

Since the focus of this book is on anti-discrimination law, another obvious question which needs to be addressed is the extent to which ethnic groups suffer similar levels of discrimination in each state and, if there are different patterns, whether there may be any tentative correlation between such differences and the differences in the nature of settlement and immigration. A fourth question relates to the nature of domestic law itself. The earlier chapters showed a multiplicity of approaches to anti-discrimination law in both civil and criminal provision, in the inclusion or exclusion of indirect discrimination, in the incorporation or otherwise of international obligations, in a piecemeal or comprehensive approach to legal provision, in the provision or otherwise of an enforcement agency, and even in the extent to which discrimination against ethnic minority groups is tolerated as lawful.

While recent studies on ethnicity and nationhood do not conclude that there is any atavistic imperative towards particular and exclusive territorial identities as was suggested by Robert Ardley, there remain legitimate questions about ethnicity and national identity and about what the sociologists call in-groups and out-groups at a national level.[1] Smith has suggested that ethnicity is the precursor of nationalism with modern states extending, deepening and streamlining the ways in which ethnic groups associate and communicate. The civic state today, he argues, has not transcended ethnicity or national sentiments.[2] Clearly there is a danger that a single focus on human rights inadvertently ignores this issue. It is apparent nonetheless that the practice of exclusion by discrimination reinforces alienation, which ultimately manifests itself in loss of cultural respect and identity.

Most legislation represents a form of compromise between the desire for non-intervention in the private affairs of the individual or the group on the one hand, and the need to regulate and protect those values, interests and approaches which the state deems important on the other. While each state will have its own view as to what priorities it must protect, the extent of protection provided will also reflect the state's political views on the appropriateness of state intervention. It is also evident that anti-discrimination law itself need not be the sole, nor indeed the most, important aspect of state policy in the promotion of equal opportunities; the state may use a panoply of initiatives, apart from legislation, such as programmes promoting multi-cultural education, resourcing community centres, providing low-cost housing, creating job incentives and providing family support structures. These may do as much to promote real equality of opportunity as any desiccated formal legislative provision, left to dry out on the non-priority shelving of hollow commitments. Nonetheless, because such positive programmes are frequently associated with enabling legislation, effective anti-discrimination law is likely to be part and parcel of a more concerted approach towards equal opportunities; it may therefore be important to

---

1. See, for example, A. Smith, *The Ethnic Origins of Nations*, Blackwell, Oxford, 1988, and J. Kellas, *The Politics of Nationalism and Ethnicity*, Macmillan, London, 1991.
2. Smith, *The Ethnic Origins of Nations*, pp. 215–216.

question the extent to which anti-discrimination law and positive action programmes are interlinked.

Finally, this chapter concludes with a view of what the European experience in individual states adds up to in the context of the evolving European Community. Thus if the provisions of Article 119 and the Equal Pay Directive provided a stimulus to promote equality of opportunity for women and the Social Chapter suggests an ineluctable European movement towards a statement of common human rights and fundamental freedoms, we must ask not only whether anti-discrimination law will have a European umbrella, but what that common framework must entail and how it should be shaped and developed.

Patterns of Immigration and Settlement

Three of the four core states examined in Chapters Six and Seven, namely France, the Netherlands and the UK, share a not wholly enviable history as colonial powers and an experience in patterns of ethnic minority immigration, which reflect both the general opportunities provided for employment by post-Second World War industrial reconstruction and the specific access provided to 'citizens' and non-nationals resident in dependencies to visit and/or settle in the 'mother country'. Thus in France a number of French citizens are of Moroccan and Algerian origin, in the Netherlands the colonial history is reflected in the settlement of Moluccans and Surinamese as well as Dutch Antilleans from the Caribbean, while in Britain the Caribbean, Pakistani, Bangladeshi, Indian, Chinese and East African Asian population similarly reflects UK's colonial past.

Nonetheless there are other factors which have affected settlement, particularly in France and the Netherlands. In France the proximity to North Africa and to Spain and Portugal, together with work opportunities provided to Turkish nationals, has resulted in French ethnic minority groups being much more than a reflection of the country's colonial history. Similarly in Holland, while the Surinamese form the largest immigrant group, the significant number of Turkish and Moroccan residents qualifies any view that colonialism has dictated all aspects of immigration and settlement patterns. The fourth core state, Germany, and Spain and Portugal are similarly populated by both 'colonial' ethnic groups and others who have sought employment, principally from Turkey and North Africa. While Italy has not been a recent colonial power, it too has been subject to immigration by minority groups from North Africa as well as the more recent influx of refugees from Albania; but Italy has also exported many of its nationals to Switzerland and Germany where they attempt to find work in more robust labour markets.

While it may be too simplistic to suggest that the colonial experience has established a permanent special relationship between host country and ethnic minorities, the creation of citizenship has conferred more immediate rights on those settled communities than on non-nationals. It may also have created particular expectations of equality of opportunity and non-discrimination which have not been sustained.[3]

In all four core countries examined, ethnic minorities comprise a significant element of the population; the proportions are respectively 5 per cent in the Netherlands, approximately 4 per cent in France, some 5 per cent in the UK and 7.8 per cent in the Federal Republic of Germany (but less than 1 per cent in the former Democratic Republic). While these proportions are not as great as those of visible minorities in the United States, for example, where the black population alone comprises 10 per cent, in three of the countries there are particular concentrations in major cities such as Paris and Marseilles, Amsterdam and Rotterdam, and London and Birmingham. As a consequence, the proportion of ethnic minority groups within the cities may be fairly high and may on occasion comprise a majority in particular districts. The host community may assume that such visible changes in the population of particular localities is reflected in similar and uniform social and cultural change. But it must be kept in mind that there may be a variety of distinct ethnic minority groups in each locale, which will not necessarily share a common language, religion or culture. In the United Kingdom, for example, there has been a tendency to classify those originating from the Indian sub-continent as 'Asian' and in doing so to submerge religious, linguistic and cultural (let alone geographical) differences within and between the Indian, Pakistani and Bangladeshi populations. Consequently there is a risk that positive measures adopted to promote the interests of 'minorities' in these areas may suffer from stereotypical assumptions about the characteristics of the 'group' and thus lead to indirect discrimination.

The common experience of discrimination based on ethnic origin, shared by post-Second World War settlers, has been characterised by:

1. The selective stemming of primary immigration, i.e. of work-seekers, from ex-colonial dependencies and elsewhere
2. Increasingly rigorous controls on immigration which impede family reunification
3. Demands, fluctuating in intensity, by the white right-wing minority parties for repatriation of black immigrants.

---

3. Malcolm Cross and Han Entzinger (eds), *Lost Illusions: Caribbean Minorities in Britain and the Netherlands*, Routledge, London, 1988.

The settlement patterns of ethnic minorities in the peripheral states of Denmark, Greece and Ireland has not been reflective of any colonial experience. The actual numbers of black settlers have, in comparative terms, been low. Thus in Denmark the largest visible minority groups are from Turkey (26,000) and from Pakistan (6,500) which, even together, comprise a very small percentage of the 3 per cent of non-citizens out of the five million resident population. In Ireland it was estimated that only .06 per cent of the population were of Asian or black origin, the same percentage as the visible minority of the Greek population, which is mostly of Turkish and Cypriot origin. There is probably less of a shared pattern of immigration and settlement in respect of the peripheral countries examined than in respect of the core. Both Ireland and Greece have poor employment prospects. The presence of Turks in Greece has a historical and geographical explanation but the Turks in Denmark came there for employment. Ireland has few applicants seeking asylum in contrast with Denmark where between 1979 and 1988 there were significant numbers of Iranians, Kurds and Tamils. Both Ireland and Greece share significant traveller populations, both of which have experienced particular difficulties with regard to employment.

Although airlines have increased the opportunities for mobility it remains an evident truth that geography, along with the colonial past, has been an important indicator of ethnic minority group settlement patterns. Thus in the case of Denmark membership of the Nordic Council and proximity to Germany has affected immigration while for Ireland its proximity to the UK, along with its historical colonial connection and its position as an island on the periphery of Europe has resulted in the UK being almost the sole factor influencing its settlement and emigration patterns. In the case of Greece the proximity of Turkey and Cyprus has been a dominant factor.

Attitudes and approaches in respect of the conferment of citizenship are slightly less easy to define, although it is clear that the peripheral states of Denmark, Ireland and Greece have been, if anything, more protectionist than the core states examined, with the important exception of Germany. While each of the other three core states has afforded citizenship to qualifying residents of dependent territories, the approaches have been far from uniform.

It remains difficult to arrive at any convincing conclusion as to whether patterns of settlement and immigration have had a direct impact on a state's preference for assimilation, integration or pluralism, but there are certainly significant differences within the core states. Germany and France are much more assimilationist than the Netherlands or Britain, despite similarities in the colonial experience and settlement of the last three. This is shown in the importance attached to citizenship as a route of access to other rights including employment in the public sector. It is also illustrated by the fact that in France it is unlawful to monitor performance by reference to race. This reinforces a colour-blind approach to discrimination, assuming a common adherence to traditional norms; the Islamic faith and its followers, for example, become a barely tolerated aberration.

Among the peripheral states, Ireland – perhaps merely reflecting a lack of any sizeable minority and any political concern – has done least to provide protection for minority groups against discrimination and is in the unenviable position of having ratified the smallest number of relevant international conventions. Accordingly, to describe the Irish stance as assimilationist is to credit the country with a greater consciousness than is merited. Although there is some official acknowledgment of the difficulties experienced by Ireland's travellers, this is not reflected in anti-discrimination law nor in a fostering of a way of life different from accepted norms.

Greece differs from Ireland in that it has not only ratified more international obligations but has also applied them directly to domestic law. To the extent that there is explicit recognition of the educationally distinctive needs of the Moslem minorities in Western Thrace, Greek government policy is not avowedly assimilationist but that pluralistic approach does not extend to other minorities in other districts. Similarly in Denmark the particular rights afforded the German minority in respect of language and education are much more a reflection of political expediency – Denmark expects like treatment for the Danish residents in Germany – than any espousal of a pluralist ideal. Indeed the dominant homogeneity of Denmark's population, a characteristic shared with Ireland, is probably a reason why the absence of any organised programme to inform ethnic minorities of their rights has so far gone unchallenged.[4]

Experience of Racism and Discrimination

The lack of systematic record-keeping in each of the countries examined must qualify any conclusions which can be drawn regarding the nature or extent of racism. Nonetheless, the following can be stated with some confidence:

1. The comparatively small size of ethnic minorities in the peripheral states has made no significant difference to the experience of racial

---

4. M. Wilkie, 'Victims of Neutrality, Race Discrimination in Denmark', *Nordic Journal of International Law*, Copenhagen, 1990, vol. 59, pp. 5–86.

harassment or discrimination. It was noted in Denmark that there was growing concern about the extent of racial prejudice and the denial of equal opportunities and violation of many international conventions. In Ireland, while some observers have suggested that the country has been 'remarkably free' from problems relating to racism and discrimination, an opinion poll of February 1991 suggested widespread prejudice on racial grounds. There is evidence of racial attacks against Jewish shops in Dublin, and harassment of travellers, Moroccans and others. In Greece there have been complaints of harassment against Moslems, and in all three countries there has been evidence of discrimination in respect of employment.

2. Experience in the UK in recording of incidents of racial harassment suggests that the figures are systematically under-estimated in comparison with actual incidents. There is evidence of a European network of fascists and right-wing groups both feeding off and contributing to racial violence in other countries, and there is also evidence that racial violence increases during periods of recession and high unemployment when ethnic minorities become a scapegoat for and the difficulties experienced by others. In each of the four core countries there is evidence of discrimination in the employment and housing markets in both public and private sectors, as well as in education and in service provisions.

3. Although citizenship is the basis for legitimate discrimination in all seven countries, it would appear that this discrimination against foreigners is more systematic in both France, as exemplified by restrictions in obtaining employment in the public service, and in Germany, as shown in the obtaining of insurance, than in the Netherlands or in the UK. Discrimination at work and in daily life has been accepted as a normal social phenomenon and reflective of the 'cold, crude, hard and reserved' behaviour of the Dutch people.[5] Mead and Simpson reported that during the first six months of 1990 in the city of The Hague alone there were 388 complaints filed on the basis of discrimination against Moroccans and Turks in employment.[6]

---

5. G. Ford, *Report of the Committee of Inquiry into Racism and Xenophobia*, Office for Official Publications of the European Communities, Luxembourg, 1991, p. 69.
6. Alan Simpson and Mel Read, *Against the Rising Tide*, Spokesman Publications, Nottingham, 1991, p. 63.

Anti-discrimination Law: The Impact of International Obligations

With the exception of Ireland, each of the states studied has ratified the United Nations Convention on Elimination of All Forms of Racial Discrimination (ICERD) and France, Denmark and the Netherlands recognise the competence of the committee constituted thereunder to receive and consider communications from individuals claiming a breach of the Convention. With the exception of the UK and Ireland, all countries studied have ratified ILO Convention No. 111 relating to anti-discrimination in employment and occupation. All seven, including both the UK and Ireland, have ratified the European Convention on Human Rights and Fundamental Freedoms, outlawing racial discrimination at least in relation to the other rights conferred by that Convention.

While the specific implications of the various international obligations are discussed in the study of each of the country's domestic provisions, one or two generalised conclusions can be drawn from their composite experience:

1. First, the pressure put on countries to become signatories to these conventions has been inadequate in overcoming various reservations expressed, particularly those expressed by Ireland. Similarly, pressure to comply with these conventions or to their protocols, or to permit individual petition, has been fairly muted.

2. While the conventions have frequently resulted in changes in domestic legislation, most importantly changes necessitated by ICERD with respect to racial incitement, the general pattern of domestic legislation has been far from uniform.

3. The reporting systems imposed on the signatories to the various conventions have proved far from onerous and have frequently been honoured in the breach. While the countries examined probably constitute a group of the more conscientious or committed spectrum of the signatories, the conventions demonstrate the frequent and very wide gaps between signature and true commitment and even between commitment and delivery.

Perhaps it is the nature of such international obligations to meet the requirements only of the lowest common denominator. But, even acknowledging such limits, the inadequacy of the enforcement provisions raises questions relating to the fundamental value of such conventions, particularly considering the resources required to secure their drafting, approval and implementation. CERD, in its report for 1992, observed that the number of times the Committee met and the amount of work it was able to undertake were curtailed by the failure of signatories to pay their dues.

In most states customary international law forms part of domestic law, but it is far from clear whether norms prohibiting racial discrimination or xenophobia have become part of customary jurisprudence. The Irish Constitution (Article 29) provides that Ireland 'accepts the generally recognised principles of international law as its rule of conduct in its relations with other states'. However, this does not extend to dealings with or between individuals within Ireland. According to Article 25 of the German Constitution, general rules of customary international law are part of German law and, as these are superior to state law, rights and duties can be derived directly from them; the situation is similar in Greece and Denmark. In Britain it was held in the case *Maclaine Watson & Co Ltd. v. Department of Trade and Industry* (1980) 3 All ER 523, that neither international agreements nor an international rule of law could confer rights enforceable by the UK courts, but in the *Parlement Belge* case (1880) 5 PD 197, the Court of Appeal for England and Wales found that mail ships, with respect to damage following a collision, benefited from immunity by customary international law. However, in common with the other countries studied, there is no case law in the UK which applies international human rights norms on discrimination, racism or xenophobia.

The only country which had incorporated ICERD into domestic law wholemeal was Greece, but there is an almost complete dearth of case law reporting relating to racial discrimination; accordingly, and acknowledging the reality of racism in Greece, it would be difficult to assert that incorporation – without separate provision for enforcement – carries any particular advantage over domestic legislation other than the obvious one of establishing uniform national responses to international obligations. In common with the constitutional position, the decision to incorporate ICERD or not had little, if anything, to do with the extent of discrimination or the perception by the state of the issues which legislation had to address. The quality of reporting by member states to the Committee for the Elimination of Racial Discrimination seems to bear out the hypothesis that states remain protective of the right to implement obligations in the manner they deem appropriate. Frequently this is on the basis, spurious or not, that the particular situation pertaining in the country demands tailor-made legislation.

Domestic Legislation

Having decided to sign an international obligation, the state is generally left to decide how this obligation should be implemented. The choice is likely to be one of the following: a) do nothing (this option presumes that the existing legislation meets all the requirements); b) incorporate the obligation into domestic law directly (some countries such as Greece automatically incorporate international obligations); or c) pass domestic legislation which seeks to implement any or all aspects of the international obligation not already covered by domestic provision.

The United Kingdom is unique among European states in not having a written constitution. As a consequence there is no provision (such as in Article 93 of the Constitution of the Netherlands) which makes treaties and decisions of international organisations binding on legal persons and directly enforceable in the domestic courts. But the constitutions in Ireland and in France do not directly implement treaty obligations, although in France the courts will interpret domestic provisions as if to comply with them and, following the decision in *Croissant* (Conseil d'Etat 7.7.78), will overrule any contradictory provisions passed prior to the obligation. In Germany it is only the self-executing provisions in a treaty which have been passed into domestic law which are then given direct effect by the courts, but because Germany has applied the European Convention alone in this way, an individual cannot invoke other conventions with respect to discrimination. Denmark has a dualist approach to international obligations; parliament may pass a special act which incorporates a treaty into domestic law verbatim, or the terms of the act may amend existing legislation or introduce new legislation in order to comply with the treaty.

The constitutions of Denmark, Ireland and, by inference, the UK provide no explicit protection for minorities or individuals against racial discrimination, while the constitutions of Greece, France and the Netherlands include some reference to such protection. In the case of Denmark it is argued that the provisions against arbitrary discrimination cover race implicitly; this may also be implied in Ireland but only with respect to the 'essential features' of an individual's existence. Setting aside the anomaly of the UK, it might be argued that those countries which have experienced relatively little immigration have not felt the need to make express reference to racial discrimination. More importantly, however, in no country which provides constitutional guarantees are those guarantees effective in providing remedies against unlawful discrimination.

Of the seven countries examined, Ireland has clearly done least to promote domestic legislation, followed by Greece. But, as noted above, Greece has ratified and incorporated ICERD. Of the peripheral countries, Denmark alone has a dedicated Race Relations Act (1971), of limited scope but supported by other provisions. Predictably, it is the core states, excepting Germany, which have attempted to address racial discrimination in a more comprehensive fashion. It is worth noting that other 'core' states such as Italy, Luxembourg and Belgium have done comparatively little to protect their minorities against discrimination. Accordingly, it would be wrong to conclude that the willingness to pass comprehensive domestic legislation is a function of the location of the state or the size or composition of its ethnic minority communities.

It is true, however, that of all the states examined, it is those core states which share a history of colonial expansion and reciprocal inward migration from their colonies which have done most to establish a legal framework not only with respect to incitement but also regarding racial discrimination. But any hypothesis that this shared experience has influenced governments to accept the passage of protective legislation will have to be tempered by the knowledge that neither Portugal nor Spain has passed anti-discrimination legislation of any width or depth. Even the questionable hypothesis that the Protestant states do more to combat racism than do Catholic states is contradicted by Germany. Accordingly, it would be wrong to suggest a simple explanation for the adoption of legislation as being related to the experience of immigration, colonial history or the dominant religion of the European states.

In Chapter 1 reference was made to different ideologies and approaches to anti-discrimination legislation and to the promotion of equal opportunities more generally. From this study, it seems more probable that these differences – and they may be significant at the level of both party politics and of the individual state – have influenced and will continue to influence the nature of domestic law.

There remain many contradictions, both between states and within them. Thus while Germany is isolated in the core states with respect to its indifferent record regarding race discrimination legislation, a brief examination of asylum law puts it in a much more favourable light. The British Conservative Government's repeated assertion of the need for 'firm but fair' immigration policies (which are in practice firm and unfair[7]) in tandem with good race relations may suggest that while governments may be reluctant to promote effective protection to minority groups when these are nationals, they do even less if a sizable minority are either non-citizens, as is the case in Germany, or are illegal, as is the situation in Spain, Portugal and Italy. It is clear that officialdom has turned a blind eye to illegal immigrants who are fuelling the economy but who are being underpaid and exploited in the process. To provide rights to these groups may imply a recognition of a residential status which governments are reluctant to concede, and also a restriction on opportunistic competition in a cutthroat labour market driven by the recession and the increasing

7. Commission for Racial Equality, *Report of Formal Investigation into the Immigration and Nationality Department of the Home Office*, CRE, London, 1983.

abolition of any form of protection for labour or capital.

The different legal provisions applying to long-stay migrants was the subject of a Council of Europe study in 1991.[8] That report made ten basic proposals to improve the position of such migrants as follows:

1. The grant of right of permanent residence after 5 years
2. The grant of rights of residence to the families of permanent residents
3. If permanent residence is restricted to 10 years, a decision on extension should be made within one year of application, with rights of appeal
4. Absence for a period of up to two years, and possibly up to four years should not affect the right to return
5. Permanent residence should equate with a work permit and confer a right to public or private employment
6. Permanent residence should confer rights to social security, education and vocational training on the same basis as nationals
7. Permanent residence should confer eligibility for citizenship
8. Those rights which are conferred should not be dependent on the issuance of permits
9. Freedom of movement for a three month period should be granted to a permanent resident
10. Regulations concerning these rights should be harmonised by member states.

Although discrimination against non-nationals in the countries studied has not been exceptional, it frequently stems from a form of xenophobia or racism which is falsely legitimated by an appeal to nationalism. A new European Convention on the Rights of Permanent Residence, incorporating the above provisions, would go some way to challenging the arbitrary division between nationals and non-nationals in the conferment of legal rights and protection.

When examining those states which have adopted penal provisions and those which have relied on the civil code, it can be seen that there has been greater reliance on the former: Denmark, Greece, the Netherlands and France place more emphasis on the criminal law than the civil. Because the anti-discrimination legal provisions in Ireland and in Germany are so slight, it may be misleading to characterise them as falling within either camp. In Britain the Race Relations Act of 1976, as amended, imposes civil remedies; but the decision to include these in the legislation was not a necessary consequence of a particular examination of issues

8. Georges-Henri Beauther, *On the Legal Position of Long-stay Migrants in Host Countries*, Council of Europe, Strasbourg, 1991, Report MG-JU (91) 3 revised.

and choice of remedies, but rather a last-minute decision based on the assumption that the American experience, in a shared common law system, was worthy of replication.[9]

Anti-racist Strategies

Comparing approaches to anti-discrimination in France and Britain, Lloyd has suggested that there is a considerable divide, which was also alluded to above. Concern has been expressed by both states about the logic of the other's approach.[10] The French tend to characterise the British approach as divisive; it fosters differences between groups and by doing so tolerates or even encourages housing ghettos.[11] The proof of Britain's mistaken policy of division is provided by the riots of the 1980s and the higher reported rates of racial incidents. In contrast, so the hypothesis continues, France has emphasised the concept of one state, one citizenship and one embracing culture, going back to the influences of the Enlightenment and to the Republican tradition; as the French *Haut Conseil a l'Integration* observed in 1991:

> The France of integration should obey a logic of equality and not a logic of minorities. The principles of identity and equality which go back to the Revolution and the Declaration of the Rights of Man and of Citizens impregnate our conception, thus founded on the principles of the equality of individuals before the law, whatever their origin, race, religion . . . to the exclusion of an institutional recognition of minorities.[12]

In contrast to the French insistence on a philosophical base as a grounding for anti-discrimination strategy, the British tend to characterise themselves as being pragmatic, evolving strategies to address particular problems, whether in education, housing, employment, services or commerce, based on the simple principles of fair play and liberalism. The existence of the Commission for Racial Equality and the fact that it receives 1,500 complaints per annum is an indication both that there is an appropriate structure to assist complainants and that it does so successfully. The lack of such an organisation and the very low number of complaints in France, the argument continues, demonstrates that French

9. See H. Street, G. Howe and G. Bindman, *Report on Anti-discrimination Legislation*, Home Office, London, 1967.

10. Cathie Lloyd, 'Concepts, Models and Anti-racist Strategies in Britain and France', *New Community*, October 1991, vol. 18, no. 1, pp. 63–73.

11. V. de Rudder, 'De Versovie a Barbes – et si le ghetto n'existait pas?', *Differences*, December, 1990.

12. HCI 1991: 10 quoted in Lloyd, 'Concepts, Models and Anti-racist Strategies in Britain and France'.

law fails to deliver.

But the reality of anti-discrimination policy in both countries should not be reduced to such stereotypical caricatures. Lloyd has suggested that, just as one may dispute the idea that the law confers privileges based on ethnicity in the British case, so one may point to the provision of resources for many ethnic minority associations in France, particularly after 1981, as well as the formulation of *ad hoc* policies in response to recent racial violence on suburban housing estates.

It is evident on occasion, however, that the French government accepts the possibility of structural causes of urban unrest, perhaps in a more profound way than the British government. The disturbances of 1981 led to the Bonnemaison Commission report in the following year, initiating the establishment of a national crime prevention council with 480 local councils and a much broader remit than the British neighbourhood watch schemes. The councils were involved in the renovation of low cost housing (HLM), which frequently followed consultation with local youth who were also provided with employment and training opportunities, workshops for vehicle repair on housing estates and even holidays to go sailing, canoeing, swimming and cross country cycling.[13] This strategy of involving local communities in the rebuilding of the physical and social fabric in areas susceptible to crime and violence was based not only on the acceptance that there was a direct correlation between unemployment (and the lack of opportunities for youth more generally) and social problems, but also that any remedy had to involve the communities concerned in strategy formulation as well as implementation.

The Scarman Report, which followed the Brixton disturbances of 1981, also recognised that structural social difficulties had been inadequately addressed by both central and local governments, but the Conservative government were not entirely enamoured of or convinced by its recommendations. Indeed, any hint of espousing a sociological analysis was emphatically refuted in the response to the Handsworth riots of 1985 when Douglas Hurd, the then Home Secretary, said that the riots were not a cry for help but a cry for loot. In setting up a police inquiry, there was an expectation that 'a clear view' would result. 'It is not a case history for sociologists to pore over', Hurd observed, 'but a case for the police.'[14]

While the obvious reluctance to seek the views of urban sociologists may support the hypothesis that the British don't want to know why things happen, only how, there is an equally obvious political divide between

13. Steve Bosely, 'Foreign Bodies', *The Guardian*, 18 November 1987.

14. John Gaffney, *Interpretation of Violence: the Handsworth Riots of 1985*, CRER, University of Warwick, Coventry, 1987.

the government and the opposition in their respective attitudes to race relations. The former profess an anti-dirigiste stance and tend to eschew an interventionist strategy, particularly with respect to employment where it may be argued that intervention would upset the self-balancing mechanisms of the free market. In contrast the Labour Party, as illustrated in the White Paper on Racial Discrimination (Home Office, 1975) and the document Urban Deprivation, Racial Inequality and Social Policy (Home Office, 1976), is much more open to a structural and 'sociological' analysis of urban malaise including issues of race relations and racial violence.[15]

If, when analysing the different responses to race relations in France and Britain, it seems wise to suspend judgment on the accuracy of the simplistic assertions that each makes about the other, it would seem equally prudent to suggest caution in promoting one approach at the expense of the other. The French have also characterised Dutch strategies as similar to the British,[16] and the approaches of the three peripheral nations examined are by no means uniform. Of the three, Denmark has probably been most proactive but the strategies adopted are not particularly distinctive; while they may resemble British strategies in their lack of an obvious theoretical underpinning, they share some similarities to the French in their assumption, albeit muted and not uncontested, that integration equates with assimilation to the dominant cultural norms.[17]

In the White Paper of 1975, which set out the intentions of the British government with respect to the amendments to the 1968 Race Relations Act which were realised in the 1976 Act, the assertion was made that while anti-discrimination law was not the only, or necessarily the most important, element in policy to promote equal opportunity, it was nonetheless a prerequisite.[18] But even if it is accepted that this assertion is true, and recognising that its veracity is difficult either to prove or to disprove, there is an argument that the character of the law, being concerned predominantly with the public domain, need not be a mirror image of other policies and practices concerned with the promotion of equal opportunity in the private domain.

The law, by definition, sets common standards of behaviour and practice to which all citizens are expected to conform. It prescribes tolerances by striving to achieve the highest common factor of shared

15. See Home Office, *Racial Discrimination*, Cmnd 6234, HMSO, London, 1975 and Home Office, *Urban Deprivation, Racial Inequality and Social Policy*, HMSO, London, 1976.

16. Cathie Lloyd, 'Concepts, Models and Anti-racist Strategies in Britain and France', *New Community*, October 1991, vol. 18, no. 1, pp. 63–73.

17. Wilkie, 'Victims of Neutrality, Race Discrimination in Denmark'.

18. See Home Office, *Racial Discrimination*.

standards, the abandonment of which are generally accepted as a threat to society warranting sanction by the courts. If the accent of the law is on commonality, does this not fit poorly with the concept of plurality of values to which a multi-cultural society must assign pre-eminence?

One method of seeking an answer to that question is to separate law from other political and social aspirations; rather than searching for the highest common factor, the law might satisfy itself with the lowest common denominator. But to achieve this in a multi-cultural society, the law must not take the dominant culture as the descriptor of acceptable practice. Instead, the law must make a sincere attempt to distance itself from the culture-bound mythology from which it has emerged, and re-evaluate the old tolerances in the light of the new. One obvious example where this process of reassessment is taking place in the UK is the law relating to blasphemy. The old tolerances are represented by the Protestant values ascribed to 'God', 'Jesus', the 'Trinity' and the 'Holy Bible'. Salman Rushdie's novel *The Satanic Verses* was said to be a blasphemy against the Moslem religion but the English courts, when asked to deliberate on whether the English law of blasphemy extended to the Koran, declined to do so. This has, understandably, increased the pressure to update the blasphemy laws so that either they encompass other religions or, conversely, abandon the unique protection afforded to the Christian religion. It is a further irony that when the Christian churches, both Protestant and Catholic, are pursuing ecumenism the Moslem religion is struggling with rifts between Sunnis and Shiites, and while the former is contemplating a less protectionist stance the latter, for a multiplicity of reasons, is apparently defensive and protectionist. An examination of that particular dialogue serves to illustrate the extent to which the legal edifice must alter if it is to show a likeness to all its adherence.

Law in a Multi-racial Society

If a goal of placing anti-discrimination law in the public domain – to establish and maintain common standards in the broader promotion of equal opportunity – is accepted, then there are a number of implications. The major implication is that the law will not countenance preferential treatment based on race, even if it is restricted to compensation for disadvantage related to racial origin. One of the major difficulties of counterbalancing racial disadvantage, that is the disproportionate experience of unemployment, comparative lack of educational qualifications, poorer housing and health (the commonly acknowledged indices of disadvantage), with positive discrimination is that in providing preferential treatment based on race, minorities are differentially incorporated into a 'mainstream society' which legitimises 'race' alone as a basis for judgment.[19]

This approach may compensate for historical disadvantage but, in perpetuating racial discrimination, it reinforces the general perception that race is not only relevant in the description of life-chances in society – a conclusion clearly justified by the evidence – but is of overriding importance in individual cases. This individualisation of cases on racial grounds may lead to both a sense of personal injustice on the part of those adversely affected, the racial inversion of life-chances illustrated by the Bakke case[20] and harm to the cause of adverse discrimination. MacEwen has illustrated how the latter might occur in housing;[21] if building societies discriminated indirectly against Asian home buyers by refusing to lend, in certain areas of the city (in this instance the 'redlining' related to houses without gardens) without good reason, simple statistical evidence of indirect discrimination would merely show a disproportionately low take-up of loans by Asians. The simple remedy of introducing differential criteria to favour Asian applicants would compensate for but not redeem the discriminatory practice. Consequently, the result is differential access by non-Asians on the basis of area preference and differential access to Asians on the basis of personal loan eligibility.

There is a fairly convincing battery of arguments which suggests that differential access on racial grounds is deeply problematic and, where promotion of equal opportunity can be achieved by other means, alternatives are preferable. But none of the countries examined, including the core states, provide preferential access to employment, education or services based on racial origin. From a legal perspective it would be inaccurate to describe Europe as accommodating positive discrimination, a prerequisite to achieve differential access.

There are a number of examples of legal systems which enable training, language support and education of ethnic minorities, but these are based either implicitly or explicitly on needs such as the lack of language skills or familiarity with domestic employment patterns. Such positive action measures, which are designed to enable fair competition by making people better qualified for employment in particular, do not offend the spirit of equal opportunity; whoever gets the job, the house or the place at university does so on the basis of merit and not simply on racial preference.

Nevertheless there remain problems about defining fair criteria for common standards which can be upheld by the law in the public domain

19. John Rex, *Race and Ethnicity*, Open University Press, Milton Keynes, 1986; and John Edwards, *Positive Discrimination*, Tavistock Publications, London, 1987.

20. *University of California Regents v. Bakke* (1978), 438 US 265.

21. M. MacEwen, *Housing, Race and Law*, Routledge, London, 1991.

which Rex defines as the main political, economic and legal institutions of society.[22] Sociologists have for some time been examining the evolution of the new abstract value systems which a large-scale society requires. Durkheim has suggested that 'organic solidarity' based on the division of labour has replaced 'mechanical solidarity', essentially kinship ties, on which smaller and simpler societies depended.[23] Weber pointed to an increasingly rationalist trend in the Calvinist religion, facilitating the development of political systems based on rational legal authority; modern capitalism, it was argued, was less dependent on kinship and traditional ties, including religion, and more functionalist in the pursuit of wealth and growth facilitating the development of an abstract morality and political and legal systems.[24] Clearly the 'abstract' concept is relative; if it is to imply more than just a flag of convenience – a shedding of responsibility to facilitate the unencumbered pursuit of capitalist endeavours – then it must also imply concessions to the expanding pluralism of the modern state.

Public morality must be reformed and severed from the sectarian interests which shaped its development. Few would contend that this process of reform has been successfully completed in any European state. As an example of the persisting ethnocentricity of the law, and the public morality which underpins it, employment law in the UK enables devout Christians to observe their sabbath but is less accommodating to the Jewish or Moslem faiths. The courts have upheld an education authority's decision to refuse time off work for a Moslem teacher to go to the Mosque for prayers on a Friday afternoon.

If there is a presumption that a 'free' labour market should reflect an irreducible minimum of social rights as a platform for fair competition, then any arbitrary discriminatory practice – including that based on religious grounds – would be unlawful. But beyond that it would be naive to assume that addressing overt discrimination, whether based on race, class, religion or gender, would make a significant impact on real outcomes.[25] In the field of housing Henderson and Karn have demonstrated that it is frequently the implicit value judgments about people's worth, and the interaction between class and race in ascribing value and merit to the individual, that determine outcomes.[26] In their study of Birmingham, the outcome was who got the better housing and in the

22. Rex, *Race and Ethnicity*, p. 122.
23. Emile Durkheim, *The Division of Labour*, The Free Press, Glencoe, 1974.
24. Max Weber, *Economy and Society*, 3 vols, Bedminster Press, New York, 1968.
25. John Rawls, *A Theory of Justice*, Oxford University Press, Oxford and New York, 1972.
26. J. Henderson and V. Karn, *Race, Class and State Housing*, Gower, Aldershot, 1987.

better locations. If there is no such concept as a 'value-free' housing market, then there is ample evidence to support the proposition that the employment market is, if anything, much more obviously flawed and 25 years of anti-discrimination legislation has done little to dent this.[27]

The liberal concept of ability, worth or talent reflects those prejudicial and individualistic values of the old school which merely disguise the fact that a free market predetermines success by defining value in racial, class and gender terms. Because discrimination on the grounds of class is not unlawful, racial and gender bias may be reclassified in terms of class (accent, schooling, associates, family 'type'), either consciously or unconsciously, and the assessment can then be authenticated for public consumption. On that basis the radicals are sceptical of the insistence by liberal reformers' on formal equal access if the practical outcome is to perpetuate discrimination.

The radical approach seeks to interfere directly in order to achieve a fair distribution of rewards on the basis that the absence of a system of fair distribution, defined by either racial or other criteria, is *ipso facto* evidence of unfair discrimination. Because the liberal concept of 'the meritocratic rise of the talented' is characterised as an ideology which legitimises social inequalities and disguises their true determinants,[28] the radicals go on to justify the abandonment not only of traditional meritocracy[29] – a logical conclusion – but, at least on some occasions, any kind of criteria which would be evenly applied to all groups.[30] But as has already been demonstrated, differential access legitimises racial discrimination (albeit compensatory) and may disguise indirect negative discrimination.

The litmus test, it is suggested, is to match a concern for the process in a formal sense (the liberal approach) with an expectation of improved outcomes (the radicals' 'bottom line'). One method of achieving this objective is to re-evaluate access criteria, drawing on the knowledge, skills and experience of local minority groups to establish both performance tests and targets for expected outcomes in the public domain. The definition of equitable criteria cannot be seen as an end in itself. It must be judged by those concerned directly with outcomes, and defined and

27. Braham, Rattansi and Skellington (eds), *Racism and Anti-racism*, Sage and The Open University, Milton Keynes, 1992.

28. See M. Flude, 'Sociological Accounts of Differential Educational Attainment', in M. Flude and J. Ahier (eds), *Educability, Schools and Ideology*, Croom Helem, London, 1976.

29. I. Berg, *Education for Jobs: the Great Train Robbery*, Penguin, Harmondsworth, 1970.

30. Jewson and Mason, 'The Theory and Practices of Equal Opportunity Policies: Liberal and Radical Approaches', in Braham, Rattansi and Skellington (eds), *Racism and Anti-racism*.

redefined by those historically disadvantaged by traditional and contemporary values. It seems, therefore, that the law must not merely provide formal equality of treatment at the individual level (the essence of present concern in all European states), it must also endorse targets of equal opportunity at the group level and impose much more onerous criteria than it does at present. Certainly the extent of persistent discrimination in all countries examined justifies the conclusion that no regime has been successful in effecting a radical improvement in the position of visible minorities. Accordingly, a radical approach to change in the legal framework appears not only justifiable but also an essential element in the promotion of equal opportunities.

There is also a potential problem in defining what constitutes the public domain – to which common standards and criteria will apply – and what constitutes the private domain where visible minorities and indeed all sections of the community may impose their own standards and expectations. If we take a working definition of the public domain as encompassing the law, the market-place (the 'economy') and politics, then legal rights, the workplace (and access to it) and participation in all critical political processes are also included. The Race Relations Act of 1976 includes the provision of goods, services and facilities to the public, and thus ensures that activities such as banking, insurance and shopping (including restaurants and pubs) are considered to be within the public domain. Similarly housing, whether in the local council, voluntary or even private sector, falls within the scope of the Act.

If we consider the three over-riding determinants of life-chances to be opportunities in employment, housing and education, then in seeking to cover the last by means of the imposition of common standards we raise important issues relating to the distinction between the public and the private domain. In truth, however, there was little soul-searching about including education within the scope of the legislation in the UK. But issues raised by and the publicity given to individual cases such as those of Ray Honeyford in Bradford and Maureen McGoldrick in Brent concerning the nature of multi-cultural provision within English schools,[31] together with the concern about parental choice, and its racist motivation, in Cleveland Educational Authority, demonstrate that while direct racial discrimination is clearly within the public domain, the imposition of common standards in the pursuit of equal opportunity is very far from an accepted norm. Moreover, both central and local government are prone to a lack of understanding and resolve about such standards, even regarding what the legislation now appears to impose as a requirement.

---

31. John Solomos, *Race and Racism in Contemporary Britain*, Macmillan, London, 1989.

The Cleveland case showed the willingness of the state to connive in allowing parents to choose their chidren's school on racial grounds, under the dubious catch-all of freedom of access. State and local government expectations of conformity to ethnocentric norms have also been illustrated in France by a series of disputes about the wearing of veils to school, and in the UK by private schools insisting on uniforms which make no concessions to cultural or religious preferences and expectations.

More fundamental issues have been raised regarding the extent to which the state should support religious schools beyond the 4,000 Christian and Jewish voluntary-aided schools in England and Wales, which receive government funds to cover running costs and up to 85 per cent of their capital spending. An application, which was seen as a test case, for funding by the Islamia primary school in Brent was refused by education minister Baroness Blatch in 1993 and the self-styled Muslim Parliament, in referring to the possibility of appeal to the European Court of Human Rights, observed that they should 'go away, organise, radicalise and come back with a strong united voice'.[32]

In Scotland there are both non-denominational and Roman Catholic state schools and in both England and Wales and in Scotland the relevant Education Acts, as recently amended, provide for religious education. The provisions are not prescriptive but there is a clear expectation that the Christian religion will dominate the multi-faith curricula. Religious instruction is no longer a requirement but there are many schools, not ostensibly 'church' schools, which in their assemblies and other gatherings make few if any concessions to non-Christian pupils. Although much needs to be done towards the development of a multi-faith curriculum – and not merely in religious studies – at a structural policy level, governments must determine whether to support only non-denominational state schools, or to provide equitable support to all schools meeting basic educational criteria irrespective of their religious affiliation. There is a strong argument for keeping religion within the private domain, thus permitting private schools alone to provide religious education as part of the approved curriculum, at least so far as that provision promotes any one faith or ideology.

Common Law and the 'Individuation' of Complaints

Lustgarden and Edwards suggest that a major reason for the relative failure of the Race Relations Act of 1976 has been its emergence from and dependence on the English common law tradition in general and in

32. Quoted in 'Muslims to set up national network of Islamic schools', article by Ben Preston in *The Times*, London, Friday 30th August 1993.

particular the problems associated with the categorisation of racial discrimination as a specific statutory 'tort' in particular (presumably this argument would extend to Scotland with its mixed law tradition where discrimination is a 'delict').[33] How law is classified, whether as primary or regulatory, affects its capacity to effect change. It was further contended that when an act is classified as criminal or when its classification has a significant impact on the status of the offender/plaintiff/defender, such as actions concerning divorce or custody, then it will be considered a primary law. Otherwise the law will be regulatory in that it facilitates or enables behaviour by declaring it to be lawful in situations where there is sufficient self-interest to secure promotion of appropriate legal behaviour; tax avoidance legislation is an example. Alternatively, the regulatory character of the law will protect the creation of rights which the weaker party, usually in a piecemeal and individual fashion, will have to assert through litigation in the civil courts.

Although the Commission for Racial Equality is empowered to investigate complaints and to represent individual complainants, British legislation, it is argued, is essentially protective and results in the individuation (or individualising) of actions and remedies which render it ineffective in reducing racial discrimination in a systemic manner. The reason legislation in the USA is more effective, particularly with regard to employment, is that there is a hierarchy of controls with the state and federal courts encouraging constructive adaptation, the courts are generally less hidebound by a narrow common law construction of the legislation and are prepared to ditch unhelpful and marginal precedence, and the concept of indirect discrimination has developed more bite through the power of class actions and the heavier resultant penalties. In the United States, therefore, it has become cheaper and easier to obey the law than be threatened with the real costs of remedying an illegal practice as it affects an entire class of litigants rather than merely having to meet the marginal costs borne by an individual litigant.[34]

It may be true that the 'protective' model of English law has proved ill-fitted to promoting anti-discrimination law but the implication that civilian traditions, reflected in virtually all other European legal systems outside the former Soviet bloc, are better equipped to tackle this problem is not supported by the evidence in this study. Conversely, examination of anti-discrimination provisions in a selection of common law-based

---

33. L. Lustgarden and J. Edwards, 'Racial Inequality and Other Limits of the Law', in Braham, Rattansi and Skellington (eds), *Racism and Anti-racism*.
34. Ibid.

countries, the USA, Canada, Australia and New Zealand,[35] suggests that one of the advantages of the common law tradition is its adaptability, particularly in combining the protective model which is essentially reactive with a proactive model, elements of which are evident in each of the countries examined.

The Way Forward

The difficulties of enforcing reactive anti-discrimination provision, particularly against indirect discrimination, are well documented in earlier chapters. A specific issue relates to information;[36] without statistical evidence both knowledge of and proof about indirect discrimination is unlikely to be evident. In the absence of any legal obligation to keep records, both public and private organisations, as noted previously, have demonstrated their reluctance to keep and publish information which, although capable of showing them to be model employers, providers of housing, education or services, may equally demonstrate their deficiencies in monitoring equal opportunity policies and changing them to ensure that targets are set and met.

The law, however, may be a much more effective tool for equal opportunity promotion than for enforcement, for the very reason that the former necessarily imposes obligations to show some tangible activity which is capable of being identified, recorded, policed and monitored. The requirements of producing corporate reports and programmes on an annual basis (or at some other specified interval of time), illustrated in the experience of both New Zealand and Canada[37] and the various initiatives required of employers in Northern Ireland for affirmative action against religious discrimination under the Fair Employment (Northern Ireland) Act of 1989, have all made significant impacts on day-to-day working practices. While these initiatives are partly uninformed by each others' experience, they owe much to the American experience of Federal Contract Compliance introduced by the Kennedy administration (Executive Order 11246) and later extended in the light of experience

35. Martin MacEwen, Ian McKenna, John Goering, Mai Chen, Meredith Wilkie and Alan Prior, *Report on Anti-discrimination Law on the Grounds of Race; A Comparative Literature Survey of Provisions in Australia, New Zealand, Canada and the USA*, CRE, London, 1994.

36. A factor also identified by Lustgarden and Edwards, 'Racial Inequality and Other Limits of the Law'.

37. MacEwen, McKenna, Goering, Chen, Wilkie and Prior, *Report on Anti-discrimination Law on the Grounds of Race; A Comparative Literature Survey of Provisions in Australia, New Zealand, Canada and the USA.*

(Executive Order 11375).[38]

In Northern Ireland failure to register with the Fair Employment Commission, failure to monitor aspects of employment on the grounds of religion, refusal to meet requests for information or failure to implement specified affirmative action requirements may lead to criminal as well as civil proceedings and the imposition of fines and other economic sanctions upon conviction. It is worth noting that the UK government is content to permit inconsistency between discrimination law in different parts of the country, with Britain outlawing race but not religious discrimination and Northern Ireland doing the reverse. The latter was influenced by the American dollar; the UK government, being threatened with loss of investment if there was no affirmative action against religious discrimination, was as a consequence much more systematic in the framing of the provisions.[39] There is no logic in these distinctions other than that derived from political pragmatism; in part, no doubt, confirming the worst suspicions of the French!

With respect to Great Britain, the statutory codes of guidance issued by the Commission for Racial Equality and approved by the Home Secretary and Parliament by way of negative resolution procedures – essentially permitting debate only when opposed – now cover employment, the original provision, and housing, both the owner-occupied and the rented sector, public, private and voluntary (Housing Associations). However, because there is no statutory obligation to follow the codes, let alone take cognisance of them as in the case of the statutory codes relating to homelessness, the courts have been reluctant to make an adverse inference, or indeed any conclusion, from their evasion.[40] At present, such codes are merely an embryo of statutory positive action programmes in the UK.

In the Netherlands a bill on equal treatment (first introduced in February 1991 and before Parliament at the time of writing) would permit positive discrimination in specific circumstances beyond the employment-related provisions of Article 429 quater of the Criminal Code, which permits minority and migrant organisations to take measures to enhance opportunities for employment.[41] While the National Bureau for Combating Racism (LBR) has no authority to draw up statutory codes of practice, it has drawn up advisory codes in various fields. Following a study into discriminatory practices in commercial employment agencies,

38. R. Osborne and R. Cormack, 'Fair Employment: Towards Reform in Northern Ireland', *Policy and Politics*, 1989, vol. 17, no. 4, pp. 287–294.

39. Lustgarden and Edwards, 'Racial Inequality and Other Limits of the Law'.

40. CRE, *Second Review of the Race Relations Act 1976*, CRE, London, 1992.

41. Roger Zegers de Beijl, *Although Equal Before the Law*, ILO Working Paper, Geneva, 1991.

the LBR drew up a code for such agencies in 1989 after consultation with the Confederation of Commercial Employment Agencies (*Algemene Bond Uitzendondernemingen*, or ABU). This code contains various directives regarding good practice, and the industry may impose its own sanctions for breach. Another code has been drawn up on car insurance in consultation with the Confederation of Car Insurance Companies (NVVA), and a general employment code is under consideration. The National Ombudsman has ruled that positive action programmes, which result in vacancies being open only to applicants from groups which are disadvantaged in the labour market, are not a violation of the principle of non-discrimination in the Constitution.[42]

However such initiatives in the field of employment, reflected in positive employment programmes in France and in various language initiatives in the four core states and in Greece and Denmark, are all enabled rather than required by law. Without a statutory framework, which requires specific action and is effectively maintained, the momentum towards change is likely to be piecemeal and slow. Unless the public sector, driven by the civil service and local authority directives and the use of economic power (principally through contract compliance), exercises a commitment to implement voluntary codes – backed by non-legal sanctions – (and there is no evidence that this has been done in a holistic fashion in any of the states studied), then a statutory framework for positive action programmes is fundamental to effecting a real shift in the life-chances of visible minorities.

Inevitably there is a caveat, and that caveat goes to the heart of the politicisation of racial issues. Governments, as was observed in the opening chapter, are frequently committed to being seen to be doing good and they may even believe in the advantages of positive action. They do not, however, wish to alienate their conservative support which, in the European context, will outnumber the 5 per cent of the voting public which comes from minority groups. Governments have consequently proved reluctant to do more than pay lip-service to the implementation of equal opportunity.

In order both to de-racialise the definition of difficulties and to neutralise the resultant solutions, governments have associated the problems of racial disadvantage with urban deprivation, class and cyclical disadvantage. There remains a fairly uniform lack of enthusiasm on the part of governments to address racial discrimination, to analyse the causes and to make a commitment to explore the value of law in promoting a more equitable and honest society.

---

42. A. C. Possel, *Rechtspraak Rassendiscriminatie 1988–1990*, Zwolle, W. E. J., Tjeenk Willink, 1991.

But all is not doom and gloom; there is a slow process of empowerment of minority groups within Europe, and national governments and the European Union will increasingly be held accountable for their ability or otherwise to ensure safety and equal opportunity for their citizens and denizens alike. There are also parallel movements to promote more effective provision for other disadvantaged groups such as women and the disabled, areas in which the Community has already accepted competence and taken initiatives. The Council of Europe, at its meeting in Vienna in October 1993, agreed an action programme for change which contained the beginnings of a process of target setting and monitoring. The European Union has not yet committed itself to a Directive on anti-discrimination law, but that item is firmly on the agenda.

In Edinburgh in December 1993 the Summary of Findings and Recommendations of an International Symposium on Anti-discrimination Law was published, suggesting that there is a common core of proposals, summarised in the Appendix, which will attract widespread support from a growing network of concerned institutions and individuals throughout Europe. In the spring of 1994 the Churches Commission for Migrants in Europe International Movement against all forms of Discrimination and Racism published a report on the use of international conventions to protect minority rights; this report comprises the papers submitted at a conference in Strasbourg the previous November along with a set of recommendations and conclusions. It was observed that states often undermine the significance of conventions, which are already a political compromise, by making reservations and by not recognising supervisory mechanisms including optional rights for individual complaint. But the potential benefits of the various conventions for minority groups were endorsed, and the European Union was encouraged to pass anti-discrimination legislation and to consider acceding to the ECHR. Accordingly, while the weaknesses of the international conventions are increasingly obvious, there is widespread support for strengthening them rather than jettisoning them; the need for a legal framework for rights at the international level as well as the national level provides a transparent standard against which current practice may be assessed.

But the law is not the only method for establishing such standards. Reebok employs tens of thousands of people around the world making and selling its products and in March 1994 the company announced the Reebok Human Rights Production Standard, built on the work of a task force which consulted the United Nations, human rights organisations and officials at Levi Strauss & Co, a company which had developed similar standards in 1993. It may be optimistic to expect a significant number of multinational conglomerates to follow such initiatives with great alacrity, but there is undoubted pressure on manufacturers from the public to be seen as behaving in an ethical fashion. Cumulatively, the work of non-state bodies (NGOs) including the Churches Council, Amnesty International and the International Commission of Jurists in particular, and of minority organisations and committed individuals will result in new international and national standards being set with respect to anti-discrimination provision. The law is also part of the process by which we measure our commitment to ethics: if we have not abandoned both national and European democracy, then we should, both collectively and individually, insist that equality of opportunity is reflected in the law of the land, the lander and the landless.

Select Bibliography

Ahier, J. and Flude, M., (eds), *Educability, Schools and Ideology,* Croom Helm: London, 1974.

Aikio, P. and Siuruainen, E., *The Laps in Finland,* Society for the Promotion of Lap Culture: Helsinki, 1977.

Anderson, B., *Imagined Communities: Reflections on the Origin and Spread of Nationalism,* Verso: London, 1983.

Baldwin, R. and McCrudden, C., (eds), *Regulation and Public Law,* Weidenfeld and Nicholson: London, 1987.

Banton, M., 'Effective Implementation of the UN Racial Convention', *New Community,* 1994, vol. 20, no. 3.

Beauther, G.-H. *On the Legal Position of Long-stay Migrants in Host Countries,* Council of Europe: Strasbourg, 1991, Report MG-JU (91) 3 revised.

Beddard, R., *Human Rights and Europe,* Sweet and Maxwell: London, 1980, 2nd edition.

Bello, J.G., 'The African Charter on Human and People's Rights', *Hague Recueil,* 194, 1985/6.

Bentham, J., *An Introduction to the Principles and Morals of Legislation,* Hart H.L.A. and Burns J.H., (eds), Athlone Press: London, 1982.

Berg, I., *Education for Jobs: the Great Train Robbery,* Penguin: Harmondsworth, 1970.

Beune, H.H.M. and Hessels, T., *Minorities and Minor Rights: An Inventory of Dutch Acts and Regulations which Distinguish between Citizens and Aliens,* Sraatsuitgeverij: The Hague, 1983, WODC no. 35.

Biddiss, M.D., (ed.) *Images of Race,* Leicester University Press: Leicester, 1979.

Bindman, G., Street, H. and Howe, G., *Report on Anti-discrimination Legislation,* Home Office: London, 1967.

Bindman, G. and Lester, A., *Race and Law,* Penguin Books: Harmondsworth, 1972.

Blauner, R., *Racial Oppression in America,* Harper and Row: New York, 1972.

Boissevain, J. and Grotenbreg, H., 'Culture, Structure and Ethnic enterprise: the Surinamese of Amsterdam' in *Lost Illusions,* Cross M., and Entzinger M., (eds), Routledge: London, 1988.

Bosely, S., 'Foreign Bodies', *The Guardian*, 18 November 1987.

Bradley, A.W., *Wade and Phillips: Constitutional and Administrative Law*, Longman: London, 1977, 9th edition.

Braham, P., Rattansi, A. and Skellington, R. (eds), *Racism and Anti-racism*, Sage and The Open University: Milton Keynes, 1992.

Brandt, W., *North-South; A programme for survival: the report of the Independent Commission on International Development Issues* , Pan Books: London and Sydney, 1980.

Bridge, J. and W. and Lasok, D., *The Introduction to the Law and Institutions of the European Communities*, Butterworths: London, 1982, 3rd edition.

Brocker, A., 'A pyramid of complaints: the handling of complaints about racial discrimination in the Netherlands', *New Community*, Commission for Racial Equality: London, 1991, vol. 17, no. 4.

Brown, C., *Black and White Britain*, Policy Studies Institute/Heinemann: London, 1984.

Brown, C. and Gay, P., *Racial Discrimination: Seventeen Years after the Act*, Policies Studies Institute: London, 1985, Paper no. 646.

Brown, C., Knox, J., McCrudden, C. and Smith, D.J., *Racial Justice at Work-the Enforcement of the Race Relations Act 1976 in Employment*, Policy Studies Institute: London, 1991.

Brownlie, I., (ed.) *Basic Documents on Human Rights*, Clarendon Press: Oxford, 1992, 3rd edition.

Buergenthal, T., Norris R. and Shelton D., *Protecting Human Rights in the Americas*, Engel: Kehl-am-Rhein, 1990.

Bunyan, T., *Statewatching the New Europe*, Statewatch: London, 1993.

Capotorti, F., Study of the Rights of Persons belonging to Ethnic, Religious and Linguistic Minorities', referred to in P. Thornberry, *International Law and the Rights of Minorities*, Clarendon Press, London, 1991.

Carr, M., 'Spain: Racism at the frontier', *Race and Class*, Institute of Race Relations, London, 1991, January/March, vol. 32, no. 3, 93–97.

Cashmore, E and Troyna, B., *Introduction to Race Relations*, The Farmer Press: Basingstoke, 1990, 2nd edition.

Cator, J. and Niessen, J. (eds), *The use of international conventions to protect the rights of migrants and ethnic minorities*, The Churches Commission for Migrants in Europe: Strasbourg, 1994.

Commission for Racial Equality, *Report of Formal Investigation into the Immigration and Nationality Department of the Home Office*, CRE Publications: London, 1985.

Commission for Racial Equality, *Second Review of the Race Relations Act 1976*, CRE Publications: London, 1992.

Cormack, R. and Osborne, R., 'Fair Employment: Towards Reform in Northern Ireland', *Policy and Politics,* School for Advanced Urban Studies: Bristol, 1989, vol. 17, no. 4.

Costa-Lascoux, J. 'Report on Racial Discrimination and the Law in EEC Countries', Runnymede Trust Report, Dummett A., (ed.), for the Social Affairs Commission of the European Economic Community, unpublished, 1986.

Costa-Lascoux, J., *Anti-discrimination in Belgium, France and The Netherlands*, report prepared for the Committee of Experts on Community Relations, Council of Europe: Strasbourg, 1990, (MG-CR).

Council of Europe, *Community and Ethnic Relaltions in Europe: Final Report of the Community Relations Project of the Council of Europe*, Council of Europe: Strasbourg, 1991, MG-CR (91)1 final E.

Cross, M. and Entzinger, H., (eds), *Lost Illusions: Caribbean Minorities in Britain and the Netherlands*, Routledge: London, 1988.

Cruz, A., *An Insight into Shengen, Trevi and other European Inter-governmental Bodies*, Churches Committee on Migrants in Europe: Brussels, 1990, CCMG, Briefing Paper no. 1.

Cruz, A., *Community Competence over Third Country Nationals residing in an EC Member State*, Brussels, 1991, CCME Briefing Paper no. 5.

Cruz, A., (ed.), *Migration News Sheet*, monthly journal of the European Information Network: Brussels, CCME, vol. 117–93, no. 1.

Danish Draft Report, 'Comparative Assessment of Legal Instruments Implemented in the various member states of the European Community to Combat all Forms of Discrimination, racism, Xenophobia and Incitement to Hatred and Racial Violence', unpublished, Danish Centre for Human Rights: Copenhagen, 1992.

Davidson, S., *Human Rights*, Open University Press: Buckingham, 1993.

De Rudder, V., 'De Versovie a Barbes-et si le ghetto n'existait pas?', *Differences*: Paris, vol. 90, no. 12.

Dhavan, R., 'Why are there so few cases? on the uses and non-uses of the Race Relations Act 1976', unpublished report submitted to the CRE: London, 1988.

Dias, R.M.W., *Jurisprudence*, Butterworths: London, 1970, 3rd edition.

Dummett, A. and Nicol, A., *Subjects, Citizens, Aliens and Others: Nationality and Immigration Law*, Weidenfeld and Nicolson: London, 1990.

Dummett, A., 'The Starting Line: A proposal for a draft Council Directive concerning the elimination of racial discrimination', *New Community*, CRE: London, 1994, vol. 20, no. 3.

Dummett, A., 'Objectives for Future European Policy' in *Strangers and Citizens*, Spencer S., (ed.), IPPR/ Rivers Oram Press: London, 1994.

Durkheim, E., *The Division of Labour,* The Free Press: Glencoe, 1974.

Dworkin, R., *Taking Rights Seriously*, Duckworth: London, 1971.

Edwards, J., *Positive Discrimination*, Tavistock Publications: London, 1987.

Edwards, J. and Lustgarden, L. 'Racial Inequality and other limits of the law', in *Racism and Anti-racism,* Braham, N. Rattansi, A. and Skellington, R. (eds), Sage and The Open University: Milton Keynes, 1992.

European Commission Report, *The European Community's relations to French Overseas Departments, European Autonomous regions, overseas countries and territories and independent countries within EEC boundaries*, European Commission: London, 1992, no. ISEC/ B33/92,

Fanon, F., *The Wretched of the Earth*, MacGibbon and Kee: London, 1965.

Flynn, J.R., *Race, IQ and Jensen*, Routledge and Kegan Paul: London, Boston and Henley, 1980.

Forbes, D., *Action on Racial Harassment: Legal Remedies and Local Authorities*, Legal Action Group and London Housing Unit: London, 1988.

Forbes, I. and Mead, G., *'Measure for Measure: A Comparative Analysis of Measures to Combat Racial Discrimination in the Member States of the European Community'*, Equal Opportunities Study Group, University of Southampton/Department of Employment: Sheffield, 1992.

Ford, G., *Report of the Committee of Inquiry into Racism and Xenophobia*, Office for Official Publications of the European Communities: Luxembourg, 1991.

Gaffney, J., *Interpretation of Violence: the Handsworth Riots of 1985,* CRER, University of Warwick: Coventry, 1987.

Gay, P. and Young, K., *Community Relations Councils: Roles and Objectives*, Policy Studies Institute in association with the Commission for Racial Equality: London, 1988.

Gomien, D. 'The Rights of Minorities under the European Convention on Human Rights and the European Charter on Regional and Minority Languages', in *The use of international conventions to protect the rights of migrants and ethnic minorities,* Cator, J. and Niessen, J., (eds), The Churches Commission for Migrants in Europe: Strasbourg, 1993.

Grant, J.P., *Independence and Devolution*, W. Green & Son Ltd: Edinburgh, 1976.

Green, A. and Sharp R., *Education and Social Control,* Routledge: London, 1976.

Greenberg, J., *Race Relations and American Law*, Columbia University Press: New York, 1959.

Guild, E., *Protecting Migrants Rights: application of EC Agreements with Third Countries*, Churches Committee for Migrants in Europe: Brussels, 1992, Briefing Paper no. 10.

Gulmann, C., 'Denmark', in *The Effect of Treaties in Domestic Law*, Jacobs, F.G. and Roberts, S., (eds), Sweet and Maxwell: London, 1987, vol. 7.

Hamlin, A., 'Complex Ruminations on the Simplest of Ideas', *The Times Higher Educational Supplement*: London, 1992, vol. 30, no. 10.

Hammer, T., *European Immigration Policy: A Comparative Study*, Cambridge University Press: Cambridge, 1985.

Hart, H.L.A., *The Concept of Law*, Clarendon Press: Oxford, 1971.

Henderson, J. and Karn, V., *Race, Class and State Housing,* Gower: Aldershot, 1987.

Herlitz, M., *Elements of Nordic Public Law*, P.A. Norstedt and Soners Forlag: Stockholm, 1969.

Hessels, T., 'Racial Discrimination in The Netherlands', Landelijk Bureau Racismebestrijding: Amsterdam, Dummett A. (ed.), 'Report on Racial Discrimination and the Law in EEC Countries', Runnymede Trust Report for the Social Affairs Commission of the European Economic Community, unpublished, 1986.

Home Office, *Racial Discrimination*, HMSO: London, 1975, Cmnd 6234.

Home Office, *Urban Deprivation, Racial Inequality and Social Policy,* HMSO: London, 1976.

House of Commons, *First Report for the Home Affairs Committee Session 1981–82 Commission for Racial Equality*, HMSO: London, Report of the Minutes of Proceedings HC46-1, vol. 1.

Huber, K.J., 'The CSCE and Minorities', in *The use of international conventions to protect the rights of migrants and ethnic minorities*, Cator, J. and Niessen, J., (eds), The Churches Commission for Migrants in Europe: Strasbourg, 1994.

Hume, D. (ed.), McNabb, D.G.C., *'A Treatise on Human Nature'*, Fontana Collins: London, 1970.

Hune, S., 'Equality of Treatment and the International Convention on the Protection of the Rights of All Migrant Workers and Members of Their Families', in *The use of international conventions to protect the rights of migrants and ethnic minorities*, Cator, J. and Niessen, J. (eds), The Churches Commission for Migrants in Europe: Strasbourg, 1994.

ICERD, *The British Twelfth Periodic Report to the Committee for the Elimination of Racial Discrimination*, United Nations Centre for Human Rights: Geneva, 1992.

ICERD, *Twelfth German Periodic Report to the Committee for the Elimination of Racial Discrimination*, United Nations Centre for Human Rights: Geneva, 1993.

International Labour Organisation, *Equality in Employment and Occupation*, Report of Committee of Experts, ILO: Geneva, 1988.

Jacobs, F.G., *The European Convention on Human Rights*, Oxford University Press: Oxford, 1979.

Jacobs, F.G. and Roberts, S., (eds), *The Effect of Treaties in Domestic Law*, Sweet and Maxwell: London, 1987, vol. 7.

Jenks, C.W., *Human Rights and International Labour Standards*, Stevens: London, 1960.

Johnson, N., *In Search of the Constitution*, Pergammon Press: Oxford, 1977.

Kartaram, S., 'Final Report on Legislation in the Netherlands Against Racism and Xenophobia', unpublished submission on behalf of Landelijk Bureau Racismebestrijding, Amsterdam to Directorate General for Work, Labour Relations and Social Affairs, European Commission: Brussels, 1992.

Katznelson, I., *Black Men, White Cities: Race, Politics and Migration in the United States 1900–30 and Britain 1948–68,* Oxford University Press: London, 1973.

Kellas, J., *The Politics of Nationalism and Ethnicity*, Macmillan: London, 1991.

Larson, A., 'The New Law of Race Relations', *Wisconsin Law Review*, University of Wisconsin: Wisconsin, 1969, vol. 1969, no. 2, 470–524.

Layton-Henry, Z., and Wilpert, C. (eds), *Discrimination, racism and citizenship: inclusion and exclusion in Britain and Germany*, The Anglo-German Foundation: London, 1994.

Lerner, N., *The International Convention on the Elimination of All Forms of Racial Discrimination*, Alphen Ann Den Rijn, Sijthoff and Noordhoff: Holland, 1980, 2nd edition.

Lillich, R., *The Human Rights of Aliens in Contemporary International Law*, Manchester University Press: Manchester, 1984.

Lloyd, C., 'Concepts, Models and Anti-racist Strategies in Britain and France', *New Community*, Commission for Racial Equality: London, 1991, vol. 18, no. 1.

MacEwen, M., *Racial Harassment, Council Housing and the Law*, SEMRU, Edinburgh College of Art/Heriot-Watt University School of Planning & Housing: Edinburgh, 1986, Research Paper no. 11.

MacEwen, M., Miller, K., McKenna, I. and White, R., (eds), *Race Discrimination Law Reports*, Commission for Racial Equality, 1990, vol. 1.

MacEwen, M., *Housing, Race and Law*, Routledge: London, 1991.

MacEwen, M. and Prior, A., *Planning and Ethnic Minority Settlement in Europe: The Myth of Thresholds of Tolerance,* SEMRU, Edinburgh College of Art/Heriot-Watt University School of Planning & Housing:

Edinburgh, 1992, Research Paper no. 40.

MacEwen, M., (ed.), *A Comparative Literature Survey of provisions in Australia, New Zealand Canada and the USA: Report on Anti-discrimination Law on the Grounds of Race*, Scottish Ethnic Minorities Research Unit (SEMRU) and Commission for Racial Equality: Edinburgh, 1994.

Mason, D. and Jewson, N., 'The Theory and Practices of Equal Opportunity Policies: Liberal and Radical Approaches', in *Racism and Anti-racism*, Braham, P., Rattansi, A. and Skellington, R., (eds), Sage and The Open University: Milton Keynes, 1992.

McCrone, D., *Understanding Scotland: The Sociology of a Nation*, Routledge: London, 1992.

McCrudden, C., 'The Commission for Racial Equality: Formal Investigations in the Shadow of Judicial Review', in *Regulation and Public Law*, Baldwin, R. and McCrudden, C., (eds), Weidenfeld and Nicholson: London, 1987.

McKean, W., *Equality and Discrimination Under International Law*, Clarendon Press: Oxford, 1983.

McKenna, I., 'Anti-discrimination Law on the Grounds of Race: Canadian Case study', in *A comparative Literature Survey of Provisions in Australia, New Zealand Canada and the USA: Report on Anti-discrimination Law on the Grounds of Race*, MacEwen, M., (ed.), Scottish Ethnic Minorities Research Unit (SEMRU) and Commission for Racial Equality: Edinburgh, 1994.

Mead, G. and Forbes, I., *Measure for Measure: A Comparative Analysis of Measures to Combat Racial Discrimination in the Member States of the European Community*, Equal Opportunities Study Group, University of Southampton/Department of Employment: Sheffield, 1992.

Mehrlander, U., 'The Development of Post-War Migration and Refugee Policy', *Strangers and Citizens*, Spencer, S. (ed.), IPPR/Rivers Oram Press: London, 1994.

Modood, T., 'The Indian Economic Success: A Challenge to Some Race Relations Assumptions', *Policy and Politics*, School for Advanced Urban Studies: Bristol, 1991, vol. 19, no. 3.

Niessen, J. and De Latour, de L., 'Equality of Treatment: the European Social Charter and the European Convention on the Legal status of Migrant Workers', in *The use of international conventions to protect the rights of migrants and ethnic minorities*, Cator, J. and Niessen, J. (eds), The Churches Commission for Migrants in Europe: Strasbourg, 1994.

Nozick, R., *Anarchy, State and Utopia*, Basic Books: New York, 1974.

O'Connor, T. and Quraishy, B. 'Denmark: No Racism by Definition',

Europe Variations on a Theme of Racism, Institute of Race Relations: London, vol. 32, no. 3.

Oakley, R., *Racial Violence and Harassment in Europe*, Council of Europe: Strasbourg, 1992, (MG-CR [91] 3 rev.2).

Offermann, (ed.) *Immigration Policy and the Right of Asylum in the Member States of the European Community*, European Parliament Directorate General for Research: Brussels, 1992, Working Papers W3.

Osborne, R., and Cormack, R., 'Fair Employment: Towards Reform in Northern Ireland' *Policy and Politics,* School for Advanced Urban Studies: Bristol, 1989, vol. 17, no. 4.

Owen, D., *The Changing Spatial Distribution of Ethnic Minorities in Britain, 1981–91*, Centre for Research in Ethnic Relations, University of Warwick: Coventry, 1993.

Pareto, W., *The Mind and Society – A Treatise on Sociology* , Dover Books: London, 1963.

Plender, R. (1985), 'Human Rights of Aliens in Europe' in the *Council of Europe Directorate of Human Rights in Europe*, Martinus Nijhoff: The Hague, 1985.

Possel, A.C., *Rechtspraak Rassendiscriminatie 1988–1990*, Zwolle, W.E.J.; Tjeenk Willink: 1991.

Ramcharan, B.G., 'Equality and Non-discrimination', in *The International Bill of Rights: the Covenant on Civil and Political Rights,* Henkin, L. (ed.), Columbia University Press: New York, 1981.

Rawls, J., *A Theory of Justice*, Oxford University Press: London, 1972.

Read, M. and Simpson, A., *Against the Rising Tide*, Spokesman Publications: Nottingham, 1991.

Rex, J., *Race and Ethnicity*, Open University Press: Milton Keynes, 1986.

Roberts, S. and Jacobs, F.G. (eds), *The Effect of Treaties in Domestic Law*, Sweet and Maxwell: London, 1987, vol. 7.

Robertson, A.H., *Human Rights in Europe*, Oceania: Manchester, 1963.

Robinson, J., *International Protection of Minorities: a Global View*, Israel Yearbook on Human Rights, Tel Aviv University: Tel Aviv, 1989, vol. 19.

Rodrigues, P. 'Racial discrimination and the law in the Netherlands', *New Community*, Commission for Racial Equality, 1994, vol. 20, no. 3.

Schwelb, E., 'The International Convention on the Elimination of all Forms of Racial Discrimination', *International and Comparative Law Quarterly*, 1966, vol. 15.

Sen, A. *Inequality Re-examined*, Clarendon Press: Oxford, 1992.

Smith, A.D., *The Ethnic Origins of Nations*, Blackwell: London, 1988.

Social Planning and Research, *Ethnic Minorities in Scotland*, The Scottish Office: Edinburgh, 1989.

Solomos, J., *Race and Racism in Contemporary Britain*, Macmillan: London, 1989.

Haralambos (ed.) *Sociology: New Directions*, Causeway Books, Lancashire, 1985.

Spencer, S., (ed.), *Strangers and Citizens*, IPPR/Rivers Oram Press: London, 1994.

Stewart P. and Whitting, G., *Ethnic Minorities and the Urban Programme*, SAUS, Bristol University: Bristol, 1983.

Thornberry, P., *International Law and the Rights of Minorities*, Clarendon Press: Oxford 1991.

Thornberry, P., *Minorities and Human Rights Law*, The Minorities Rights Group: London, 1991.

United Nations, *Report of the Committee on the Elimination of Racial Discrimination*, 22 September 1992, 47th Session Supplement no.18, General Assembly, A/47/18.

United Nations, *Study of Discrimination in Education*, Special Rapporteur Ammoun, UN Doc E/CN.4/Sub.2/181/Rev.1.

Vasak, K., 'A Thirty-Year Struggle', *UNESCO Courier*, United Nations: Geneva, 1977.

Verdoodt, A., 'Ethnic and Linguistic Minorities and the United Nations', *World Justice*, 1969, vol. 11, no. 66.

Weber, M., *Economy and Society,* Bedminster Press: New York, 1968.

Wheare, K.C., *Modern Constitutions*, Oxford University Press: Oxford, 1966, 2nd edition.

Wilkie, M., 'Discrimination in Denmark', *Nordic Journal of International Law,* The Danish Centre for Human Rights: Copenhagen, 1990, vol. 59.

Wilkie, M., 'Multiculturalism and Anti-discrimination Law in Australia', *New Community,* CRE: London, 1994, vol. 20, no. 3, 437–53.

Zegers de Beijl, R., *Although Equal Before the Law . . .*, ILO Working Paper, ILO Office: Geneva, 1991.

Name Index

Index

Index

Spencer, S. 7, 69, 145, 146
St. John, M. 104
Stewart, P. 26
Street, H. 186

Tannam, M. 102
Thatcher, M. 34
Thornberry, P. 31, 48, 49, 50, 53, 54, 56, 59, 60, 63
Tito, J.B. 107
Toubon, J. 34–5
Troyna, B. 17

Vasak, K. 37
Verdoodt, A. 59

Wallraff, G. 147
Weber, M. 191
Werth, M 106, 108
Wheare, K.C. 161, 162
White, R. 90
Whitting, G. 26
Wilkie, M. 39, 55, 90, 93, 96, 100, 179, 188, 196
Wilpert, C. 148

Young, K. 165

Zegers de Beijl, R. 135, 197
Zesco, Mr 90
Zwamborn, M. 102, 106

Subject Index

Index

Index

AMPARO MORENO SARDÀ
FLORENCIA ROVETTO GONEM
ALFONSO BUITRAGO LONDOÑO

¿DE QUIÉN HABLAN LAS NOTICIAS?

GUÍA PARA HUMANIZAR LA INFORMACIÓN

Icaria Ακαδημεια
SOCIEDAD Y OPINIÓN

La presente obra ha sido editada con subvención del Insituto de la Mujer (Ministerio de Trabajo y Asuntos Sociales):

Diseño de la cubierta: Josep Bagà
Ilustración de la cubierta: Adriana Fàbregas

© Amparo Moreno Sardà, Florencia Rovetto Gonem y Alfonso Buitrago Londoño

© De esta edición
Icaria editorial, s. a.
Arc de Sant Cristòfol, 11-23
08003 Barcelona
www. icariaeditorial. com

ISBN: 978-84-7426-955-0
Depósito legal: B-49.135-2007

Primera edición: noviembre de 2007

Fotocomposición: Text Gràfic

Impreso en Romanyà/Valls, s. a.
Verdaguer, 1, Capellades (Barcelona)

Todos los libros de esta colección están impresos sobre papel reciclado.
Printed in Spain. Impreso en España. Prohibida la reproducción total o parcial.

A las compañeras y compañeros que desde la academia se han involucrado para contribuir a humanizar la información. A las y los periodistas, que día a día nos proveen de material para hacer inteligible el mundo que nos rodea.

ÍNDICE

ÍNDICE DE TABLAS

Internet ha devuelto la voz a millones de seres humanos que hasta ahora sólo tenían ojos...

A los medios de comunicación tradicionales no les queda más remedio que investigar seriamente este aspecto crucial de la nueva era en vez de tratar de atrincherarse en las posiciones conquistadas hasta ahora y en hacer valer un prestigio como «diseminadores profesionales de información» que, previsiblemente a medio plazo, será cuestionado por la diversidad y multiplicidad de medios en la Red.

Ahora tienen la oportunidad de actuar a partir de la propia dinámica que genera la nueva infoestructura y la variedad de recursos que pueden desplegar en esa dirección.

Porque si a lo máximo que llegan es a trasladar a la Red sus actuales contenidos —y hábitos de elaborarlos—, no hace falta ser un profeta para augurar los problemas que deberán afrontar.

Luis Ángel FERNÁNDEZ-HERMANA, *Los monasterios del siglo XXI*, Revista En.red.ando, 23-I-1996

I. PRESENTACIÓN*
¿POR QUÉ ES NECESARIO HOY HUMANIZAR LA INFORMACIÓN?

Amparo Moreno Sardà**

A lo largo del siglo XX, especialmente en las últimas décadas, se han producido cambios decisivos en las sociedades democráticas. Por una parte, se ha modificado la consideración de las personas a las que se reconoce los derechos políticos, que pueden ser electores o que pueden concurrir a las elecciones para acceder a diferentes cargos públicos. El derecho de voto, restringido primero a los *pater familiae* que disponían de patrimonios (sufragio censitario), se ha ido extendiendo a todos los hombres y mujeres de edades cada vez más jóvenes (sufragio universal).

Ahora bien, la intensificación de los procesos de globalización han favorecido las movilidades de numerosos colectivos por toda la Tierra y ha generado unas sociedades en las que hoy convivimos mujeres y hombres de una gran diversidad de procedencias y situaciones personales y sociales. Estos cambios obligan a revisar el concepto de *ciudadano*, que inicialmente se refería sólo a los varones adultos acomodados y que se suele utilizar como genérico del conjunto de ciudadanas y ciudadanos, y a adecuar el lenguaje a las nuevas realidades sociales: es necesario hablar de una *ciudadanía plural*, término que expresa mejor la gran variedad de situaciones de mujeres y hombres que componen las sociedades actuales.

---

* Las investigaciones de base para la elaboración de esta Guía han sido financiadas por el Instituto de la Mujer (Ministerio de Trabajo y Asuntos Sociales), y el Institut Català de les Dones (Generalitat de Catalunya).

** Catedrática de Historia de la Comunicación. Departamento de Periodismo y Ciencias de la Comunicación. Universidad Autónoma de Barcelona

Estas transformaciones en las relaciones sociales y políticas han repercutido en las instituciones democráticas y en las formas de gestión del poder político que ya no se dirime sólo en las altas esferas de los Estados nacionales, como sucedía con las burguesías decimonónicas que impulsaron las democracias censitarias, sino también en instancias supraestatales que se han constituido desde principios del siglo XX paralelamente a las democracias de masas.

Esta situación conduce a que las decisiones que afectan a las personas de forma individual y colectiva ya no dependan sólo de los representantes políticos en el marco de los Estados, sino de otras personas que acceden a los puestos de poder por su formación técnica, su posición económica u otras razones. Quizás por eso cada día se advierte más la necesidad de fortalecer el papel de las instituciones más próximas, locales y supralocales. Y es en estas relaciones de proximidad donde se plantea el reto de ampliar los derechos políticos a la *ciudadanía plural*, primer paso para profundizar y adecuar el sistema democrático a las nuevas realidades sociales.

Ciertamente, si tenemos en cuenta el papel de los medios de comunicación en las sociedades democráticas, como instrumentos que han de proporcionar día a día conocimientos significativos con los que la ciudadanía pueda fiscalizar las decisiones de sus representantes políticos, podemos pensar que estos cambios sociales e institucionales se han de poner de manifiesto de forma clara en las informaciones. Un ejemplo: el acceso de las mujeres a los espacios públicos y a los escenarios del poder político, económico, cultural..., de los que hasta no hace mucho estábamos excluidas, tendría que traducirse en una mayor presencia también en la prensa llamada *de información general* y restantes medios de comunicación que dan cuenta de los debates y actuaciones públicos.

Sin embargo, la lectura atenta de la prensa, intentando detectar cómo da cuenta día a día de los cambios y también de las pervivencias, nos dice que esto no es así. La representación de la realidad social en los diarios parece impermeable a las situaciones sociales más decisivas para la vida cotidiana de las personas, si bien es cierto que no todos los medios de comunicación, ni todas las secciones de los periódicos, ni por supuesto todos los periodistas ponen de manifiesto la misma miopía ante los cambios que las mujeres hemos protagonizado en los últimos cien años.

14

Una mirada rápida a las portadas que se ofrecen en cualquier kiosco permite advertir que, curiosamente, la prensa considerada *seria*, la que centra su atención en los escenarios públicos en los que se dirimen los problemas y las posibilidades de la democracia y en los personajes que detentan los poderes políticos, económicos y culturales, es más impermeable y manifiesta mayor resistencia a dar cuenta de las aportaciones que hemos hecho y hacemos las mujeres; mientras que la prensa *del corazón* o la prensa *femenina* y en general la prensa considerada *frívola*, así como la publicidad comercial, sí que dan cuenta al menos de la mayor presencia de las mujeres en más y más espacios sociales, realizando nuevas actuaciones y comportamientos, aunque a menudo lo hace porque las considera no tanto como ciudadanas sino como consumidoras.

Es probable que todo esto no sea ajeno al hecho de que la prensa *seria* sólo despierte el interés de unas minorías, y parece haber llegado al tope de su difusión, mientras otras publicaciones consideradas *frívolas* llegan a las mayorías y amplían sus mercados. En cualquier caso, la falta de reconocimiento de las aportaciones de las mujeres falsea la realidad y pone en cuestión la *objetividad* que se atribuye a la prensa *seria*. Además, supone un déficit para la democracia ya que dificulta que la mayoría de las personas se puedan identificar como sujetos políticos activos y puedan ejercer plenamente los derechos y deberes que les son reconocidos por las leyes.

Con el objetivo de probar la validez de estas sospechas y comprender por qué se produce esta falta de adecuación de la información respecto a los cambios sociales, y también con la intención de encontrar soluciones, hemos realizado en los últimos años diversas investigaciones que nos han servido de base para elaborar esta *Guía para humanizar la información*.

Las investigaciones se han centrado en distintos tipos de periódicos publicados en España o en algunos países de América Latina desde mediados del siglo XX.[1] En todos los casos hemos partido

---

1. Esta *Guía* es el resultado de un largo y provechoso trabajo de equipo en el que han colaborado diversas personas, desde hace más de tres décadas. Los primeros problemas surgieron cuando nos propusimos comprender el papel de la prensa de sucesos, evitando incurrir en los prejuicios clasistas habituales en el mundo académico en relación a los medios de comunicación de mayor audiencia. Opté por aplicar el

de la pregunta que sirve de título a esta Guía: *¿De quién hablan las noticias?* Esto es: ¿qué mujeres y qué hombres de distintas edades, procedencias y condiciones personales y sociales son considerados como protagonistas de las noticias? Esta pregunta básica sobre la información comporta otra de carácter político: ¿qué mujeres y qué hombres pueden reconocerse en la prensa como sujetos agentes y partícipes de la democracia?

Para responder a estas preguntas hemos desarrollado una metodología minuciosa, compleja y muy laboriosa,[2] de la que presentamos en esta *Guía para humanizar la información* una versión sencilla y fácil de utilizar por cualquier persona interesada en la prensa, como

---

análisis hemerográfico que había desarrollado Jacques Kayser, y me planteé informatizar el tratamiento de los datos, procedimiento que exige clarificar con precisión las categorías con las que se registra y organiza la información para su tratamiento.

En el verano de 1981 formulé la hipótesis de que las dificultades para comprender la cultura de masas estaban enraizadas en el orden androcéntrico del discurso académico. Pude validarla en la Tesis Doctoral que defendí en la Facultad de Geografía e Historia de la Universidad de Barcelona (1984).

Esta crítica al androcentrismo fue aplicada al análisis de la prensa en diferentes trabajos, a partir de mediados de los 80. Los cursos de doctorado del Departamento de Periodismo de la UAB han permitido realizar diversas Tesis de Licenciatura, Tesis de Doctorado e investigaciones que han contribuido a clarificar la metodología que se propone en esta Guía.

Hay que destacar el proyecto I+D+I sobre *La representación de las relaciones entre mujeres y hombres y del recambio generacional en la prensa, de 1974 a 2004*, financiado por el Instituto de la Mujer (2001-2004), realizado por un equipo formado por Amparo Moreno Sardà, directora (UAB), Natividad Abril (UPV), Isabel Alonso, Manel López (UAB) y las becarias de investigación Patricia Gomez, Gloria Quinayás, Nuria Simelio y M. Soledad Vargas.

Esta investigación se completó con el trabajo que elaboraron para la asignatura del curso de doctorado: Elvira Barreto, Alfonso Buitrago, J. Edson Moreira y Florencia Rovetto Gonem (2004), *Ejercicio de lectura crítica no-androcéntrica de cuatro ejemplares de la revista Lecturas (1974, 1984, 1994 y 2004).*

A partir del año 2004 hemos realizado talleres en los que se ha experimentado la metodología de análisis de la información tal como se expone en esta Guía, gracias al apoyo del Institut Català de les Dones y del Instituto de la Mujer.

La información sobre la trayectoria del Feminario Mujer y Cultura de Masas de la UAB (Feminari Dones i Cultura de Masses), y sobre otras aportaciones feministas al análisis de los medios de comunicación pueden consultarse en: https://masters.oaid.uab.es/feminari - http://antalya.uab.es/mhmc.

2. Metodología de análisis hemerográfico diacrónico automático, en MORENO SARDÀ, A. (1998), *La mirada informativa,* Barcelona: Bosch.

7090002
161
269550

LA INFORMACION.

son Ref 4479492-012

AST

Supplier   Daws(
Order Date   11/1(
Quantity   2
Unit Price   18.0(
Instructions £2X

Author   MORE
Title   DE Q

Volume
Format
Shelf Mark
Site   3MAI
Fund   SPAB
Sequence
Loan Type   7DAY
Quantity   2

profesional o lectora: el *Test* para la evaluación de la *Amplitud,* la *Diversidad* y la *Sensibilidad Humana* de la *mirada informativa,* o *Test ADSH.*

La principal dificultad estriba en que obliga a leer y releer atentamente las noticias con un ritmo muy distinto del habitual, más sosegado que el que seguimos cuando consumimos las informaciones cotidianamente. Sólo así podemos evitar conclusiones precipitadas que responden más a nuestros hábitos de pensamiento que a lo que está en los ejemplares, y clarificar quién o quiénes aparecen realmente como protagonistas de las noticias, a quién o quiénes se enfoca y se considera realmente sujetos de los verbos que expresan las acciones que se representan como noticiables, y qué tratamiento reciben.

Los resultados de las investigaciones que hemos realizado sobre prensa *de información general* pueden parecer evidentes para cualquier persona habituada a la lectura de diarios: las mujeres apenas aparecen como protagonistas de los hechos que se consideran noticiables; su presencia en la prensa no se ha incrementado proporcionalmente a su incorporación a los escenarios públicos, económicos, políticos, culturales…; cuando aparecen, suelen ser representadas como víctimas pasivas y pacientes, en situaciones anecdóticas o como objeto de ironía. Por tanto, podemos concluir que la prensa resulta impermeable a los cambios sociales que las mujeres protagonizamos.

Ahora bien, que sea así no significa que no pueda ser de otro modo y que no tengamos que trabajar para que la información se ajuste más a la realidad y aporte luz sobre el conjunto diverso de la sociedad. Ciertamente, la presencia de las mujeres en las noticias sólo adquiere pleno significado cuando se relacionan con la atención que reciben los hombres, y se aborda la representación de mujeres y hombres en el conjunto del periódico. Porque el problema no se puede situar en las mujeres y considerarlas víctimas una vez más, ahora de la prensa. Tampoco se puede reducir a una cuestión de *género*: no todos los hombres son considerados protagonistas y sujetos agentes de las noticias, ya que la mayoría de hombres corren una suerte similar a la de las mujeres.

De hecho, la prensa también se muestra impermeable a las actuaciones de los numerosos y diversos colectivos de mujeres y hombres de distintas edades, procedencias y condiciones personales y sociales, que constituyen hoy la *ciudadanía plural*: su presencia en la prensa no se ha incrementado proporcionalmente a los cambios sociales que provocan con sus decisiones de movilidad, y al igual que las mujeres y las criaturas no adultas, también la mayoría de los hombres suelen ser representados como víctimas en situaciones dramáticas. En fin, la mayor presencia de las mujeres en los diarios, en los últimos años… se registra en las páginas de anuncios breves de contactos y relax, para algunos periódicos la principal fuente de ingresos.

Para comprender por qué quienes elaboran las noticias parecen refractarios a dar cuenta de las transformaciones sociales promovidas por las mujeres y la mayoría de hombres, hay que centrar la atención en la otra cara del problema: la prensa considerada *seria*, al igual que los textos académicos y políticos, hablan poco de la mayoría de mujeres y hombres porque centran su atención en unas minorías de varones adultos que constituyen los colectivos que ejercen el poder en los escenarios centrales, políticos, económicos y culturales.

Pero además, las actuaciones de estos varones son valoradas como actos noticiables positivos, capaces de influir en toda la sociedad con una aureola de superioridad a pesar de que a menudo, y según son enfocados por la prensa, incrementan los conflictos en lugar de hacer aportaciones para solucionarlos. Los periódicos se convierten así, en los escenarios de debates o disputas entre grupos políticos y económicos, mayoritariamente, liderados por hombres. Por el contrario, las noticias que se relacionan con el resto de mujeres y hombres suelen recibir valoraciones negativas y aparecen como ejemplos de lo inferior que hay que repudiar o combatir, o propio de víctimas de quienes detentan el poder legalmente o contra la ley.

Lo que dicen y hacen unos pocos se presenta como trascendental para toda la sociedad aunque a menudo no son más que escenificaciones de actos retóricos en el mejor de los casos vacíos de contenido; por el contrario, lo que hace y dice la mayoría de mujeres y hombres cotidianamente para resolver los problemas, llegar a acuerdos y mejorar las condiciones de vida, carece de valor como noticia o es utilizado como ejemplo de lo anormal, lo amenazante, o propio de víctimas pasivas y pacientes.

Según esta versión, unos hacen la historia día a día y son considerados protagonistas activos de la información; la mayoría la padece o constituye algún peligro o lacra para la sociedad. Y esta forma de explicar la realidad, en lugar de fomentar el papel activo de la ciudadanía plural en el control de la democracia, reduce las posibilidades de intervención a unos pocos y exalta formas de poder despóticas, restringidas a las minorías de los países y grupos sociales que acumulan las riquezas.

Es más. Pensemos en la presencia de las mujeres como víctimas de lo que se ha dado en llamar *violencia de género* o *violencia doméstica*. Con este término se elude focalizar la atención sobre los hombres como sujetos agentes y responsables de estos actos criminales contra las mujeres hasta no hace mucho amparadas por la ley y por la costumbre. Además, se evita sacar a la luz pública que estas situaciones también ponen de manifiesto que las mujeres responden activamente contra estas situaciones.

Se diría que nos encontramos ante una especie de juego del *mundo al revés*, en el que para poder valorar a unos seres humanos como superiores es preciso valorar a otros como inferiores, procedimiento simbólico que pone de manifiesto la falsedad en la que se basa la afirmación de superioridad, aunque la hayamos asumido como normal e incuestionable.

Ciertamente, la valoración positiva de las actuaciones de los varones que participan en el poder o se enfrentan por el poder, como si fueran superiores y cargadas de significado, *significativas,* sea en el terreno informativo, como en el político, social, cultural, etc., sólo se puede sustentar construyendo simbólicamente en negativo, como si fuera inferior e *in-significante,* todo lo que aportan al funcionamiento de la sociedad la mayoría de mujeres y hombres que no forman parte de estos colectivos.

Se trata de una construcción simbólica primigenia, de carácter mítico, que fue reelaborada por los filósofos griegos realzando como concepto de *lo humano superior* un modelo humano particular e idealizado que identificaron con los varones adultos que formaban parte del ejército y participaban en la política, varones a los que consideraban libres y a los que reconocían el derecho a conquistar y esclavizar a las mujeres, hombres y criaturas de otros pueblos. Aristóteles lo explicó con claridad cuando afirmó que *para hacer grandes cosas hay que ser tan superior como lo es el hombre a la mujer, el padre a los hijos y el amo a los esclavos,* frase que pone de manifiesto que se trata, obviamente, de una aseveración falsa, ya que la afirmación de la superioridad sólo se puede pronunciar definiendo a otras y otros como inferiores.

Este concepto de *lo humano superior*, que condensa a la vez rasgos racistas y clasistas, sexistas y adultos, corresponde a la palabra griega *aner, andrós*, y a la palabra latina *vir, viri*, términos que en sentido estricto corresponden a un *arquetipo viril* cuyo sistema de valores es el dominio de otras y otros, no puede aplicarse al conjunto de hombres, ni al conjunto de seres humanos, sino sólo de forma exclusiva y excluyente a los varones adultos que ejercen el poder.

Y ha pervivido hasta nuestros días en la memoria colectiva, ya que se transmite generacionalmente y lo asumimos individualmente, como *yo cognoscente,* en el proceso de escolarización, de formación académica y de incorporación a los colectivos adultos, como *concepto de lo humano objetivo.*

En consecuencia, constituye la pieza clave de los criterios compartidos por los profesionales de las explicaciones míticas y racionales sobre la existencia humana, a partir de los cuales se establece qué es o no es una noticia, un hecho histórico, un dato significativo. Por eso las mujeres periodistas, igual que las historiadoras, las sociólogas y otras profesionales, asumimos los mismos criterios que nuestros compañeros, y podemos continuar ancladas en el punto de vista androcéntrico, si en lugar de ir a la raíz simbólica compleja de este sistema de pensamiento racista y clasista, sexista y adulto,[3] nos limitamos a sustituir el enfoque *de género,* que privilegia a los hombres, por otro que sólo invierte los términos y mira preferentemente a las mujeres.

La persistencia de esta construcción simbólica androcéntrica está en la base de unas explicaciones académicas, profesionales,

---

3. En la Tesis Doctoral que leímos en 1984 en la Facultad de Geografía e Historia de la Universidad de Barcelona demostramos la construcción histórica del concepto de lo humano como un Arquetipo Viril, a partir de un análisis atento de *La Política* de Aristóteles comparado con obras actuales de Historia del Pensamiento en las que se puede advertir la asimilación de este modelo en los ambientes académicos, que se caracterizan por un androcentrismo más opaco, ya que generalizan como humano lo que no es sino un modelo particular. Ver MORENO SARDÀ, Amparo (1988), *La otra 'Política' de Aristóteles*, Barcelona: Icaria.

periodísticas, que aparecen ajenas a los cambios, anquilosadas en un punto de vista fijo y obsoleto, que ya no son capaces de dar cuenta de las transformaciones que han conducido a las actuales sociedades plurales, diversas y en constante transformación, y de colaborar a pensar en cómo resolver los nuevos problemas que tenemos planteados.

Pero además, en las investigaciones que hemos realizado sobre la representación de las relaciones sociales entre mujeres y hombres en periódicos publicados en España, desde la transición hasta la actualidad,[4] partíamos de la hipótesis de que las noticias no hablan de cómo las mujeres se han incorporado a espacios que antes les habían sido vedados, y ese punto de vista compartido por los y las profesionales de la información, que por tanto podemos considerar propio de *la mirada informativa*, se ha focalizado cada vez más en los últimos años en unos círculos reducidos de varones y mujeres que actúan en los despachos de los escenarios del poder, y a menudo se ha limitado a reproducir sus declaraciones y comunicados oficiales.

No nos resultó fácil advertir que éste no era el único problema. Tuvimos que modificar nuestra pregunta e interrogarnos no sólo sobre *de quién hablan las noticias*, sino también *de qué* otros fenómenos que englobamos como *no humanos*, para agrupar una diversidad de instituciones, entidades, seres animados e inanimados, acciones, datos…, que cada vez más aparecen como los protagonistas activos y los sujetos agentes de las acciones noticiables. Un grupo de protagonistas heterogéneo en el que predominan una serie de instituciones, entidades y corporaciones desde las que se ejerce el poder en distintas esferas, y también datos abstractos, estadísticas, acciones diversas que a menudo, en lugar de enriquecer la información, suplantan a los seres humanos responsables y presentan determinadas situaciones y actuaciones como si fueran asépticas o inapelables; en definitiva, hacen la información más opaca, más alejada de la realidad, más deshumanizada.

---

4. MORENO SARDÀ, A. (dir.); LOPEZ, M.; ABRIL, N.; ALONSO, I.; SIMELIO, N.; GOMEZ, P.; VARGAS, M. S.; QUINAYAS, G.; CORCOY, M. (2004) «La representación de las relaciones entre mujeres y hombres y del recambio generacional en la prensa, de 1974 a 2004». Proyecto I+D+I Nº 07/01 financiado por el Instituto de la Mujer. Dep. Periodismo, Facultad de Ciencias de la Información, Universidad Autónoma de Barcelona (sin publicar).

La mirada informativa, especialmente la que se considera más «seria», se ha hecho impermeable a las transformaciones que se han producido en las relaciones entre mujeres y hombres de diferentes edades, condiciones sociales y procedencias, porque se ha desviado cada vez más de las personas hacia las instituciones y los datos abstractos. En consecuencia la información, especialmente la considerada «seria», se ha deshumanizado.[5]

Esta pudiera ser la razón de fondo por la que la prensa, en lugar de proporcionar un conocimiento diverso y matizado de la compleja sociedad actual, base para un debate plural, colabora a polarizar las posiciones, a agudizar los conflictos, a *crispar las situaciones*, como se dice ahora, y sobre todo, ahonda y aumenta las distancias entre la ciudadanía plural, y quienes gestionan el poder desde los múltiples despachos, personas que acaso un día fueron elegidas como representantes pero de cuyos nombres ya nadie se acuerda y a las que cada vez resulta más difícil pedir responsabilidades de unas acciones u omisiones que parecen realizadas por entes abstractos, fuera del alcance de cualquier ciudadana o ciudadano.

De ahí la necesidad urgente de modificar ese punto de vista supuestamente objetivo, de desplazarlo para hacer visible el conjunto de la sociedad, en definitiva, de trabajar para que *la mirada informativa* se torne más amplia, más diversa y más sensible a cuanto hacemos y repercute en el conjunto de los seres humanos.

Resulta imprescindible, por tanto, *humanizar la información*. Por ello, como resultado de nuestras investigaciones nos propusimos esta tarea,[6] sin ignorar que reclamar que las noticias vuelvan a despertar el

---

5. Conclusiones investigación I+D+I Nº 07/01. «La representación de las relaciones entre mujeres y hombres y del recambio generacional en la prensa, de 1974 a 2004», (pp. 724).

6. La presentación de los resultados del proyecto I+D+I sobre *La representación de mujeres y hombres en la prensa (1974-2004)*, realizada en el I Simposio «Periodisme i Ciutadania plural: rutines i reptes», celebrado en Barcelona los días 25 y 26 de octubre de 2004, nos hizo advertir la necesidad de dotar a las y los profesionales del periodismo de nuevas herramientas de evaluación de su trabajo. La realización de talleres para elaborar informaciones no androcéntricas nos motivó a desarrollar el proyecto *Guía per a humanitzar la informació. Elaboració de materials per a la*

interés humano puede provocar el desprecio de los profesionales más honorables de la academia y el periodismo, o la condena a la hoguera del silencio por frivolidad o sensacionalismo. Esta *Guía...* quiere ser una aportación, una herramienta para humanizar la información con el máximo respeto a las personas como seres activos y responsables de decisiones personales y colectivas.

En esta tarea, el primer paso consiste en detectar la propia miopía de *la mirada informativa* respecto a las mujeres, y en advertir que este problema no se limita a las mujeres, o al *género*, sino que se deriva de una construcción simbólica compleja androcéntrica enraizada en esas estructuras mentales que, como advirtió Fernand Braudel, *constituyen prisiones de larga duración*: unos prejuicios interiorizados como hábitos de pensamiento y rutinas profesionales compartidas que operan como mecanismos de autocensura.

Para ello es imprescindible llevar la crítica a una autocrítica sistemática. Porque sólo un ejercicio de autocrítica consciente y muy atento nos permite asumir cómo nos afectan estos pre-juicios, condición imprescindible para poder ampliar nuestra mirada al conjunto de seres humanos, situarlos en el centro de nuestra atención, explorar nuevos enfoques más amplios, más diversos y con una mayor sensibilidad humana, y ensayar nuevas formas de hacer información fruto de nuevos criterios acerca de lo que se puede considerar o no se puede considerar noticia.

En esta *Guía para humanizar la información* presentamos el Test ADSH y lo aplicamos a una muestra reducida de noticias que fueron destacadas en las portadas y contraportadas de unos cuantos diarios publicados en Madrid y Barcelona el primer viernes del mes de febrero de tres años separados por una década, 1984, 1994 y 2004.

No los hemos elegido porque los consideremos especialmente problemáticos, sino como un ejemplo de cómo se hace la información habitualmente, y para que sirvan como pre-textos para ejercitar

---

producció d'informacions des de perspectives no-androcèntriques, financiado por el Institut Català de les Dones (2005), que sirvió de base para elaborar esta Guía... y las tesinas de doctorado leídas por Florencia Rovetto Gonem (2006) *La representación del trabajo de las mujeres en la prensa (1984-2004)*, y Alfonso Buitrago Londoño (2006) *De las 5W y 1H a las 5Q. Diferentes aplicaciones del Test ADSH*.

la autocrítica. Este Test permite evaluar la Amplitud, la Diversidad y la Sensibilidad Humana de *la mirada informativa*. Cada cual puede utilizarlo con textos propios o ajenos, pero siempre con el objetivo de descubrir su propia *mirada informativa*, esto es, la posición que adopta, como profesional de la información, en el enfoque y tratamiento que hace de la realidad social.

Estos ejercicios, a la vez que permiten desentrañar cuáles son las rutinas que deshumanizan la información, proporcionan pistas para explorar otros enfoques y utilizar otros criterios que permitan hacer una información más humana, de manera que las mujeres y hombres que formamos hoy la *ciudadanía plural* podamos disponer de conocimientos significativos para identificar cómo podemos actuar e intervenir en la mejora de la democracia, desde los espacios más próximos hasta los más lejanos y globales e impulsar una profunda renovación de la democracia.

No se trata de una receta cerrada y definitiva, sino de un texto abierto al debate y a la exploración cooperativa: unos primeros apuntes que esperamos completar a medida que utilicemos esta herramienta en talleres y sesiones de trabajo con profesionales y con otras personas interesadas, de forma presencial o virtual.

Tortosa, enero de 2006*

---

* Han transcurrido casi dos años desde que cerramos el texto de esta Guía…, y escribí esta presentación. En este tiempo se ha tomado conciencia de que el periodismo ha de transformarse, y algunos de los diarios analizados en este trabajo han introducido cambios para prestar mayor atención a sus lectores y lectoras, incluso para tener en cuenta sus comentarios.

Esperamos que nuestra aportación colabore a que el periodismo recupere el papel que le corresponde como instrumento para restituir a mujeres y hombres como sujetos activos del debate y el control democrático.

II. TEST PARA LA EVALUACIÓN DE LA AMPLITUD, LA DIVERSIDAD Y LA SENSIBILIDAD HUMANA DE LA MIRADA INFORMATIVA

El propósito principal del *Test* que presentamos en esta *Guía* es facilitar a quien lo quiera utilizar, sea profesional de la información lectora o lector, cómo detectar fácilmente de qué personas *hablan las noticias* y qué tratamiento les dan. Esto es, qué mujeres y hombres de distintas edades, condiciones personales, sociales y procedencias, se presentan como protagonistas en relación con qué actuaciones que se consideran noticiables, y qué valoraciones positivas o negativas se hace de unas y otros como sujetos agentes o pacientes de la vida social.

Puntos de partida

Partimos de la base de que toda explicación, ya sea una noticia, un documental, una investigación sociológica, una película…, es el resultado de los dos procedimientos básicos que orientan cualquier mirada sobre la realidad. Primero, de *enfocar* a unas personas, grupos de personas, o a unos aspectos de la realidad desde un determinado punto de vista, que corresponde a una determinada posición social. Y además, de realizar determinado *tratamiento* con el fin de poner de relieve y valorar determinados comportamientos, actuaciones y aspectos positiva o negativamente, apelando preferentemente a los sentimientos o a los argumentos racionales.

Consideramos cada ejemplar de periódico no como una colección de temas,[1] sino como un conjunto de explicaciones que hacen referencia a distintos protagonistas que establecen relaciones diversas entre sí, personales u colectivas. Una especie de *representación cartográfica* de lo que acontece en la realidad social,[2] que sirve para generar debates públicos entre quienes producen y quienes leen cada periódico y entre los distintos colectivos.

Desde esta perspectiva, todo periódico es el fruto de enfocar y resaltar distintos escenarios de la vida social, ya se trate de los escenarios de las actuaciones públicas, de aquellos que se reservan para las relaciones privadas o interpersonales, o de espacios marginales. Y estos escenarios aparecen, además, ocupados por personajes, por actores que se ajustan o no a unos papeles o guiones preestablecidos, según reglas que han sido elaboradas a lo largo de los tiempos.

En consecuencia, la lectura cotidiana del periódico nos lleva a rememorar los comportamientos (los gestos, las palabras, los ornamentos...) considerados socialmente pertinentes en las distintas coordenadas espacio-temporales y, en consecuencia, a recordar también aquellos que debemos considerar impertinentes. La representación imaginaria de la realidad social que ofrecen las páginas de los periódicos revierte, así, en el comportamiento personal y colectivo.

Una lectura atenta de un ejemplar de un periódico cualquiera puede ayudarnos a percibir qué merece atención prioritaria para lo que podemos definir como *la mirada informativa:* qué personajes aparecen haciendo qué, en qué escenarios, y cuáles son marginados o incluso excluidos.[3]

---

1. Los planteamientos sobre la agenda temática impiden ver que la prensa habla fundamentalmente de las personas... Deshumaniza la investigación y la hace abstracta.

2. Este planteamiento lo expusimos por primera vez en MORENO SARDÀ, A. (1986), «Realidadad histórica» y «realidad informativa». *La reproducción de la realidad social en la prensa,* I Encuentro de Historia de la Prensa en Bilbao, Facultad de Ciencias de la Información, Universidad del País Vasco.

3. MORENO SARDÀ, (1998), *La mirada informativa,* Barcelona: Bosch, (pp. 74-75).

El análisis de textos de distintos tipos de publicaciones periodísticas, diarios y semanarios considerados *de información general,* dominicales, revistas del corazón, de sucesos…, siguiendo estos criterios, nos ha permitido concluir que los cambios que se advierten en la representación de los protagonistas de las noticias, y en las actuaciones por las que son considerados noticiables, más allá de estos hechos, remiten de alguna manera a transformaciones que se han producido en las relaciones sociales. Sin embargo, ningún periódico, ninguna explicación, por más que se presente como objetiva o científica, refleja con transparencia estos cambios. Unos periódicos son más favorables que otros a enfocar y hacer visibles en sus páginas a los distintos protagonistas y a valorar sus actuaciones positiva o negativamente. Y según los colectivos sociales a los que se dirigen, unos periódicos presentan a algunos protagonistas realzando sus actuaciones en sentido positivo, como modelos idealizados de lo *que se debe hacer* para conseguir la integración social, y presentan a otros protagonistas poniendo de relieve sus actuaciones en sentido negativo, como modelos de *lo que no se debe hacer* so pena de incurrir en la marginación.

Desde esta perspectiva, podemos considerar los protagonistas valorados positivamente como modelos a imitar para conseguir la integración social, y los protagonistas valorados negativamente como modelos a rechazar, que pueden conducir a la marginación social. De manera que los distintos *modelos positivos* y *negativos* proporcionan referencias de los cambios sociales que se producen en los comportamientos, a medida que las personas protagonizan *procesos de movilidad social* a lo largo de sus vidas, de la infancia a la adolescencia, la vida adulta y la senectud, y en el recambio de las generaciones.

Estos planteamientos nos permiten comprender que los distintos medios de comunicación, los diferentes periódicos, incluso cada sección o programa, se dirigen a colectivos sociales específicos con los que ponen en común estos *criterios de valoración social* y negocian día a día su actualización. Y en todos los casos, mientras en las informaciones se ofrece un repertorio variado de modelos positivos y negativos, en la publicidad se representan los modelos de comportamiento idealizados como superiores, que representan el grado máximo de integración social ya que permiten acceder al paraíso del consumo.

También nos permiten considerar el conjunto de ejemplares publicados por una cabecera a lo largo del tiempo, como distintas capas de un atlas histórico que recoge las particulares representaciones cartográficas que ha ofrecido, día a día, de las *permanencias* y los *cambios sociales*, y de las *situaciones de integración y marginación* que han afectado a los colectivos humanos en los *procesos de movilidad social*.

Además, cuando nos preguntamos *de quién hablan las noticias* y cómo lo hacen, podemos identificar también *la mirada informativa* del profesional que las ha elaborado: el punto de vista que ha adoptado, por tanto, la posición social en que se sitúa y desde la que ha enfocado a unos u otros seres humanos y ha valorado sus actuaciones positiva o negativamente, o las ha excluido por considerarlas carentes de significado, insignificantes. Este punto de vista no depende sólo de cada periodista, sino que hay que relacionarlo con el periódico o el medio de comunicación que, a su vez, ofrece una cierta pluralidad de enfoques y de voces sobre la realidad social en las distintas secciones o programas.

Así, no podemos concluir sin más que los diarios enfocan de forma muy reducida a las mujeres, sino que hemos de tener en cuenta que este enfoque limitado se produce en las informaciones, mientras que las mujeres ocupan una buena proporción de la publicidad, y especialmente de los anuncios por palabras: en este enfoque de conjunto se pone de manifiesto la amplitud, la diversidad y la sensibilidad humana de *la mirada informativa* de cada periódico o medio de comunicación.

Esta forma de entender las explicaciones permite examinar la prensa con una cierta distancia crítica, y también, aplicar la misma distancia crítica a lo que escribimos. De este modo, podemos detectar cómo hemos aprendido a explicar la realidad, de acuerdo con qué criterios y rutinas profesionales; y sólo entonces estamos en condiciones para explorar nuevos enfoques y nuevos tratamientos de la realidad, en lugar de repetir rutinas asumidas inconscientemente. Por eso, el *Test* constituye el primer ejercicio imprescindible para ampliar y diversificar la mirada informativa, y dotarla de mayor sensibilidad humana.

En definitiva, el *Test ADSH* está pensado como una herramienta que obliga a realizar lecturas pausadas y cuidadosas para promover la crítica autocrítica que nos permita repensar la labor periodística y hacer más transparente la propia *mirada informativa* que hemos asumido como profesionales.

La selección de la muestra

El *Test ADSH* se puede utilizar con cualquier tipo de información noticiosa. La selección de la muestra depende de los propósitos o intereses de la persona o grupo que quiera hacer uso de él. Así, un periodista puede hacer una selección de informaciones de elaboración propia a lo largo del tiempo para hacerse una auto evaluación; un editor puede evaluar un repertorio de informaciones producidas por varios periodistas para valorar el trabajo de la redacción en su propia cabecera y compararla con otras; y una lectora o lector puede realizar lecturas críticas de un tipo de noticias o medio. Esta herramienta resulta especialmente interesante y útil para hacer comparaciones entre periódicos de distintas cabeceras publicados en una misma fecha o a lo largo del tiempo. Estas comparaciones permiten establecer «noticias paradigmáticas» o «noticias tipo», que se refieren a cierto tipo de personas o protagonistas y se repiten en más de un periódico, y ver diferencias o reiteraciones en el enfoque y el tratamiento de un determinado aspecto de la realidad social.

Existen varias posibilidades para escoger el material que nos proponemos analizar. Para ilustrar esta *Guía...* hemos seleccionado una muestra aleatoria de periódicos compuesta por distintas cabeceras de diarios considerados de información general, cuya difusión tiene distinto alcance. La muestra completa está integrada por *quince ejemplares* correspondientes a *siete cabeceras*, publicados el *primer viernes del mes de febrero* de tres años separados por una década: *1984, 1994 y 2004. ABC, La Vanguardia, El Periódico y El País*, que ya se publicaban en los dos primeros años; y tres de aparición más reciente, un diario comarcal, *El Punt*, y dos diarios de distribución gratuita en Barcelona, *Metro Directe y 20 Minutos,* de los que sólo analizamos las portadas del día seleccionado de 2004:

Viernes 3 de febrero de 1984: ABC - La Vanguardia - El Periódico - El País

Viernes 4 de febrero de 1994: ABC - La Vanguardia - El Periódico - El País

Viernes 6 de febrero de 2004: ABC - La Vanguardia - El Periódico - El País - El Punt - Metro Directe - 20 Minutos

Con el *Test* se puede analizar el contenido completo de la publicación, como hemos hecho en algunas investigaciones, o una parte, sea la información que se presenta en la primera y última páginas, o en algunas secciones. Los titulares o las noticias completas, las fotografías o los pies. Igualmente se puede hacer una selección de *noticias tipo* en las que se involucra a cierto tipo de personas en un contexto determinado, y comparar cómo se tratan en varios periódicos. En cualquier caso, noticias, anuncios y comentarios son resultados de enfoques diversos que saltan a la vista de quien las lee o las mira, realzadas mediante diversos recursos tipográficos de color o imágenes.

En esta *Guía...* hemos aplicado el *Test ADSH* a todas la unidades redaccionales (UR) que se presentaron en las portadas y en las contraportadas, ya que son las páginas que los mismos periódicos consideran de mayor importancia, para destacar la información y también la publicidad: las ventanas de acceso a la información que cada periódico presenta como más relevante del día. El análisis de las portadas y contraportadas nos permite ver lo que cada periódico quiere hacer más visible. No obstante, en el último ejercicio examinamos minuciosamente algunas *noticias tipo* teniendo en cuenta no sólo lo que aparece en portada, sino también el material de continuidad que se ofrece en las páginas interiores del ejemplar.

Insistimos en que el objetivo que nos proponemos es clarificar *de quién hablan las* noticias, esto es, qué personas son consideradas protagonistas en las noticias por parte de los profesionales que elaboran los periódicos. Este objetivo significa adoptar unos criterios diferentes de los que suelen ser habituales, cuando lo que se pretende es examinar los temas de que tratan las publicaciones, o la agenda.

Consideramos que la cuestión fundamental en unas explicaciones que se dirigen a las personas para que puedan conocer e intervenir en el funcionamiento de la sociedad es, en primer lugar, detectar cómo son representados los distintos colectivos y así, qué modelos de comportamiento se propone a lectores y lectoras como positivos o negativos, para que puedan tomarlos como referencia de lo que es considerado socialmente aceptable o rechazable y puedan valorar sus posibilidades de participación en el funcionamiento de la sociedad.

TABLA 1
DATOS GENERALES DE LA MUESTRA

1984	Total UR portada	Total UR contraportada	Total elementos gráficos portada	Total elementos gráficos contraportada
ABC	1	0	10	0
El País	11	2	2	1
La Vanguardia	4	0	2	0
El Periódico	8	2	2	2

1994	Total UR portada	Total UR contraportada	Total elementos gráficos portada	Total elementos gráficos contraportada
ABC	2	0	3	0
El País	10	2	1	1
La Vanguardia	4	3	2	7
El Periódico	6	1	3	2

2004	Total UR portada	Total UR contraportada	Total elementos gráficos portada	Total elementos gráficos contraportada
ABC	6	0	3	0
El País	9	2	1	1
La Vanguardia	6	1	1	1
El Periódico	4	0	2	0
El Punt	9	2	2	1
Metro Directe	15	0	6	0
20 Minutos	23	0	5	0
Gran total	**118**	**15**	**45**	**16**

1984

Portada *ABC*
Viernes 03/02/1984

Contraportada *ABC*
Viernes 03/02/1984

Portada *El País*
Viernes 03/02/1984

Contraportada *El País*
Viernes 03/02/1984

Portada *La Vanguardia*
Viernes 03/02/1984

Contraportada *La Vanguardia*
Viernes 03/02/1984

Portada *El Periódico*
Viernes 03/02/1984

Contraportada *El Periódico*
Viernes 03/02/1984

1994

Portada *ABC*
Viernes 04/02/1994

Contraportada *ABC*
Viernes 04/02/1994

Portada *El País*
Viernes 04/02/1994

Contraportada *El País*
Viernes 04/02/1994

Portada *La Vanguardia*
Viernes 04/02/1994

Contraportada *La Vanguardia*
Viernes 04/02/1994

Portada *El Periódico*
Viernes 04/02/1994

Contraportada *El Periódico*
Viernes 04/02/1994

Portada *ABC*
Viernes 06/02/2004

Contraportada *ABC*
Viernes 06/02/2004

Portada *El País*
Viernes 06/02/2004

Contraportada *El País*
Viernes 06/02/2004

Portada *La Vanguardia*
Viernes 06/02/2004

Contraportada *La Vanguardia*
Viernes 06/02/2004

Portada *El Periódico*
Viernes 06/02/2004

Contraportada *El Periódico*
Viernes 06/02/2004

Portada *El Punt*
Viernes 06/02/2004

Contraportada *El Punt*
Viernes 06/02/2004

Portada *Metro Directe*
Viernes 06/02/2004

Contraportada *Metro Directe*
Viernes 06/02/2004

Portada *20 Minutos*
Viernes 06/02/2004

Contraportada *20 Minutos*
Viernes 06/02/2004

Las unidades de análisis

Una vez definida la muestra, el paso siguiente es distinguir los tipos de unidades que componen las páginas de cada ejemplar: unidades redaccionales, unidades publicitarias y unidades administrativas. Además, en este análisis hemos diferenciado especialmente aquellas unidades redaccionales que incorporan elementos gráficos (imágenes o infografías).

Unidades Redaccionales (UR): Por Unidad Redaccional entendemos lo que conocemos habitualmente como noticias, crónicas, reportajes, entrevistas, artículos, críticas, comentarios y opiniones de los columnistas. En el tipo de periódicos que hemos seleccionado para esta guía generalmente son fáciles de distinguir y constituyen el principal contenido de sus páginas. En los dominicales de estos mismos periódicos o en otras publicaciones, puede resultar más difícil distinguir entre las UR y las unidades publicitarias (UP).

Hemos considerado especialmente las unidades que contienen ilustraciones, sea una fotografía, un dibujo, un cuadro o un gráfico, ya que estos *elementos gráficos* hacen visibles a los protagonistas de forma diferente a como lo hacen los textos. En los diarios analizados suelen formar parte de las UR que van encabezadas por un titular y explicadas en un breve texto o pie. En algunos casos pueden constituir unidades independientes, a veces apoyadas en un pie de foto que hace al mismo tiempo de titular.

Unidades Publicitarias (UP): Consideramos Unidades Publicitarias cualquier anuncio comercial, oficial o clasificado. También incluimos la publicidad que hace el periódico de sí mismo o de los productos o servicios que ofrece como valor agregado para los lectores.

Unidad Administrativa (UA): Por Unidad Administrativa entendemos cualquier información sobre el periódico o la empresa: cabecera, eslogan, fundadores, propietarios, personal, localización, índice sumario, etc.

En el análisis que presentamos en esta *Guía* no hemos incluido las unidades publicitarias ni administrativas, aunque consideramos que la evaluación completa de un periódico ha de tener en cuenta el total del material que presenta en sus páginas.

Cinco preguntas para evaluar *la mirada informativa*

Para responder a la pregunta fundamental que nos planteamos en la *Guía*, *¿de quién hablan las noticias?*, y evaluar qué visión ofrece la prensa de los diversos seres humanos como modelos de comportamiento positivos o negativos que merecen ser imitados o repudiados, hemos de plantearnos dos interrogantes básicos:

A. *¿Quién, quiénes*, o *qué* aparece representado como protagonista de las noticias? y

B. *¿Qué tratamiento reciben* los distintos seres humanos en las noticias?

La respuesta al primer interrogante nos conduce a detectar tanto el punto de vista adoptado por quien ha elaborado la noticia, como el enfoque que ha hecho de la sociedad, más amplio o más reducido y orientado a una mayor o menor diversidad de seres humanos. Por tanto, de este primer interrogante se derivan dos preguntas concretas: *quién enfoca,* y *a quién enfoca.* A estas dos preguntas hemos respondido en los tres primeros ejercicios.

Además, cualquier enfoque pone de manifiesto el interés de quien elabora una explicación por unas personas u otras, y la valoración que hace de determinadas actuaciones que considera noticiables por algún motivo, y que se desarrollan en distintos escenarios sociales. Por tanto, podemos completar la pregunta *a quién enfoca* con otras dos: *haciendo qué* y *en qué escenarios.* De este modo podemos detectar el *tratamiento* que se hace de unas u otras personas en función de valoraciones positivas o negativas que tienen que ver con las distintas condiciones sociales, profesionales, estatus…

Estas son las 5 preguntas básicas que permiten evaluar la amplitud, la diversidad y la sensibilidad humana de *la mirada informativa: ¿quién enfoca?, ¿a quién enfoca?, ¿en qué actuaciones?, ¿en qué escenarios?* y *¿utilizando qué fuentes?* La primera y la última pregunta se refieren al o a la profesional que elabora la información, y las tres restantes a las mujeres y hombres, o a lo que se presenta como protagonistas de las noticias.

Para registrar los datos de una forma sistemática conviene, en cualquier investigación, preparar unas fichas que serán las herramientas que utilizaremos para organizar los datos con los mismos criterios en todos los casos, y para hacer posteriormente balances cuantitativos y evaluaciones cualitativas. Todos los datos que se recogen deben ser anotados literalmente, tal como están escritos y no según nos parece a partir de una lectura rápida y acrítica. Acercarse a las noticias con paciencia y dejarlas hablar por sí mismas nos traerá sorpresas muy reveladoras.

Test ADSH

Evaluación de la Amplitud, la Diversidad y la Sensibilidad Humanas
de la mirada informativa

Evaluación realizada por: ....
Publicación evaluada: ....
Fecha de la publicación: ....

UNIDAD Titular y página	¿QUIÉN ENFOCA? Autoría y lugar donde se situa la noticia	¿A QUIÉN SE ENFOCA Términos literales de identificación y características atribuidas a los protagonistas	¿EN QUÉ ACTUACIONES? Expresiones literales que indican las acciones por las que se consideran a los protagonistas	¿EN QUÉ ESCENARIOS? Lugares públicos o privados en los que se sitúa a los protagonistas, (o lugares geográficos)	¿UTILIZANDO QUÉ FUENTES? Mencionadas explícitamente	OBSERVACIONES Ausencias ¿qué no se dice, a quién no se menciona?

Ficha de recogida de datos

Test para la evaluación de la Amplitud, la Diversidad y la Sensibilidad Humanas

de la mirada informativa (ADSH)

Ejemplo:

Evaluación realizada por: ....

Periódico evaluado: *El Periódico*

Fecha de la publicación: 3 de febrero de 1984

UNIDAD Titular y página	¿QUIÉN ENFOCA? Autoría y lugar donde se sitúa la noticia	¿A QUIÉN SE ENFOCA Términos literales de identificación y características atribuidas a los protagonistas	¿EN QUÉ ACTUACIONES? Expresiones literales que indican las acciones por las que se consideran a los protagonistas	¿EN QUÉ ESCENARIOS? Lugares públicos o privados en los que se sitúa a los protagonistas, (o lugares geográficos)	¿UTILIZANDO QUÉ FUENTES? Mencionadas explícitamente	OBSERVACIONES
PER 1984 UR 01 (pág. 1) Quejido unánime ...	No consta	Quejido unánime Movilización de 300.000 personas en más de veinte localidades... La policía... Líderes de Comisiones Obreras del PCE...	...de la España «reconvertida» participación en los paros y movilizaciones convocados ...para protestar por la aplicación de la ley de reconversión industrial ...utilizó balas de goma ...estuvieron muy activos	En más de 20 localidades Gijón; varios puntos de Galicia, País Vasco, Cantabria, Andalucía, Madrid y Comunidad Autónoma Valenciana	No consta	*Imagen:* Mapa de la protesta contra el «plan Solchaga» Un mapa de España con los puntos marcados de las ciudades donde se desarrolló el conflicto. En la UR de portada hay una descripción de la adhesión a la huelga ciudad por ciudad y sector de la producción: astilleros, fábricas, comercios, escuelas, universidades.

Criterios para registrar los datos

Para registrar los datos hemos de establecer unos criterios que aplicaremos de forma sistemática:

UNIDAD: nombre de la cabecera, número de registro de la unidad y número de página en la que se presenta.

¿QUIÉN ENFOCA?: Cada ejemplar de un periódico incluye varias voces que en ocasiones pueden manifestar diferencias, discrepancias e incluso contradicciones. El enfoque de la realidad social que se presenta en cada ejemplar es el resultado de un trabajo colectivo en el que intervienen tanto la empresa, como el equipo de dirección y las personas concretas que elaboran cada unidad utilizando distintas fuentes, que pueden aparecer identificadas o no. Esta diversidad de perspectivas y voces que ofrece un periódico tiene que ver también con el lugar donde se encuentra la persona concreta que elabora la información, ya que su explicación varía según esté en la sede central del periódico, o haga el papel de corresponsal o enviado especial que trabaja en la capital de algún estado, en una pequeña población, etc.

¿A QUIÉN ENFOCA?: Palabras literales usadas para identificar y describir a quién, o qué se enfoca y se considera protagonista de la información, como sujetos o como objetos de las acciones noticiables, que aparecen con nombres, adjetivos... Como hemos dicho, pueden ser humanos, en cuyo caso hemos de distinguir si aparecen identificados con nombre y apellidos o no, o pueden ser colectivos, y también pueden ser protagonistas que englobamos como no humanos: nombres de instituciones, conceptos o datos abstractos... que aparecen como sujeto de la acción. Respecto a los protagonistas humanos, podemos tomar nota de si aparecen acompañados de referencias expresas a la edad, el sexo, la nacionalidad, el origen étnico, la religión, y que suelen utilizarse con connotaciones negativas, o al estilo de vida, la profesión, el rol social o posición jerárquica, que suelen utilizarse con connotaciones positivas.

¿EN QUÉ ACTUACIONES?: Palabras literales usadas para expresar las acciones por las que los protagonistas son mencionados o citados: principalmente verbos. Advertir qué tipo de acciones expresan, y si se trata de verbos en forma activa o pasiva, y si indican acciones valoradas positiva o negativamente.

¿EN QUÉ ESCENARIOS?: Lugares geográficos y espacios definidos socialmente, públicos o privados, y otras circunstancias en los que los protagonistas son presentados (suelen identificarse en el predicado de la oración).

¿UTILIZANDO QUÉ FUENTES?: Sólo se registran cuando son mencionadas literalmente. Hay que advertir si coinciden con los protagonistas, o si tienen una posición complementaria o antagónica.

OBSERVACIONES: En la ficha se ha previsto un apartado para incluir otros datos de interés como la sección en que la unidad es ubicada por el periódico y las imágenes que incluye. Asimismo, se pueden introducir anotaciones acerca de las exclusiones e inclusiones que se observan: ¿Qué no se dice? ¿Quién está incluido y quién está excluido? ¿Quiénes son los protagonistas, antagonistas y qué relación los vincula? ¿Existe alguna relación entre los protagonistas y las fuentes de información mencionadas? ¿Qué fuentes se excluyen? Etcétera.

La selección de los protagonistas

Consideramos *protagonistas humanos* a cualquier persona identificada con un nombre común o un nombre propio, con nombre y apellidos o con otras palabras literales que se refieren a una persona o grupo de personas. Ejemplo: *el Rey, un policía muerto, un general mexicano, un obispo ortodoxo catalán, Dolores Fernández Feijoo, los vecinos del Liceo, 11 ecologistas, el 68% de los enfermos...*

Este tipo de protagonistas humanos se diferencia de otro, en el que englobamos los que hemos definido como *protagonistas no humanos*, en los casos en que las acciones noticiables se atribuyen a cualquier organización, institución, compañía, corporación, gobierno, ministerio, tribunal, país, ciudad, pueblo, animal, fenómeno natural o cualquier otra palabra. Ejemplo: *un pacto social..., la pasividad de la policía..., la Comisión Mixta..., el dólar..., una farmacia..., la influencia de...*

Para determinar quién o qué aparece como protagonistas en una Unidad Redaccional hemos de seguir la misma lógica que muestra la unidad de análisis, no la que se nos viene a la cabeza: hemos de identificar quién, o quienes, o qué, aparecen literalmente como sujetos o receptores de los verbos que expresan las acciones. Además, hemos de tener en cuenta que el grado de importancia que se atribuye a un protagonista disminuye desde los titulares, antetítulos y subtítulos, al cuerpo del texto que se suele organizar jerárquicamente en una pirámide invertida. De la misma manera, la presencia en las imágenes da cuenta de los protagonistas a los que se enfoca en la unidad. Esta presencia no siempre corresponde exactamente con lo que se dice en el texto escrito al pie, que en principio debería explicar la imagen.

III. ¿DE QUIÉN HABLAN LAS NOTICIAS?

Presentamos a continuación una serie de ejercicios básicos que permiten utilizar el *Test ADSH* para evaluar paso a paso *la mirada informativa*. Estos ejercicios pueden aplicarse a noticias elaboradas por cada profesional que utilice el *Test* para evaluar sus propias informaciones, o a informaciones publicadas por cualquier periódico o medio de comunicación que analicemos.

Insistimos en que el objetivo de este *Test* no es descalificar el trabajo de otros periodistas. El objetivo primero y principal es realizar *ejercicios de autocrítica* de los propios hábitos asumidos; por tanto, hemos de utilizar el análisis atento de lo que han escrito o elaborado otras personas como un espejo que nos permite contrastar nuestros propios hábitos y prejuicios. Es decir: no se trata de llegar a la conclusión de *cuántos prejuicios tiene este periódico* o *aquel periodista*, porque esta frase sólo sirve para reforzar la pretensión de superioridad y pone de manifiesto la incapacidad de cuestionar la propia mirada androcéntrica.

El ejercicio sólo habrá cumplido su objetivo después de varias relecturas atentas que nos ayuden a percibir lo que a primera vista no habíamos advertido o no se explica de forma clara. Se trata, por tanto, de un procedimiento que hay que realizar con muchas ganas, con paciencia, con calma, leyendo, pensando, releyendo, pensando otra vez, buscando otros enfoques que nos hemos acostumbrado a considerar inexistentes o menospreciar porque los valorábamos automáticamente, inconscientemente, como insignificantes.

Para facilitar la aplicación de este *Test* acompañamos los ejercicios con reproducciones del material analizado, las fichas en las que hemos registrado los datos y unas tablas al final de cada ejercicio con el resumen de los datos obtenidos.

Ejercicio 1
La *AMPLITUD* de *la mirada informativa* ¿A quién o a qué se presenta como protagonista en los titulares?

El primer ejercicio consiste en registrar literalmente los titulares de cada unidad y extraer datos que respondan a la pregunta básica: *¿De quién hablan las noticias?* Esto es, ¿a qué mujeres y a qué hombres presentan como protagonistas? Y en el caso de protagonistas que no sean seres humanos, ¿qué instituciones, entidades, acciones, fenómenos naturales, datos, cosas, abstracciones... son presentados como protagonistas de las noticias?

En la ficha 1 registramos, en las columnas de la izquierda, la relación completa de titulares de la muestra elegida, precedida por la cabecera en la que han aparecido. En las columnas de la derecha, indicamos cómo hemos considerado a los distintos protagonistas que aparecen en cada noticia siguiendo los criterios que ya hemos explicado. Hemos distinguido ente los protagonistas humanos y los protagonistas no humanos; y entre los primeros, hemos diferenciado los que se presentan de forma individual, mujeres y hombres, y los que se presentan de forma colectiva:

**MUJERES, HOMBRES, COLECTIVOS HUMANOS
y PROTAGONISTAS NO HUMANOS**

De esta manera, quien lea esta *Guía* puede advertir cómo hemos clasificado a los protagonistas, y pensar si comparte o no los criterios que hemos seguido, que no siempre son fáciles de aplicar debido a la ambigüedad con que a menudo utilizamos el lenguaje. También puede valorar los resultados numéricos de nuestra investigación que aparecen agrupados al final de la selección de las noticias en cada periódico, en cada año, y globalmente en las tablas y gráficos.

FICHA 1
TITULARES UNIDADES REDACCIONALES AÑO 1984

Periódicos	Titulares (unidades redaccionales)	Elementos gráficos	Humanos Individuales M	Humanos Individuales H	Colectivos	No humanos
ABC	«Cumbre» iberoamericana en Caracas	X X X X X				X
Contraportada	Publicidad	X X X X X				
Subtotal ABC		**10**	**0**	**0**	**0**	**1**
El País	**Manifestaciones de trabajadores y críticas patronales contra** la **política del Gobierno**	X				XXX
	El **PSC** acusa a **Pujol** de financiar una campaña contra los municipios			X		X
	Jaime Lusinchi propugna un **pacto social** entre los venezolanos			X		X
	Pasividad de la policía francesa en la búsqueda de «**etarras**» que deben ser confinados				X	X
	Ronald Reagan no detendrá la **subida del dólar**			X		X
	Westinghouse negocia la venta de **su filial española** a una **compañía británica**					XXX
	Probable declaración conjunta de los 12 magistrados del Tribunal Constitucional ante el **Supremo**					XX
	Guardia civil muerto, por error de **un compañero**, en la persecución de **tres atracadores**			XX	X	
	La Comisión Mixta aprueba la **transferencia de las cámaras agrarias, las universidades** y **los espectáculos**					XXXX
	Un general mexicano asesina a un **obispo ortodoxo catalán**			XX		
	Dolores Fernández Feijoo. La última artesa maragata teje mantas y cobertores ayudada por **su madre**, de 93 años, y de **una tía**, de 83	X	XXX			
Contraportada	Gente. **Peach de Rohan, Julio Anguita, José Hernández Quero, Fernando Esteso**	X		XXXX		
	Claustrofilia, **Juan Cueto**			X		
Subtotal El País		**3**	**3**	**12**	**2**	**16**

49

| Periódicos | Titulares (unidades redaccionales) | Elementos gráficos | Humanos | | | No huma- nos |
| | | | Individuales | | Colectivos | |
			M	H		
La Vanguardia	**Movilizaciones sindicales** contra la **política del Gobierno**	XX				XX
	Barcelona: cada día es atracada **una farmacia**					XX
	Más protección para los **mandos del Ejército**				X	X
	Crece **la influencia del Opus Dei** en la Iglesia					X
Contraportada	Publicidad					
Subtotal La Vanguardia		2	0	0	1	6
El Periódico	**Quejido unánime** de la **España 'reconvertida'**	X				XX
	Felipe critica en Venezuela **el informe de Kissinger**			X		X
	Escolta policial					X
	El PSC acusa					X
	Educación física					X
	El Barça pincha					X
	Encarcelan a un **cabo de Lloret** por vender armas			X		
	Sumario secreto en el caso **Salomó**	X				XX
Contraportada	**La OTAN** a coloquio con **Ángel Viñas**	X		X		X
	Verdes. **Antonio Álvarez Solís**	X		X		
Subtotal El Periódico		4	0	4	0	10
Total cabeceras 1984		19	3	16	3	33

FICHA 2
TITULARES UNIDADES REDACCIONALES AÑO 1994

Periódicos	Titulares (unidades redaccionales)	Elementos gráficos	Humanos Individuales M	Humanos Individuales H	Colectivos	No huma-nos
ABC	El Tribunal Supremo acude al arbitraje del Rey ante su conflicto con el Tribunal Constitucional	XXX				XXX
	El fondo de garantía de depósitos, oferta pública y subasta serán los tres tramos de la ampliación de Banesto					XXXX
Contraportada	Publicidad					
Subtotal ABC		3	0	0	0	7
El País	El Tribunal Supremo se rebela contra el Constitucional y apela al Rey			X		XX
	Desencuentro en la Moncloa	X				X
	El Fondo de Garantía cambiará sus normas para vender Banesto					XX
	La inminente expropiación encrespa a los vecinos del Liceo				X	
	Uno de los policías de la matanza de Nigrán planeaba liquidar a su cómplice			XX		
	Rusia tendrá tres bases militares en Georgia					XX
	Los conductores que circulen por las aceras en Barcelona serán juzgados				X	
	Creado el Consejo Asesor de Medio Ambiente, que contará con 11 ecologistas				X	X
	El Betis elimina de la Copa a un impotente Barça					XX
	Londres embarga al ex presidente de KIO por 500 millones de dólares			X		X
Contraportada	La camiseta, Juan José Millás			X		
	Salir en la «tele» por guarros. Los vitorianos que ensucien la calle verán su infracción por la pequeña pantalla como castigo	X			X	XX
Subtotal El País		2	0	5	4	14

Periódicos	Titulares (unidades redaccionales)	Elementos gráficos	Humanos Individuales M	Humanos Individuales H	Colectivos	No humanos
La Vanguardia	Pujol y Roca censuran al PP por su actitud con el catalán			XX		X
	Felipe González no cede ante los sindicatos	X		X		X
	El policiá acusado de asesinato tenía grandes deudas en el póquer	X		X		X
	Otra sorpresa en la copa: el Betis elimina al Barça					XXX
Contraportada	Aires escandinavos. Fallece Ruben Mattus el creador de Häagen-Dazs	X		X		X
	Pulso bursátil y financiero	X				X
	El semáforo, Edmond Alphandeéry, Manuel Conté, Joaquín Moyá-Angeler, Jean-Luc Dehnaene, Eduardo Abellán	XXXXX		XXXXX		
Subtotal La Vanguardia		9	0	10	0	8
El Periódico	Redondo y Gutiérrez salen frustrados de l Moncloa	X		XX		
	La movilidad de los funcionarios se pondrá en marcha de inmediato					X
	El Supremo denuncia ante el Rey al Tribunal Constitucional			X		XX
	Acuerdo de todos los partidos para que el nuevo Liceu sea público					XX
	Un segunda elimina al Barça de la Copa en el Camp Nou (0-1)	X				XX
	La policía no encuentra la pistola del crimen de Galicia	X				XX
Contraportada	El ruedo es acosado por la piqueta	XX				XX
Subtotal El Periódico		5	0	3	0	11
Total cabeceras 1994		19	0	18	4	40

FICHA 3
TITULARES UNIDADES REDACCIONALES AÑO 2004

Periódicos	Titulares (unidades redaccionales)	Elementos gráficos	Humanos Individuales M	Humanos Individuales H	Colectivos	No humanos
ABC	**La CIA asegura** que **Iraq** era una amenaza potencial pero no inminente					XX
	Funeral por el **comandante Pérez García**	X		X		X
	Los malos tratos provocaron **117 denuncias diarias** en 2003	X				XX
	España, entre los países que practican más **turismo sexual con menores**					XX
	Viernes de Estreno, **Cold Mountain** con **Nicole Kidman** abrió la Berlinale		X			X
	Falso directo: **ABC** y **CBS** emitirán con media hora de retraso las ceremonias de los Oscar y los Grammy para evitar incidentes	X				XX
Contraportada	Publicidad					
Subtotal ABC		3	1	1	0	10
El País	**El jefe de la CIA** afirma que nunca habló de **Iraq** como amenaza inminente	X		X		X
	Decenas de heridos en las protestas de los astilleros andaluces				X	
	Los malos tratos a mujeres generaron **más de 50,000 denuncias** el año pasado					XX
	EE UU deja a **España** fuera del contrato millonario para equiparar al nuevo Ejército iraquí					XX
	Salud asegura que el **anterior gobierno de CiU** ocultó **las listas de espera reales**					XXX
	Funeral por el **comandante de la Guardia Civil** herido mortalmente en **Iraq**			X		X
	El PP europeo pide que **los políticos del Este** revelen su pasado comunista				X	X
	El Gobierno francés amenaza con requisar **500.000 pisos vacíos** si no salen al mercado					XX
	Un hombre mata a **su madre**, la entierra en cal viva y vive con el cadáver más de un año en su casa		X	X		
	Guerra entre los **Blair** y lo **Bush**	X			XX	X
Contraportada	El «mandao», **Juan José Millás**			X		
Subtotal El País		2	1	4	4	13

FICHA 3
TITULARES UNIDADES REDACCIONALES AÑO 2004 *(Continuación)*

Periódicos	Titulares (unidades redaccionales)	Elementos gráficos	Humanos Individuales M	Humanos Individuales H	Colectivos	No humanos
La Vanguardia	La CIA dice que **Iraq** no era un peligro inminente					XX
	Casi 60.000 catalanes están en **lista de espera** para ser operados				X	X
	Letizia vestirá **Pertegaz**	X	X	X		
	Las muertes por violencia doméstica crecen un 30%					X
	Más de 30.000 españoles hacen **turismo sexual infantil**				X	X
	Unió lidera una rebelión democristiana en el **PPE**					XX
Contraportada	«Un árbol puede ser malvado». **Alexandre Hollan**	X		X		
Subtotal La Vanguardia		2	1	2	2	7
El Periódico	**Sanitat** garantiza **las operaciones** antes de 6 meses	X				XX
	Vinallop: aquí empezará **el trasvase**	X				XX
	La CIA afirma que nunca dijo que **Sadam** fuera un peligro inminente			X		X
	Un hombre tuvo 15 meses en cal viva **el cadáver de su madre**		X	X		
Contraportada	Publicidad					
Subtotal El Periódico		2	1	2	0	5
Total ABC, El País, La Vanguardia, El Periódico		9	4	9	6	35

54

FICHA 3
TITULARES UNIDADES REDACCIONALES AÑO 2004 *(Continuación)*

Periódicos	Titulares (unidades redaccionales)	Elementos gráficos	Humanos			No huma- nos
			Individuales		Colectivos	
			M	H		
El Punt	El gobierno regulará la actividad de las colonias escolares*					XX
	Un hombre mata a la madre y oculta el cuerpo más de un año en su casa, en Esplugues*	X	X	X		
	Gracia quiere convertir la plaza del Diamante en un espacio de recuperación de la memoria histórica*					XX
	Mieras apuesta por un hombre de las casas regionales para dirigir la cultura tradicional y popular*		X	X		
	Gorbatxov dice que una nueva «perestroika» haría un mundo más justo*			X		X
	Geli dice que las listas de espera son el doble de largas de lo que decía CiU*		X			X
	Las universidades catalanas ofrecerán carreras de tres años el próximo curso*					XX
	Trasladar el zoo de Barcelona a Sabadell cuesta 120 millones según un estudio*					X
	Treinta mil españoles practicaron turismo sexual con menores durante el año 2001*	X			X	X
Contraportada	Viaje en cercanías. Toni Sala*			X		
	Madrid. Enric Serra*			X		
Subtotal El Punt		2	3	5	1	10
Metro Directe	Plan para reducir las listas de espera a seis meses*					XX
	5.000 niños, obligados a ejercer la prostitución				X	X
	Dalí, genial	X		X		
	Entrevista a El Canto del Loco	X			X	
	Un best seller en la carretera					X
	De Mortimers en Nou Barris				X	
	I Congreso Nacional de Prensa Gratuita					X
	Los españoles, los que menos duermen				X	
	La Cia contradice a Bush por el supuesto arsenal de Sadam	X		XX		X

* En catalán en el original.

55

Periódicos	Titulares (unidades redaccionales)	Elementos gráficos	Humanos Individuales M	Humanos Individuales H	Colectivos	No humanos
Metro Directe *(continuación)*	**ERC** y **ICV** se oponen al túnel de Horta*	X				XX
	Mata a **su madre** y la entierra en casa durante 18 meses	X	X			
	«Hay que hacer tests psicológics a los jueces». **Enrique Arias Vega**			X		
	El Barça de Pesic gana y pasará como líder del grupo					X
	Rafael Nadal, el degutante más joven de la Davis	X		X		
	El tiempo*					X
Contraportada	Publicidad					
Subtotal Metro Directe		6	1	5	4	10
20 Minutos	**El 65% de los enfermos** en lista de espera está en el área de Barcelona				X	
	España, uno de los cinco países de la UE con más **turismo sexual infantil**					XX
	Llevaban **mujeres inmigrantes** al Raval y las violaban si no se prostituían*				X	
	Los socios del gobierno de Clos rechazan **el plan del alcalde** para hacer el túnel de Horta*				X	X
	Perfumes y **productos del hogar**, pasan de las rebajas					XX
	68 mujeres asesinadas (y **106 casi**) por su pareja en 2003				XX	
	Guarda a **su madre** en cal viva más de un año tras matarla		X			
	Duras críticas de **la mujer de Tony Blair** contra los **Bush**		X		X	
	Censura en **los Grammy** y **los Oscar** por el pecho de **Janet**	X	X			XX
	Seàbucuit. Galopando hacia el Oscar	X				X
	«Deborah saca mi parte salvaje», **Javier**	X		X		
	Pochettino. «La situación es difícil y vine a ayudar»	X		X		
	Martirio & Rinaldi. Une **el tango** y **la copla**	X	XX			XX
	Minghella. Llega a la Berlinale sin **Kidman**		X	X		

* En catalán en el original.

FICHA 3
TITULARES UNIDADES REDACCIONALES AÑO 2004 *(Continuación)*

Periódicos	Titulares (unidades redaccionales)	Elementos gráficos	Humanos Individuales M	Humanos Individuales H	Colectivos	No humanos
20 Minutos *(continuación)*	MÁS CINE. **Samuráis de risa** en Zatoichi				X	
	TEATRO. **De 7 vidas al Romea**					X
	Mayumana, percusión y humor				X	
	MÚSICA. **Serafín**, el índice de Londres				X	
	ARTE. **Fotografía soviética**					X
	Modigliani en el Diocesà			X		
	TELE. **Toda la programación**					X
	Primitiva, ONCE, Trío					X
	Sol y temperatura más agradable					X
Contraportada	Publicidad					
Subtotal 20 Minutos		5	6	4	9	15
Gran total		23	14	23	20	70

TABLA 2
RESULTADOS FINALES DEL EJERCICIO 1. LA *AMPLITUD* DE *LA MIRADA INFORMATIVA* EN CIFRAS

Año 1984 Periódicos	Total UR	Protagonistas Humanos individuales M y H	%	Protagonistas Humanos colectivos	%	Protagonistas No Humanos	%
ABC	1	0	0	0	0	1	100
El País	13	15	45	2	6	16	49
La Vanguardia	4	0	0	1	14	6	86
El Periódico	10	4	29	0	0	10	71
Total	**28**	**19**	**35**	**3**	**5**	**33**	**60**

Año 1994 Periódicos	Total UR	Protagonistas Humanos individuales M y H	%	Protagonistas Humanos colectivos	%	Protagonistas No Humanos	%
ABC	2	0	0	0	0	7	100
El País	12	5	22	4	17	14	61
La Vanguardia	.7	10	59	0	0	8	41
El Periódico	7	3	21	0	0	11	79
TOTAL	**28**	**18**	**30**	**4**	**6**	**40**	**64**

TABLA 2
RESULTADOS FINALES DEL EJERCICIO 1. LA *AMPLITUD* DE *LA MIRADA INFORMATIVA* EN CIFRAS *(continuación)*

Año 2004 Periódicos	Total UR	Protagonistas Humanos individuales M y H	%	Protagonistas Humanos colectivos	%	Protagonistas No Humanos	%
ABC	6	2	17	0	0	10	83
El País	11	5	23	4	18	13	59
La Vanguardia	7	3	25	2	17	7	58
El Periódico	4	3	37	0	0	5	63
SUBTOTAL	**28**	**13**	**24**	**6**	**11**	**35**	**65**
El Punt	11	8	42	1	5	10	53
Metro Directe	15	6	30	4	20	10	50
20 Minutos	23	10	31	9	25	15	44
TOTAL	**77**	**37**	**30**	**20**	**15**	**70**	**55**

TABLA 3
TOTALES DEL EJERCICIO 1

	1984	1994	2004		Total
Total humanos individuales	19	18	37	(13)*	74
Total humanos colectivos	3	4	20	(6)	27
Total no humanos	33	40	70	(35)	143
Total protagonistas	**55**	**62**	**127**	**(54)**	**244**

* Los números entre paréntesis equivalen a los datos de las cuatro cabeceras (ABC, El País, La Vanguardia i El Periódico) que se repiten en los tres años analizados.

REPRESENTACIÓN GRÁFICA DE LA AMPLITUD DE *LA MIRADA INFORMATIVA* EN LOS EJEMPLARES ANALIZADOS

Año 1984

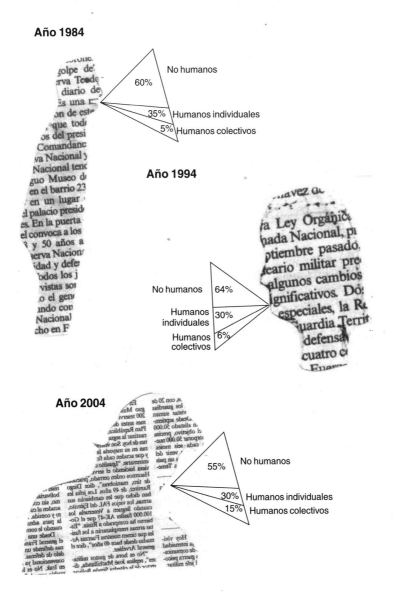

60% — No humanos

35% — Humanos individuales

5% — Humanos colectivos

Año 1994

No humanos — 64%

Humanos individuales — 30%

Humanos colectivos — 6%

Año 2004

55% — No humanos

30% — Humanos individuales

15% — Humanos colectivos

Comentarios al ejercicio 1

Como hemos explicado, la primera pregunta que nos hicimos fue *¿de quién hablan las noticias?* Pero al examinar atentamente cada titular para registrarlos literalmente en la ficha nos dimos cuenta que debíamos ajustar la pregunta, ya que las noticias, además de hablar de *seres humanos*, hablan también de una diversidad de instituciones, acciones, entidades, datos, fenómenos, cosas... que hemos englobado como *no humanos*. Es decir, que para evaluar la amplitud de *la mirada informativa* hemos de preguntarnos *quién, quiénes*, o *qué* son considerados protagonistas en las noticias.

En cuanto a los seres humanos, a veces las noticias hablan de seres *humanos individuales*, sean mujeres u hombres identificados o no con nombre y apellidos, y otras veces de *colectivos*.

El análisis de los titulares de las 133 unidades redaccionales que aparecen en portada y contraportada de las cabeceras de los ejemplares correspondientes a la muestra de los tres años analizados nos permite advertir que, en términos generales, las noticias publicadas hablan menos de protagonistas humanos que de protagonistas no humanos. La representación gráfica de los datos muestra con claridad que *la mirada informativa* enfoca con mayor *amplitud* a los protagonistas no humanos, con índices que van entre el 55% y el 64%.

Esta relación es mucho más evidente en los ejemplares analizados de los diarios que se repiten en los tres años (*ABC, El País, La Vanguardia y El Periódico*), en los que el porcentaje de protagonistas no humanos está entre el 60% y el 64% del total. Las únicas excepciones se dan en *El País* de 1984 y *La Vanguardia* de 1994, donde el porcentaje de protagonistas humanos es mayor que el de no humanos (51% humanos frente a 49% de no humanos y 59% humanos frente a 41% no humanos, respectivamente). También en el ejemplar analizado de *La Vanguardia* de 2004 la representación de ambos tipos de protagonistas es similar (42% humanos frente a 58% no humanos).

En los ejemplares analizados de 2004 que no aparecían en la muestra de la década anterior, *El Punt, Metro Directe y 20 Minutos*, la relación es más equilibrada. *El Punt* presenta un porcentaje de protagonista humanos de 47% frente a un 53 % de protagonistas no humanos. En *Metro Directe* la relación es de uno a uno, y en *20 Minutos*, los protagonistas humanos superan a los no humanos en una relación de 56% frente a 44%, el único caso junto con los ejemplares de *El País* de 1984 y de *La Vanguardia* de 1994. Por tanto, sólo tres ejemplares de los 15 analizados presentan una mirada informativa más amplia hacia los seres humanos.

En general, el enfoque a los protagonistas humanos no supera el 35%, y representa, preferentemente, a protagonistas individuales. Los protagonistas colectivos no superan el 15% del total de los protagonistas registrados en la muestra. Y en algunos casos los protagonistas humanos no aparecen.

Por ejemplo, los ejemplares analizados de *ABC* de 1984 y 1994 no presentan a ningún ser humano como protagonista de sus titulares de portada (presenta seres humanos en las imágenes, aunque en este ejercicio nos limitamos a analizar los textos); *La Vanguardia* de 1984 presenta solamente un colectivo humano: *«los mandos del ejército»*; en el mismo año 1984, el ejemplar analizado de *El Periódico* sólo presenta protagonistas hombres, y las mujeres solamente son consideradas como protagonistas en la contraportada de *El País*.

En la muestra de 1994, las mujeres desaparecen completamente. Ninguno de los cuatro ejemplares analizados presenta mujeres como protagonistas en la portada ni en la contraportada. Asimismo, en este año, el único caso en que los protagonistas humanos superan a los no humanos se da en *La Vanguardia*. Los protagonistas colectivos sólo aparecen en *El País*, donde representan casi la mitad del total de protagonistas humanos.

En 2004, en los ejemplares de la muestra de los cuatro periódicos que se repiten en años anteriores, *ABC, El País, La Vanguardia y El Periódico*, solamente se presentan una mujer como protagonista en los titulares de las noticias. El número de mujeres aumenta en los ejemplares de *El Punt* y *20 Minutos* y se mantiene en el ejemplar de *Metro Directe*. En todos los casos, el número de hombres es mayor al número de mujeres. En todos los casos, exceptuando *Metro Directe* y *20 Minutos*, los protagonistas no humanos superan a los protagonistas humanos. Igualmente, es en las cabeceras gratuitas donde aparecen más como protagonistas, los colectivos humanos.

También podemos apreciar las diferencias en la cantidad de unidades redaccionales que presentan en sus portadas las distintas cabeceras. El diario *El País* es, en todos los años, uno de los que presenta mayor número de unidades. En *ABC* aumenta el número de unidades mientras que en *El Periódico* disminuye. Las portadas de las cabeceras gratuitas, también, son las que mayor número de unidades presentan. Estos datos expresan la representación que los ejemplares de la muestra hacen de los protagonistas a los que enfocan, y en ningún caso se pueden generalizar, si bien, otras investigaciones que hemos realizado nos permiten concluir que estos datos son bastante habituales y ponen de manifiesto rutinas compartidas por los y las profesionales respecto al enfoque que hacen de la realidad social.

Las contraportadas, además de ser espacios en el que la publicidad desempeña un papel importante, se hallan desligadas, en cierta manera de la presión de la actualidad que rige las portadas, y presentan diversos protagonistas humanos, hombres y mujeres, identificados con nombres y apellidos. Aparte de las tradicionales secciones de opinión de los periódicos, en las contraportadas se suelen presentar una serie de autores, a veces colaboradores, no siempre redactores de plantilla de los periódicos y no necesariamente periodistas de profesión, a los que hemos considerado como protagonistas de las unidades que ellos mismos escriben, porque estas voces también representan la multiplicidad coral que compone un diario. El matiz informativo personalizado o personalista que encontramos en las contraportadas nos presenta este espacio como un lugar dedicado a una visión más humana de los acontecimientos noticiosos y en algunos casos también al humor.

Es muy posible encontrar en esta sección perfiles de hombres y mujeres que se destacan por sus acciones, como «un exitoso empresario» o la «última artesana maragata». Sin entrar en este apartado en el tratamiento informativo ni en las acciones que se le atribuyen a protagonistas hombres y mujeres presentes en las contraportadas, podemos decir que en esta página se presenta proporcionalmente un mayor número de seres humanos, y más mujeres protagonistas que en las portadas.

Ejercicio 2
La *DIVERSIDAD* de *la mirada informativa* en los titulares

Después de evaluar la *Amplitud* de *la mirada informativa*, en este ejercicio vamos a evaluar la **Diversidad** de los protagonistas a los que se enfoca en los titulares de las noticias.

Para hacer este análisis más detallado, realizamos el ejercicio paso a paso, en tres fases en las que nos detenemos a examinar específicamente quiénes son los seres humanos individuales, colectivos, o los protagonistas no humanos que aparecen en los titulares de las noticias. Los datos pueden contrastarse en las fichas que incluimos, concebidas para seleccionar los casos concretos que corresponden a las preguntas específicas de cada fase.

En la **primera fase** del ejercicio seleccionamos todos los titulares que presentan un protagonista humano individual, y distinguimos entre humanos identificados con nombre y apellidos, y humanos no identificados, ya que la presentación con nombre y apellido siempre tiene una connotación más positiva que la presentación anónima. Esta identificación permite distinguir también entre mujeres (M) y hombres (H).

En la **segunda fase**, seguimos el mismo procedimiento con los protagonistas humanos colectivos.

Finalmente, en la **tercera fase** examinamos los protagonistas no humanos, y diferenciamos entre instituciones y entidades diversas formadas por seres humanos, y el resto de cosas y fenómenos.

En cada fase, reproducimos las portadas y hacemos un *zoom* de algunas noticias, para facilitar que quien lea esta guía pueda contrastar los criterios que hemos aplicado con los materiales originales. Al final del ejercicio, se incluye una tabla con los resultados de las tres fases, en la que podemos ver comparativamente la diversidad de *la mirada informativa* que se ofrece en los titulares de los ejemplares de los diarios analizados.

Primera fase
¿A qué mujeres y hombres individuales, con o sin nombre y apellido, se presenta como protagonistas en los titulares?

En esta primera fase nos detenemos a examinar qué protagonistas individuales son identificados con nombre y apellido, o con términos genéricos. De esta manera, podemos evaluar a qué seres humanos se atribuye una identidad propia y a qué seres humanos se considera anónimos, como si su identidad no fuera significativa. Al mismo tiempo, los distinguimos entre mujeres y hombres.

PROTAGONISTAS HUMANOS INDIVIDUALES DE LOS TITULARES
(AÑO 1984)

Periódicos	Protagonistas de los titulares	Humanos Individuales	
		Con nombre y apellido	Sin nombre y apellido
ABC		-	-
Subtotal		0	0
El País	El PSC acusa a **Pujol** de financiar una campaña contra los municipios	H	
	Jaime Lusinchi propugna un pacto social entre los venezolanos	H	
	Ronald Reagan no detendrá la subida del dólar.	H	
	Guardia civil muerto, por error de **un compañero**, en la persecución de tres atracadores		HH
	Un general mexicano asesina a **un obispo** ortodoxo catalán		HH
	Claustrofilia. **Juan Cueto**	H	
	Dolores Fernández Feijoo. La última artesa maragata teje mantas y cobertores ayudada por **su madre**, de 93 años, y de **una tía**, de 83	M	MM
	Gente. **Peach de Rohan, Julio Anguita, José Hernández Quero, Fernando Esteso**	HHHH	
Subtotal		9	6
La Vanguardia		-	-
Subtotal		0	0
El Periódico	**Felipe** critica en Venezuela el informe de Kissinger	H	
	La OTAN a coloquio con **Ángel Viñas**	H	
	Verdes. **Antonio Álvarez Solís**	H	
	Encarcelan a **un cabo de Lloret** por vender armas		H
Subtotal		3	1
Total		12	7

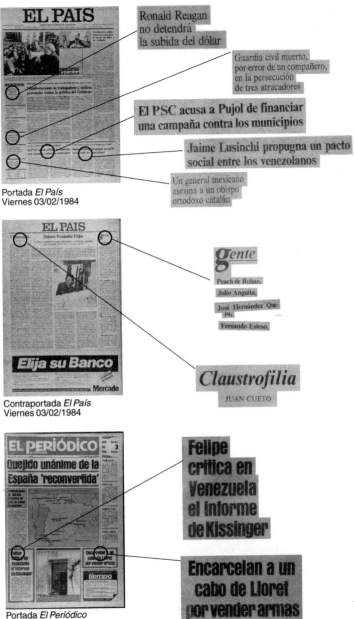

Portada El País
Viernes 03/02/1984

Ronald Reagan no detendrá la subida del dólar

Guardia civil muerto, por error de un compañero, en la persecución de tres atracadores

El PSC acusa a Pujol de financiar una campaña contra los municipios

Jaime Lusinchi propugna un pacto social entre los venezolanos

Un general mexicano asesina a un obispo ortodoxo catalán

Contraportada El País
Viernes 03/02/1984

*g*ente

Peach de Rohan,
Julio Anguita,
José Hernández Quero,
Fernando Esteso,

Elija su Banco

Mercado

Claustrofilia

JUAN CUETO

Portada El Periódico
Viernes 03/02/1984

Felipe critica en Venezuela el informe de Kissinger

Encarcelan a un cabo de Lloret por vender armas

65

FICHA 5
PROTAGONISTAS HUMANOS INDIVIDUALES DE LOS TITULARES
(AÑO 1994)

Periódicos	Protagonistas de los titulares	Humanos Individuales	
		Con nombre y apellido	Sin nombre y apellido
ABC		-	-
Subtotal		0	0
El País	El Tribunal Supremo se rebela contra el Constitucional y apela **al Rey**		H
	Uno de los policías de la matanza de Nigrán planeaba liquidar a **su cómplice**		HH
	Londres embarga al **ex presidente** de KIO por 500 millones de dólares		H
	La camiseta. **Juan José Millás**	H	
Subtotal		1	4
La Vanguardia	**Pujol** y **Roca** censuran al PP por su actitud con el catalán	HH	
	Felipe González no cede ante los sindicatos	H	
	El **policía acusado** de asesinato tenía grandes deudas en el póquer		H
	El semáforo. **Edmond Alphandeéry, Manuel Conté, Joaquín Moyá-Angeler, Eduardo Abellán, Jean-Luc Dehnaene**	HHHHH	
	Aires escandinavos. Fallece **Ruben Mattus** el creador de Häagen-Dazs	H	
Subtotal		9	1
El Periódico	**Redondo** y **Gutiérrez** salen frustrados de la Moncloa	HH	
	El Supremo denuncia ante **el Rey** al Tribunal Constitucional		H
Subtotal		2	1
Total		12	6

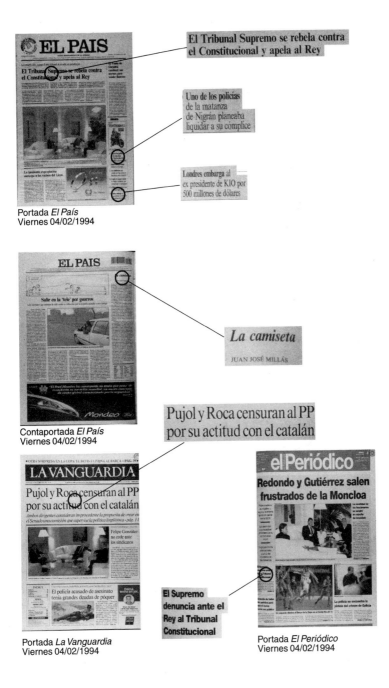

Portada *El País*
Viernes 04/02/1994

El Tribunal Supremo se rebela contra
el Constitucional y apela al Rey

Uno de los policías
de la matanza
de Nigrán planeaba
liquidar a su cómplice

Londres embarga al
ex presidente de KIO por
500 millones de dólares

Contraportada *El País*
Viernes 04/02/1994

La camiseta

JUAN JOSÉ MILLÁS

Pujol y Roca censuran al PP
por su actitud con el catalán

Portada *La Vanguardia*
Viernes 04/02/1994

El Supremo
denuncia ante el
Rey al Tribunal
Constitucional

Redondo y Gutiérrez salen
frustrados de la Moncloa

Portada *El Periódico*
Viernes 04/02/1994

PROTAGONISTAS HUMANOS INDIVIDUALES DE LOS TITULARES
(AÑO 2004)

Periódicos	Protagonistas de los titulares	Humanos Individuales	
		Con nombre y apellido	Sin nombre y apellido
ABC	Viernes de Estreno. Cold Mountain con **Nicole Kidman** abrió la Berlinale	M	
	Funeral por **el comandante Pérez García**	H	
Subtotal		2	0
El País	**El jefe de la CIA** afirma que nunca habló de Iraq como amenaza inminente		H
	Un hombre mata a **su madre**, la entierra en cal viva y vive con el cadáver más de un año en su casa		HM
	Funeral por **el comandante de la Guardia Civil** herido mortalmente en Iraq		H
	El «mandao». **Juan José Millás**	H	
Subtotal		1	4
La Vanguardia	**Letizia** vestirá **Pertegaz**	MH	
	«Un árbol puede ser malvado». **Alexandre Hollan**	H	
Subtotal		3	0
El Periódico	La CIA afirma que nunca dijo que **Sadam** fuera un peligro inminente.	H	
	Un hombre tuvo 15 meses en cal viva el cadáver de **su madre**		HM
Subtotal		1	2
Total		7	6
El Punt	**Un hombre** mata a **la madre** y oculta el cuerpo más de un año en su casa, en Esplugues*		HM
	Mieras apuesta por **un hombre** de las casas regionales para dirigir la cultura tradicional y popular*	M	H
	Gorbatxov dice que una nueva «perestroika» haría el mundo más justo*	H	

* En catalán en el original.

EL PAIS

El jefe de la CIA afirma que nunca habló de Irak como amenaza inminente

> El jefe de la CIA
> afirma que nunca
> habló de Irak como
> amenaza inminente

Funeral por el comandante de la Guardia Civil herido mortalmente en Irak

UN HOMBRE mata a su madre, la entierra en cal viva y vive con el cadáver más de un año en su casa

Portada *El País*
Viernes 06/02/2004

EL PAIS

Guerra entre los Blair y los Bush

El 'mandao'

JUAN JOSÉ MILLÁS

Contraportada *El País*
Viernes 06/02/2004

el Periódico

Sanitat garantiza las operaciones antes de 6 meses

Un hombre tuvo 15 meses en cal viva el cadáver de su madre

La CIA afirma que nunca dijo que Sadam fuera un peligro inminente

Portada *El Periódico*
Viernes 06/02/2004

69

PROTAGONISTAS HUMANOS INDIVIDUALES DE LOS TITULARES
(AÑO 2004) *(continuación)*

Periódicos	Protagonistas de los titulares	Humanos Individuales	
		Con nombre y apellido	Sin nombre y apellido
El Punt *(continuación)*	**Geli** dice que las listas de espera son el doble de largas de lo que decía CiU*	M	
	Viaje en cercanías. **Toni Sala***	H	
	Madrid. **Enric Serra***	H	
Subtotal		**5**	**3**
Metro Directe	**Dalí**, genial	H	
	La CIA contradice a **Bush** por el supuesto arsenal de **Sadam**	HH	
	Mata a su **madre** y la entierra en casa durante 18 meses		M
	«Hay que hacer tests psicológicos a los jueces». **Enrique Arias Vega**	H	
	Rafael Nadal, el debutante más joven de la Davis	H	
Subtotal		**5**	**1**
20 Minutos	Guarda a **su madre** en cal viva más de un año tras matarla		M
	«Deborah saca mi parte salvaje», **Javier**	H	
	Duras críticas de la **mujer de Tony Blair** contra los Bush		M
	Censura en los Grammy y los Oscar por el pecho de **Janet**	M	
	Pochettino. «La situación es difícil y vine a ayudar»	H	
	Martirio & **Rinaldi**. Unen el tango y la copla	MM	
	Minghella. Llega a la Berlinale sin **Kidman**	HM	
	Modigliani en el Diocesà	H	
Subtotal		**8**	**2**
Gran total		**25**	**12**

* En catalán en el original.

Mieras aposta per un home de les cases regionals per dirigir la cultura tradicional i popular

Geli diu que les llistes d'espera són el doble de llargues del que mantenia CiU

Gorbatxov diu que una nova «perestroika» faria el món més just

Portada *El Punt*
Viernes 06/02/2004

la columna | ENRIC SERRA
Madrid

Contraportada *El Punt*
Viernes 06/02/2004

Guarda a su madre en cal viva más de un año tras matarla

Portada *20 Minutos*
Viernes 06/02/2004

71

Comentarios a la primera fase

Al preguntarnos por las mujeres y hombres que aparecen identificados o no con nombres y apellidos, en los titulares de las noticias publicadas en las portadas de los ejemplares seleccionados, vemos claramente que los hombres son siempre mayoría: en las fichas que registran los datos de los protagonistas de 1984 y 1994 predominan los hombres (H) casi por completo (1984) o de forma exclusiva (1994). La ficha correspondiente a los ejemplares del año 2004 presenta más variaciones.

En los titulares de los ejemplares de 1984 aparecen 4 mujeres y 15 hombres. De las 4 mujeres, 2 aparecen identificadas con nombre y apellidos, Dolores Fernández Feijoo y Peach de Rohan, y 2 no identificadas, la madre, de 93 años, y una tía, de 83, de Dolores Fernández, todas en la contraportada de *El País*. De los 15 hombres que se presentan en los titulares de *El País* y *El Periódico*, 10 aparecen identificados (Pujol, Jaime Lusinchi, Ronald Reagan, Juan Cueto, Julio Anguita, José Hernández Quero, Fernando Esteso, Felipe, Ángel Viñas, y Antonio Álvarez Solís) y 5 sin identificar (guardia civil muerto, un compañero, un general mexicano, un obispo ortodoxo catalán, un cabo de Lloret). *La Vanguardia* y *ABC* no presentan ni un solo ser humano como protagonista en los textos de los titulares de las noticias.

En las portadas de los titulares de los ejemplares analizados de 1994 no aparece ninguna mujer como protagonista, mientras que los hombres aparecen en 18 ocasiones: 12 identificados con nombre y apellidos (Juan José Millás, Pujol, Roca, Felipe González, Edmond Alphandeéry, Manuel Conté, Joaquín Moyá-Angeler, Eduardo Abellán, Jean-Luc Dehnaene, Redondo, Gutiérrez y Ruben Mattus), y 6 sin nombre y apellido (en dos ocasiones el Rey, uno de los policías de la matanza de Nigrán, su cómplice, el policía acusado de asesinato, el ex presidente de KIO), aunque en el caso del Rey y el ex presidente de KIO se identifican por su posición jerárquica. En el ejemplar del diario *ABC* de este año tampoco se presentan protagonistas humanos en los textos de los titulares.

El análisis de los 7 ejemplares seleccionados de 2004 permite ver que la preponderancia del protagonismo de los hombres se mantiene: de 37 protagonistas, 14 son mujeres y 23 hombres. Podemos constatar que, cuantitativamente, el protagonismo de las mujeres ha aumentado considerablemente con respecto a los años anteriores, aunque el número de hombres considerados protagonistas son casi el doble que el de mujeres. No obstante, los datos ponen de manifiesto que la presencia de mujeres en los titulares no es equitativa respecto a la de los hombres.

Si examinamos por separado las cifras de las cuatro cabeceras analizadas también en los años anteriores, *ABC, El País, La Vanguardia* y *El Periódico*, encontramos 13 protagonistas: 4 mujeres y 9 hombres, lo que significa un cambio notable respecto a los datos de años anteriores, al menos cuantitativamente. En los titulares de las nuevas cabeceras que incorporamos a la muestra de ejemplares analizados del año 2004, *El Punt, Metro Directe y 20 Minutos*, aparecen 24 protagonistas, de los cuales 10 son mujeres y 14 hombres.

¿Quiénes son estas mujeres y hombres de los que hablan los titulares de las noticias publicadas en las portadas y contraportadas de los ejemplares seleccionados de 2004? *ABC, El País, La Vanguardia* y *El Periódico*, enfocan 4 mujeres, dos son presentadas con nombres y apellidos en los textos de los titulares de las portadas, Nicole Kidman (*ABC*) y Letizia (*La Vanguardia*), y dos no son identificadas, se trata de una madre que fue asesinada por su hijo, de la que se habla en *El País* y en *El Periódico*.

En cuanto a los hombres, de los 4 identificados con nombre y apellido, 2 aparecen en los textos de los titulares de las portadas, Sadam (*El Periódico*) y Pertegaz (*La Vanguardia*); y otros 2 en las contraportadas, Juan José Millás, autor de una columna en la contraportada de *El País*, y Alexandre Hollan al que se hace una entrevista en la de *La Vanguardia*. Y los 3 hombres no identificados son el jefe de la CIA y un hombre que mata a su madre, en la portada de *La Vanguardia*, y el mismo hombre en la portada de *El Periódico*, del que se dice que «*tuvo 15 meses en cal viva el cadáver de su madre*».

En cuanto a las cabeceras de *El Punt, Metro Directe y 20 Minutos*, que no existían en la muestra de los años anteriores, hemos visto que enfocan una mayor cantidad de protagonistas humanos individuales (24 protagonistas frente a los 13 de las otras cuatro cabeceras). También se puede apreciar que las 6 mujeres identificadas con nombre y apellidos (las conselleras de la Generalitat de Catalunya, Mieras y Geli, en la portada de *El Punt*, y las artistas Martirio y Rinaldi, la actriz Kidman y la cantante Janet en la portada de *20 Minutos*) superan por primera vez a las 4 mujeres no identificadas (la mujer-madre asesinada que aparece en las tres portadas y la mujer de Tony Blair). Y de los 14 hombres que aparecen como protagonistas, solamente 2 no son identificados con nombres y apellidos, se presentan como personajes anónimos en la portada de *El Punt* (el hombre que mató a su madre, y un hombre de las casas regionales al que la consellera Mieras encargó la dirección de las casas regionales). Los otros 12, aparecen identificados: en la portada de *El Punt*, Gorvatxov, y en la contraportada, dos autores, Toni Sala y Enric Serra; en la portada de *Metro Directe*, Dalí, Bush, Sadam, Enrique Arias Vega, Rafael Nadal; y en la primera de *20 Minutos*, Javier, Pochettino, Minghella y Modigliani.

Podemos concluir que, en relación con los protagonistas individuales identificados o no, cuantitativamente se ha producido una mayor amplitud y diversidad de *la mirada informativa* tanto en relación con las mujeres como con los hombres al incorporarse nuevas cabeceras en 2004. Si bien los hombres continúan siendo mayoría en todos los ejemplares de los tres años seleccionados, en 2004 el protagonismo de las mujeres aumenta considerablemente, aunque el número de hombres en este año sea casi el doble que el de mujeres, y la presencia de mujeres y hombres no es equitativa.

Segunda fase
¿A que seres humanos colectivos se presenta como protagonistas en los titulares?

En esta segunda fase seleccionamos los titulares de las noticias en las que se enfoca a colectivos humanos como protagonistas.

FICHA 7
PROTAGONISTAS COLECTIVOS DE LOS TITULARES (AÑO 1984)

Periódicos	Protagonistas de los titulares	Colectivos
ABC		-
El País	Pasividad de la policía francesa en la búsqueda de «etarras» que deben ser confinados	X
	Guardia civil muerto, por error de un compañero, en la persecución de tres atracadores	X
La Vanguardia	Más protección para los mandos del Ejército	X
El Periódico		-
Total		3

Pasividad de la policía francesa en la búsqueda de 'etarras' que deben ser confinados

Portada *El País*
Viernes 03/02/1984

Más protección para los mandos del Ejército

Portada *La Vanguardia*
Viernes 03/02/1984

75

PROTAGONISTAS COLECTIVOS DE LOS TITULARES (AÑO 1994)

Periódicos	Protagonistas de los titulares	Colectivos
ABC		-
El País	La inminente expropiación encrespa a **los vecinos del Liceo**	X
	Los conductores que circulen por las aceras en Barcelona serán juzgados	X
	Creado el Consejo Asesor de Medio Ambiente, que contará con **11 ecologistas**	X
	Salir en la «tele» por guarros. **Los vitorianos** que ensucien la calle verán su infracción por la pequeña pantalla como castigo	X
La Vanguardia		-
El Periódico		-
Total		4

Portada *El País*
Viernes 04/02/1994

PROTAGONISTAS COLECTIVOS DE LOS TITULARES (AÑO 2004)

Periódicos	Protagonistas de los titulares	Colectivos
ABC		-
El País	**Decenas de heridos** en las protestas de los astilleros andaluces	X
	El PP europeo pide que **los políticos del Este** revelen su pasado comunista	X
	Guerra entre los **Blair y los Bush**	XX
La Vanguardia	**Casi 60.000 catalanes** están en lista de espera para ser operados	X
	Más de 30.000 españoles hacen turismo sexual infantil	X
El Periódico		-
Subtotal		6
El Punt	**Treinta mil españoles** parcticaron turismo sexual con menores durante el año 2001*	X
Metro Directe	**5.000 niños**, obligados a ejercer la prostitución	X
	Los españoles, los que menos duermen	X
	Entrevista a **El Canto del Loco**	X
	De Mortimers en Nou Barris	X
20 Minutos	**El 65% de los enfermos** en lista de espera está en el área de Barcelona	X
	Llevaban **mujeres emigrantes** al Raval i las violaban si no se prostituían*	X
	Los socios del gobierno de Clos rechazan el plan del alcalde para hacer el Tunel de Horta*	X
	68 mujeres asesinadas (y 106 casi) por su pareja en 2003	XX
	Duras críticas de la mujer de Tony Blair contra **los Bush**	X
	MÁS CINE. **Samuráis** de risa en Zatoichi	X
	Mayumana, percusión y humor	X
	MÚSICA. **Serafín**, el indie de Londres	X
Gran total		20

* En catalán en el original.

EL PAÍS

El jefe de la CIA afirma que nunca habló de Irak como amenaza inminente

EL PP EUROPEO pide que los políticos del Este revelen su pasado comunista

Portada *El País*
Viernes 06/02/2004

LA VANGUARDIA

La CIA dice que Iraq no era un peligro inminente

Las muertes por violencia doméstica crecen un 30%

Portada *La Vanguardia*
Viernes 06/02/2004

Casi 60.000 catalanes están en lista de espera para ser operados

Más de 30.000 españoles hacen turismo sexual infantil

metro

Pla per reduir les llistes d'espera a sis mesos

Los españoles, los que menos duermen

De Mortimers en Nou Barris

5.000 niños, obligados a ejercer la prostitución

Portada *Metro Directe*
Viernes 06/02/2004

20 minutos Barcelona

El 65% de los enfermos en lista de espera está en el área de Barcelona

El 65% de los enfermos en lista de espera está en el área de Barcelona

68 mujeres asesinadas (y 106 casi) por su pareja en 2003

MÁS CINE Samuráis de risa en *Zatoichi*

MÚSICA Serafín, el indie de Londres

Portaven **dones immigrants** al Raval **i les violaven** si no es prostituïen

NOS CASAMOS

Portada *20 Minutos*
Viernes 06/02/2004

Comentarios a la segunda fase

Como podemos ver, la presencia de protagonistas humanos colectivos en los titulares es generalmente escasa en toda la muestra y en todos los años analizados, según evidencia el volumen de información registrado en estas fichas, muy inferior al de de las fichas de la fase anterior y de la fase siguiente de este ejercicio. Visto desde otra perspectiva, en los titulares de las portadas y contraportadas, *la mirada informativa* enfoca preferentemente a protagonistas individuales, la mayoría identificados.

En 1984 sólo aparecen tres protagonistas colectivos, dos en la portada de *El País* (etarras y tres atracadores) y uno en la de *La Vanguardia* (mandos del ejército).

En 1994 aparecen cuatro protagonistas colectivos, todos en *El País* (los vecinos del Liceo, los conductores, 11 ecologistas y los vitorianos), y no aparece ninguno ni en las portadas ni en las contraportadas de los ejemplares analizados de *ABC, El Periódico* y *La Vanguardia*.

Sin embargo, en 2004 advertimos un aumento considerable. Si bien, *ABC* y *El Periódico* siguen sin mencionar ningún protagonista colectivo, los restantes diarios analizados sí los incluyen: tres en *El País* (decenas de heridos, los políticos del Este, los Blair y los Bush), 2 en *La Vanguardia* (60.000 catalanes, 30.000 españoles), uno en *El Punt* (trenta mil espanyols), otros cuatro en *Metro Directe* (5.000 niños, los españoles, El canto del loco, De Mortimers) y nueve en *20 Minutos* (el 65 % de los enfermos, mujeres inmigrantes, los socios del gobierno de Clos, 68 mujeres asesinadas (y 106 casi), los Bush, samurais, Mayumana y Serafín).

En el caso de *20 Minutos*, *El País* y *La Vanguardia*, los protagonistas humanos colectivos alcanza un número muy similar al de hombres y mujeres en conjunto (4 protagonistas colectivos y 5 humanos individuales en *El País*; 9 protagonistas colectivos y 10 humanos individuales en *20 Minutos* y 2 protagonistas colectivos y 3 humanos individuales en *La Vanguardia*). *Metro Directe* presenta 4 protagonistas colectivos en los titulares y 6 protagonistas humanos individuales.

Los diarios *ABC* y *El Periódico* no hacen referencia a colectivos humanos en ningún titular de las páginas analizadas. Hemos de destacar también las escasas referencias a colectivos no adultos habitualmente excluidos en los titulares, como los 5.000 niños (de los que no se explicita el sexo) a los que sólo se menciona como protagonistas en la portada de *Metro Directe*, y las referencias a los colectivos femeninos: las mujeres inmigrantes, y las 68 mujeres asesinadas (y 106 casi) que aparecen como protagonistas en la portada de *20 Minutos*.

Tercera fase
¿Qué otros protagonistas no humanos son presentados en los titulares?

Finalmente, en esta tercera fase examinamos esos otros protagonistas que hemos agrupado como *no humanos*, a los que también enfoca *la mirada informativa* y se presenta en los textos de los titulares de las noticias.

Entre estos protagonistas no humanos hemos distinguido entre las instituciones o entidades que agrupan a seres humanos (partidos políticos, instituciones del gobierno, del Estado o de carácter internacional, empresas…), y «otros», englobando en esta categoría todo lo demás, especialmente los sujetos y predicados de las oraciones que hacen mención a lugares, reuniones o acciones, etc.

FICHA 10
PROTAGONISTAS NO HUMANOS DE LOS TITULARES (AÑO 1984)

Periódicos	Protagonistas de los titulares	No Humanos	
		Instituciones	Otros
ABC	**«Cumbre» iberoamericana** en Caracas	-	X
Subtotal		0	1
El País	**Manifestaciones de trabajadores y críticas patronales** contra la política del **Gobierno**		XXX
	El PSC acusa a Pujol de financiar una campaña contra los municipios	X	
	Jaime Lusinchi propugna un **pacto social entre los venezolanos**		X

80

FICHA 10
PROTAGONISTAS NO HUMANOS DE LOS TITULARES (AÑO 1984)
(continuación)

Periódicos	Protagonistas de los titulares	No Humanos	
		Instituciones	Otros
El País *(continuación)*	**Pasividad de la policía francesa** en la búsqueda de «etarras» que deben ser confinados		X
	Ronald Reagan no detendrá la **subida del dólar**		X
	Westinghouse negocia la **venta de su filial española** a una **compañía británica**	XXX	
	Probable declaración conjunta de los 12 magistrados del Tribunal Constitucional ante **el Supremo**	X	X
	La Comisión Mixta aprueba la transferencia de las **cámaras agrarias, las universidades y los espectáculos**	XXXX	
Subtotal		9	7
La Vanguardia	**Movilizaciones sindicales** contra la **política del Gobierno**	-	XX
	Barcelona: cada día es atracada **una farmacia**		XX
	Más protección para los mandos del Ejército		X
	Crece la influencia del Opus Dei en la Iglesia	-	X
Subtotal		0	6
El Periódico	**Quejido unánime** de la **España 'reconvertida'**		XX
	Felipe critica en Venezuela **el informe de Kissinger**		X
	Escolta policial		X
	El PSC acusa	X	
	Educación física		X
	El Barça pincha	X	
	Sumario secreto en el **caso Salomó**		XX
	La OTAN a coloquio con Ángel Viñas	X	
Subtotal		3	7
Total		12	21

Portada *El País*
Viernes 03/02/1984

Westinghouse negocia la venta de su filial española a una compañía británica

Probable declaración conjunta de los 12 magistrados del Tribunal Constitucional ante el Supremo

La Comisión Mixta aprueba la transferencia de las cámaras agrarias, las universidades y los espectáculos

Contraportada *La Vanguardia*
Viernes 03/02/1984

Barcelona: cada día es atracada una farmacia
(Página 22)

Crece la influencia del Opus Dei en la Iglesia
(Página 4)

Portada *El Periódico*
Viernes 03/02/1984

Escolta policial

El PSC acusa

Educación Física

El Barça «pincha»

82

FICHA 11
PROTAGONISTAS NO HUMANOS DE LOS TITULARES (AÑO 1994)

Periódicos	Protagonistas de los titulares	No Humanos	
		Instituciones	Otros
ABC	El Tribunal Supremo acude al arbitraje del Rey ante su conflicto con el Tribunal Constitucional	XX	X
	El fondo de garantía de depósitos, oferta pública y subasta serán los tres tramos de la ampliación de Banesto	X	XXX
Subtotal		3	4
El País	El Tribunal Supremo se rebela contra el Constitucional y apela al Rey	XX	
	Desencuentro en la Moncloa		X
	El Fondo de Garantía cambiará sus normas para vender Banesto	XX	
	La inminente expropiación encrespa a los vecinos del Liceo		X
	Rusia tendrá tres bases militares en Georgia		XX
	Creado el Consejo Asesor de Medio Ambiente, que contará con 11 ecologistas	X	
	El Betis elimina de la Copa a un impotente Barça	XX	
	Londres embarga al ex presidente de KIO por 500 millones de dólares		X
	Salir en la «tele» por guarros. Los vitorianos que ensucien la calle verán su infracción por la pequeña pantalla como castigo		XX
Subtotal		7	7
La Vanguardia	Pujol y Roca censuran al PP por su actitud con el catalán	X	
	Felipe González no cede ante los sindicatos	X	
	El policía acusado de asesinato tenía grandes deudas en el póquer		X
	Otra sorpresa e la copa: el Betis elimina al Barça	XX	X
	Aires escandinavos. Fallece Reuben Mattus, el creador de los helados Häagen-Dazs		X
	Pulso bursátil y financiero		X
Subtotal		4	4

PROTAGONISTAS NO HUMANOS DE LOS TITULARES (AÑO 1994)
(continuación)

Periódicos	Protagonistas de los titulares	No Humanos	
		Instituciones	Otros
El Periódico	**La movilidad de los funcionarios** se pondrá en marcha de inmediato		X
	El Supremo denuncia ante el Rey al **Tribunal Constitucional**	XX	
	Acuerdo de todos los partidos para que el nuevo **Liceu** sea público	X	X
	Un segunda elimina al **Barça** de la Copa en el Camp Nou (0-1)	XX	
	La policía no encuentra **la pistola del crimen** de Galicia	X	X
	El ruedo acosado por **la piqueta**		XX
Subtotal		6	5
Total		20	19

Portada *ABC*
Viernes 04/02/1994

EL FONDO DE GARANTÍA DE DEPÓSITOS, OFERTA PÚBLICA Y SUBASTA SERÁN LOS TRES TRAMOS DE LA AMPLIACIÓN DE BANESTO

El Fondo de Garantía cambiará sus normas para vender Banesto

EL PAIS

El Tribunal Supremo se rebela contra el Constitucional y apela al Rey

Rusia tendrá tres bases militares en Georgia

El Betis elimina de la Copa a un impotente Barça

Portada *El País*
Viernes 04/02/1994

Portada *La Vanguardia*
Viernes 04/02/1994

Portada *El Periódico*
Viernes 04/02/1994

FICHA 12

PROTAGONISTAS NO HUMANOS DE LOS TITULARES (AÑO 2004)

Periódicos	Protagonistas de los titulares	No Humanos	
		Instituciones	Otros
ABC	**La CIA** asegura que **Iraq** era una amenaza potencial pero no inminente	X	X
	Funeral por el comandante Pérez García		X
	Los malos tratos provocaron **117 denuncias diarias** en 2003		XX
	España, entre los países que practican más **turismo sexual**		XX
	Viernes de Estreno. **Cold Mountain** con Nicole Kidman abrió la Berlinale		X
	Falso directo: **ABC** y **CBS** emitirán con media hora de retraso las ceremonias de los Oscar y los Grammy para evitar incidentes	XX	
Subtotal		**3**	**7**

PROTAGONISTAS NO HUMANOS DE LOS TITULARES (AÑO 2004)
(continuación)

Periódicos	Protagonistas de los titulares	No Humanos	
		Instituciones	Otros
El País	El jefe de la CIA afirma que nunca habló de **Iraq** como amenaza inminente		X
	Los malos tratos a mujeres generaron **más de 50.000 denuncias** el año pasado		XX
	EEUU deja a **España** fuera del contrato millonario para equipar al nuevo Ejército iraquí		XX
	Salud asegura que el anterior **gobierno de CiU** ocultó las **listas de espera reales**	XX	X
	Funeral por el comandante de la Guardia Civil herido mortalmente en Iraq		X
	El PP europeo pide que los políticos del Este revelen su pasado comunista	X	
	El Gobierno francés amenaza con requisar **500.000 pisos** vacíos si no salen al mercado	X	X
	Guerra entre los Blair y los Bush		X
Subtotal		4	9
La Vanguardia	**La CIA** dice que **Iraq** no era un peligro inminente	X	X
	Casi 60.000 catalanes están en **lista de espera** para ser operados		X
	Las muertes por violencia doméstica crecen un 30%		X
	Más de 30.000 españoles hacen **turismo sexual infantil**		X
	Unió lidera una **rebelión democristiana** en el PPE	X	X
Subtotal		2	5
El Periódico	**Sanitat** garantiza **las operaciones** antes de 6 meses	X	X
	Vinallop: aquí empezará **el trasvase**		XX
	La CIA afirma que nunca dijo que Sadam fuera un peligro inminente	X	
Subtotal		2	3
Total		11	24

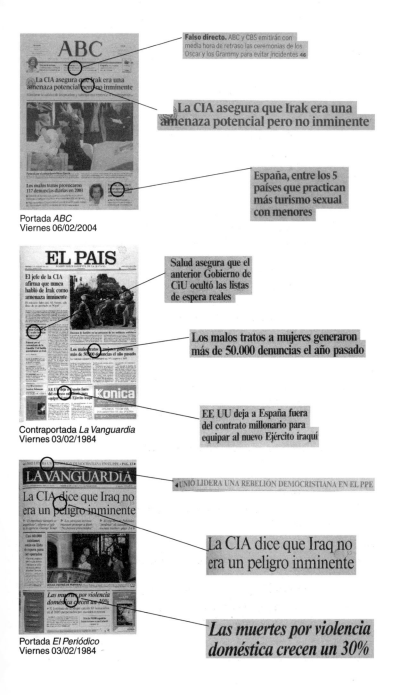

Falso directo. ABC y CBS emitirán con media hora de retraso las ceremonias de los Oscar y los Grammy para evitar incidentes 46

La CIA asegura que Irak era una amenaza potencial pero no inminente

España, entre los 5 países que practican más turismo sexual con menores

Portada *ABC*
Viernes 06/02/2004

Salud asegura que el anterior Gobierno de CiU ocultó las listas de espera reales

Los malos tratos a mujeres generaron más de 50.000 denuncias el año pasado

EE UU deja a España fuera del contrato millonario para equipar al nuevo Ejército iraquí

Contraportada *La Vanguardia*
Viernes 03/02/1984

◀UNIÓ LIDERA UNA REBELIÓN DEMOCRISTIANA EN EL PPE

La CIA dice que Iraq no era un peligro inminente

Las muertes por violencia doméstica crecen un 30%

Portada *El Periódico*
Viernes 03/02/1984

87

PROTAGONISTAS NO HUMANOS DE LOS TITULARES (AÑO 2004)
(continuación)

Periódicos	Protagonistas de los titulares	No Humanos	
		Instituciones	Otros
El Punt	**El gobierno** regulará la actividad de las **colonias escolares***	X	X
	Gracia quiere convertir **la plaza del Diamante** en un espacio de recuperación de la memoria histórica*		XX
	Geli dice que las **listas de espera** son el doble de largas de lo que decía CiU*		X
	Las universidades catalanas ofrecerán **carreras de tres años** el próximo curso*	X	X
	Trasladar el zoo de Barcelona a Sabadell cuesta 120 millones según un estudio*		X
	Treinta mil españoles practicaron **turismo sexual con menores** durante el año 2001*		X
	Gorbatxov dice que **una nueva «perestroika»** haría el mundo más justo*		X
Subtotal		2	8
Metro Directe	**Plan** para reducir las **listas de espera** a seis meses*		XX
	Un best seller en la cartelera		X
	5.000 niños, obligados a ejercer **la prostitución**		X
	I Congreso Nacional de Prensa Gratuita	X	
	La CIA contradice a Bush por el supuesto arsenal de Sadam	X	
	ERC e ICV se oponen al túnel de Horta*	XX	
	El Barça de Pesic gana y pasará como líder del grupo	X	
	El tiempo*		X
Subtotal		5	5
20 Minutos	**España**, uno de los cinco países de la UE con más **turismo sexual infantil**	-	XX
	Los socios del gobierno de Clos rechazan el **plan del alcalde** para hacer el túnel de Horta		X

* En catalán en el original.

PROTAGONISTAS NO HUMANOS DE LOS TITULARES (AÑO 2004)

(continuación)

Periódicos	Protagonistas de los titulares	No Humanos	
		Instituciones	Otros
20 Minutos	**Perfumes** y **productos del hogar**,		
(continuación)	pasan de las rebajas		XX
	Censura en los **Grammy** y los **Oscar** por el pecho de Janet		XX
	Seabiscuit. Galopando hacia el Oscar		X
	Martirio & Rinaldi. Unen el **tango** y la **copla**		XX
	TEATRO. **De 7 vidas al Romea**		X
	ARTE. **Fotografía soviética**		X
	TELE. **Toda la programación**		X
	Primitiva, ONCE, Trío		X
	Sol y temperatura más agradable		X
Subtotal		0	15
Gran total		**18**	**52**

Portada *El Punt*
Viernes 06/02/2004

El govern regularà l'activitat de les colònies escolars

Les universitats catalanes oferiran carreres de tres anys el pròxim curs

Trenta mil espanyols van practicar turisme sexual amb menors durant l'any 2001

Gràcia vol convertir la plaça del Diamant en un espai de recuperació de la memòria històrica

I Congreso Nacional de Prensa Gratuita

Pla per reduir les llistes d'espera a sis mesos

Un *best seller* en la cartelera

ERC i ICV s'oposen al túnel d'Horta

el temps

Portada *Metro Directe*
Viernes 06/02/2004

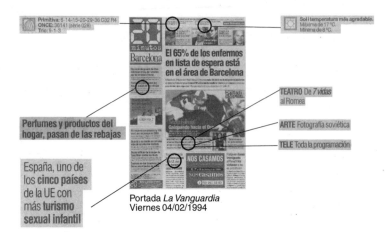

Primitiva: 6-14-15-20-29-36 C32 R4
ONCE: 36141 (sèrie 028)
Trio: 9-1-3

El 65% de los enfermos en lista de espera está en el área de Barcelona

Sol i temperatura més agradable. Màxima de 17 °C. Mínima de 8 °C.

Perfumes y productos del hogar, pasan de las rebajas

España, uno de los **cinco países** de la UE con más **turismo sexual infantil**

TEATRO De *7 vidas* al Romea

ARTE Fotografía soviética

TELE Toda la programación

NOS CASAMOS

Portada *La Vanguardia*
Viernes 04/02/1994

Comentarios a la tercera fase

Recordemos que, como ya hemos visto en los resultados del primer ejercicio, los protagonistas no humanos son generalmente privilegiados con respecto a los humanos, en los titulares de toda la muestra, y este enfoque se incrementa, aunque debemos matizar que este aumento aparece relacionado con el mayor número de cabeceras analizadas en 2004.

Este predominio de protagonistas no humanos se observa a simple vista ante la cantidad de fichas en las que hemos registrado los titulares, mayor que la de los ejercicios anteriores. En las fichas también resaltan los protagonistas no humanos no institucionales sobre las instituciones.

Si examinamos los resultados globales de los ejemplares de las cuatro cabeceras analizadas en los tres años, *ABC, El País, La Vanguardia* y *El Periódico*, advertimos que los datos se mantienen con un ligero incremento: 33 protagonistas no humanos en 1984, 39 en 1994 y 35 en 2004; y en las tres cabeceras nuevas en la muestra de 2004 los protagonistas no humanos suman 35, por tanto, siguen la misma orientación.

El País es la cabecera que presenta mayor número de protagonistas no humanos en los titulares de las portadas y contraportadas de los tres años, con una ligera tendencia a disminuir (16 protagonistas no humanos en 1984, 14 en 1994 y 13 en 2004). Este planteamiento es compartido por *El Periódico*, aunque con datos inferiores (10 protagonistas no humanos en 1984, 11 en 1994 y 5 en 2004). Por su parte, se advierte un notable incremento en *ABC* (de 1 protagonista no humano en 1984, pasa a 7 en 1994 y a 10 en 2004) mientras que *La Vanguardia* se mantiene en cifras similares (6 protagonistas no humanos en 1984, 7 en 1994 y 7 en 2004).

En cuanto a las cabeceras que se incorporan a la muestra seleccionada del año 2004, las tres adoptan el mismo enfoque: *El Punt* presenta a 10 protagonistas no humanos, *Metro Directe* también 10, y es en el ejemplar de *20 Minutos* en el que encontramos la mayor cantidad de protagonistas no humanos del conjunto de ejemplares de 2004 (15, seguido de *El País* con 13). En consecuencia, la cantidad absoluta de protagonistas no humanos aumenta en 2004.

Si examinamos con atención los dos tipos de protagonistas no humanos que hemos distinguido, esto es, en un grupo las instituciones o entidades que agrupan a seres humanos (partidos políticos, instituciones del gobierno, del Estado o de carácter internacional, empresas…), y en otro grupo todo lo demás, sujetos y predicados de las oraciones que hacen mención a lugares, reuniones o acciones, en las fichas, vemos que en los años 1984 y 2004 predominan los segundos: es decir, que en los titulares el enfoque a las instituciones es inferior al enfoque a los restantes protagonistas no humanos. Sólo *El País* de 1984 y el *Metro Directe* de 2004 presenta un equilibrio entre los dos tipos de protagonistas. Igualmente es en el año 1994 donde se presenta un equilibrio entre estos dos tipos de protagonistas, con un total de 20 instituciones y 19 otros. En este año, en *El Periódico* y *La Vanguardia* las instituciones superan a los demás protagonistas no humanos y en *El País* están igualados. Solamente el *ABC* presenta un menor número de instituciones.

En 1984 y en 2004 las instituciones y entidades suponen aproximadamente una tercera parte del total de protagonistas no humanos (12 de 33 en 1984, 18 de 70 en 2004) y en 1994 poco más de la mitad (20 de 39). En definitiva, destaca el enfoque preferente hacia «otros» en los titulares de 1984 y 2004.

Un análisis más detallado permite valorar las preferencias que ponen de manifiesto las distintas cabeceras, y quienes son unos y otros protagonistas no humanos enfocados.

Los protagonistas institucionales en los que se centra la atención en los titulares de las portadas y contraportadas, son los siguientes:

En los ejemplares analizados de 1984, *ABC* y *La Vanguardia* no presentan ningún protagonista institucional. *El País* presenta 9 (El PSC, Westinghouse que negocia la venta de su filial española a una compañía británica, el Supremo, La Comisión Mixta que aprueba la transferencia de las cámaras agrarias, las universidades y los espectáculos). *El Periódico* presenta 3 (El Barça, El PSC, y La OTAN).

Todos los ejemplares analizados de 1994 enfocan a protagonistas institucionales. El que presta más atención es de nuevo El País, que presenta el mismo número de protagonistas institucionales y no institucionales, 7 en cada caso. Los institucionales son: el Tribunal Supremo se rebela contra el Constitucional y apela al arbitraje del Rey, El Fondo de Garantía cambiará sus normas para vender Banesto, Creado el Consejo Asesor de Medio Ambiente, que contará con 11 ecologistas, El Betis elimina de la Copa a un impotente Barça. En segundo lugar, *El Periódico*, que presenta 6 protagonistas institucionales y 5 de los restantes. Los institucionales son: El Supremo denuncia ante el Rey al Tribunal Constitucional,...el nuevo Liceu sea público, Un segunda elimina al Barça..., La policía no encuentra la pistola del crimen de Galicia. *La Vanguardia* presenta 4 protagonistas institucionales: Pujol y Roca censuran al PP por su actitud con el catalán, Felipe González no cede ante los sindicatos,...el Betis elimina al Barça. Finalmente, *ABC* presenta 3 protagonistas institucionales: El Tribunal Supremo... en conflicto con el Tribunal Constitucional, la ampliación de Banesto.

De los ejemplares analizados de 2004, sólo uno, *20 Minutos*, no presenta ningún protagonista institucional, si bien presenta 14 protagonistas no humanos que hemos clasificado como otros. En el resto *sí* aparecen. Destaca *Metro Directe*, con 5: I Congreso Nacional de Prensa Gratuita, La CIA..., ERC i ICV..., El Barça de Pesic..., *El País*, con 4: Salud asegura que el anterior gobierno de CiU..., El PP europeo..., El Gobierno francés... *ABC*, con 3: La

CIA..., ABC y CBS... En las restantes cabeceras encontramos dos protagonistas institucionales en cada una. *La Vanguardia* habla de La CIA... y Unió...; *El Periódico* de Sanidad... y La CIA... Y *El Punt* de El gobierno... y Las universidads catalanas...

En cuanto a los restantes protagonistas no humanos, los datos indican que merecen una atención preferente en los titulares de las portadas y contraportadas de casi todos los ejemplares de la muestra, como hemos dicho. Son los siguientes:

En 1984 destaca *El País*, con 7 protagonistas: Manifestaciones de trabajadores y críticas patronales contra la política del Gobierno, ...un pacto social entre los venezolanos, la pasividad de la policía francesa..., la subida del dólar, y la probable declaración conjunta de los 12 magistrados... *La Vanguardia* presenta 6 protagonistas: Movilizaciones sindicales contra la política del Gobierno, Barcelona, donde cada día es atracada una farmacia, Más protección para los mandos del Ejército, y la influencia del Opus Dei que crece en la Iglesia. También encontramos 7 protagonistas en *El Periódico*: el Quejido unánime de la España 'reconvertida', ...el informe de Kissinger, la Escolta policial, la Educación física, y el Sumario secreto en el caso Solomo... Y *ABC* sólo presenta uno: La Cumbre iberoamericana...

En 1994 también *El País* es el diario que presenta más protagonistas no humanos, 14 en total, 7 institucionales y 7 del resto. Estos son: el Desencuentro en la Moncloa, La inminente expropiación..., Rusia que tendrá tres bases militares en Georgia, Londres..., Salir en la «tele» por guarros. Los vitorianos que ensucien la calle verán su infracción por la pequeña pantalla... En segundo lugar encontramos *El Periódico*, con 5 protagonistas de este tipo: La movilidad de los funcionarios..., un Acuerdo de todos los partidos...,...la pistola del crimen de Galicia, El ruedo acosado por la piqueta. Finalmente, estos protagonistas también adquieren un papel destacado en *ABC*: El arbitraje del Rey..., El fondo de garantía de depósitos, oferta pública y subasta. Y en *La Vanguardia*, Otra sorpresa en la copa..., Aires escandinavos..., y Pulso bursátil y financiero.

La mayor cantidad de cabeceras analizadas en 2004 hace que se incremente considerablemente el número de protagonistas no humanos, que ascienden en total a 70, de los cuales 18 son institucionales y 52 son de los restantes. Este tipo de protagonistas destaca en 20 Minutos, que presenta un total de 15: España, uno de los países de la UE con más turismo sexual infantil,...el pla de l'alcalde..., Perfumes y productos del hogar...,...los Grammy y los Oscar..., Seabiscuit,...el tango y la copla, De 7 vidas al Romea, Fotografía soviética, Toda la programación, Primitiva, ONCE, Trío, Sol i temperatura... La segunda posición corresponde a *El País*, con 9: Iraq..., Los malos tratos a mujeres generaron más de 50.000 denuncias..., EEUU deja a España fuera del contrato..., las listas de espera reales de sanidad. El funeral por el comandante de la Guardia Civil..., 500.000 pisos vacíos..., y la Guerra entre los Blair y los Bush. Le sigue *El Punt*,* con 8: ...la actividad de las colonias escolares, Gracia quiere convertir la plaza del Diamante en un espacio...,...las listas de espera...,...carreras de tres años, el coste de trasladar el zoo de Barcelona a Sabadell, y el turismo sexual con menores... *ABC* presenta 7 protagonistas de este tipo: Iraq..., el Funeral..., Los malos tratos provocaron 117 denuncias... España, entre los países que practican más turismo sexual, y Cold Mountain... *La Vanguardia*, 5: ...Iraq..., la lista de espera..., Las muertes por violencia doméstica..., el turismo sexual infantil, y una rebelión democristiana en el PPE. Igualmente, *Metro Directe*, presenta 5: Plan para reducir las listas de espera*..., Un best seller..., y El tiempo* y 5.000 niños obligados a ejercer la prostitución. Finalmente, encontramos a *El Periódico*, con 3: ... las operaciones..., y Vinallop, el lugar donde empezará el trasvase.

Conclusiones ejercicio 2

Después de observar detenidamente la distribución de protagonistas en las distintas fichas mediante las cuales realizamos un primer acercamiento a las noticias seleccionadas de las portadas y las contraportadas, vemos como la aplicación cuidadosa del *Test ADSH* nos muestra las preferencias e inclinaciones de *la mirada informativa*.

El protagonismo de los hombres predomina sobre el de las mujeres en los tres años analizados. En 1984 apenas encontramos

---

* En catalán en el original.

protagonistas mujeres en una contraportada y en el año 1994 no aparecen en ninguna de las cabeceras analizadas. Encontramos más mujeres en las cabeceras analizadas del año 2004, pero este incremento no supera el volumen de protagonistas hombres.

Asimismo vemos como los colectivos humanos apenas aparece en toda la muestra. En 1984 y 1994 solamente se registran en una cabecera. Nuevamente es el año 2004 donde encontramos más protagonistas colectivos.

En cuanto a los protagonistas no humanos, vemos que son más abundantes y predominantes en casi la totalidad de la muestra.

TABLA 4
RESULTADOS FINALES DEL EJERCICIO 2. LA DIVERSIDAD DE LOS PROTAGONISTAS HUMANOS Y NO HUMANOS DE LA MIRADA INFORMATIVA EN CIFRAS

Año 1984 Periódicos	Mujeres		Hombres		Colectivos	No Humanos	
	Identific.	No identif.	Identific.	No identif.		Instituciones	Otros
ABC	0	0	0	0	0	0	1
El País	2	2	7	4	2	9	7
La Vanguardia	0	0	0	0	1	0	6
El Periódico	0	0	3	1	0	3	7
Total	**2**	**2**	**10**	**5**	**3**	**12**	**21**

Año 1994 Periódicos	Mujeres		Hombres		Colectivos	No Humanos	
	Identific.	No identif.	Identific.	No identif.		Instituciones	Otros
ABC	0	0	0	0	0	3	4
El País	0	0	1	4	4	7	7
La Vanguardia	0	0	9	1	0	4	4
El Periódico	0	0	2	1	0	6	5
Total	**0**	**0**	**12**	**6**	**4**	**20**	**20**

TABLA 4
**RESULTADOS FINALES DEL EJERCICIO 2. LA DIVERSIDAD
DE LOS PROTAGONISTAS HUMANOS Y NO HUMANOS
DE LA MIRADA INFORMATIVA EN CIFRAS** *(continuación)*

Año 2004 Periódicos	Mujeres		Hombres		Colectivos	No Humanos	
	Identific.	No identif.	Identific.	No identif.		Instituciones	Otros
ABC	1	0	1	0	0	3	7
El País	0	1	1	3	4	4	9
La Vanguardia	1	0	2	0	2	2	5
El Periódico	0	1	1	1	0	2	3
Subtotal	**2**	**2**	**5**	**4**	**6**	**11**	**24**
El Punt	2	1	3	2	1	2	8
Metro Directe	0	1	5	0	4	5	5
20 Minutos	4	2	4	0	9	0	15
Total	**8**	**6**	**17**	**6**	**20**	**18**	**52**

Ejercicio 3
La *AMPLITUD* y la *DIVERSIDAD* de *la mirada informativa* ¿A quién o qué se presenta como protagonista en las imágenes y en los pies de foto?

En ese ejercicio evaluamos *la mirada informativa* que se pone de manifiesto en las imágenes y otros elementos gráficos. Para ello analizamos primero los pies de foto de los elementos gráficos que acompañan a algunas de las unidades redaccionales de portada y contraportada de la muestra. De esta forma, podemos apreciar fácilmente las diferencias entre los distintos enfoques que se pueden ofrecer en una misma noticia (en los textos de los titulares, en los pies de foto y en las imágenes).

Como se puede ver en los totales generales recogidos en las tablas 1 (página 31) y gráficamente en las fichas 1, 2 y 3 (páginas 49-57), de las 133 unidades redaccionales analizadas en toda la muestra, 43 de ellas presentan 61 elementos gráficos en total.

En las fichas 13, 14 y 15, siguiendo el esquema de las fichas de los ejercicios anteriores, hemos recogido los textos de los pies de foto de las imágenes que aparecen en las portadas y contraportadas de toda la muestra. En la tabla 6 se recogen los datos totales de esta selección comparados con los datos de los protagonistas que se presentan en los textos de los titulares de las unidades redaccionales acompañadas de elementos gráficos.

Finalmente, después de cada ficha, correspondiente a cada año de la muestra, presentamos las reproducciones de las unidades redaccionales con elementos gráficos. En ellas se puede apreciar fácilmente las diferencias en los enfoques de los protagonistas que se presentan en los titulares, los pies de foto y las imágenes mismas.

FICHA 13
PROTAGONISTAS DE LOS PIES DE FOTO (AÑO 1984)

Periódicos	Protagonistas de los pies de foto	Humanos M	Humanos H	Colectivos	No humanos
ABC	**Felipe González**, presidente del Gobierno de España; **Jaime Luscinchi,** presidente de Venezuela; **Luis Alberto Monge**, presidente de Costa Rica, **Belisario Betancur**, presidente de Colombia; **Hernán Siles Suazo**, presidente de Bolivia; **Daniel Ortega**, coordinador de la Junta Sandinista; **Jorge Blanco**, presidente República Dominicana, **Ricardo de la Espriella**, presidente de Panamá, **Raúl Alfonsín**, presidente de Argentina.		XXXX XXXX X		
Subtotal		0	9	0	0
El País	**Marcelino Camacho**, secretario general de CC OO lanzó ayer duros ataques **al Gobierno** ante **los trabajadores** que respondieron a la convocatoria de huelga general en la localidad madrileña de Getafe.		X	X	X
	Por su lado, **José Antonio Segurado** coincidió con Camacho en sus **críticas a la política económica gubernamental** en la asamblea anual de la Confederación Empresaria Independiente de Madrid		X		X
Contraportada	**Dolores Fernández Feijoo**	X			
Subtotal		1	2	1	2

PROTAGONISTAS DE LOS PIES DE FOTO (AÑO 1984) *(continuación)*

| Periódicos | Protagonistas de los pies de foto | Humanos | | Colectivos | No |
		M	H		humanos
La Vanguardia	Cerca de **un millar de trabajadores** del sector naval se manifestaron ante la sede de la Junta de Andalucía contra **la política de reconversión industrial**			X	X
	Jornaleros andaluces continúan su **huelga de hambre** en la catedral de Sevilla en protesta por el **nuevo subsidio del empleo**			X	XX
Subtotal		0	0	2	3
El Periódico	**Mapa de la protesta** contra el «**Plan Solchaga**»				XX
	Sumario secreto en el caso **Salomó – Enric** y **Mayte** (en la foto) hijos de **Enric Salomó**, acudieron ayer a declarar al juzgado de Reus sin llevar escolta. El juez que lleva el caso del **asesinato de Teresa Mestre** declaró **secreto el sumario**	X	XX		XXXX
Contraportada	**España** debe explotar en la **OTAN** su situación geopolítica				XX
	Antonio Álvarez Solís		X		
Subtotal		1	3	0	8
Total		2	14	4	13

Portada *ABC*
Viernes 03/02/1984

Portada del *ABC* de 1984 con los elementos gráficos. Nueve ilustraciones de hombres identificados con nombre, apellidos y cargo reposan sobre la ilustración de un mapa de latinoamérica. El titular de la noticia no hace referencia a los seres humanos.

Portada *El País*
Viernes 03/02/1984

Dolores Fernández Feijoo

La última artesana maragata teje mantas y cobertores ayudada
por su madre, de 93 años, y una tía, de 83

Es la última artesana del Val de San Lorenzo, un pueblo maragato con una vieja industria tradicional de mantas y cobertores. El rítmico traqueteo de los telares eléctricos se oye en cualquier calle del pueblo, pero Dolores Fernández Feijoo nunca quiso electrificar el suyo: es una reliquia del pasado ("era de mi bisabuelo, y tiene más de 200 años").

Dolores tiene 62 primaveras y unos hermosos ojos grises chispeantes y llenos de vida. Teje mantas y cobertores de colores vivos, ayudada por su madre, Carolina Feijoo, que, pese a haber cumplido los 93 años, hila todos los días en el pequeño taller familiar, y por su tía Antonia, de 83, que es la encargada de hacer las canillas.

Dolores Fernández Feijoo.

Contraportada *El País*
Viernes 03/02/1984

En la contraportada de *El País* encontramos la primera mujer identificada con nombre y apellidos tanto en el titular como en el pie de foto y también es la protagonista de la imagen.

Portada *La Vanguardia*
Viernes 03/02/1984

En esta portada vemos como la imagen enfoca un colectivo humano mientras el titular hace referencia a unas «movilizaciones sindicales» sin sujeto definido.

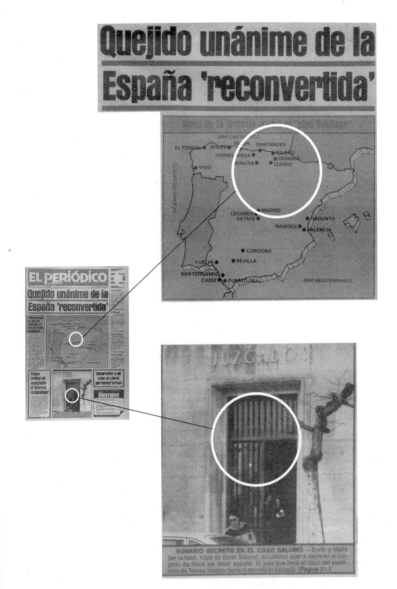

Portada *El Periódico*
Viernes 03/02/1984

La portada del periódico presenta tanto en su titular como en la imagen central a protagonistas no humanos.

Contraportada *El Periódico*
Viernes 03/02/1984

FICHA 14
PROTAGONISTAS DE LOS PIES DE FOTO (AÑO 1994)

Periódicos	Protagonistas de los pies de foto	Humanos M	Humanos H	Colectivos	No humanos
ABC	**Pascual Sala**. Presidente del Tribunal Supremo		X		
	No consta (Fotografía del **Rey de España**)		X		
	Miguel Rodríguez-Piñero. Presidente del Tribunal Constitucional		X		
Subtotal		0	3	0	0

PROTAGONISTAS DE LOS PIES DE FOTO (AÑO 1994) *(continuación)*

Periódicos	Protagonistas de los pies de foto	Humanos		Colectivos	No
		M	H		humanos
El País	**Desencuentro en La Moncloa.** Ninguno varió su posición. Dos horas en La Moncloa no consiguieron conciliar las posturas de **Felipe González y los líderes sindicales.** El no por previsto menos sonoro fracaso de la cumbre de ayer prueba que González no piensa alterar su política de reforma laboral tras la huelga de hace una semana. La actitud del Gobierno según **Antonio Gutiérrez** (a la izquierda en la foto) y **Nicolás Redondo** cierra el camino a una resolución.		XXX	X	X
Contraportada	**Un inspector de Vitoria** fotografía desde un coche camuflado a un infractor de las ordenanzas de limpieza		X		
Subtotal		0	4	1	1
La Vanguardia	**Antonio Gutiérrez, Felipe González y Nicolás Redondo** posan para los fotógrafos con expresión de circunstancias		XXX	X	
	Manuel Lorenzo fotografiado por su ex amante en la playa en 1991	X	X		
Contraportada	**Edmond Alphandeéry, Manuel Conté, Joaquín Moyá-Angeler, Eduardo Abellán, Jean-Luc Dehnaene**		XXXXX		
	Pulso bursátil y financiero				X
	La firma cuenta con **18 tiendas en España**				XX
Subtotal		1	9	0	3
El Periódico	**Antonio Gutiérrez, Felipe González y Nicolás Redondo** con caras serias. **La reforma laboral** sigue adelante.		XXX		X
	Un segunda elimina al **Barça** de la Copa en el Camp Nou (0-1)				XX
	Manuel Lorenzo. Uno de los policías detenidos		X		
Contraportada	**La plaza de toros Las Arenas.** El edificio fue una de las primeras construcciones de la plaza España				X
	Detalle del escudo de la puerta principal				X
Subtotal		0	4	0	5
Total		1	20	1	9

Portada *ABC*
Viernes 04/02/1994.

Portada y contraportada *El País*
Viernes 04/02/1994.

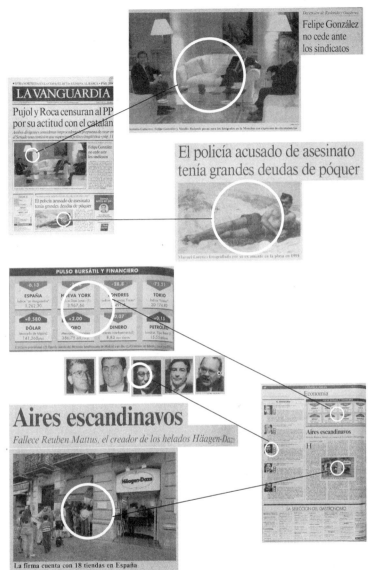

Portada y contraportada *La Vanguardia*
Viernes 04/02/1994

Todos los protagonistas de esta cabecera son hombres identificados con nombres y apellidos o son protagonistas no humanos.

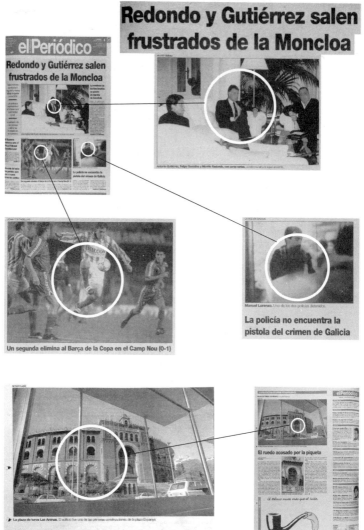

Portada y contraportada *El Periódico*
Viernes 04/02/1994

En esta dos portadas vemos otra vez como las imagenes enfocan a hombres identificados con nombres, apellidos y cargos mientras los titulares hacen referencia a protagonistas no humanos.

PROTAGONISTAS DE LOS PIES DE FOTO (AÑO 2004)

Periódicos	Protagonistas de los pies de foto	Humanos M	Humanos H	Colectivos	No humanos
ABC	**Funeral** por **el comandante Pérez García**. El presidente del Gobierno, **José María Aznar, miembros del Ejecutivo y líderes de los principales partidos políticos** acompañaron ayer a la **familia del comandante** de la Guardia Civil Gonzalo Pérez García en el solemne funeral celebrado por su alma en la sede de la Dirección General del Benemérito Instituto. En la imagen, **la viuda del oficial** muerto consuela a **su hija mayor** ante el féretro con los restos mortales de Pérez García.	XX	XX	XXX	X
	Cristina Alberdi	X			
	Viernes de estreno. «**Cold Mountain**», con **Nicole Kidman**, abrió la Berlinale	X			X
Subtotal		4	2	3	2
El País	**Decenas de heridos** en las protestas de los astilleros andaluces			X	
Contraportada	**Cherie Blair** (izquierda) saluda al **matrimonio Bush** en noviembre	X			X
Subtotal		1	0	2	0
La Vanguardia	**Letizia** vestirá de **Pertegaz**. Manuel Pertegaz, el maestro de alta costura, diseñará el traje de boda de Letizia. En la foto tomada ayer, la novia del Príncipe deja el taller del diseñador en la Diagonal de Barcelona	X	X		
Contraportada	**Alexandre Hollan**		X		
Subtotal		1	2	0	0
El Periódico	**Vinallop:** aquí empezará **el trasvase. Medio Ambiente** marca en este paraje próximo a Tortosa el punto exacto donde se extraerá el agua del Ebro				XXX
	La cola de pacientes	X			
Subtotal		0	0	0	4
Total ABC, El País, La Vanguardia y El Periódico		6	4	5	6

PROTAGONISTAS DE LOS PIES DE FOTO (AÑO 2004) *(continuación)*

Periódicos	Protagonistas de los pies de foto	Humanos M	Humanos H	Colectivos	No humanos
El Punt	Empieza el **juicio** por el **caso Marlès***				XX
	Gorbatxov dice que una **nueva** «**perestroika**» haría un mundo más justo*		X		X
Contraportada	**Un grupo de usuarios**, esperando para subir al tren en el andén de Renfe a Belvitge*			X	
Subtotal		0	1	1	3
Metro Directe	No consta (**una pareja de hombres jóvenes** cantando)		XX		
	No consta (una persona caminando frente a una obra de arte)				
	Bush reza durante una plegaria		X		
	«Hay que hacer test psicológicos a los jueces». **Enrique Arias Vega**		X		
	Rafael Nadal, el debutante más joven de la Davis		X		
	La vivienda, lugar del crimen				X
Subtotal		0	5	0	1
20 Minutos	**Seabiscuit**. Galopando hacia el Oscar. Llega a nuestras pantallas una de las candidatas a mejor película además de optar a otras seis estatuillas				X
	«Deborah saca mi parte salvaje». Se llama **Javier**, presenta MTV Hot y es contertulio de *La selva de los famosos*		X		
	Pochettino. «La situación es difícil y vine a ayudar». Entrevista al defensa tras la vuelta al **Espanyol**		X		X
	Martirio & **Rinaldi**. Unen el **tango** y **la copla**	XX			XX
	Minghella. Llega a la Berlinale sin **Kidman**. El director abrió el festival con *Cold Mountain*		X	X	X
Subtotal		2	3	1	5
Gran total		8	13	7	15

* En catalán en el original.

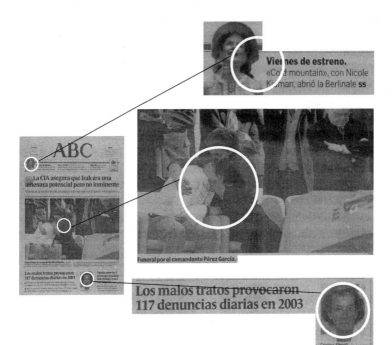

Portada *ABC*
Viernes 06/02/2004

En la portada del ABC vemos cuatro mujeres que son enfocadas como protagonistas. Dos está identificadas con nombre y apellido, Nicole Kidman y Cristina Alberdi, las otras dos que aparecen en la imagen central identificadas como «viuda» e «hija».

Decenas de heridos en las protestas de los astilleros andaluces

Portada *El País*
Viernes 06/02/2004

109

Guerra entre los Blair y los Bush

Cherie Blair (izquierda) saluda al matrimonio Bush en noviembre. / AP

Contraportada *El País*
Viernes 06/02/2004

En la contraportada de El País encontramos otra mujer identificada con nombre y apellido, junto a la pareja Bush.

LETIZIA VESTIRÁ DE PERTEGAZ.

Portada *La Vanguardia*
Viernes 06/02/2004

La imagen central de la portada de la Vanguardia presenta una mujer identificada con nombre y apellido y por su condición de «novia del Príncipe».

110

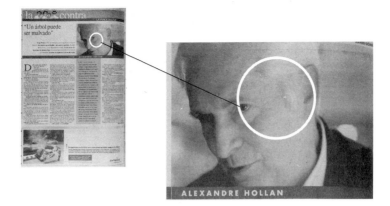

Contraportada *La Vanguardia*
Viernes 06/02/2004

Portada *El Periódico*
Viernes 06/02/2004

Tanto el título como la imagen central de la portada hacen referencia a protagonistas no humanos. En este caso la imagen no contribuye a «humanizar» la información.

Viatge en Rodalies

ical dels trens, que sovint resulta mes una molestia que un atractiu per als usuaris

Un grup d'usuaris, esperant per pujar al tren al baixador de Renfe a Bellvitge. GABRIEL MAS-BARÀ

Portada y contraportada *El Punt*
Viernes 06/02/2004

En la portada y contraportada de El Punt vemos nuevamente que mientras las imagenes enfocan seres humanos, los titulares presentan protagonistas no humanos.

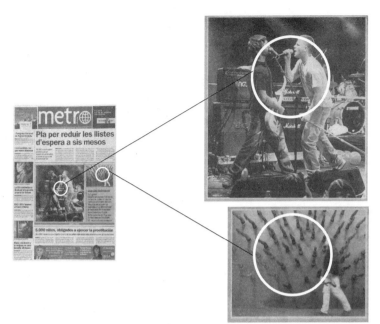

Portada *Metro Directe*
Viernes 06/02/2004

Las imágenes de la portada del Metro Directe no presentan pie de foto ni titular que las identifiquen.

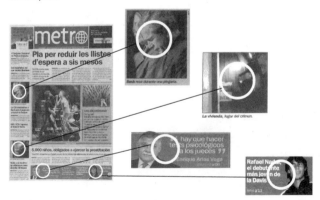

Portada *Metro Directe*
Viernes 06/02/2004

La portada del Metro Directe nos presenta las imágenes de varios protagonistas hombres identificados con nombres y apellidos

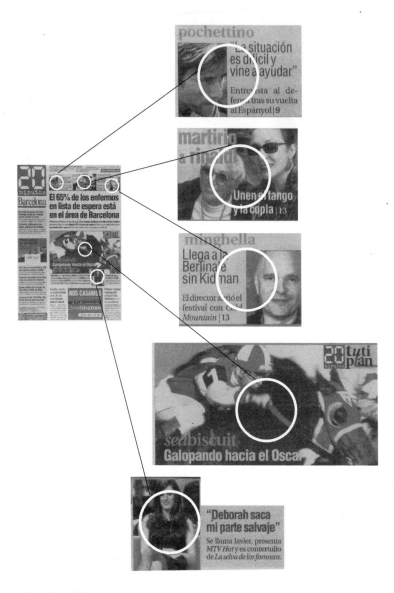

Portada *20 Minutos*
Viernes 06/02/2004

Las imágenes de la portada de 20 Minutos presenta hombres y mujeres identificados y por primera vez un protagonista travesti.

TABLA 5
PROTAGONISTAS DE LOS ELEMENTOS GRÁFICOS EN CIFRAS
(TITULARES)

1984	UR	Elementos Gráficos	Mujeres	Hombres	Colectivos	No Humanos
ABC	1	10	0	0	0	1
El País	2	3	3	0	0	3
La Vanguardia	1	2	0	0	0	2
El Periódico	4	4	0	2	0	5
Total	8	19	3	2	0	11

1994	UR	Elementos Gráficos	Mujeres	Hombres	Colectivos	No Humanos
ABC	1	3	0	0	0	3
El País	2	2	0	0	1	3
La Vanguardia	5	9	0	8	0	3
El Periódico	4	5	0	2	0	6
Total	12	19	0	10	1	15

2004	UR	Elementos Gráficos	Mujeres	Hombres	Colectivos	No Humanos
ABC	3	3	1	1	0	4
El País	2	2	0	0	3	1
La Vanguardia	2	2	1	2	0	0
El Periódico	2	2	0	0	0	4
Subtotal	9	9	2	3	3	9
El Punt	3	3	0	1	0	3
Metro Directe	6	6	1	5	1	1
20 Minutos	5	5	3	3	0	3
Total	23	23	6	12	4	16

TABLA 6
PROTAGONISTAS DE LOS PIES DE FOTO EN LAS UNIDADES
REDACCIONALES CON ELEMENTOS GRÁFICOS EN CIFRAS

1984	Mujeres	Hombres	Colectivos	No humanos
ABC	0	9	0	0
El País	1	3	1	2
La Vanguardia	0	0	2	3
El Periódico	1	3	0	8
Total	2	14	3	13

TABLA 6
PROTAGONISTAS DE LOS PIES DE FOTO EN LAS UNIDADES
REDACCIONALES CON ELEMENTOS GRÁFICOS EN CIFRAS
(continuación)

1994	Mujeres	Hombres	Colectivos	No humanos
ABC	0	3	0	0
El País	0	4	1	1
La Vanguardia	1	9	0	3
El Periódico	0	4	0	5
Total	**1**	**20**	**1**	**9**

2004	Mujeres	Hombres	Colectivos	No humanos
ABC	4	2	3	2
El País	1	0	2	0
La Vanguardia	1	2	0	0
El Periódico	0	0	0	4
Subtotal	6	4	5	6
El Punt	0	1	2	2
Metro Directe	0	3	0	1
20 Minutos	2	3	1	5
Total	**8**	**11**	**8**	**14**

Si damos una mirada general a las portadas y contraportadas de todas las cabeceras de la muestra, vemos como el color y los elementos gráficos ganan terreno en todos los años analizados. Mientras en 1984 tan sólo *El Periódico* presentaba color en su portada, todas las cabeceras de 2004, excepto *El Punt*, presentan color e imágenes en color en sus portadas. Sin embargo, es en 1994 cuando aparece el mayor número de unidades redaccionales con elementos gráficos: 12 noticias con 19 elementos gráficos en total.

En este mismo año es *La Vanguardia* la que más noticias con elementos gráficos presenta: 5 noticias con 9 elementos gráficos; en portada presenta dos fotografías que enfocan a hombres como protagonistas y en la contraportada presenta cinco fotografías de hombres, un gráfico y una fotografía de un local comercial. En los dos años restantes, 1984 y 2004, es el *ABC* la cabecera que presenta más noticias con elementos gráficos. En el ejemplar del año 1984, encontramos en la portada del *ABC* nueve retratos ilustrados de hombres sobre la ilustración de un mapa de Latinoamérica, mientras que la portada del año 2004 presenta tres fotografías de mujeres.

Así mismo podemos observar como el carácter de los elementos gráficos pasa de ser meramente ilustrativo en 1984 a convertirse en elemento central de la información, como sucede con la unidad redaccional: desencuentro en La Moncloa de *El País* de 1994, en la que el pie de foto constituye a su vez el texto de la unidad redaccional. Este esquema se repite en el 2004 con Funeral por el comandante Pérez García del *ABC*; Decenas de heridos en los astilleros andaluces de *El País*; Letizia vestirá Pertegaz de *La Vanguardia*; Vinallop: Aquí empezará el transvase de *El Periódico* y Seabiscuit galopando hacia el Oscar en *20 Minutos*.

En las contraportadas de todas las cabeceras de la muestra encontramos imágenes. De las 15 contraportadas analizadas, 7 están totalmente cubiertas por anuncios publicitarios: las contraportadas del *ABC* y *La Vanguardia* de 1984; la del *ABC* de 1994 y las del *ABC*, *El Periódico*, *Metro Directe* y *20 Minutos*. De todos los protagonistas de los pie de fotos identificados en las fichas 13, 14 y 15, tres de ellos aparecen sin identificar con nombre ni sexo: el juez en un pie de foto de la portada de *El Periódico* de 1984; un infractor en la contraportada de *El País* de 1994, y una persona caminando en la portada del *Metro Directe* de 2004.

Las 10 imágenes de la portada del ejemplar analizado de *ABC* de 1984 están relacionadas con la noticia que se anuncia en el titular: Cumbre Iberoamericana en Caracas. Sobre un mapa de América del Sur que cubre toda la portada, se destacan recuadrados 9 dibujos de los rostros de los presidentes de gobierno que participan en la reunión; de acuerdo con el pie, se trata de Felipe González, presidente de Gobierno de España; Jaime Luscinchi, presidente de Venezuela; Luis Alberto Monge, presidente de Costa Rica; Belisario Betancur, presidente de Colombia; Hernán Siles Suazo, presidente de Bolivia; Daniel Ortega, coordinador de la Junta Sandinista; Jorge Blanco, presidente República Dominicana; Ricardo de la Espriella, presidente de Panamá; y Raúl Alfonsín, presidente de Argentina. Por tanto, mientras el titular enfoca a un protagonista no humano, la «Cumbre Iberoamericana», una reunión, las imágenes enfocan a 9 varones adultos que ejercen el poder político, identificados con nombre y apellido y el cargo que ocupan, sobre un protagonista no humano, un mapa.

Las dos imágenes que aparecen en la portada del ejemplar analizado de *El País* están relacionadas con una noticia que se anuncia en un titular, Manifestaciones de trabajadores y críticas patronales contra la política del gobierno, que presenta como protagonistas tres acciones. Sin embargo, en las dos fotografías se enfoca a seres humanos. En una, a Marcelino Camacho hablando a un grupo de trabajadores (de acuerdo con el pie: Marcelino Camacho, secretario general de CC OO lanzó ayer duros ataques al Gobierno ante los trabajadores que respondieron a la convocatoria de huelga general en la localidad madrileña de Getafe); y en la otra, a José Antonio Segurado hablando ante un atril (en el pie se explica: Por su lado, José Antonio Segurado coincidió con Camacho en sus críticas a la política económica gubernamental en la asamblea anual de la Confederación Empresaria Independiente de Madrid). Es decir, que mientras el titular presenta tres protagonistas no humanos, las imágenes hacen visibles a seres humanos, individualizados e identificados con nombre y apellidos, en dos casos, y como colectivo, en otro. Sólo en la contraportada aparece la imagen de una mujer que es identificada en el titular y en el pie con su nombre y apellidos: Dolores Fernández Feijoo.

La portada del ejemplar analizado de *La Vanguardia* de 1984 también ofrece dos imágenes relacionadas con la misma información que destaca la portada de *El País*. El titular también presenta dos protagonistas no humanos: Movilizaciones sindicales contra la política del gobierno. Por el contrario, las fotografías hacen visibles a los seres humanos como colectivos, tal como explican los pies de foto: Cerca de un millar de trabajadores del sector naval se manifestaron ante la sede de la Junta de Andalucía contra la política de reconversión industrial; y Jornaleros andaluces continúan su huelga de hambre en la catedral de Sevilla en protesta por el nuevo subsidio del empleo.

Por el contrario, la imagen de la portada del ejemplar analizado de *El Periódico* de 1984 que se relaciona con esta misma noticia presenta un protagonista no humano; tal como se indica en el pie, un mapa de España, el Mapa de la protesta contra el «Plan Solchaga». Este tipo de protagonista no humano coincide con los que se resaltan en el titular, Movilizaciones sindicales contra la política del gobierno. En otra fotografía de esta portada sí que se ven seres humanos, dos hombres y una mujer saliendo de la puerta del juzgado: según se explica en el pie, se trata del Sumario secreto en el caso Salomó – Enric y Mayte (en la foto) hijos de Enric Salomó, acudieron ayer a declarar al juzgado de Reus sin llevar escolta. El juez que lleva el caso del asesinato de Teresa Mestre declaró secreto el sumario. Los seres humanos también son representados en las imágenes de la contraportada de este diario: Antonio Álvarez Solís, encabezando la columna que escribe, y en torno a una mesa de reuniones numerosos varones de la OTAN. En total, vemos en un lugar preferente un protagonista no humano, un mapa, 4 varones adultos, una mujer, y un protagonista colectivo.

En las portadas y contraportadas de los ejemplares analizados de 1994 observamos un notable incremento de imágenes. Sólo una contraportada, la de *ABC*, está dedicada íntegramente a un anuncio publicitario.

La portada de ABC resalta 3 imágenes relacionadas con la noticia que se destaca con el siguiente titular: El Tribunal Supremo acude al arbitraje del Rey ante su conflicto con el Tribunal Constitucional. Los tres protagonistas no humanos con los que se compone este titular aparecen identificados con las imágenes de otros tantos varones adultos que ofrecen la cara humana de la noticia, y cuya identidad se explica en dos pies de foto, Pascual Sala. Presidente del Tribunal Supremo, a la izquierda de la página, y Miguel Rodríguez-Piñero. Presidente del Tribunal Constitucional, a la derecha, mientras que la imagen del Rey, en el centro, no está acompañada de ninguna indicación.

En la portada de *El País* vemos una fotografía relacionada con una noticia que se presenta con el siguiente titular: Desencuentro en la Moncloa, que abre el pie de la imagen: Ninguno varió su posición. Dos horas en La Moncloa no consiguieron conciliar las posturas de Felipe González y los líderes sindicales. El no por previsto menos sonoro fracaso de la cumbre de ayer prueba que González no piensa alterar su política de reforma laboral tras la huelga de hace una semana. La actitud del Gobierno según Antonio Gutiérrez (a la izquierda en la foto) y Nicolás Redondo cierra el camino a una resolución. Por tanto, de nuevo los titulares de los textos centran la atención en protagonistas no humanos (el desencuentro), mientras que las imágenes ofrecen los rostros humanos de los responsables de las acciones noticiables, en este caso, tres varones adultos, Felipe González, Antonio Gutiérrez y Nicolás Redondo.

Los mismos personajes en el mismo escenario aparecen en la portada del ejemplar analizado de *La Vanguardia* de 1994, con la diferencia de que el titular (Felipe González no cede ante los sindicatos) realza a uno de los protagonistas humanos identificado, que también aparece en la fotografía, y a unos protagonistas no humanos pero formados por seres humanos, los sindicatos, cuyos líderes aparecen en la fotografía, tal como se explica en el pie: Antonio Gutiérrez, Felipe González y Nicolás Redondo posan para los fotógrafos con expresión de circunstancias. Una segunda imagen presenta también a otro varón adulto relacionado con la noticia encabezada con el siguiente titular, (El policía acusado de asesinato tenía grandes deudas en el póquer), que aparece identificado en el siguiente pie: Manuel Lorenzo fotografiado por su ex amante en la playa en 1991. En definitiva, tanto los titulares como las imágenes de esta portada enfocan preferentemente a seres humanos, todos ellos varones adultos. A unos por su posición jerárquica al frente del gobierno y de los sindicatos, y a otro por ser el autor de un delito. Este enfoque preferente a varones adultos se incrementa con los rostros de 5 protagonistas que aparecen en la contraportada, en la sección El Semáforo. En esta página vemos también a un grupo de gente en la calle ante un establecimiento comercial, en relación con una noticia titulada: Aires escandinavos. Fallece Ruben Martus, el creador de Häagen-Dazs.

En la portada del ejemplar analizado de *El Periódico* del mismo año 1994 también se enfoca exclusivamente a varones adultos. En la fotografía más destacada aparecen los tres varones adultos relacionados con la misma noticia realzada por los dos diarios anteriores en el mismo escenario, con un titular que enfoca a dos de los protagonistas: Redondo y Gutiérrez salen frustrados de la Moncloa, con el siguiente pie de foto: Antonio Gutiérrez, Felipe González y Nicolás Redondo con caras serias. La reforma laboral sigue adelante. En otra fotografía, bajo el titular La policía no encuentra la pistola del crimen de Galicia, se ve el rostro de otro varón al que se identifica en el siguiente pie, Manuel Lorenzo. Uno de los policías detenidos. Y una tercera fotografía enfoca a un grupo de cinco varones jóvenes jugando al fútbol que se explica en el siguiente título del pie de foto: Un segunda elimina al Barça de la Copa en el Camp Nou (0-1). En la contraportada vemos dos fotos de un protagonista no humano, una plaza de toros.

El incremento de imágenes continúa en los ejemplares analizados de 2004. De las 7 cabeceras, 4 dedican sus contraportadas a un gran anuncio (*ABC, El Periódico, Metro Directe* y *20 Minutos*), y 3 a informaciones y opinión (*La Vanguardia, El País* y *El Punt*). Además, también destaca a simple vista la presencia de imágenes de mujeres, de las que hasta ahora sólo habían aparecido dos, una en la portada de *El Periódico* y otra en la contraportada de *El País*, ambas de 1984.

Las mujeres son las principales protagonistas de las imágenes de la portada del ejemplar analizado de *ABC* de 2004. En el centro, una gran fotografía con un pie que se abre con el siguiente titular: Funeral por el comandante Pérez García. El texto del pie explica: El presidente del Gobierno, José María Aznar, miembros del Ejecutivo y líderes de los principales partidos políticos acompañaron ayer a la familia del comandante de la Guardia Civil Gonzalo Pérez García en el solemne funeral celebrado por su alma en la sede de la Dirección General del Benemérito Instituto. En la imagen, la viuda del oficial muerto consuela a su hija mayor ante el féretro con los restos mortales de Pérez García. En la parte inferior de la página vemos la fotografía de una mujer a la que se identifica en el pie como Cristina Alberdi, entre dos titulares. A la izquierda, un titular, Los malos tratos provocaron 117 denuncias diarias en 2003, que encabeza dos subtítulos: el primero, Detenido un hombre que asesinó a su madre hace un año en Espulgues y mantuvo el cadáver en su casa enterrado en cal viva; y el segundo que explica el motivo de la fotografía: Aguirre nombra a Cristina Alberdi presidenta del Observatorio contra la Violencia de Género. Y a la izquierda otro titular, España, entre los países que practican más turismo sexual. En la parte superior de la página, bajo la cabecera, el rostro de otra mujer, la actriz Nicole Kidman, con el siguiente titular: Viernes de estreno. «Cold Mountain», con Nicole Kidman, abrió la Berlinale.

La portada del ejemplar analizado de *La Vanguardia* de 2004 también ofrece la imagen de una mujer que resalta entre un grupo. Letizia vestirá de Pertegaz. Manuel Pertegaz, el maestro de alta costura, diseñará el traje de boda de Letizia. En la foto tomada ayer, la novia del Príncipe deja el taller del diseñador en la Diagonal de Barcelona.

En la portada de *El Punt*, dos fotografías en las que se enfoca a seres humanos entre los que también se pueden ver mujeres. En una, un grupo de gente en una sala y una explicación en el pie de foto: Comença el judici pel cas de Marlès. Y en otra, se ve el rostro de un hombre adulto con el siguiente titular: Gorbatxov diu que una nova «perestroika» faria el món més just.

En la portada de *20 Minutos* vemos 5 imágenes en las que se enfoca a 6 seres humanos, entre ellos a dos mujeres. La foto de un jinete en un caballo aparece encabezada con el siguiente titular que a la vez es pie de foto: Seabiscuit. Galopando hacia el Oscar. Llega a nuestras pantallas una de las candidatas a mejor película además de optar a otras seis estatuillas. En otra fotografía vemos a un hombre vestido de mujer: Deborah saca mi parte salvaje». Se llama Javier, presenta MTV Hot y es contertulio de La selva de los famosos. Los rostros de dos hombres aparecen acompañados de los respectivos titulares-pies de foto: Pochettino. «La situación es difícil y vine a ayudar». Entrevista al defensa tras la vuelta al Espanyol; y Minghella. Llega a la Berlinale sin Kidman. El director abrió el festival con Cold Mountain. También encontramos el rostro de dos mujeres con el siguiente titular: Martirio & Rinaldi. Unen el tango y la copla.

Por el contrario, en la portada del ejemplar analizado de *El País* de 2004 no aparece ninguna mujer. Sólo aparece una fotografía en la que se ve a un grupo de hombres adultos, bajo el siguiente titular que también funciona a la vez como pie de foto: Decenas de heridos en las protestas de los astilleros andaluces.

Tampoco aparece ninguna mujer en la portada de *Metro Directe*, en la que vemos 6 fotografías. Dos, en el centro de la página en un recuadro con varios titulares que se engloban en otro, Cap de Setmana. En la más destacada, dos jóvenes cantando relacionados con el siguiente titular: Entrevista a El Canto de El Loco. En otra, una persona delante de una instalación artística que parece corresponder con el titular: Dalí genial. En la parte inferior de la página, otras dos imágenes con los rostros de dos varones. Uno, de Enrique Arias Vega con la siguiente frase: «Hay que hacer test psicológicos a los jueces»; y otro, de Rafael Nadal, el debutante más joven de la Davis. Además, en la columna de la izquierda encontramos dos fotografías: en una vemos a un varón adulto con el siguiente pie: Bush reza durante una plegaria, sobre un titular que explica que La CIA contradice a Bush por el supuesto arsenal de Sadam. Y en la otra, una puerta y una cámara de televisión con el siguiente pie:

La vivienda, lugar del crimen, que corresponde al titular Mata a su madre y la entierra en casa durante 18 meses.

Finalmente, las imágenes que aparecen en la portada de *El Periódico* de 2004 son un ejemplo de cómo las imágenes no siempre son utilizadas para hacer visibles a los seres humanos. Bajo la cabecera, un gráfico que presenta los datos de La cola de pacientes, acompaña una noticia que anuncia Plan de choque contra las listas de espera en Catalunya. Sanitat garantiza las operaciones antes de seis meses. Y en el centro de la página, la más destacada, una fotografía de un paisaje con un pie de foto que explica: Vinallop: aquí empezará el trasvase. Medio Ambiente marca en este paraje de un barrio del municipio de Tortosa, el punto exacto donde se extraerá el agua del Ebro. Curiosamente, este paisaje sin ninguna persona se utiliza para ilustrar un acontecimiento que ha estado acompañado por un amplio movimiento popular.

Si comparamos los resultados del análisis de los titulares de portada y contraportada con los textos de los pies de foto, y en algunas ocasiones con las imágenes y fotografías, vemos que las fotografías tienden a enfocar a un mayor número de seres humanos, aunque no siempre se utilizan con este fin. También vemos claramente una mayor cantidad de protagonistas varones adultos vinculados con el ejercicio del poder.

En la muestra seleccionada de 1984, todos los titulares, los pies de foto y las imágenes entran en contradicción sobre a quién se considera protagonista. La noticia principal de portada coincide en las portadas de *El País*, *La Vanguardia y El Periódico*: en todos los casos se enfoca a una mayor cantidad de protagonistas humanos en los pies de foto y en las fotografías, que en los titulares, que no presentan protagonistas humanos.

Si analizamos, por ejemplo, la fotografía principal de estas cabeceras, que comparten la misma noticia más destacada del día, vemos también las diferencias que se presentan entre los enfoques de las diferentes cabeceras. *El País* presenta a un líder sindical y un líder de las patronales en primer plano. Por su parte, la fotografía principal de *La Vanguardia* presenta dos colectivos de protagonistas humanos anónimos. Finalmente, *El Periódico* de este año no presenta protagonistas humanos ni en los titulares, ni en los pies de foto, ni en las imágenes de su noticia más destacada, ya que ilustra la unidad redaccional con un mapa de España.

Mientras en los pies de fotos de todas las unidades con elementos gráficos de portada y contraportada se presenta a 17 protagonistas humanos individuales (2 mujeres y 15 hombres) en los titulares se presenta a 5 protagonistas individuales (3 mujeres y 2 hombres). Las mujeres se presentan en los pies de foto de la contraportada de *El País*, Dolores Fernández Feijoo y en la portada de *El Periódico*, Mayte. Entre los hombres tenemos los 9 presidentes que aparecen en la portada del *ABC* mencionados arriba; Marcelino Camacho y José Antonio Segurado, que aparecen en la portada de *El País*; Enric y Enric Salomó en la portada de *El Periódico* y Antonio Álvarez Solís, en la contraportada del mismo diario. Las tres mujeres que son presentadas en los titulares aparecen en la contraportada de *El País*, Dolores Fernández Feijoo, su madre y una tía; los dos hombres aparecen en la contraportada de *El Periódico*, Ángel Viñas y Antonio Álvarez Solís. En este año, los protagonistas colectivos solamente aparecen en los pies de foto, 3 en total y ninguno en los textos de los titulares. Aparecen protagonistas colectivos en la portada de *El País*, los trabajadores; en la portada de *La Vanguardia*, un millar de trabajadores y jornaleros andaluces. Igualmente se presenta un mayor número de protagonistas no humanos en los pie de foto, 13 en total, frente a 11 que se presentan en los textos de los titulares, aunque la diferencia no es tan notable como en el caso de los protagonistas humanos.

Por su parte, en la portada de *ABC* de 1984 las imágenes presentan nueve protagonistas humanos, varones adultos que ejercen el poder político: Felipe González, Jaime Lusinchi, Luis Alberto Monge, Belisario Betancur, Hernán Siles Suazo, Daniel Ortega, Jorge Blanco, Ricardo de la Espriella y Raúl Alfonsín y, en la portada de 1994 de la misma cabecera, tres protagonistas humanos, varones adultos que ejercen el poder: Pascual Sala y Miguel Rodríguez-Piñero y en medio una imagen sin identificación del Rey de España, mientras que los titulares de estas noticias presentan como sujetos agentes a protagonistas que hemos considerado como no humanos: en 1984, 'Cumbre' Iberoamérica en Caracas, y en 1994, el Tribual Supremo, el Tribunal Constitucional y el arbitraje del Rey.

En 1994, podemos apreciar la misma tendencia a presentar mayor número de seres humanos individuales como protagonistas en los pies de foto y en las imágenes que en los titulares. Los pies de foto presentan 21 protagonistas humanos individuales (1 mujer y 20 hombres) mientras los titulares presentan a 10 protagonistas individuales (ninguna mujer y 10 hombres). La única mujer aparece en la portada de La Vanguardia, como una «ex amante» y ese mismo periódico presenta 9 hombres identificados con nombres y apellidos, 4 en la portada (Antonio Gutiérrez, Felipe González, Nicolás Redondo y Manuel Lorenzo) y 5 en la contraportada (Edmond Alphandeéry, Manuel Conté, Joaquín Moya-Angeler, Eduardo Abellán y Jean-Luc Dehnaene). Los protagonistas colectivos son presentados equitativamente, uno en los pies de foto, «los trabajadores» en la portada de El País, y uno en los titulares, «los vitorianos» en la contraportada del mismo periódico. En este año se presenta un menor número de protagonistas no humanos en los pies de foto, 9 en total, mientras en los titulares se presentan 15 de ellos.

Comparando las cuatro cabeceras que seleccionamos en el año 2004 y que se repiten en los otros dos años (ABC, El País, La Vanguardia y El Periódico) vemos que la tendencia se mantiene. Son presentados 10 protagonistas humanos individuales en los pies de fotos (6 mujeres y 4 hombres) y 5 protagonistas individuales en los textos de los titulares (2 mujeres y 3 hombres). Las mujeres aparecen en los pies de fotos de la portada del ABC, «la viuda del oficial muerto», «su hija mayor», Cristina Alberdi y Nicole Kidman; en la contraportada de El País, Cherie Blair y en la portada de La Vanguardia, Letizia. Las dos mujeres que aparecen en los titulares son presentadas por el ABC, Nicole Kidman y La Vanguardia, Letizia.

Asimismo, se presenta un mayor número de protagonistas colectivos en los pies de fotos, 5 en total frente a los 3 presentados en los titulares. El ABC presenta en un pie de foto de la portada a «miembros del Ejecutivo», «líderes de los principales partidos políticos», «la familia del comandante…»; El País, habla de «decenas de heridos» en la portada y del «matrimonio Bush» en la contraportada. Los tres protagonistas colectivos presentados en los titulares aparecen en la portada y contraportada de El País, «Decenas de heridos» y «los Blair» y «los Bush». Con respecto a los protagonistas no humanos, en este año también son presentados en mayor medida en los textos de los titulares que en los pies de foto, 9 y 6 respectivamente.

Algunos ejemplos que ilustran la preponderancia de los protagonistas hombres en portada y contraportada los encontramos en los titulares, los pies de foto y las imágenes de todas las cabeceras de 1994, también en El Periódico de 1984 y el Metro Directe de 2004.

Además, como señalamos al principio, en las imágenes y pies de fotos del *ABC* de 1984 y 1994, los 12 protagonistas son hombres identificados con nombres y apellidos vinculados a las más altas jerarquías del poder político e institucional de las sociedades a las que pertenecen.

El protagonismo de las mujeres es muy inferior al de los hombres, aparece generalmente en las imágenes y muy pocas veces en los textos, y más en las contraportadas que en las portadas. De los 15 ejemplares de la muestra, sólo en 6 portadas vemos mujeres: 2 corresponden a 1984: portada de *El Periódico* y contraportada de *El País*; y 4 se presentan en las portadas del año 2004. Por lo tanto, en ninguna portada de del año 1994 ni en 3 portadas del año 2004 aparece ninguna mujer. La falta de atención de *la mirada informativa* hacia las mujeres en los titulares, a diferencia de las imágenes, la advertimos en la portada de *ABC* de 2004, donde los titulares presentan varias instituciones y a un hombre no identificado como protagonista, mientras las imágenes muestran a tres protagonistas mujeres.

Además, las mujeres son consideradas protagonistas por sus roles en relación con los hombres. La imagen central de la portada de *La Vanguardia* de 2004 muestra a la hoy princesa Letizia, a quien se menciona como la novia del Príncipe, en su visita al taller del modisto que prepara su traje de boda; mientras que la imagen central de *ABC* muestra en primer plano a dos mujeres que se identifican en el pie como la viuda del oficial muerto, y su hija mayor. Las otras dos fotografías de *ABC* muestran una conocida estrella de Holywood identificada con nombres y apellido, y a Cristina Alberdi de la que también se menciona su posición social y estatus: nombrada presidenta del Consejo Asesor del Observatorio contra la violencia de Género. Otro ejemplo de la forma de presentar a las mujeres en las portadas lo encontramos en *20 Minutos*, en el que aparece un titular que hace referencia a la mujer de Tony Blair, identificada con el nombre y apellido de su marido. Además, se muestra la imagen de dos cantantes identificadas son sus nombres artísticos: Martirio y Rinaldi. Esta es también la única portada de toda la muestra donde se presenta la fotografía de un personaje travesti, famoso presentador de televisión.

Los seres humanos presentados como colectivos son mostrados pocas veces como protagonistas tanto en los titulares como en los pies de foto y en las imágenes. Además de las imágenes mencionadas de *El País* y *La Vanguardia* de 1984, solamente vemos colectivos humanos en las imágenes de portada de *El País* y *El Punt* de 2004. La primera, muestra un grupo de trabajadores enfrentándose a la policía; y la segunda, el desarrollo de un juicio con acusados, abogados y jueces y también vemos colectivos humanos en la contraportada de *El Periódico* de 1984 y en la contraportada de *El Punt* de 2004. La primera muestra una reunión de la OTAN y la segunda un grupo de usuarios de Renfe esperando un tren.

Por tanto, en general, los elementos gráficos hacen más visibles a los seres humanos, humanizan la información, pero especialmente a los varones adultos individualizados e identificados y en menor proporción a las mujeres y a los colectivos; además, las imágenes también se pueden utilizar para deshumanizar la información, como se puede advertir en las portadas de *El Periódico* de 1984 y 2004.

Ejercicio 4. La *SENSIBILIDAD* humana de *la mirada informativa:* enfoque y tratamiento

En los ejercicios anteriores hemos evaluado la amplitud y la diversidad de protagonistas de los que hablan las noticias en los titulares, las imágenes y los pies de foto. En este ejercicio nos proponemos completar este análisis examinando la Sensibilidad Humana que se pone de manifiesto en *la mirada informativa*. Para ello, hemos seleccionado algunas *noticias tipo*, relacionadas con distintos grupos sociales de protagonistas que suelen ser enfocados en relación con diferentes actuaciones en distintos escenarios. Hemos ampliado nuestro análisis a los titulares, imágenes y textos que dan continuidad a las noticias de portada en las páginas interiores de los ejemplares y les hemos aplicado el cuestionario completo del *Test ADSH*, agrupando las 5 preguntas fundamentales en dos:

A. ¿A quién, a quiénes o a qué se considera protagonista, haciendo qué y en qué escenarios? Hemos resaltado los protagonistas, y distinguido los verbos que indican haciendo qué, y los escenarios en los que se enfoca a los protagonistas.

B. ¿Quién enfoca y utilizando qué fuentes?

Las respuestas a estos dos interrogantes son complementarias. La primera, al preguntar a quién se presenta como protagonista y las acciones noticiables con las que se identifica, así como la valoración que merece, proporciona información sobre el punto de vista y la posición social que adopta cada cabecera y cada profesional concretos. A la vez, esta información se complementa cuando examinamos las fuentes que se han utilizado, las fuentes que ofrecen datos parciales y a partir de las cuales se valoran las acciones positiva o negativamente. En definitiva, a quién o qué se presenta como protagonistas, y la sensibilidad con la que se valora, pone de manifiesto de forma clara cuáles son los modelos positivos o negativos asumidos como *«yo cognoscente»* por cualquier profesional.

Primera noticia tipo
Un ejemplo de 1984 sobre conflictos entre varones adultos en los escenarios públicos del poder político y sindical.
La primera noticia que hemos seleccionado fue destacada como noticia principal en las portadas de tres de los cuatro diarios analizados de 1984: *El País, La Vanguardia* y *El Periódico*.

Marcelino Camacho, secretario general de CC.OO, lanzó ayer duros ataques al Gobierno ante los trabajadores que respondieron a la convocatoria de huelga general en la localidad madrileña de Getafe. Por su lado, José Antonio Segurado coincidió con Camacho en sus críticas a la política económica gubernamental en la asamblea anual de la Confederación Empresarial Independiente de Madrid.

Medio millón de personas protestó contra la reconversión industrial, según CC OO

Manifestaciones de trabajadores y críticas patronales contra la política del Gobierno

Portada *El País* - Viernes 03/02/1984

128

Movilizaciones sindicales contra la política del Gobierno

Portada *La Vanguardia* - Viernes 03/02/1984

Portada *El Periódico* - Viernes 03/02/1984

El ejemplar del diario *El País* destinó una unidad redaccional en la portada con el siguiente título: *Manifestaciones de trabajadores y críticas patronales contra la política de Gobierno.* Esta noticia continúa en la página 35, en la sección Economía - Trabajo, con el siguiente titular: *Medio millón de trabajadores secundó ayer la jornada de protesta contra la política de reconversión industrial.*

El ejemplar del diario *La Vanguardia* de ese mismo día presentó esta noticia en portada acompañada de dos fotografías y este titular: *Movilizaciones sindicales contra la política del Gobierno.* Continúa en la página 3: *Huelga general en los sectores en reconversión.* Y continúa en la sección Economía de la página 35: *Varias ciudades españolas quedaron paralizadas por las movilizaciones contra la reconversión.*

En la portada de *El Periódico* vemos: *Quejido unánime de la España reconvertida.* Y en la página 3, en la sección Tema del Día encontramos los siguientes titulares: *Rebelión en 22 ciudades contra la reconversión industrial* y *Marcelino Camacho está satisfecho por la respuesta.*

Veamos con qué sensibilidad se trató este acontecimiento en los distintos diarios, respondiendo a las preguntas que hemos planteado más arriba.

A. ¿A quién, a quiénes o a qué se considera protagonista, haciendo qué en qué escenarios?

EL PAÍS

El titular de la portada de *El País* presenta como protagonistas no a los seres humanos en sí mismos sino sus acciones: *Manifestaciones de trabajadores y críticas patronales* [que actúan] *contra la política del Gobierno.* Los titulares de páginas interiores centran la atención en protagonistas humanos colectivos: *Medio millón de trabajadores* secundó *ayer la jornada de protesta contra la política de reconversión industrial.*

Por tanto, los sujetos agentes de las acciones noticiables no son los trabajadores o los patronos, sino las manifestaciones realizadas por unos y las críticas de otros. En sentido estricto, la única referencia a seres humanos como sujetos activos es *Medio millón de trabajadores*, si bien no aparecen como actores que deciden algo, sino que *secundan* una acción que adoptaron otros de los que no se dice nada en los titulares.

130

En consecuencia, el potencial de actuación humano queda amortiguado al identificar a *las manifestaciones...*, *las críticas...*, *la política...*, *la jornada...*, como sujetos o como objetos protagonistas de las actuaciones en contra de; esto es, al identificar como protagonistas y agentes no a los seres humanos, sino a las acciones que parece que se producen sin intervención humana.

El enfoque y el tratamiento se humanizan en las fotografías y en los textos que las explican al pie. En la portada de *El País* se publican 2 fotografías que centran la atención en *Marcelino Camacho* hablando por megáfono a una *multitud de gente*; y en *José Antonio Segurado* en un estrado.

Estos dos varones adultos, identificados con nombre y apellido, y el conjunto de personas que escuchan las palabras del primero, son los protagonistas a los que se enfoca también en el pie de foto con el siguiente texto: *Marcelino Camacho, secretario general de CC OO lanzó ayer duros ataques al Gobierno ante los trabajadores que respondieron a la convocatoria de huelga general en la localidad madrileña de Getafe. Por su lado, José Antonio Segurado coincidió con Camacho en sus críticas a la política económica gubernamental en la asamblea anual de la Confederación Empresaria Independiente de Madrid.* Podemos advertir en este texto un enfoque más humano, que resalta positivamente las actuaciones de dos varones, uno porque *lanzó duros ataques,* y otro porque *coincidió con él en sus críticas,* y de sujetos colectivos como *los trabajadores* que *respondieron a la convocatoria de huelga general.*

En cuanto a los escenarios en los que se desarrollan estas acciones, se trata de escenarios públicos que se localizan uno geográficamente, *en la localidad madrileña de Getafe,* y otro en relación a su carácter institucional, *en la asamblea anual de la Confederación Empresaria Independiente de Madrid*

La Vanguardia

En ningún titular de *La Vanguardia* aparecen seres humanos como sujetos activos, sino que la capacidad de actuación humana queda amortiguada al atribuir el papel de sujetos activos o de objetos a cuatro términos que remiten a acciones. En los titulares de la portada y de la sección de Economía en la página 35, las noticias atribuyen el protagonismo a las *Movilizaciones sindicales contra la política del*

Gobierno y *la reconversión*; y también en la página 35 se presenta como sujeto pasivo a *Varias ciudades españolas* [que] *quedaron paralizadas por las movilizaciones contra la reconversión*. En la página 3 aparece como protagonista activo la *Huelga general* [que se produce] *en los sectores en reconversión*.

En cuanto a las 2 fotografías que se publican en la portada de *La Vanguardia*, en una se enfoca a una *multitud de hombres* alrededor de una pancarta, y en otra a un grupo de 7 hombres no identificados con nombre y apellido sentados en el suelo. Los pies de foto explican estas imágenes: *Cerca de un millar de trabajadores del sector naval se manifestaron ante la sede de la Junta de Andalucía contra la política de reconversión industrial*. Y *Jornaleros andaluces continúan su huelga de hambre en la catedral de Sevilla en protesta por el nuevo subsidio del empleo*

De nuevo podemos observar que la información se humaniza en las fotografías y en los pies de foto, y que además, los colectivos humanos aparecen relacionados con acciones con sentido positivo (*se manifestaron…, y continúan su huelga de hambre en protesta por el nuevo subsidio del empleo*).

En cuanto a los escenarios, se trata de nuevo de escenarios públicos, uno de tipo político, *ante la sede de la Junta de Andalucía*, y otro de tipo religioso, *en la catedral de Sevilla*.

Notemos que, a diferencia de *El País, La Vanguardia* no identifica ningún protagonista individualmente con nombre y apellidos.

EL PERIÓDICO

En el titular principal de la portada, *Quejido unánime de la España reconvertida*, y en el de la página 3, *Rebelión en 22 ciudades contra la reconversión industrial*, no se hace referencia explícita a seres humanos. También en la página 3, otro titular ofrece la única referencia a un ser humano como sujeto activo, un hombre identificado con nombre y apellidos: *Marcelino Camacho está satisfecho por la respuesta*. En los restantes titulares aparecen como sujetos activos protagonistas no humanos, aunque se trata de acciones protagonizadas por seres humanos.

La imagen que se publica en la portada de *El Periódico*, no enfoca a ningún ser humano sino que presenta un *mapa de España* en el que aparecen marcadas las ciudades en las que se ha producido el acto noticiable. El pie de foto, *Mapa de la protesta contra el «Plan Solchaga»*, también identifica como protagonista al mapa, y aunque utiliza el apellido del ministro Solchaga para identificar el objeto contra el que se protesta, su papel como sujeto responsable queda diluido en una acción, el *«Plan Solchaga»*.

De este modo, las actuaciones de protesta protagonizadas por tantas personas contra una decisión del gobierno, y de la que es responsable especialmente uno de los ministros, quedan desprovistas del potencial humano al realzarse la representación cartográfica y el plan de un ministro. El único protagonista humano al que se atribuye una acción positiva y un papel responsable con la situación es un hombre adulto, *Marcelino Camacho* [que] *está satisfecho por la respuesta*. Los escenarios de las acciones son *22 ciudades* que aparecen representadas en el mapa de España (imagen de portada).

En el titular interior de la página 3, en la sección Tema del Día, leemos, *Rebelión en 22 ciudades contra la reconversión industrial,* sin protagonistas humanos, mientras que en el subtítulo sí aparece un protagonista humano colectivo: *Más de 300.000 personas secundan en toda España la protesta convocada por Comisiones Obreras.*

En la misma página, tres fotografías humanizan *la mirada informativa.* Una, muestra una multitud de gente detrás de una pancarta con este pie: *En Valencia se manifestaron trabajadores y se produjeron grandes atascos en el centro de la ciudad.* Otra fotografía más pequeña muestra un grupo de personas reunidas y se explica al pie: *Protesta ante la Junta de Andalucía...* Y por último, ocupando toda la foto, el retrato de Marcelino Camacho acompañado por el siguiente pie de foto: *El líder de Comisiones Obreras critica la falta de participación de UGT en la protesta contra la reconversión.*

Este análisis permite evaluar la distinta sensibilidad humana que muestra cada uno de los diarios en el enfoque y tratamiento de un mismo acontecimiento social. En las tres cabeceras, los titulares de portada y de las páginas interiores presentan como protagonistas principalmente accione*s* y no seres humanos, excepto un titular de *El Periódico* en la página 3 que dice que *Marcelino Camacho está satisfecho…,* y otro titular de *El País* de la página 35, en la sección Economía – Trabajo, que habla de *Medio millón de trabajadores secundó la jornada de protesta.* Notemos la mayor sensibilidad humana para realzar con contundencia el papel del representante sindical (*El*

Periódico), y de los trabajadores (*El País*), que el resto de los titulares que ponen el acento en las acciones, por ejemplo, *Movilizaciones sindicales contra la política del Gobierno* y *la reconversión* en el ejemplar de *La Vanguardia*.

Estas informaciones se complementan con fotografías y pies de foto en las que sí se realza la dimensión humana. En *El País* se enfoca a protagonistas individuales varones con nombre y apellido, *Marcelino Camacho* y *José Antonio Segurado*, y a protagonistas colectivos, *multitud*. Y en *La Vanguardia* sólo a colectivos, tanto en las imágenes como en los pie de foto. No obstante, la imagen y el pie de foto de la portada de *El Periódico* también permite advertir que, aunque en general las imágenes humanizan la información no siempre se utilizan así.

En definitiva, la información de portada que presenta de *El Periódico* resulta más deshumanizada, mientras que *La Vanguardia* es el diario que atribuye un protagonismo más positivo a colectivos humanos, y *El País* enfoca preferentemente como sujetos agentes a dos varones adultos identificados con nombres y apellidos, *Marcelino Camacho* y *José Antonio Segurado*.

Además, en los tres casos, *la mirada informativa* no abarca a las mujeres ni a las criaturas no adultas, como si no existieran o no hubieran participado en absoluto en este acontecimiento, o no tuvieran nada que decir o nada que hacer al respecto, o su participación, si la hubo, no tuviera interés noticiable, o tampoco sufrieran las consecuencias derivadas de este acontecimiento. Nos hallamos, por tanto, ante una *mirada androcéntrica*, restringida a unos cuantos varones adultos que se confrontan en los escenarios públicos, y parcialmente deshumanizada.

Portada *El País*
Viernes 03/02/1984

El País - página 37
Viernes 03/02/1984

Portada *El Periódico*
Viernes 03/02/1984

El Periódico - página 3
Viernes 03/02/1984

La Vanguardia - página 35
Viernes 03/02/1984

Portada *La Vanguardia*
Viernes 03/02/1984

La Vanguardia - página 3
Viernes 03/02/1984

136

B. ¿Quién enfoca y utilizando qué fuentes?

El País es el diario que presenta esta *noticia tipo* elaborada por una mayor cantidad de autores, periodistas —corresponsales— identificados con nombre y apellido y por ciudades.

Dos son mujeres: María José Porteire (Vigo), Marita Martín (Huelva), y cuatro son hombres: Carlos Fuentes (Gijón), Manuel Rivas (El Ferrol), Manuel Muñoz (Sagunto), José Ángel Bermejo (Cádiz)

En *La Vanguardia*, de las tres UR destinadas a este acontecimiento sólo encontramos un autor hombre identificado con nombre y apellido en la información que aparece en la página 35, el corresponsal Vicente González.

Por su parte en el ejemplar de *El Periódico* no encontramos ningún autor de las noticias destinadas a cubrir este acontecimiento.

Para identificar fácilmente *utilizando qué fuentes*, hemos elaborado una tabla que recoge la información textual referida a las fuentes citadas en la noticia, donde distinguimos: *Fuentes humanas identificadas con nombre y apellidos*, y *Fuentes institucionales, agencias, etc....*

TABLA 7
FUENTES DE LA NOTICIA TIPO 1984

Cabecera	Fuentes humanas identificadas con nombre y apellidos	Fuentes no humanos (institucionales, agencias...)
El País	• Carlos Ferrer Salat, presidente de la cúpula patronal • José Antonio Segurado, presidente de los empresarios madrileños • Rafael Termes, presidente de la patronal bancaria	• CC OO • Europa Press
La Vanguardia	• Antonio Puerta, secretario general de UGT - Metal	• Comisiones Obreras • Los sindicatos
El Periódico	• Marcelino Camacho, líder de comisiones obreras • Gerardo Iglesias, secretario general del PCE	• Agencias de Noticias

Esta tabla permite notar que las fuentes consultadas son mayoritariamente varones adultos identificados con nombre y apellido que ocupan posiciones jerárquicas de carácter económico, político y sindical, en instituciones implicadas en la confrontación, y también fuentes institucionales, como los sindicatos y las agencias de noticias.

En todos los casos, excepto en el de las agencias de noticias, las fuentes humanas e institucionales consultadas coinciden con los protagonistas enfocados en las informaciones, si bien estas fuentes mantienen posiciones diferentes e incluso opuestas respecto a la noticia. Por tanto, aunque la información que se ofrece aparece contrastada con distintas fuentes con posiciones enfrentadas, todas ellas son de carácter institucional.

No aparece consultada ninguna mujer como fuente, ni trabajadoras afectadas por las medidas del plan de gobierno, o que forman parte de los sindicatos, ni siquiera como componentes de las familias en las que repercuten las consecuencias del plan de reconversión.

Segunda noticia tipo
Un ejemplo de 2004 sobre conflictos en las relaciones personales entre mujeres y hombres adultos, y criaturas no adultas

De las siete portadas analizadas de los ejemplares de la muestra del año 2004 hemos seleccionado un conjunto de noticias que algunos diarios presentan relacionadas entre sí mediante recuadros u otros recursos tipográficos, y que, de acuerdo con los titulares, hablan de distintos conflictos en las relaciones entre mujeres y hombres adultos, y criaturas no adultas, de países considerados del «centro» y de las «periferias». Noticias, por tanto, en las que la *mirada informativa* no se reduce a los espacios centrales en los que se dirimen los conflictos entre varones adultos por el poder político, económico y sindical, como en el caso anterior, sino que se amplía, se diversifica y abarca al conjunto de la población.

En las portadas de todos los diarios analizados aparece al menos una de estas informaciones, pero en la mayoría encontramos más de una, y, en ocasiones, se presentan vinculadas entre sí. Una característica común a todas ellas es que están desarrolladas en el interior del cuerpo del ejemplar en las secciones Sociedad, España o Nacional y casi todas presentan los mismos protagonistas y citan a las mismas fuentes humanas e institucionales.

Los malos tratos provocaron 117 denuncias diarias en 2003

● Detenido un hombre que asesinó a su madre hace un año en Esplugues y mantuvo el cadáver en su casa enterrado en cal viva

● Aguirre nombra a Cristina Alberdi presidenta del Consejo Asesor del Observatorio contra la Violencia de Género Editorial, 10 y 11

Cristina Alberdi

España, entre los 5 países que practican más turismo sexual con menores

Portada *ABC*
Viernes 06/02/2004

Los malos tratos a mujeres generaron más de 50.000 denuncias el año pasado

UN HOMBRE mata a su madre, la entierra en cal viva y vive con el cadáver más de un año en su casa

Portada *El País*
Viernes 06/02/2004

Las muertes por violencia doméstica crecen un 30%

Más de 30.000 españoles hacen turismo sexual infantil

Portada *La Vanguardia*
Viernes 06/02/2004

Un hombre tuvo 15 meses en cal viva el cadáver de su madre

Portada *El Periódico*
Viernes 06/02/2004

139

Un home mata la mare i
oculta el cos més d'un any
a casa seva, a Esplugues

Les universitats
catalanes oferiran
carreres de tres anys
el pròxim curs

El govern regularà l'activitat de les colònies escolars

Portada *El Punt*
Viernes 06/02/2004

5.000 niños, obligados a ejercer la prostitución

Portada *Metro Directe*
Viernes 06/02/2004

**Mata a su madre y
la entierra en casa
durante 18 meses**

España, uno de
los **cinco países**
de la UE con
más **turismo
sexual infantil**

**68 mujeres asesinadas (y 106
casi) por su pareja en 2003**

Portaven **dones
immigrants**
al Raval **i les
violaven** si no
es prostituïen

Portada *20 Minutos*
Viernes 06/02/2004

140

A. ¿A quién, a quiénes o a qué se considera protagonista, haciendo qué en qué escenarios?

ABC

El ejemplar del diario *ABC* es el que presenta, en la portada, más titulares y fotografías que centran la atención en mujeres y criaturas: concretamente, vemos la imagen de cuatro mujeres, y una referencia a menores en un titular. En la parte inferior izquierda de la portada tres titulares: uno más destacado, *Los malos tratos provocaron 117 denuncias diarias en 2003*. Otras dos noticias distintas se insertan como subtítulos: *Detenido un hombre que asesinó a su madre hace un año en Esplugues y mantuvo su cadáver en su casa en cal viva*; y *Aguirre nombra a Cristina Alberdi presidenta del Consejo Asesor del Observatorio contra la Violencia de Género*. Esta noticia va acompañada de la fotografía del rostro de Cristina Alberdi.

Estas informaciones continúan en la editorial, en página 4, en la sección Nacional, en páginas 10 y 11, y en la sección Sociedad en la página 44. En el primer titular, la actuación de las mujeres enfrentándose a un problema queda atenuado porque la atención que se centra en unas acciones: *los malos tratos, y 117 denuncias*.

Las acciones aparecen ejemplificadas en el segundo titular con la noticia sobre *un hombre* [que] *asesinó* a *su madre y mantuvo su cadáver* en su casa, ejemplo que no obstante elude identificar a los protagonistas con nombre y apellidos. Se completa este conjunto de noticias anunciando una medida de carácter institucional que se presenta con dos protagonistas mujeres identificadas con nombre y apellidos, una de las cuales aparece con una fotografía: la ministra *Aguirre* que *nombra* a *Cristina Alberdi presidenta del Consejo Asesor del Observatorio contra la Violencia de Género*.

Junto a este bloque de noticias, también en la parte inferior de la portada a la derecha, pero diferenciado del grupo anterior, se anuncia: *España entre los países que practican más turismo sexual con menores*.

Los tres primeros titulares se amplían en el interior del ejemplar. En la editorial de la página 4 con el título, *Violencia familiar* y en la sección Nacional, en las páginas 10 y 11. La noticia central ocupa toda la página 10 y su titular dice: *Durante 2003 se produjeron 117 denuncias diarias de media por malos tratos en España*. Los protagonistas de portada se repiten en el titular del interior, pero se invierte el orden

141

en el que son presentados, y el verbo está en voz pasiva: *se produjeron 117 denuncias diarias de media por malos tratos.*

El lugar *[en España]* es el escenario donde se produce el acontecimiento noticioso. Esta información está acompañada por una infografía titulada: *Las huellas del drama*, que muestra la silueta dibujada en blanco sobre negro de una «víctima» (similar a la que se realizan en las investigaciones policiales) acompañada con texto, datos numéricos y gráficos que expresan las estadísticas sobre: la edad de la víctima y del agresor; vinculación de la pareja; método utilizado para cometer el crimen; actitud tras cometer el crimen; etc.…

En la página 11, a una columna, se presenta la información que hace referencia al nombramiento por parte de Esperanza Aguirre, de Cristina Alberdi, con el título: *Aguirre «ficha» a la ex ministra Cristina Alberdi.* Esta información reproduce la misma fotografía de C. Alberdi que se presenta en la portada del diario.

La segunda información que encontramos en las página 11 hace referencia al «parricidio» de Esplugues con el siguiente título: *Asesinó a su madre y tuvo su cadáver en casa un año cubierto de cal viva.* El subtítulo proporciona más detalles del protagonista *hombre* que se presentó en el titular de la portada: *El hijo, de 46 años, dice que la mató por dinero y porque lo obligó a prostituirse.* Una fotografía muestra un hombre con la cabeza cubierta y otros tres hombres de espaldas que le introducen en una furgoneta. En el pie se identifica al protagonista con su apellido: *Rus, con la cabeza cubierta; hizo ayer la reconstrucción de los hechos.*

Por último, en la sección Sociedad, en la página 44, se amplía otra información de portada, y que incluimos en este análisis, sobre turismo sexual con criaturas no adultas. Esta información presenta dos noticias interiores, la central y de mayor tamaño se titula: *España se encuentra entre los cinco países del mundo que más turismo sexual practica con menores,* y esta acompañada de una fotografía que muestra a dos mujeres y un hombre, en el pie de foto se lee: *Dos de cada diez meretrices adultas en España confiesan que empezaron a ejercer la prostitución cuando sólo eran niñas.* El protagonista de la información en el titular es no humano, *España,* cuya acción es ser uno de *los cinco países del mundo que practica más turismo sexual.* El titular hace referencia a un país como protagonista activo, eludiendo el sexo, la edad, la clase social, etc. de los humanos responsables de «practicar turismo sexual» invisibles y englobados en el término *España.* Otros protagonistas son los receptores de la acción: los *menores,* que se presentan como un colectivo humano sin identificar, un término ambiguo que no proporciona información sobre sexo, procedencia, condición social…

Podemos concluir que en los titulares de *ABC,* tanto el protagonista activo como el receptor de su acción, no son identificados. Sin embargo en el pie de foto se presenta a protagonistas mujeres caracterizadas con un rol profesional: *Dos de cada diez meretrices adultas* que cuando *sólo eran niñas empezaron a ejercer la prostitución.* Es llamativo que el protagonismo de las mujeres (adultas y niñas) se presente asociado a la prostitución, mientras que el protagonismo de los hombres no aparezca ni en el texto de los titulares ni en el pie de foto, pero sí en la fotografía.

El País

La portada del ejemplar de *El País* del mismo día presenta un enfoque menos amplio y diverso y más deshumanizado. En el centro de la página, dos titulares separados: *Los malos tratos a mujeres generaron más de 50.000 denuncias el año pasado*; y en una columna a la izquierda, más pequeño: *Un hombre mata a su madre, la entierra en cal viva y vive con el cadáver más de un año en su casa».* Ninguna información presenta imágenes. En la primera el protagonismo de hombres y mujeres queda desplazado por las acciones de *los malos tratos,* y las *denuncias.* En la segunda aparece la dimensión humana [*un hombre* y *su madre*] aunque los protagonistas no son identificados con nombre y apellidos.

La información en portada referida a los «malos tratos» se amplía en la sección Sociedad, en la página 26: *España registró más de 50.000 denuncias por malos tratos a mujeres en 2003.* A diferencia del titular de portada, en el encabezado interior se agrega *España,* como protagonista y escenario donde se *registraron más de 50.000 denuncias* y se presenta a los mismos protagonistas como fuentes de la información. Esta noticia está acompañada por un recuadro con gráficos que se titula: *Víctimas de la violencia doméstica. Por el cónyuge o análogo.* El gráfico presenta la curva ascendente y la expresión en datos numéricos de las denuncias por malos tratos, las mujeres asesinadas desde el año 1997 al 2003.

Otras dos noticias ocupan el resto del espacio en la página 26. Una hace referencia a que *Finlandia y Noruega tienen la mayor tasa de homicidios* en Europa. En la otra, el titular expresa la voz de un protagonista hablando en primera persona: *Aguanté veinte años de*

143

malos tratos y acabó matando a mi hija. Aunque en esta información se otorga la palabra a una mujer, la acción expresada en el titular remite a la pasividad [*Aguanté*] y al padecimiento [*acabó matando a mi hija*].

Por último, el diario *El País* también habla en portada de una noticia que se desarrolla en la página 1 de la sección Cataluña: «*Metió a su mamá, una 'madame', en cal viva y, borracho, la lloraba por las noches*». Este titular contiene connotaciones negativas para la mujer «victima», asesinada por su hijo: *'una madame'*.

LA VANGUARDIA

En relación con estas mismas noticias, *La Vanguardia* presenta, en la parte inferior de la portada, los siguientes titulares: *Las muertes por violencia doméstica crecen un 30%*, con un subtítulo que dice: *El Instituto de la Mujer calcula 68 homicidios en el 2003 perpetrados por maridos o novios*; y en un recuadro más pequeño: *Más de 30.000 españoles hacen turismo sexual infantil*. Como en otras ocasiones, *la mirada informativa* aparece deshumanizada, ya que presenta como protagonistas no a los seres humanos, sino a las actuaciones [*Las muertes por violencia doméstica, 68 homicidios, turismo sexual infantil*], los datos [*un 30%, 68 homicidios*] y las instituciones [*El Instituto de la Mujer*]. No obstante, esta portada se diferencia de las anteriores porque enfoca a varones adultos [*maridos o novios*] como responsables de la acción [*homicidios... perpetrados*]. También, presenta a *Más de 30.000 españoles* como responsables de la acción, porque *hacen turismo sexual infantil*. En cualquier caso, si bien la información de esta portada se humaniza, las mujeres y los menores de edad no aparecen como sujetos agentes sino como víctimas pasivas incluidas implícitamente en los datos [*un 30%, 68 homicidios*] o como receptores de las acciones de los *30.000 españoles* que hacen *turismo sexual infantil*.

Estas noticias continúan en las páginas 29 y 30 de la sección Sociedad. Ocupando una cuarta parte de la página 29, al lado de una necrológica, se puede leer el siguiente titular: *Más de 30.000 españoles practican turismo sexual infantil en Latinoamérica cada año*. Nuevamente en el interior se presenta como protagonista de la acción [*practican*] al colectivo genérico *españoles*, que incluye tanto a hombres como mujeres diversos, sobre los cuales no se proporciona más información, aunque sí se aporta el escenario y el tiempo de la acción: *en Latinoamérica cada año*.

Por último, en la página 30 leemos: *Las muertes de mujeres a manos de su pareja crecen un 30% en 2003.* Las protagonistas, una vez más, no son las mujeres sino *Las muertes de mujeres* que *crecen un 30% en 2003. Sus parejas,* también aparecen como protagonistas. Esta información se acompaña de una fotografía que muestra un coche de la policía y en cuyo pie de foto podemos leer: *En este barranco de Palma se halló anteayer el cadáver de M.I. Ferrer.* Presumimos que por el titular *el cadáver de M.I. Ferrer* corresponde al cuerpo de una mujer asesinada.

Destacamos que la información en esta cabecera se humaniza, aunque en ningún titular se hace referencia a que las muertes de las mujeres puedan ser consecuencia de acciones positivas de ellas, de su resistencia a los malos tratos.

EL PERIÓDICO

En la portada de *El Periódico* del mismo día sólo encontramos una de las informaciones que hemos visto en otras portadas. Un pequeño titular en el centro de la columna de la derecha anuncia: *Un hombre tuvo 15 meses en cal viva el cadáver de su madre.* El titular centra la atención en dos seres humanos, un hombre y una mujer, *su madre,* que, como en los casos anteriores, tampoco son identificados con sus nombres y apellidos. Las restantes noticias destacadas por las otras cabeceras y que analizamos en este grupo, no han merecido la atención de este diario.

En el interior de *El Periódico,* dos unidades redaccionales amplían la información de portada en la página 32 en la sección Cosas de la Vida. La primera titula: *Un parricida ocultó 15 meses el cadáver de su madre.* El protagonista aparece definido por su acción, *Un parricida.* La noticia está acompañada de tres fotografías. El pie de foto señala: *El inmueble donde estaba el cadáver y a la derecha, el precinto y el buzón de la vivienda.* La otra noticia que amplia esta información es una crónica titulada *El Norman Bates de Espulgues,* donde se presenta el escenario y se equipara al protagonista a un conocido personaje de ficción del cine de terror. Ambas informaciones están enmarcadas con un antetítulo que las precede: *La violencia familiar – Descubrimiento de un crimen truculento.* La frase *violencia familiar,* que había sido utilizada por *ABC* en su editorial del mismo día haciendo referencia a la información sobre «malos tratos» a las mujeres, aparece aquí asociada al «parricidio».

EL PUNT*

El Punt destaca en portada dos de las noticias que hemos analizado en este segundo grupo. En la parte inferior de la página, a dos columnas, titula: *Un hombre mata a la madre y oculta el cuerpo más de un año en su casa, en Esplugues*. Esta noticia continúa en la página 5, en la sección Països Catalans con el siguiente titular: *Un hombre mata a su madre y la oculta más de un año enterrada con cal viva en su casa*, que se repite casi idéntico en la página interior, salvo por que omite el escenario [*en Esplugues*] y aporta nueva información, *enterrada en cal viva*. La noticia es acompañada con la fotografía de un edificio y el titular: *El escenario del crimen*.

La otra información de este grupo de noticias se presenta en portada a la izquierda con un pequeño titular: *Treinta mil españoles practicaron turismo sexual con menores durante el año 2001*. Esta información se amplia en la página 34, en la sección Europa – Món con este título: *Francia y el Estado español encabezan la lista de países que practican más turismo sexual con menores*. Así, mientras en el titular de portada se enfoca a seres humanos, [*Treinta mil españoles*] como protagonistas responsables [*practicaron turismo sexual*] de una acción que repercute sobre otro colectivo humano indeterminado [*con menores*], el titular del interior se deshumaniza al enfocar a los países [*Francia y el Estado español*] en lugar de las personas, hombres y mujeres, como responsables de las acciones. Sin embargo, en la foto que presenta dos mujeres caminando, el enfoque se humaniza y se refuerza en el pie: *El informe sostiene que más de 30.000 españñoles van al extranjero para tener relaciones con nniños*.

Por último, mencionaremos una noticia destacada sólo en la portada de *El Punt*, que también hace referencia a las criaturas no adultas: *El gobierno regulará la actividad de las colonias escolares*. Este titular a tres columnas encuadra una fotografía en la que se ve un grupo de personas sentadas en el interior de un juzgado, y en el pie de foto se explica: *Empieza el juicio por el caso Marlès*. La información se complementa con otros subtítulos: *Fijará una norma para minimizar los riesgos que oferecen las empresas de ocio; Bargalló lo anuncia el día del inicio del juicio por la muerte de dos niños en unas convivencias; La normativa no afectará al funcionamiento de los «esplais» y grupos «escoltes»; y La Generalitat quiere dejar a punto el nuevo marco en esta legislatura*. La noticia continúa en la página 3 en

146

la sección *Punto y aparte* con el titular: *Los acusados por la tragedia de Merlès todavía no se explican que falló*. Por primera vez se menciona a los protagonistas humanos como responsables de los acontecimientos. Este tratamiento se refuerza con la fotografía que acompaña la información (similar a la de portada), cuyo pie de foto señala: *Los dos acusados sentados ayer en el banco del juzgado de Vic*.

Destacamos que la noticia del juicio por la muerte de dos niños cuya vista se inicia (información resaltada en portada y acompañada con una fotografía central), queda relegada a un segundo plano, favoreciendo el enfoque de otros protagonistas a los que se destaca en el titular principal y en los subtítulos: el gobierno de la Generalitat de Catalunya y su representante, Bargalló que anuncian intervenciones de futuro *(regulará la actividad de las colonias escolares, fijará una norma para minimizar los riesgos…)*. De este modo, las criaturas que murieron y sus familiares quedan fuera del enfoque de una *mirada informativa* más atenta a los varones que actúan en los escenarios públicos de carácter político, que al conjunto de la sociedad.

METRO DIRECTE

En la portada del diario gratuito *Metro Directe* encontramos dos de las noticias que hemos analizado en otras portadas del mismo día. La más destacada, en la parte inferior de la página, a cuatro columnas, presenta el siguiente titular: *5.000 niños, obligados a ejercer la prostitución*. Un subtítulo aclara: *Una ONG denuncia que España es uno de los países más aficionados al turismo sexual con menores*. Por primera vez, una información de portada pone el acento en los niños (sin especificar sexo ni edad) como protagonistas activos, aunque obligados a ejercer la prostitución. Este enfoque cambia y se deshumaniza en el titular de la página 2 de la sección España, que hace referencia nuevamente a un país: *España, entre los países más adictos al turismo sexual*.

El otro titular de portada anuncia: *Mata a su madre y la entierra en casa durante 18 meses*. Una fotografía muestra una puerta y una cámara de televisión, en el pie se explica: *La vivienda, lugar del crimen*. En la página 6, en la sección Barcelona, encontramos el siguiente titular: *Mata a la madre por venganza y conserva el cadáver año y medio**. Esta información se acompaña con la fotografía de un edificio cuyo pie de foto anuncia: *Pocos vecinos sospechaban que convivían con un matricida**.

20 Minutos

El diario gratuito *20 Minutos* anuncia en portada tres de las noticias que hemos analizado: *España, uno de los cinco países de la UE con más turismo sexual infantil; 68 mujeres asesinadas (y 106 casi) por su pareja en 2003; Guarda a su madre en cal viva más de un año tras matarla.* Y además, otra noticia que no encontramos en los restantes diarios pero que incluimos en este grupo por el tipo de protagonistas y el tratamiento que les da, con el siguiente titular: *Llevaban mujeres inmigrantes al Raval y las violaban si no se protituían.* *

En la página 6, en la sección Actualidad, se amplía una de las informaciones: *España, a la cabeza de la UE en el turismo sexual con menores.* Como en otras cabeceras, los protagonistas quedan englobados en el término *España.* En la página 7, también en la sección Actualidad, continúa otra de las noticias: *68 asesinadas por sus parejas en 2003.* Luego en negrita y destacado al principio como subtítulo se complementa la información: *Y trece hombres.* Este es el único ejemplar que destaca la violencia ejercida contra los hombres y también la cuantifica. En la página 2, en la sección Barcelona, continúa la tercera noticia seleccionada: *Mata a su madre y convive con su cadáver en casa durante un año.* Otro titular habla de *Psicosis en el número 30*, asociando nuevamente el crimen a un relato de ficción, la película de Alfred Hitchcock. La fotografía que acompaña estas dos unidades redaccionales muestra la puerta de una vivienda y este pie de foto: *Una cámara de televisión graba, ayer, imágenes de la puerta precintada por la Policía del piso donde se produjo el matricidio.*

Por último, esta cabecera presenta en portada una noticia que no hemos encontrado en ninguna de las otras seis cabeceras analizadas, que hace referencia a un colectivo de mujeres inmigrantes. En el interior, en la sección Barcelona, en la página 3, encontramos el siguiente titular: *Cae un grupo que introducía emigrantes con pasaportes robados y las prostituía,** que hace referencia a una banda que, como se señala en la portada, operaba en el Raval. Ambos titulares no aportan información ni de la cantidad de mujeres obligadas a prostituirse, ni de sus edades, o procedencias; estas mujeres son enfocadas como un colectivo receptor y padeciente de las acciones de un grupo (del que tampoco se aportan datos en los titulares): *que las violaban si no es prostituían; las introducía; y las prostituía.**

148

OTRAS CONSIDERACIONES

El diario *ABC* es el único ejemplar que presenta un titular en el que se enfoca como protagonistas activas a dos mujeres identificadas con nombre y apellido, *Esperanza Aguirre* y *Cristina Alberdi*, mujeres a las que se les reconoce su capacidad de tomar decisiones en el ámbito de la política.

También encontramos otras referencias a las mujeres en los ejemplares de *ABC*, *El País* y *La Vanguardia*, aunque su protagonismo se desplaza hacia *los malos tratos, las muertes por violencia doméstica, 117 denuncias diarias, las muertes a mujeres*, mientras que el diario gratuito *20 Minutos* centra la atención en *68 asesinadas y (106 casi) por su pareja en 2003*.

En dos noticias, los hombres reciben un tratamiento poco habitual, como responsables de acciones contra las mujeres y las criaturas que, de acuerdo con el sistema simbólico androcéntrico, aparecen como sujetos pasivos y víctimas, como seres sin capacidad para actuar y reaccionar. Todos los diarios, excepto *La Vanguardia*, hacen referencia a una noticia cuyo protagonista activo se presenta como *un hombre* que ejerce una acción [*mata, guarda, convive, tuvo*] sobre una mujer *su madre*. Y también todas las portadas, menos las de *El País* y *El Periódico*, se hacen eco de otra noticia que en los titulares del *ABC*, *Metro Directe* y *20 Minutos* habla de que *España practica turismo sexual con menores*. Mientras que *La Vanguardia* y *El Punt*, humanizan la información haciendo alusión a *30.000 españoles*.

En definitiva, este conjunto de noticias publicadas en las portadas de la muestra seleccionada de 2004, indica una ampliación y una diversidad mayor en el enfoque. No obstante, persiste la misma sensibilidad humana que pone de manifiesto la otra cara del sistema simbólico androcéntrico, que valora como inferiores y pasivos a las mujeres y hombres y a las criaturas que nos forman parte de los círculos centrales del poder, y representa dramáticamente las situaciones que viven. En ningún caso se presentan como sujetos activos con capacidad de resolver sus problemas individual o colectivamente.

---

* En catalán en el original.

149

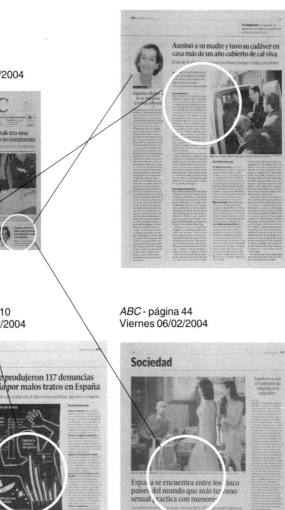

Portada *ABC*
Viernes 06/02/2004

El País - página 26
Viernes 06/02/2004

Portada *El País*
Viernes 06/02/2004

El País - página 1. Sección Cataluña
Viernes 06/02/2004

Portada *La Vanguardia*
Viernes 06/02/2004

152

Portada *El Periódico*
Viernes 06/02/2004

El Periódico - página 32
Viernes 06/02/2004

El Punt - página 34
Viernes 06/02/2004

Portada *El Punt*
Viernes 06/02/2004

El Punt - página 5
Viernes 06/02/2004

154

Metro Directe - página 2
Viernes 06/02/2004

Portada *Metro Directe*
Viernes 06/02/2004

Metro Directe - página 6
Viernes 06/02/2004

Metro Directe - página 9
Viernes 06/02/2004

155

Mata a su madre y convive con su cadáver en casa durante un año

Psicosis en el número 30

Gorbatxov reclamà una nova 'perestroika' al món i fer més humà el procés de globalització

Los Mossos multarán a los incívicos en Santa Coloma

Los vecinos se quejan porque el Ajuntament rechaza sus ideas

Portada *20 Minutos*
Viernes 06/02/2004

El 65% de los enfermos en lista de espera está en el área de Barcelona

Cau un grup que introduïa immigrants amb passaports robats i les prostituïa

Perfumes y productos del hogar son los que menos se cambian

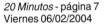

B. ¿Quién enfoca utilizando qué fuentes?

En la siguiente tabla hemos registrado las fuentes utilizadas por los periódicos para cada una de las noticias que hablan de conflictos en las relaciones personales entre mujeres y hombres adultos y criaturas no adultas. Este agrupamiento distingue las informaciones que hacen referencia a «malos tratos», «parricidio» y «turismo sexual con niños». Al mismo tiempo analizamos las autorías en relación con las fuentes utilizadas.

TABLA 8.
FUENTES DE LAS NOTICIAS TIPO DE 2004

Cabecera	Fuentes humanas identificadas con nombre y apellido	Fuentes no humanas (instituciones, agencias…)
ABC	**Malos tratos**	
	• Micaela Navarro (secretaria de Igualdad del PSOE) • María Jesús Sainz (portavoz del grupo Popular en la Comisión Mixta de Derechos de la Mujer) • Montserrat Comas (presidenta del Observatorio sobre Violencia Doméstica) • Cristina Alberdi (ex ministra socialista) • Rafael Simancas (Secretario de la Federación socialista madrileña)	• Encuestas • Observatorio de violencia Doméstica • Centro Reina Sofía para el estudio de la violencia • PP • PSOE
	Parricidio	
	• Vecinos del barrio	
	Turismo sexual con niños	
	• Pedro Núñez Morgades (Defensor del Menor de la comunidad de Madrid) • Zapatero (líder de la oposición)	• Save the Children • Ministerio del Interior • Plataforma de Organizaciones de la Infancia
El País	**Malos tratos**	
	• Miriam Tey (Directora del instituto de la Mujer) • Enriqueta Chicano (Presidenta de la Federación de Mujeres Progresistas)	• Datos del ministerio del Interior recogidos por el Instituto de la Mujer • Gobierno • PSOE

TABLA 8.

FUENTES DE LAS NOTICIAS TIPO DE 2004 *(continuación)*

Cabecera	Fuentes humanas identificadas con nombre y apellido	Fuentes no humanas (instituciones, agencias…)
El País	**Malos tratos** *(continuación)*	

	• Rosa Pérez Villar Aparicio (Portavoz de la organización Themis)	• Internacional de Mujeres Progresistas
	• Ana pastor (Ministra de sanidad y Consumo)	• Izquierda Unida
	• Micaela Navarro (secretaria de Igualdad del PSOE)	• Estudio del Centro Reina Sofía con datos del año 2000
	• José Bono (Presidente de Castilla la Mancha, dirigente socialista)	• Televisión Canaria
	• Gaspar Llamazares (líder de izquierda Unida)	
	• Araceli Hurtado («víctima» que se presenta como fuente de la Televisión canaria)	

Parricidio

	• Isabel Polo, vecina del inmueble	• Fuentes policiales
	• Vecinos	

La Vanguardia	**Malos tratos**	

	• Montserrat Comas (presidenta del Observatorio sobre Violencia Doméstica, Miembro de Consejo General del Poder Judicial)	• Instituto de la Mujer
	• José María Michavila (Ministro de Justicia)	• Federación de Asociaciones de Mujeres Separadas y Divorciadas
	• Eduardo Zaplana (titular de Trabajo y Asuntos Sociales)	
	• Ana Pastor (Ministra de Sanidad)	

Turismo sexual con niños

		• ONG Save the Children

El Periódico	**Parricidio**	

	• Enrique Rus Sánchez (su único hijo)	
	• Los vecinos	

El Punt	**Parricidio**	

	• Enrique Rus, (el fill, l'arrestat)	• Policía
	• La propiètaria de una de botiga	
	• Veïna del primer pis	
	• Isabel Polo, veïna del entresol	
	• Propietari bar Bohemia	

TABLA 8.
FUENTES DE LAS NOTICIAS TIPO DE 2004 *(continuación)*

Cabecera	Fuentes humanas identificadas con nombre y apellido	Fuentes no humanas (instituciones, agencias...)
El Punt *(contiuación)*		**Turisme sexual amb nens**
		• ONG Save the Children
Metro Directe		**Parricidio**
	• El detingut • El veïns • Els sociòlegs	• La Policía
		Turismo sexual con niños
		• ONG Save the Children • Organización Mundial de Turismo (fuente citada por la ONG) • Red Internacional de Erradicación de la Explotación sexual Infantil • Ministerio del Interior (fuente citada por la Red Internacional de Erradicación de la Explotación sexual Infantil)
20 Minutos		**Malos tratos**
		• Instituto de la Mujer • Observatorio sobre Violencia Doméstica
		Parricidio
	• Vecinos • Isabel Polo	
		Turismo sexual con niños
		• Informe ONG Save the Children
		Prostitución mujeres inmigrantes
		• Policía

La mayoría de las unidades redaccionales no presentan autoría definida. Las autorías registradas por tipo de información y por cabecera se comentarán al hablar de las fuentes citadas para construir la información. Cabe destacar, como puede verse en la tabla, que las noticias que se repiten en dos o más periódicos citan prácticamente a las mismas personas y/o instituciones como fuentes de la información.

160

ABC

Como hemos señalado más arriba, la portada de esta cabecera es la única que presenta vinculadas entre si tres informaciones que hacen referencia a los conflictos en las relaciones interpersonales. Las tres noticias se amplían en la editorial de la página 4 titulada *Violencia familiar* y en la sección Nacional de las páginas 10 y 11 del diario.

En la página 10 la información que titula *Durante 2003 se produjeron 117 denuncias diarias de media por malos tratos en España*, presenta como autor a M.A. Barroso, cuyo sexo no se identifica. Las fuentes con las que se construye esta información son principalmente institucionales: el Observatorio de Violencia Doméstica, el Centro Reina Sofía para el estudio de la Violencia, los partidos políticos mayoritarios y las encuestas proporcionadas por dichas instituciones. Además, esta cabecera presenta como fuentes a tres mujeres identificadas con nombre y apellido y por el cargo político institucional que ocupan: Micaela Navarro (secretaria de Igualdad del PSOE); María Jesús Sainz (portavoz del grupo Popular en la Comisión Mixta de Derechos de la Mujer); Montserrat Comas (presidenta del Observatorio sobre Violencia Doméstica). Las mujeres como fuentes de esta información representan la voz de las instituciones de las que forman parte. A las mujeres afectadas por las acciones noticiables no se les da voz, y no se las considera como fuentes.

En cuanto a la imagen infográfica que acompaña a la noticia de la página 10, titulada *Las huellas del drama,* su autor es el propio diario *ABC,* y la fuente, el Centro Reina Sofía para el estudio de la Violencia.

En página 11, sin autoría, se presenta la información que hace referencia al nombramiento, por parte de la presidenta de la Comunidad de Madrid, *Esperanza Aguirre,* de *Cristina Alberdi* para presidir el Consejo asesor del Observatorio autonómico contra la Violencia de Género. Esta información ocupa el tamaño de una columna con recuadro y no presenta autoría. Las fuentes en este caso también son los partidos políticos mayoritarios, la propia protagonista de la información, Cristina Alberdi, y un hombre, Rafael Simancas, secretario de la Federación Socialista madrileña.

La última información registrada en la misma página 11, que hace referencia al «parricidio» de Espulgues, es la única que presenta autoría, una mujer, Dolors Massot, y las fuentes consultadas son los vecinos (no identificados) del piso donde vivían la madre y el hijo.

Por último, en la sección Sociedad de la página 44 se amplía la noticia presentada en portada sobre el turismo sexual. Esta información presenta dos noticias interiores cuyas autorías son identificadas con iniciales: E.M. firma la noticia central y de mayor tamaño que titula *España se encuentra entre los cinco países del mundo que más turismo sexual practica con menores*; y G.L.A. firma el recuadro que ocupa media columna con el titular *Zapatero acusa al gobierno de «negligencia culpable»*. Respecto a las fuentes humanas citadas en ambas noticias, sólo se presentan hombres, con cargos institucionales: en la primera, Pedro Núñez Morgades (Defensor del Menor de la comunidad de Madrid) y en la segunda, Luis Rodríguez Zapatero. Mientras que las fuentes institucionales citadas en la primera noticia son la ONG Save the Children y el Ministerio del Interior, y en la segunda noticia se presenta como fuente institucional la Plataforma Organizaciones de la Infancia.

EL PAÍS

El País presenta a un hombre, Antonio Fraguas (Madrid) y a las Agencias como autores de la información central sobre «malos tratos» publicada en portada que se amplía en la sección Sociedad de la página 26: *España registró más de 50.000 denuncias por malos tratos a mujeres en 2003*. El cuerpo del texto está dividido entre diferentes agentes involucrados, que son citados tanto como protagonistas y como fuentes: Miriam Tey (Directora del instituto de la Mujer); Enriqueta Chicano (Presidenta de la Federación de Mujeres Progresistas); Rosa Pérez Villar Aparicio (Portavoz de la organización Themis); Ana Pastor (Ministra de Sanidad y Consumo); Micaela Navarro (secretaria de Igualdad del PSOE); José Bono (Presidente de Castilla la Mancha, dirigente socialista); Datos del ministerio del Interior recogidos por el Instituto de la Mujer; Gobierno; PSOE; Internacional de Mujeres Progresistas; Izquierda Unida; Gaspar Llamazares (líder de izquierda Unida). En cuanto a su rol como fuentes de la información, igual que en el caso anterior, se trata de hombres y mujeres que ocupan cargos políticos e institucionales y por tanto hablan en nombre de las instituciones a las que representan. También quedan excluidas como fuentes las mujeres que están

162

afectadas por esta acción noticiable. Esta noticia está acompañada por un recuadro con gráficos que se titula: *Víctimas de la violencia doméstica. Por el cónyuge o análogo* cuyo autor es el propio diario *El País* y las fuentes son dos instituciones oficiales: el Ministerio del Interior y *el* Instituto de la Mujer.

Otras dos noticias ocupan el resto del espacio en la página 26, una que hace referencia a la tasa de homicidios en Europa *Finlandia y Noruega tienen la mayor tasa de homicidios.* La autoría corresponde a otro hombre, Jaime Prats (Valencia), y la fuente consultada coincidiendo con la de otras cabeceras, un Estudio del Centro Reina Sofía.

Y la última información, firmada por J.M.P. (Santa Cruz de Tenerife) *Aguanté veinte años de malos tratos y acabó matando a mi hija*, cita como fuentes a la protagonista, Araceli Hurtado (madre de la pequeña Natalia) y a otro medio de comunicación, la Televisión Canaria. Respecto a las autorías, en *El País* la mayoría son hombres y la mayoría de las fuentes consultadas son institucionales.

Otra información que incluimos en este grupo y que *El País* también enfoca como acontecimiento noticioso es la relacionada con el «parricidio» de Esplugues. Esta información publicada en portada se amplía en la página 1 de la sección Cataluña. La autoría corresponde a una mujer Dulce Valero, que en el interior titula: «*Metió a su mamá, una 'madame', en cal viva y, borracho, la lloraba por las noches*». Las fuentes son: una mujer identificada con nombre y apellido, Isabel Polo, vecina del inmueble, otros vecinos sin identificar, y fuentes policiales.

LA VANGUARDIA

De las informaciones que estamos analizando, la que hace referencia a los «malos tratos» ampliada en la sección Sociedad de la página 30, la firma un hombre, Luis Izquierdo (Madrid). Las fuentes consultadas son casi las mismas que las utilizadas por las cabeceras anteriores. Es decir que, además de repetir el esquema de equiparar fuentes y protagonistas, las fuentes corresponden a instituciones o a personas consultadas en su carácter de portavoces institucionales: Instituto de la Mujer; Federación de Asociaciones de Mujeres Separadas y Divorciadas; Montserrat Comas (presidenta del Observatorio sobre Violencia Doméstica y miembro del

Consejo General del Poder Judicial); José María Michavila (Ministro de Justicia); Eduardo Zaplana (titular de Trabajo y Asuntos Sociales); Ana Pastor (Ministra de Sanidad). Entre las fuentes consultadas por esta cabecera se puede destacar la inclusión por primera vez de la Federación de Asociaciones de Mujeres Separadas y Divorciadas que, si bien sigue siendo una fuente institucional, no pertenece a organismos oficiales y representa la voz de un numeroso sector de mujeres.

La segunda información que se presenta en portada y continúa en página 29 de la sección Sociedad hace referencia al «turismo sexual con niños». Aparece firmada por una mujer, Cecilia López, que utiliza como fuente a la ONG Save the Children.

EL PERIÓDICO

Como ya hemos señalado, de las noticias que analizamos en este ejercicio, *El Periódico* sólo presenta en portada la información del «parricidio» de Esplugues. La autoría de esta noticia que continúa en la página 32 corresponde a un hombre, Xavier Adell. Esta información, junto con la que presenta el periódico gratuito *Metro Directe*, son las únicas que presentan como fuente a un hombre identificado con nombre y apellido y del que se indican otras características sociodemográficas: Enrique Rus, el hijo, de 46 años, autor del crimen y por tanto protagonista de la información. Además, como en los casos anteriores, otras fuentes son los vecinos de la finca donde se produjeron los acontecimientos.

La otra noticia destinada a ampliar esta información es una Crónica-Reportaje titulada *El Norman Bates de Esplugues* a cuyo autor corresponden las iniciales X. A. (las siglas del autor), y es, a su vez, la fuente profesional del reportaje.

EL PUNT*

La información acerca del «parricidio» que se desarrolla en la página 5 de la sección Países Catalanes, titulada *Un hombre mata a su madre y la oculta más de un año enterrada con cal viva en su casa*, presenta como autor a un hombre, Miquel A. Luque y no menciona ninguna fuente.

La noticia sobre «el turismo sexual» presenta como autores a una persona con sexo indeterminado U. Comas y a la Agencia EFE (Madrid). La información se amplía en la página 34 de la sección Europa-

Mundo y se titula «*Francia y el Estado español encabezan la lista de países que practican más turismo sexual con menores*», presentando como única y recurrente fuente de la información, a la ONG Save the Children.

METRO DIRECTE

La información que hace referencia al «turismo sexual» aparece ampliada en página 2 en la sección España con el titular *España, entre los países más adictos al turismo sexual*. La autoría corresponde a la propia cabecera Metro (Madrid) y las fuentes mencionadas son: la Red Internacional de Erradicación de la Explotación Sexual Infantil que cita como su propia fuente al Ministerio del Interior y la ONG Save the Children que, a su vez, cita como su propia fuente a otra institución, la Organización Mundial de Turismo.

La información sobre los acontecimientos de Esplugues *Mata a su madre por venganza y conserva el cadáver año y medio*,* presenta como autor a una persona cuyo sexo no podemos identificar: J. Silvestre; y como fuentes a la policía, el detenido, los vecinos y los sociólogos.

20 MINUTOS

Esta cabecera no presenta autoría en las unidades redaccionales que hacen referencia al *turismo sexual* y a *mujeres emigrants obligadas a prostituirse en el Raval*.* Respecto a las fuentes, la primera información cita como fuente el Informe ONG Save the Children y la segunda a la policía.

En cambio, un hombre, Juan Bravo, firma la información referida al parricidio de Esplugues *Mata a su madre y convive con su cadáver en casa durante un año*. Las fuentes citadas para construir esta información son nuevamente los vecinos sin identificar, y una vecina, Isabel Polo, identificada con nombre y apellido.

OTRAS CONSIDERACIONES

En las noticias que hacen referencia a «malos tratos» predominan las fuentes institucionales, y en casi todos los ejemplares analizados, las autorías corresponden a hombres.

---

* En catalán en el original.

Respecto al uso de fuentes institucionales, el análisis demuestra que se reiteran en casi todos los ejemplares analizados, por ejemplo: el Instituto de la Mujer, el Centro Reina Sofía para el estudio de la Violencia y el Observatorio sobre la Violencia Doméstica.

Entre las fuentes humanas más citadas por todos los periódicos, para construir la información sobre «malos tratos», hay un predominio de las mujeres como portavoces o representantes de instituciones políticas y sociales. Los casos más recurrentes son: Micaela Navarro (secretaria de Igualdad del PSOE) y Montserrat Comas (Presidenta del Observatorio sobre la Violencia Doméstica). También se citan como fuentes humanas a algunos hombres vinculados al mundo de la política como José Bono, Gaspar Llamazares, o Rafael Simancas. El único periódico que cita a una mujer identificada con nombre y apellido como fuente de la información, que no tiene un cargo político o institucional, sino que es una mujer que relata en primera persona su «padecimiento como víctima» (Araceli Hurtado) es *El País*.

En las informaciones que hacen referencia al «turismo sexual», las autorías son mayoritariamente indeterminadas. Por ejemplo las dos unidades redaccionales que dedica el diario *ABC* a esta noticia presentan como autores las siglas E.M. y G.L.A. Así mismo, *El Punt* registra como autor humano sin identificar a U. Comas, y como autor institucional a la Agencia EFE. Por su parte la información que presenta el diario *20 Minutos* no indica autoría. Sin embargo, *La Vanguardia* presenta la única autoría identificada con nombre y apellido: Cecilia López.

Respecto a las fuentes, todas citan el informe de la ONG Save the Children y en la mayoría de los casos es la única. La excepción la encontramos en el diario *ABC* que incluye otras fuentes; dos hombres: Pedro Núñez Morgades (Defensor del Menor de la comunidad de Madrid) y Zapatero (líder de la oposición), y entre las instituciones, además de la ONG Save the Children, se cita al Ministerio del Interior y a la Plataforma de Organizaciones de la Infancia.

Por otra parte, en las cinco cabeceras que hacen referencia al «parricidio de Esplugues» las autorías correspondientes a hombres y mujeres se equiparan: *ABC* y *El País* presentan como autoras a dos mujeres, mientras que en *El Periódico* y *El Punt* a dos hombres. Por su parte, *Metro Directe* presenta una autoría no identificada.

Excepcionalmente, en esta información se destaca que en casi todos los periódicos, menos en *La Vanguardia*, se cita como fuentes a las personas. *El Periódico* y *El Punt*, a su vez, presentan como fuente al mismo protagonista, Enrique Rus Sánchez, y en todos los ejemplares se recoge la voz de los vecinos del inmueble donde sucedió el acontecimiento. La única fuente institucional citada es la policía.

Después del análisis de este grupo de noticias tipo, podemos constatar que aunque se amplía el enfoque y se diversifica *la mirada informativa* incluyendo a mujeres y hombres de distintas edades e incluso procedencias, persiste una sensiblidad humana androcéntrica que se traduce en el sistema simbólico que excluye a mujeres y criaturas como sujetos agentes y fuentes reconocidas y las reduce a víctimas pasivas y pacientes, a las que no se pide su versión de las acciones noticiables que protagonizan. Se silencia su voz y no se reconoce su capacidad de hacer y decir.

Este tratamiento a la mayoría de mujeres y hombres constituye el contrapunto simbólico que permite presentar a los varones adultos que ejercen el poder como protagonistas de acciones consideradas superiores.

IV. CRITERIOS Y HERRAMIENTAS PARA UNA INFORMACIÓN CON INTERÉS HUMANO

El diagnóstico

Los ejercicios anteriores nos han permitido explicar con casos prácticos los criterios que consideramos básicos para poder responder con rigor a la pregunta de la que parte esta *Guía para humanizar la información*: ¿De quién hablan las noticias?; o mejor en primera persona: ¿de quién hablamos cuando elaboramos noticias?, y también, ¿en quién centramos la atención cuando las leemos y las comentamos? Y hemos presentado estos criterios como una herramienta sencilla, el Test ADSH, consciente de que la principal dificultad para responder a esta pregunta radica en la predisposición para la autocrítica de los propios hábitos de pensamiento, especialmente entre los profesionales (ya lo advirtió Aristóteles, «es más difícil olvidar lo aprendido que aprender por primera vez»).

La aplicación de este Test a las noticias de las portadas y contraportadas de 15 ejemplares de 7 cabeceras de diarios, publicados un día cualquiera de 1984, 1994 y 2004, nos ha proporcionado un diagnóstico minucioso sobre la amplitud y la diversidad del enfoque y la sensibilidad humana que se pone de manifiesto en el tratamiento de las mujeres y hombres de diversas edades, procedencias y condiciones sociales a quienes se enfoca como protagonistas en relación con diferentes actuaciones consideradas noticiables, o que se menosprecia y excluye.

Los resultados confirman la existencia de una *mirada informativa* compartida, aunque con matices, por los distintos periódicos y periodistas, que adopta un enfoque reducido y limitado a unos pocos colectivos más o menos homogéneos que comparten algunos rasgos comunes: están formados predominantemente por varones adultos que ocupan distintas posiciones jerárquicas en los escenarios del poder político, económico, cultural… o que, en todo caso, se organizan para confrontarse con éstos y acceder a estos escenarios del poder. Y este enfoque parece insensible e impermeable a los cambios protagonizados por la mayoría de mujeres y hombres, y resulta cada día más obsoleto, como anclado en las democracias decimonónicas que sólo reconocían el derecho de voto a los *pater familiae* y cada vez más alejado de la realidad humana y la ciudadanía plural que compone las sociedades actuales. Además, podemos considerarlo deshumanizado porque presta más atención a los datos abstractos, las acciones, las instituciones y entidades, que a los seres humanos responsables en última instancia de unas decisiones que aparecen, así, como si fueran autónomas y ante las que ya no se sabe a quién se puede reclamar.

Queda claro que no se trata de un problema que pueda reducirse al «género» ni a las relaciones entre mujeres y hombres, sino de un sistema simbólico androcéntrico, construido articulando diversas divisiones sociales que afectan al sexo y la edad, la clase social y los pueblos de procedencia. En consecuencia, a la hora de revisarlo para construir nuevas explicaciones que abarquen al conjunto de la población, no podemos limitarnos a la variable del *«género»*, sino que hemos de tener en cuenta esta diversidad compleja.

El análisis pone de manifiesto también que este enfoque persiste incluso cuando *la mirada informativa* abarca otras y otros mujeres y hombres. En primer lugar, porque estos protagonistas suelen merecer un tratamiento negativo, como víctimas pasivas y pacientes, o como seres amenazantes, o como anécdotas humorísticas a menudo sanguinarias, en cualquier caso, merecedoras de menosprecio. Pero además, porque esta ampliación siempre es limitada, y en las contadas ocasiones en que se habla de las mujeres y hombres que forman las mayorías, son tratados como seres pasivos o amenazantes, y pocas veces se tienen en cuenta como agentes sociales activos en sentido positivo. Un ejemplo claro es el tratamiento de los numerosos colectivos de emigrantes que con sus decisiones están transformando las sociedades actuales, así como de los pueblos de los que proceden.

De este modo, unos pocos varones y algunas mujeres homologadas, y cada vez más las instituciones y entidades públicas y privadas que gestionan el poder, o los datos abstractos, aparecen como los sujetos activos y responsables del funcionamiento social, mientras que la mayoría de la población es tratada como víctimas pasivas y pacientes, como peligros para la sociedad o simplemente como datos estadísticos. En consecuencia, concluimos que la información carece hoy de interés humano porque la mayoría de mujeres y hombres no puede apreciar en las noticias referentes que les facilite comprender las necesidades y problemas sociales que encuentran para resolver los problemas cotidianos e intervenir en la vida política.

Ante esta oferta de noticias y opiniones consideradas serias, no ha de extrañar que resulten más atractivas, aunque sólo sea porque son menos abrumadoras, las informaciones valoradas como frívolas y sensacionalistas que sí hablan de seres humanos concretos en relación con sus vivencias cotidianas… En ambos casos, la mayoría de mujeres y hombres quedan reducidos a meros receptores pasivos ante unos espectáculos que ensalzan, con distintos formatos, ese juego del mundo al revés al que nos referíamos en la presentación, en el que para que unos pocos varones adultos y mujeres aparezcan como superiores y con capacidad de intervenir en la sociedad, se presenta a la mayoría de mujeres y hombres como inferiores, víctimas o como seres amenazantes. Unas y otras noticias apelan a la sentimentalidad inconsciente, de forma clara, sin tapujos en las informaciones frívolas y sensacionalistas y en los discursos conservadores; de forma encubierta tras la máscara de la supuesta objetividad, en las informaciones serias y presuntamente progresistas.

Este sistema simbólico androcéntrico, como hemos visto, distorsiona *la mirada informativa* y contamina la pretendida objetividad hasta el punto de que la hace insensible, impermeable e incapaz de dar cuenta de las transformaciones sociales que han conducido a un sistema social vasto y complejo en el que convivimos una pluralidad diversa de mujeres y hombres. Por eso las noticias, en lugar de dar cuenta de la realidad, aparecen cortadas por unos moldes que adaptan la realidad a las rutinas asumidas por unos profesionales que, como explicó Foucault, se encuentran atrapados en un orden discursivo al servicio de perpetuar el poder y bloquear cualquier posible cambio. Las noticias se convierten, así, en un compendio de alabanzas a mayor honra y gloria de quienes gestionan unas instituciones que, en lugar de estar al servicio de la mayoría, son utilizadas por unas minorías para perpetuar sus intereses de grupo, por su capital o porque forman parte de las burocracias públicas o privadas. Y en lugar de colaborar al debate plural y a la resolución de los conflictos, polarizan las posiciones y acentúan así los problemas de nuestras sociedades.

En definitiva, si consideramos la prensa como una especie de representación cartográfica de la realidad, que periódicamente, con sus explicaciones de lo que acontece ha de facilitar que la ciudadanía se oriente en sus actuaciones personales e intervenga en la gestión democrática de los asuntos públicos, a la vista de los resultados de las investigaciones hemos de concluir que estos mapas en lugar de orientar, desorientan y confunden.

Porque estas representaciones contienen errores que no son simples erratas puntuales: amplifican unas zonas y las describen minuciosamente, mientras que otras zonas mucho más extensas son minimizadas o excluidas y decoradas con imágenes que apelan al victimismo, al miedo o a la burla nunca inocente. Las zonas representadas con todo tipo de detalles están ocupadas por las minorías que acumulan las riquezas y pueden disfrutar de los paraísos del consumo que exhibe la publicidad; por el contrario, las zonas por las que transitamos la mayoría de mujeres y hombres, y a partir de las que nos ubicamos en la sociedad y actuamos para resolver los problemas derivados de unas condiciones sociales cada día más injustas, estas zonas vastas y diversas sólo se adivinan en los bordes, separadas de aquellas por abismos cada vez más profundos. En el mejor estilo de aquellos mapas antiguos en los que las tierras conquistadas y supeditadas al poder que los financiaba aparecían como parajes idílicamente ordenados, rodeados por monstruos irascibles y amenazantes que poblaban las tierras ignotas del más allá.

Estas representaciones gozan de credibilidad porque están legitimadas como objetivas y racionales por los profesionales y los políticos, a pesar de que, como comprobamos al aplicar el Test ADSH, son reduccionistas, parciales y partidistas. Y esta credibilidad bloquea la capacidad de reconocer y valorar como significativos esos otros territorios poblados por otras muchas gentes.

Conviene insistir en los resultados del análisis para no engañarnos más: el análisis atento de la muestra, aunque reducida, permite constatar que los criterios que se aplican para definir qué protagonistas y actuaciones son considerados noticiables y merecen un tratamiento positivo o negativo, no dependen de una u otra cabecera, ni de que el periodista sea mujer u hombre. Todas las cabeceras y profesionales compartimos básicamente el mismo enfoque y tratamiento.

Por tanto el diagnóstico es claro: no se trata de un problema individual, propio de la mejor o peor voluntad, o de la mayor o menor formación intelectual de cada profesional; tampoco se puede atribuir a la posición de cada cabecera en el abanico ideológico convencional de derecha e izquierda; ni siquiera depende de un censor oficial. Se trata de unas rutinas enraizadas en el *yo cognoscente* y compartido por el colectivo profesional, que forma parte de estructuras de pensamiento asumidas en el proceso de aprendizaje de una racionalidad que se legitima como si fuera objetiva, pero que sólo proporciona visiones parciales y partidistas. Y estas estructuras de pensamiento operan en el inconsciente como una autocensura, encubiertas por una particular racionalidad sobre la que se sustenta la definición de lo significativo como noticia.

Por eso las noticias, tal como se producen y difunden hoy, alimentan una opinión pública que sólo despierta el interés humano apelando a la sentimentalidad primigenia, polarizando las posiciones y alimentando los conflictos, en lugar de fomentar el debate plural para encontrar soluciones y llegar a acuerdos.

A pesar de todo, como decimos en la presentación, que sea así no quiere decir que no pueda ser de otro modo y que no tengamos que trabajar para que la información despierte el interés entre la ciudadanía y fomente su voluntad de participar en la vida política. El periodismo no ha sido siempre como lo conocemos hoy, ha cambiado constantemente para adaptarse a las transformaciones sociales, y hoy también ha de cambiar.

El tratamiento

Pero ¿qué hay que hacer para poner remedio a esta situación? ¿Qué tratamiento hay que aplicar? No estamos en condiciones de ofrecer ninguna receta capaz de solucionar el problema detectado, y seguramente no exista. Pero si podemos indicar algunas líneas de actuación para humanizar la mirada informativa.

En primer lugar, es imprescindible re-visar unos hábitos que nos conducen a hacer enfoques reducidos y tratamientos viciados por un sistema de valores al servicio de la perpetuación de los poderes establecidos de unas minorías, y nos abocan a ignorar que formamos parte de sociedades constituidas por una ciudadanía plural. Por tanto, el Test es el primer remedio para el tratamiento de este mal endémico de la información, con toda la dificultad que implica la autocrítica y el des-aprendizaje de hábitos asumidos individualmente y compartidos por los colectivos profesionales. Tomar conciencia individualmente de que hay otros territorios ocupados por seres humanos diversos, explorar lo excluido, perder el miedo incluso a perderse, dar significado y valorar positivamente lo que hemos aprendido a menospreciar, es una tarea imprescindible para humanizar la información.

Por tanto, las soluciones personales son necesarias. Pero no son suficientes. Y resulta especialmente difícil aplicarlas si tenemos en cuenta el ambiente de una profesión periodística muy individualista y competitiva, y en la que cualquier disonancia puede conducir a la exclusión, especialmente si se reclama una información de interés humano, desliz que puede merecer la hoguera de la frivolidad o el sensacionalismo, no importa que la seriedad informativa se haya reducido a la mera apariencia de superioridad… Esta presión del colectivo se acentúa hoy debido a que la precariedad laboral, la prisa por cerrar ediciones, y la invasión de comunicados procedentes de los gabinetes de comunicación de las instituciones y las empresas…, marcan un ritmo de trabajo frenético y difícil de eludir que fomenta el simplismo por falta de tiempo para explorar y contrastar distintas fuentes y la utilización de las tecnologías como máquinas de copiar y pegar.

En consecuencia, hay que pensar en compromisos colectivos, que han de ser asumidos por las personas que forman parte de instituciones públicas como las Universidades y los medios de comunicación públicos, o por instancias profesionales como los Colegios, las Asociaciones y los Sindicatos de Periodistas.

Afortunadamente, hoy disponemos de herramientas que hacen posible y facilitan construir otras formas de informar y de explicar la realidad. Y estas herramientas no se han desarrollado sin saber cómo ni porqué ni para qué: las tecnologías digitales han sido concebidas y perfeccionadas por ingenieros e informáticos porque son necesarias para registrar, almacenar, organizar, tratar y difundir los datos necesarios para las actuales sociedades diversas e interconectadas por redes personales e institucionales de alcance global. El déficit afecta a la organización conceptual de la información, a los contenidos, que aparecen anquilosados y obsoletos porque los profesionales del periodismo y los expertos en explicaciones humanísticas y sociales, parece que no nos hemos enterado de que la sociedad ha cambiado y de que son necesarios otros mapas... Son necesarios, y además son posibles.

Luis Ángel Fernández Hermana, en la revista electrónica En.red.ando que publicaba cada semana desde 1996, comparaba el desafío que tenía el periodismo a partir de Internet con el que tuvieron:

> Los benedictinos y otras órdenes religiosas que durante la Edad Media montaron el más vasto y prolífico negocio editorial del que tengamos memoria. Hasta que un tal Juan Gensfleisch, conocido como Gutemberg, les sacó del libro de la historia y los metió en los museos al inventar la imprenta de tipos móviles en 1440. Por irónico que parezca, los bellísimos códices murieron estrangulados por la alfabetización... Hoy volvemos a tener otra vez este tipo de desafío delante de nuestras narices...[1]

Diez años después las cosas no han mejorado sustancialmente, excepto porque resulta ineludible buscar soluciones colectivas para transformar el sistema de pensamiento androcéntrico que se consolidó en las Universidades europeas bajo la mirada vigilante de una iglesia y unas órdenes religiosas que impusieron un Índice de Libros que fue preservado por el tribunal de la Inquisición que arrojaba a la hoguera las páginas que contenían pensamientos contrarios a su ortodoxia. Y estas mismas órdenes construyeron la superioridad imaginaria de los varones como concepto clave de un discurso que

---

1. Fernández Hermana, Luis Ángel (1998), *En.red.ando*, Ediciones B, Grupo Z, Barcelona.
2. Varela, Julia...

legitimó la expulsión de las mujeres de las aulas y las cátedras, y persiguió a otras hasta el escarnio y la muerte en las plazas públicas.

Quizás por eso, corresponde hoy a las Universidades, y especialmente a las mujeres que hemos accedido a ellas, tener la iniciativa de promover este cambio profundo en el pensamiento humanístico y social androcéntrico, y en la formación de las y los jóvenes que se preparan para ser profesionales de la comunicación. La nueva orientación pedagógica que se plantea con motivo de la convergencia europea constituye una oportunidad que no podemos desperdiciar limitándonos a los reductos especializados en *estudios de género* y otros conocimientos fragmentados. Hemos de convertir las Universidades en espacios de reflexión y debate y laboratorios de experimentación e innovación para formular un nuevo humanismo plural.

Este proceso de renovación también se ha de producir en los medios de comunicación financiados con recursos públicos, colectivos. Ya no pueden ser simples máquinas de propaganda política al servicio de los partidos y caudillos que han ganado en las últimas contiendas electorales. Se han de convertir en auténticos instrumentos al servicio de una democracia orientada a la justicia social, la participación democrática y la mejora de la cualidad de vida para la ciudadanía plural. También aquí las mujeres podemos hacer aportaciones siempre que no nos limitemos a emular y repetir lo que se viene haciendo.

En fin, este proceso quizás tendría que estar liderado por organismos profesionales como los Colegios, Asociaciones y Sindicatos de Periodistas. Pero para ello, estas entidades han de dejar de ser los ambientes cerrados que son hoy y se han de abrir a las nuevas necesidades sociales.

Esta Guía se ha pensado como un texto que sintetiza diversos trabajos de investigación realizados en los últimos años por varias mujeres y hombres en el marco del Feminario sobre Mujer y Cultura de Masas del Departamento de Periodismo de la Universidad Autónoma de Barcelona, y quiere ser una aportación a este proceso innovador y abierto al debate plural.

Para que quede constancia de todas las aportaciones que se han hecho y de la trayectoria del grupo, las mencionamos ordenándolas cronológicamente en la siguiente Bibliografía.

BIBLIOGRAFÍA

BUITRAGO LONDOÑO, Alfonso (2006), *De las 5W y 1H a las 5Q. Diferentes aplicaciones del Test ADSH.* Trabajo de doctorado. Departamento de Periodismo de la Facultad de Ciencias de la Información (UAB).

CORCOY i RIUS, Marta; CARRASCO, Mavi; GÁMEZ, Isabel y GO-MEZ, Patricia (2002), *Les administracions locals i la informació pública (1979-2000): anàlisi de butlletins i webs municipals.* Departamento de Periodismo de la Facultad de Ciencias de la Información (UAB).

DE FONTCUBERTA, Mar; MORENO SARDÀ, Amparo (1990), «Prensa para mujeres o el discurso de lo privado: el caso del grupo HYMSA», en Garitaonandia, C.; De La Granja, J. L. y De Pablo, S. (ed.) *Comunicación, cultura y política durante la República y la Guerra Civil: España (1931-1921)*, Bilbao, Servicio ediciones, Universidad del País Vasco.

FERNÁNDEZ HERMANA, Luis Á. (1998), «Los monasterios del siglo XXI», En.redando, Barcelona, Ediciones B, Grupo Z.

GÓMEZ, Patricia (2005), *Herramientas metodológicas para el análisis de la prensa. Usos y aplicaciones del método hemerográfico diacrónico,* Trabajo de doctorado, Departamento de Periodismo de la Facultad de Ciencias de la Información (UAB).

GONZÁLEZ ESCUDERO, Elena (1994), *Un asesinato para la historia. Lucrecia Pérez, 13 de noviembre de 1992,* Trabajo de doctorado, Departamento de Periodismo de la Facultad de Ciencias de la Información (UAB).

QUINAYAS MEDINA, Gloria (2002), *EL CASO, Semanario de sucesos. Una crónica de los procesos de movilidad social durante la Dictadura de Franco,* Trabajo de doctorado, Departamento de Periodismo de la Facultad de Ciencias de la Información (UAB).

MOLINA, Pedro (1995), *Utilización didáctica de la prensa del corazón en la etapa instrumental de la formación básica de adultos,* Departamento de Periodismo de la Facultad de Ciencias de la Información (UAB).

MORENO SARDÀ, A. (1973), *La prensa de sucesos en España,* Tesis de Grado de la Escuela Oficial de Periodismo de Barcelona.

— (1975), *Historia de la prensa de sucesos en España,* Tesis de Licenciatura, Facultad de Geografía e Historia de la Universidad de Barcelona.

— (1982), «Problemas metodológicos de la historia de la prensa. Aplicación de la informática al análisis de las publicaciones», en VV AA, *Metodología de la historia de la prensa española,* Madrid, Siglo XXI.

— (1986), «*Realidad histórica» y «realidad informativa», La re-producción de la realidad a través de la prensa,* en Tuñón de Lara, M. (dir.), *La prensa en los siglos XIX y XX,* Bilbao, Universidad del País Vasco.

— (1986), *Prensa de sucesos y modelos de comportamiento: la mediación del Arquetipo Viril.* Bellaterra. Estudis Semiòtics n. 9, Universidad Autónoma de Barcelona.

— (1986), *El arquetipo viril protagonista de la historia. Ejercicios de lectura no-androcéntrica,* Barcelona, Edicions LaSal.

— (1988), *La otra «política» de Aristóteles. Cultura de Masas y divulgación del Arquetipo Viril,* Barcelona, Editorial Icaria.

— (1989), «En torno a la comprensión histórica de la cultura de masas (I): El orden androcéntrico del saber académico», en *Anàlisi: Quaderns de comunicació i cultura* (12), Universitat Autónoma de Barcelona, Facultat de Ciències de la Informació, Bellaterra.

— (1992), «En torno a la comprensión histórica de la cultura de masas (II): Paradigmas para una historia de la comunicación social (no-androcéntrica)», en *Anàlisi: Quaderns de comunicació i cultura* (14), Universitat Autónoma de Barcelona, Facultat de Ciències de la Informació, Bellaterra.

— (1994), «Premsa de sucessos: Models de marginació i integració social en els processos de movilitat social», en *Anàlisi: Quaderns de comunicació i cultura* (16), Universitat Autónoma de Barcelona, Facultat de Ciències de la Informació, Bellaterra.

— (1998), *La mirada informativa,* Barcelona, Bosch.

— (2007), *De qué hablamos cuando hablamos del hombre 30 años de crítica y alternativas al pensamiento androcéntrico,* Barcelona, Icaria.

MORENO SARDÀ, A. (dir.); LOPEZ, M.; ABRIL, N.; ALONSO, I.; SIMELIO, N.; GOMEZ, P.; VARGAS, M. S.; QUINAYAS, G.; CORCOY, M. (2004), *La representación de las relaciones entre mujeres y hombres y del recambio generacional en la prensa, de 1974 a 2004,* Proyecto I+D+I Nº7/01 Instituto de la Mujer. Departament de Periodisme i Ciències de la Comunicació de la Universitat Autònoma de Barcelona.

OSORIO PORRAS, Zenaida (2002), Las imágenes del periódico, Trabajo de doctorado, Departamento de Periodismo de la Facultad de Ciencias de la Información (UAB).

ROVETTO GONEM, Florencia (2006), *La representación del trabajo de las mujeres en la prensa (1984-2004),* Trabajo de doctorado, Departamento de Periodismo de la Facultad de Ciencias de la Información (UAB).

SAN MARTIN RODRÍGUEZ, Luis E. de (2002), *La mirada informativa del vespertino TAL CUAL sobre la sociedad venezolana* (2000-2001). Trabajo de doctorado. (2005), *La mirada informativa de los vespertinos TAL CUAL y EL MUNDO sobre la sociedad venezolana (2000-2002),* Tesis Doctoral. Departamento de Periodismo de la Facultad de Ciencias de la Información (UAB).

SIMELIO i SOLÀ, Núria (2001), *Paper i influència de la premsa diària d'informació general durant la transició espanyola (1973-1983),* Trabajo de doctorado. (2006), *Prensa de información general durante la transición política (1974-1984): pervivencias y cambios en la representación de las relaciones sociales,* Tesis Doctoral, Departamento de Periodismo de la Facultad de Ciencias de la Información (UAB).

SÁNCHEZ MENÉNDEZ, Joaquín (1998), *La representación de realidades sociales marginales en prensa diaria: la prostitución en EL PERIODICO y LA VANGUARDIA (I-VI-1995).* Trabajo de doctorado.

Departamento de Periodismo de la Facultad de Ciencias de la Información (UAB).

SUÑÉ I BALCELLS, Ramón (1992), *Anàlisi hemerogràfica diacrònica automatitzada: aplicació a EL PAÍS 1976-1991*. Trabajo de doctorado. Departamento de Periodismo de la Facultad de Ciencias de la Información (UAB).

VARGAS CARRILLO, Mª. Soledad (2006), «Estilos de vida, ética y estética en los dominicales de los diarios *ABC*, *La Vanguardia* y *El País* (1974-1999)», Tesis Doctoral. Departamento de Periodismo de la Facultad de Ciencias de la Información (UAB).

VEGA SURIAGA, Edgar (2001), *La construcción social del cuerpo andrógino en los vídeos clips de Madona y Michael Jackson*, Trabajo de doctorado. Departamento de Periodismo de la Facultad de Ciencias de la Información (UAB).